CONSUMER BANKRUPTCY

ALSO BY HENRY J. SOMMER

Consumer Bankruptcy Law and Practice

Collier Family Law and the Bankruptcy Code

CONSUMER BANKRUPTCY

The Complete Guide to Chapter 7 and Chapter 13 Personal Bankruptcy

Henry J. Sommer

John Wiley & Sons, Inc.

New York ▪ Chichester ▪ Brisbane ▪ Toronto ▪ Singapore

This text is printed on acid-free paper.

This publication is designed to provide accurate and authoritative information in regard to the subject matter covered. It is sold with the understanding that the publisher is not engaged in rendering legal, accounting, or other professional service. If legal advice or other expert assistance is required, the services of a competent professional person should be sought. *From a Declaration of Principles jointly adopted by a Committee of the American Bar Association and a Committee of Publishers.*

Library of Congress Cataloging-in-Publication Data:

Sommer, Henry J.
    Consumer bankruptcy : the complete guide to chapter 7 and chapter 13 personal bankruptcy / Henry J. Sommer.
        p. cm.
    Includes index.
    ISBN 0-471-58528-9 (acid-free paper) — ISBN 0-471-58527-0 (paper, acid-free paper)
        1. Debtor and creditor—United States—Popular works.
    2. Bankruptcy—United States—Popular works.   I. Title.
    KF1539.Z9S66   1994
    346.73'078—dc20
    [347.30678]   93-19661

Printed in the United States of America

10 9 8 7

This book is dedicated to my parents,
Moses and Ruth Sommer

PREFACE

This guide provides a detailed explanation of the tools that bankruptcy provides to consumer debtors. Most of what follows is also applicable to debtors who have had small businesses; many consumer debtors are, after all, simply businesspeople who have fallen on hard times and no longer operate their businesses. However, although this guide may be of some use to debtors who seek to continue operating their businesses, they will have to look elsewhere for assistance in handling the more complex problems that can arise.

The guide was written for consumers who are considering bankruptcy for the first time and are not yet ready to consult an attorney. Many consumers are understandably nervous about the prospect of bankruptcy and want to know more before they contact an attorney. Others may not even know how to find a competent attorney.

This book provides the information necessary to make the important decision about whether to file a bankruptcy case, when to file, and whether to file under chapter 7 or chapter 13. It describes what is likely to happen in a bankruptcy case to help those who are thinking about filing, those who have already filed, and those who are caught up in a bankruptcy case filed by someone else. And it does so in much greater detail than would be available in a consultation with an attorney, explaining all of the steps involved and how the law would be applied in a wide variety of situations.

Although no book is guaranteed to answer every question, this guide's detailed discussion of bankruptcy law and practice addresses most of the issues that arise in consumer bankruptcy. The text is based on a legal practice manual written by the same author for bankruptcy attorneys, *Consumer Bankruptcy Law and Practice*, published by the National Consumer Law Center in Boston, Massachusetts. That manual, now in its fourth edition, has probably been used by more attorneys who practice under the Bankruptcy Code than any other book of its type. Because it was written primarily for lawyers, *Consumer Bankruptcy Law and Practice* contains extensive citations to the law and court decisions as well as other materials that have been omitted from this guide. (It is also considerably more expensive!) Readers who seek even greater detail than that provided here should consider ordering a copy from the National Consumer Law Center.

Although this guide is primarily oriented toward cases filed by consumer debtors, the final chapter provides a basic explanation of the rights of consumers as creditors when a merchant, landlord, or other provider of goods or services files a bankruptcy case. The treatment of this topic in Chapter 15 is far from exhaustive, and anyone who seeks a full explanation of corporate bankruptcy is encouraged to use other resources as well.

PURPOSE OF THE GUIDE

This guide is intended to provide information to nonlawyers about what happens in bankruptcy cases. It is meant to provide both a quick overview of bankruptcy for those who want to know only the basics and also a more detailed explanation for those who want to know what will happen in a particular situation, whether in their own possible bankruptcy case, that of a friend, or that of someone who owes them money. It also discusses the alternatives to bankruptcy and the likely consequences of those alternatives. Finally, it explains the effects of bankruptcy on credit and on other rights of people who have filed.

This guide is not intended to be a substitute for consulting with or retaining an attorney. Only a consultation can provide firm and definitive answers about how local laws and practices, possible changes in the law, and court decisions will affect a particular case. This guide can make a consultation with an attorney more productive and effective, however, by eliminating the need for much explanation and focusing the discussion on important issues and questions, some of which the attorney might otherwise overlook.

Although this guide would undoubtedly be useful to someone attempting to file a bankruptcy case without a lawyer, it is not meant to be a do-it-yourself book. Only those debtors who have no way of obtaining legal representation in a bankruptcy case should consider representing themselves. Although it is theoretically possible to file a bankruptcy case *pro se* (without a lawyer), it is almost never a good idea. There are numerous pitfalls along the way, and creditors frequently take advantage of those who are not represented. Consumers who represent themselves in bankruptcy sometimes wind up in far worse situations after their bankruptcies than before they filed.

Even more importantly, a person filing a bankruptcy case without an attorney might miss ways in which further benefits can be derived from the case. Often, the cost of mistakes or lost opportunities that a competent lawyer would point out far exceeds the money that would be saved by not paying an attorney's fee.

Going to a lawyer is a lot like going to a doctor. Both professionals have had specialized training that other people do not have. Although it is sometimes possible for patients to treat themselves successfully, the consequences of a mistake can be extremely serious and occasionally fatal. Complicated problems may call for major surgery that no layperson should attempt. Even if a patient does figure out how to cure an illness, there might well have been a quicker or better treatment. A lawyer, like a doctor, can recognize complicated situations that call for different treatment and can suggest the most effective solution.

Obtaining the services of a competent attorney cannot be too strongly recommended, if only for the peace of mind that comes from knowing that the case will be handled in the best possible way. Chapter 14 deals extensively with how to find a good bankruptcy attorney and how to get the most out of your relationship. It also describes how to avoid incompetent lawyers and debt- or bankruptcy-related rip-off schemes.

To facilitate its use, this guide is divided into three parts. Part I, consisting of the first three chapters, is intended to provide an introductory nuts-and-bolts understanding of how bankruptcy works. To keep these chapters relatively nontechnical, they contain many cross-references to in-depth discussions in later chapters.

The second part, Chapters 4 through 7, contains a step-by-step description of the papers and proceedings in a case, from the moment that bankruptcy is first considered to events that occur after the case is over. The first seven chapters should provide the reader with a basic knowledge of what happens in a typical consumer bankruptcy.

The reader may then consult Part III to deal with specific issues of interest. Chapters 8 through 13 contain a more detailed discussion of the legal issues that frequently arise in consumer bankruptcy cases. Many of these issues are fairly complicated, and courts do not always agree on their resolution. Also, the law may have changed since this book was written, especially if the edition you are reading was published more than a year or two ago. Therefore, even after reading these chapters, it is important to check with an attorney on points that are important in your case.

Chapter 14 explains how to find and work with a good bankruptcy lawyer. Chapter 15 addresses issues pertaining to the rights of consumers as creditors when a merchant, landlord, or other entity is in bankruptcy.

Appendix A contains a list of the major types of property that can be claimed as exempt in each state. The issues relating to exemptions, as well as the federal exemptions available in some cases, are discussed at length in Chapter 9. Appendix B contains a set of the Official Forms federally mandated to be used in every consumer bankruptcy case. They are included to give you an idea of the type of paperwork that is involved in a bankruptcy case and the questions that are asked. These forms are discussed further in Chapter 6.

ACKNOWLEDGMENTS

This book is adapted from *Consumer Bankruptcy Law and Practice*, fourth edition, a manual for attorneys published by the National Consumer Law Center (NCLC) in Boston, Massachusetts. That book could not have been written without the help of numerous people at NCLC and elsewhere, particularly Joan Plonski, who typed the original manuscript; Gary Klein, who co-authored the revisions for the last two editions; Robert Sable, who wrote portions of Chapter 16; and Jonathan Sheldon and Judy O'Donnell, who helped put it all together. In addition, the editing efforts of Judith Mara Riotto were extremely helpful in transforming that book into something a layperson could understand. Finally, this book could not have been written without the cooperation and support of my wife, Beth, and my sons, Ethan and Aaron.

ATTENTION

CONTENTS

Part I.   Overview of Bankruptcy   **1**

    1. What Is Bankruptcy?   3
    2. Chapter 7 Bankruptcy (Straight Bankruptcy): The Basic Steps   17
    3. Chapter 13 Bankruptcy: The Basic Steps   27

Part II.   Bankruptcy Step by Step   **39**

    4. Knowing All the Facts about Your Financial Picture   41
    5. Does Bankruptcy Provide the Best Solution?   53
    6. The Bankruptcy Forms   81
    7. After the Papers Are Filed   99

Part III.   Legal Issues in Bankruptcy   **119**

    8. Automatic Stays and Turnover of Property   121
    9. Exemptions   141
   10. Dealing with Secured Creditors   171
   11. Issues Arising in Chapter 13 Cases   189
   12. Other Types of Litigation in the Bankruptcy Court   215
   13. The Bankruptcy Discharge: Protecting It and Using It   227
   14. Attorneys and Their Fees in Consumer Bankruptcy Cases   269
   15. Consumers' Rights in Business Bankruptcy Cases   281

Appendix A: Major State and Local Exemptions Available in Bankruptcy   **289**

Appendix B: Official Consumer Bankruptcy Forms   **307**

Index   **329**

Part I

OVERVIEW OF
BANKRUPTCY

Chapter 1

WHAT IS BANKRUPTCY?

BANKRUPTCY AS A REMEDY FOR CONSUMER DEBTORS

The 1980s saw an explosive increase in the already easy availability of consumer credit in the United States. The inevitable economic downturn of the 1990s has brought enormous financial difficulties for consumers. Aggressive creditors regularly threaten to throw people's lives into chaos through foreclosures, repossessions, levies, executions, garnishments, collection harassment, and utility shutoffs.

Bankruptcy is sometimes the only option that will bring order, rational planning, and permanent, or at least temporary, relief to people who are under immense financial pressure. Bankruptcy provides an effective means of leveling the playing field between debtors and creditors, and it profoundly improves the well-being of individuals and families.

It should come as no surprise, then, that more than 900,000 consumer bankruptcy cases were filed in the United States in 1992, and even greater numbers are anticipated in the future. As credit expands and bankruptcy becomes increasingly central to our economic and legal systems, larger numbers of consumers and businesses seek assistance with bankruptcy. Bankruptcy gives them an opportunity to reorder their finances and obtain a fresh start.

It has become impossible to ignore bankruptcy. Not only is it an important option for those with financial difficulties, but it also frequently affects nondebtors who become involved through employment, marriage, a tenancy, or a consumer relationship or as party to a lawsuit. Bankruptcy can wipe out both long- and short-term debts, with a minimum of effort in many cases, and can upset the firmest of expectations about consumer, landlord-tenant, and even marital relationships. Even large municipal governments, like the City of Bridgeport, Connecticut, have filed bankruptcy cases with potentially significant implications for all city residents.

As the importance of bankruptcy increases, so does the need for consumers and people with small businesses to be familiar with the world of bankruptcy. This book is intended to guide those who are considering filing a bankruptcy case, who are affected by the bankruptcy case of another person or business, or who simply want to know more about this important element of our legal and economic systems.

Despite its potential importance to consumers, the use of bankruptcy law was virtually unheard of in many areas before 1978. Many lawyers saw bankruptcy as an intimidating maze of paperwork in an unfamiliar and sometimes (for rural lawyers) inconvenient court. For some consumers, a touch of the old-time stigma remained from the early days of bankruptcy law. They saw bankruptcy as a lazy cop-out for the debtor—and perhaps as a bit immoral.

This view of bankruptcy is rapidly changing. The widespread use of bankruptcy has frequently been the subject of press coverage. Lawyer advertising, which became acceptable at about the same time that the Bankruptcy Code was passed, has informed people of their right to deal with financial problems through bankruptcy. The knowledge that bankruptcy cases have been filed by famous celebrities, large corporations, and perhaps a few friends and neighbors has done much to eliminate the stigma of filing.

THE BENEFITS OF BANKRUPTCY FOR CONSUMERS

Bankruptcy has provided millions of people with relief from the incessant collection calls, letters, and other harassment tactics that accompany unpaid debts. Bankruptcy is sometimes the best way to prevent the loss of housing, utility service, income, a car or driver's license, and even one's freedom, since imprisonment may result from the failure to comply with orders to pay support or other indebtedness. Bankruptcy can save a family thousands of dollars, a home, a car, or a job, and it may accomplish these desired results better, faster, and with less expenditure of time and money than any other means.

Probably at least as important is the impact of bankruptcy practice on creditor behavior. The ever-present possibility of bankruptcy will cause many creditors to become more reasonable in settling cases and in dealing with their customers. A creditor faced with the possibility that a consumer will file a bankruptcy case will usually become more flexible, because if the consumer does file a bankruptcy case the creditor will likely receive little or nothing on the claim.

Of course, this is not to suggest that bankruptcy is always the preferable course of action. There are sometimes other ways to deal effectively with debt problems. (Some of these options are discussed in Chapter 5.)

THE LAW GOVERNING BANKRUPTCY CASES

On October 1, 1979, a new and far-reaching consumer protection law went into effect. That law, the federal Bankruptcy Code, may well be the most important federal legislation ever passed in terms of its benefits for consumers. It far surpasses the federal Consumer Credit Protection Act and other statutes designed to protect consumers. In its first years, the Code demonstrated its enormous potential as a source of quick, concrete, and far-reaching relief in the day-to-day cases of financially troubled individuals. The burgeoning number of bankruptcies in recent years has been matched by a host of court cases interpreting this important new law.

The Bankruptcy Code has been amended several times since it was enacted, mostly at the behest of the consumer credit industry. Within a year of the Code's passage, creditors began mounting a lobbying and public relations drive to cut back on the Code's protections. So far the Code has remained largely intact, although such efforts to limit consumers' rights never cease.

Although the Bankruptcy Code is the most important law governing bankruptcy, many decisions in bankruptcy cases are also based on local, state, or other federal laws, including laws that establish the rights of property owners, debtors, and creditors. For example, every state has exemption laws concerning how much property debtors are allowed to protect from their creditors, and these laws may be applied in bankruptcy cases. (The exemption laws are discussed in Chapter 9.)

Also important in determining the course of bankruptcy cases are the Federal Rules of Bankruptcy Procedure, promulgated in 1983 by the Supreme Court and amended various times since then. These rules provide detailed guidelines in many areas that are not specifically covered by the Code. They cover procedures not only for administering the bankruptcy petitions themselves, but also for the legal proceedings that sometimes take place in conjunction with the principal bankruptcy case. In addition to the Bankruptcy Rules, there are often supplemental local rules or unusual local procedural practices in bankruptcy court.

A series of Official Forms is appended to the rules. The rules provide that all papers filed must conform substantially to the Official Forms. Blank copies of some of the forms filed in consumer bankruptcy cases are included in Appendix B.

Finally, bankruptcy law is interpreted in decisions of the courts, all the way up to the Supreme Court. Since 1978, thousands of decisions from the bankruptcy courts have been published. Numerous decisions of appellate courts below the Supreme Court have also been rendered, and these decisions are binding on the courts below them.

All of these materials are available in a good law library, along with numerous treatises and texts on bankruptcy. However, legal training is generally necessary to understand and utilize them fully in bankruptcy cases.

WHAT IS BANKRUPTCY?

In essence, a voluntary bankruptcy case is a legal proceeding filed by a debtor who seeks relief specifically provided for by a federal law, the Bankruptcy Code. (Involuntary bankruptcy cases may also be brought against debtors, but they are very rare in nonbusiness situations.) The bankruptcy proceeding must be brought in U.S. District Court and is normally referred to the bankruptcy court for that district. The bankruptcy court is a unit of the district court.

The Relief Available in Bankruptcy

For an individual, two types of relief are commonly available. The first is liquidation under chapter 7 of the Code. In a liquidation case, which is often called a *straight bankruptcy*, all of the debtor's nonexempt assets are converted to cash and distributed to creditors according to certain statutory rules. (Chapter 9 discusses which assets are exempt.) At the end of the proceeding, the debtor receives a discharge, which absolves him or her from the responsibility to pay most debts and also provides various other protections.

The second type of relief is a reorganization, or adjustment, of the debtor's financial affairs. Although a reorganization may be available to individuals under both chapters 11 and 13 of the Code, chapter 13 is more beneficial for virtually every consumer debtor. It is less expensive, and it offers a number of protections not found in chapter 11. In a chapter 13 case, the debtor proposes a plan for payment of some or all of the debts, within certain guidelines that are set by the law. (These guidelines are discussed in Chapters 6, 10, and 11.) The plan is then carried out under court supervision. The court protects the debtor and, usually, all of the debtor's property from creditors. At the end of the case, as in a chapter 7 case, the debtor receives a discharge from personal liability on most debts, as well as other protections.

Neither discharge by itself protects the debtor's property from creditors with valid liens on it. However, the Code offers a number of ways, particularly in chapter 13, for debtors to obtain full or partial relief from such liens in most cases.

The Purposes of Bankruptcy

The purposes of bankruptcy are usually described as twofold: (1) a fresh start for the debtor and (2) equity among creditors. In most cases involving consumer debtors, the first is by far the more significant because there are typically few assets to be distributed, equitably or otherwise, to the creditors involved.

The fresh start concept encompasses the law's goal of allowing individuals who have become mired in debt to free themselves and to engage in newly productive lives, unimpaired by their past financial problems. It avoids the kind of permanent discouragement that would prevent a person from becoming reestablished as a hard-working member of society. In *Local Loan Co. v. Hunt*, the Supreme Court described the fresh start as "a new opportunity in life, unhampered by the pressure and discouragement of pre-existing debt." Bankruptcy thus serves to grease the wheels of a capitalist economy, offering a safety net that somewhat tempers its harshness for those who do not fare well in free-market competition. At the same time, it adds to the dynamism of the society, encouraging risk-taking and expansion of new enterprises by limiting the risk involved and by offering a new start to those who fail.

The goal of equity among creditors is achieved by the fair distribution of the debtor's assets according to established rules, set forth in the law, that guarantee identical treatment to similarly situated creditors. This guarantee and various provisions that require creditors to disgorge certain assets seized by them shortly before bankruptcy are meant to discourage creditors from rushing to be the first to try to seize property or to repossess their collateral from a struggling individual or business. Thus, the specter of bankruptcy sometimes causes creditors to negotiate with debtors because the aggressive dismemberment of debtors' assets could force them to seek relief from the bankruptcy court.

THE BANKRUPTCY COURT

Status Under the Amended Bankruptcy Reform Act

Under the 1984 amendments to the Bankruptcy Reform Act, the bankruptcy court continues to be a unit of the federal district court in each judicial district. Its powers, however, are far less than those that were originally contemplated by the drafters of the 1978 Bankruptcy Reform Act. Bankruptcy judges are appointed for terms of 14 years by the courts of appeals, which have jurisdiction over the various districts; the judges have a status and power roughly equivalent to U.S. Magistrates, that is, less than the full power of a federal judge. Because the bankruptcy court is a part of the district court, laws applicable to the federal district courts, as well as federal rules of evidence, generally apply in bankruptcy proceedings.

Powers of the Bankruptcy Court

A principal goal of the 1978 Bankruptcy Reform Act was to simplify the court structure, which had caused endless litigation for the previous 80 years under the Bankruptcy Act of 1898. This simplification was to be accomplished by giving the bankruptcy court broad and pervasive powers over all matters related in any way to the bankruptcy case. But this broad power did not meet the requirements of Article III of the Constitution (lifetime tenure for judges and Senate confirmation of judicial appointments). It was found unconstitutional by the Supreme Court in a case called *Northern Pipeline Construction Co. v. Marathon Pipe Line Co.*, often called the *Marathon* case.

The 1984 amendments attempted to meet the Supreme Court's objections in a variety of ways, most of which involved limiting the types of disputes that the bankruptcy court could decide. Under the amendments, all matters arising under the Bankruptcy Code (or arising in or related to cases under the Bankruptcy Code) are initially referred by the district court to the bankruptcy court. They may also arrive there by removal from another court. However, some matters will not stay in bankruptcy court. The statute now provides for a complex system of mechanisms to transfer matters to the district court or to state courts, depending on the type of proceeding involved. These include old and new devices that allow the bankruptcy court to abstain from (refuse to decide) some issues and the district court to withdraw others; the latter are then decided by the district court. In some proceedings, bankruptcy judges are permitted to enter final orders, and in others they are allowed only to submit recommended findings of fact and conclusions of law to the federal district judge, who then accepts or rejects them before deciding the case.

These jurisdictional complexities do not affect most routine bankruptcy cases, which are fully heard in the bankruptcy court. However, for more unusual matters, the statute's many twists and turns will probably cause at least as much confusion and litigation as existed before 1978, thus ending the hopes of many that such wasteful expenditures of time and money had finally been eliminated.

Corresponding to the court's broad initial jurisdiction are provisions that allow bankruptcy-related lawsuits to be filed across state lines. Many proceedings arising in or related to a bankruptcy case may be commenced in the court in which that case is pending, even if that court is in Maine and the defendant is in Hawaii. However, a case or proceeding may be transferred to another district in the interest of justice or for the convenience of the parties.

Furthermore, lawsuits in progress elsewhere may be removed by a party to the district court that has bankruptcy jurisdiction. This provision may be of tremendous assistance in obtaining a better forum or other procedural advantages for a litigant. It should be noted, though, that the receiving court may choose to remand the proceeding. Such a decision is not reviewable by appeal or otherwise, except by the district court.

Appeals

There are two possible avenues for appeals from the bankruptcy court. The process selected depends on the wishes of the parties and the practice adopted by the federal district and judicial circuit in which the case is pending.

In the case of a final judgment order or decree, where a bankruptcy court is authorized to enter one, an appeal is normally taken to the federal district court for that state or part of a state. Further appeals from the district court decision may then be taken to the court of appeals that handles appeals for the district, provided that the district court's order is a final order. There are often technical disputes about whether an order is a final order and therefore appealable. No provision in the law explains exactly what is or is not a final order, judgment, or decree, and some uncertainty remains.

The only exception to this general rule occurs when an appellate panel of three bankruptcy judges has been established by the circuit council of the court of appeals that governs the district in which the appeal is pending. (At present, only the court of appeals covering the Ninth Circuit—the states of California, Oregon, Washington, Montana, Arizona, Hawaii, and Idaho—has established such a panel.) An appeal from a bankruptcy court order may be taken to this panel instead of to the district court only when (1) all parties consent and (2) the district judges for the district, by majority vote, authorize referral of appeals to the appellate panel.

Appellate procedure for nonfinal orders and decrees is somewhat different. An appeal to either a three-judge panel or the district court (whichever is applicable) is permitted only with permission of that panel or district court. At least one bankruptcy appellate panel has held that only exceptional circumstances justify the granting of such leave to appeal. However, when the district court or appellate panel takes an appeal of an interlocutory (nonfinal) order, the parties have a further right of appeal to the court of appeals for that jurisdiction.

The procedure for appeals to a district court or bankruptcy appellate panel is governed by the Federal Rules of Bankruptcy Procedure. These rules are similar to the rules for other federal court appeals, but they differ in several significant respects, most notable the ten-day time limit for bankruptcy appeals. Appeals to courts of appeals are governed by the normal rules for appeals to those courts.

THE BANKRUPTCY ESTATE

The term *bankruptcy estate* describes the aggregation of property rights that can be administered by the court in a bankruptcy case. The estate is created on the commencement of the case, and it generally consists of all of the debtor's interests in any kind of property as of that time. It includes interests in community property and some types of property that cannot be seized by creditors under state law, such as the right to receive various kinds of income in the future.

If only one spouse in a community-property state files a bankruptcy petition, the bankruptcy estate may sometimes include the other spouse's share of all community property. In addition, the estate includes property recovered by the bankruptcy trustee, proceeds or rents of property already in the estate, the debtor's right to sue others for prebankruptcy claims, interests in insurance policies, and various other types of property interests, as set forth in the Bankruptcy Code. (The bankruptcy trustee is an official appointed to administer a bankruptcy case. The trustee is given powers to recover certain property that the debtor transferred before the bankruptcy case was filed.)

Most property acquired by the debtor after commencement of the case does not come into the estate. However, there are exceptions for certain types of property acquired within 180 days of filing the bankruptcy case. These include property acquired by bequest or inheritance, through a spousal property settlement or divorce decree, or as a beneficiary of life insurance. In a chapter 13 case, all property and earnings acquired during the pendency of the case (until the case is ended or converted to another chapter) belong to the estate.

Even very limited and remote property interests are included in the debtor's bankruptcy estate. For example, bare legal title to property, as a trustee for another person or as a co-owner merely for convenience, brings an interest in that property into the estate. Similarly, mere possession of property without legal title is sufficient to bring property into the estate. Such property may not be available for actual distribution to creditors, however, because the estate's interest is usually limited to the debtor's interest. The nature of that interest is generally determined under state law. If the debtor has no right under state law to transfer the property, the trustee usually does not have that right either.

Significant issues may arise when two or more people jointly own property and only one of the co-owners files bankruptcy. Although the debtor's partial interest in the property clearly comes into the estate, the Code mandates some protection of the interests of the nondebtor co-owner. In such cases, the court may have to balance the co-owner's needs with the possible benefits to creditors that would result from a sale of the property and a division of the proceeds.

The person who files the bankruptcy papers must exercise care in identifying and listing the debtor's various interests in property. Failure to list correctly property of the estate in the debtor's schedules may be grounds to deny or revoke the debtor's discharge and may give rise to claims by creditors or the trustee against the unlisted property.

Most consumer debtors find that they can exempt all or almost all of their property from the estate. Even property that cannot be exempted is often of little interest to the trustee because of the cost of liquidation. It is often abandoned (left to those who owned it before bankruptcy) or sold back to the debtor.

Pensions and Spendthrift Trusts

Particularly thorny issues arise in evaluating whether the beneficiary's interest in pensions, retirement funds, certain employee benefit accounts, and spendthrift trusts come into the bankruptcy estate. The Bankruptcy Code provides that "[a] restriction on the transfer of a beneficial interest of the debtor in a trust that is enforceable under applicable nonbankruptcy law is enforceable in a case under this title." This means that where the beneficiaries of a trust cannot lose their interests in that trust to a creditor outside the bankruptcy, they are equally protected in the bankruptcy case.

For many years, courts reached various conclusions about whether the language quoted above protects pension plans established under the federal Employee Retirement Income Security Act (ERISA), which covers most employer pension plans, by excluding them from a debtor's bankruptcy estate. The issue was whether the "anti-alienation" provision, which protects ERISA-qualified pensions from creditors, constitutes "applicable nonbankruptcy law." If so, then those pensions could not be transferred to a debtor's bankruptcy estate.

In 1992, the Supreme Court cleared up the morass of court decisions in the area and concluded that ERISA does protect debtors' pensions. The Court held that a debtor's interest in an ERISA-qualified pension does not become a part of the debtor's bankruptcy estate.

Some issues nevertheless remain. The Court pointed out, for example, that at least two types of retirement accounts do not qualify under ERISA and therefore are not entitled to its protection. These are certain pensions established by government entities or religious organizations and individual retirement accounts (IRAs). These types of retirement funds, along with other employee benefit plans that are not subject to ERISA's anti-alienation language, must continue to be analyzed on a case-by-case basis.

It should be noted, however, that some government and church pensions may have been established with provisions similar to the anti-alienation provisions in ERISA plans or may receive protection under state law. Similarly, IRAs may also be protected from alienation under state law.

Nonretirement employee benefit plans may also be protected, depending on whether they come within the scope of ERISA's anti-alienation language or alternative protections of the plan or state law. The benefits under some plans may be unvested so that they cannot be made available to debtors or their estates. Other plans may qualify as state law "spendthrift trusts," trusts containing money that neither the person who benefits from the trust nor creditors can obtain without the trustee's consent. These trusts cannot be alienated for the purpose of bankruptcy. A critical issue may be whether receipt of the funds from the benefit plan will occur only after additional services from the debtor or some other future event. If that is the case, the court will usually decide that the debtor does not yet have the right to receive the money, and it will not become a part of the bankruptcy estate.

The laws regarding spendthrift trusts vary widely from one jurisdiction to another. Most states allow trusts to be established that protect the beneficiary's interest from creditors as long as the beneficiary has no right to obtain trust funds whenever he or she desires. Those trusts are excluded from the debtor's bankruptcy. However, once funds are distributed or withdrawn from a qualified trust account, they presumably lose their protection.

The debtor must list pensions and other trust interests in Schedule B of the bankruptcy schedules whether or not they come into the estate. Any argument that the interest is outside the estate should be carefully noted on the schedule.

Issues will also continue to arise concerning the exemptibility of retirement funds or other trust interests that do come into the estate. It should not be assumed that no exemption applies. There are usually exemption provisions covering all or part of the debtor's rights to future income. (These exemptions are discussed in Chapter 9.) Nothing prevents a debtor from claiming that property is outside the estate, but the debtor should nevertheless list an applicable exemption in case the court decides otherwise.

Tax Refunds and the Earned Income Tax Credit

The right to receive a tax refund is clearly property of the bankruptcy estate. The debtor may also have a property interest in excessive withholding for the then-current tax year. When excessive withholdings result in a refund due after the filing of the bankruptcy, the refund is often prorated over the entire year, and the prebankruptcy portion is considered to be property of the estate. However, in some parts of the country, no one will check into excessive withholding from the debtor's pay during the tax year when the bankruptcy case is filed.

The debtor's right to various tax credits that arise prepetition has also been held to come into the estate, but there is some precedent for distinguishing the right to an earned income tax credit. The courts that have concluded that the earned income tax credit is always excluded from the estate presumably based their decision on a belief that a debtor can have no legal or equitable interest in the credit before receiving it.

Because the right to a credit cannot be determined until the end of the tax year, the argument that it should not be included in the estate is strongest when bankruptcy is filed before the end of the relevant tax year. A slightly weaker argument can be made when the debtor files bankruptcy before claiming the credit by filing a return, since the credit does not exist until it is claimed. It is also plausible to argue that the mere filing of the return does not create an interest in the credit because the credit does not come into existence until it is determined by the government. It would follow, then, that the credit does not come into the estate unless it is actually mailed or received before the bankruptcy case is filed.

Before commencing a bankruptcy case, the debtor should consider how a tax refund will be treated in the bankruptcy process. Careful efforts should be made to set up the case in a way that maximizes the debtor's ability to obtain the benefit of any refund or credit.

The simplest way of ensuring that a debtor will retain control over a tax refund, whether or not it includes an earned income tax credit, is to wait for the refund to be received before filing bankruptcy. Most debtors are able to use such funds for consumable necessities or for tangible property that can be exempted once bankruptcy is filed.

Obviously, this strategy may not be appropriate if the tax refund is subject to interception by the Internal Revenue Service on a government claim. In certain circumstances, the government can seize both an overpayment of earnings and the earned income tax credit for obligations such as overdue child support and student loans.

If the refund is seized, the debtor may be able to use a provision of the Code to reverse the transfer. However, the potential interception of a tax return can be a consideration in favor of filing sooner rather than later.

It is always a good idea to evaluate whether there is an applicable exemption that would protect a refund or tax credit. A debtor can sometimes claim an exemption for a tax refund or earned income tax credit based on the federal wild-card exemption. Similarly, the earned income tax credit may be exemptible based on state or federal exemptions for public assistance benefits. (Such exemptions are discussed in Chapter 9.)

THE BANKRUPTCY TRUSTEE

In most cases under chapter 7 and chapter 13, a bankruptcy trustee is appointed by the United States trustee. (In two states—Alabama and North Carolina—the bankruptcy judge appoints the trustee.) The trustee's basic role is to represent the interests of the unsecured creditors (those who do not have liens on the debtor's property).

The trustee's duties in carrying out this role are set forth in the Bankruptcy Code. They can include collecting property of the estate, invalidating certain transfers made by the debtor before bankruptcy, objecting to a claim that property is exempt, objecting to the debtor receiving a discharge of debts, liquidating (normally by selling) any nonexempt property and distributing it to creditors with valid claims, and making a final accounting to the court and the U.S. trustee. The bankruptcy trustee may sue or be sued as the representative of the estate in order to determine claims by or against the estate.

In a typical chapter 7 consumer case, there is no nonexempt property, so the trustee's duties are more limited. In such cases, the trustee evaluates the debtor's schedules, statements, and claim of exemptions and ensures that the debtor carries out the stated intentions with respect to property on which creditors have liens. The trustee participates in and, in many districts, presides at the meeting of creditors, an event that occurs in every case. (The meeting of creditors is discussed in Chapter 7.) Finally, in some places, the trustee also files a report with the court stating any objection to the discharge or exemption claims.

The chapter 13 trustee has considerably more to do. Unlike in chapter 7 cases, where the trustee is one of a number who can be chosen from a panel in each district, there is usually only one trustee, called a *standing trustee*, to handle all chapter 13 cases in a particular district or part of a district. In addition to most of the duties of a chapter 7 trustee, the chapter 13 trustee must also attend all hearings on the value of property subject to liens and on confirmation or modification of the debtor's plan. The trustee receives and disburses payments according to the debtor's plan, makes sure that the debtor is making payments, advises the debtor on non-legal matters, and assists the debtor in performance of the plan. In the past, the diligence of chapter 13 trustees in performing the last two duties has varied widely among districts.

Both chapter 13 and chapter 7 trustees are accountable for the performance of their statutory duties and may generally be held liable for failure to perform them. Courts have differed on the extent of a bankruptcy trustee's immunity from being sued for damages.

Depending on the type of case involved, then, the trustee may be either a friend or a foe of the debtor. It is obviously important to distinguish these situations carefully and to be familiar with how the trustee sees his or her role. An active trustee may closely scrutinize the debtor's affairs, sometimes to help the debtor and sometimes to help the creditors. Some trustees may be interested in asserting the debtor's counterclaims or defenses, and others may not. As will be seen in the following chapters, knowing the predilections of a particular trustee may be of considerable help in choosing the correct bankruptcy strategy.

THE UNITED STATES TRUSTEE

In 1986, amendments to the Bankruptcy Code and related legislation made permanent and expanded nationwide the United States trustee program, which had been created as a pilot project in 1979. By the end of a seven-year phase-in period, every judicial district in the country (with the exception of those in Alabama and North Carolina) will be part of a larger U.S. Trustee District, served by a U.S. trustee and one or more assistant U.S. trustees. For political reasons, neither Alabama nor North Carolina will have a U.S. trustee until the year 2002, at least.

The function of the U.S. trustee is to remove the bankruptcy court from administrative matters, leaving the court with its primary function of resolving disputes that arise between parties in the bankruptcy case and related proceedings. Thus, the U.S. trustee takes over such functions as appointing and supervising trustees, convening the meeting of creditors, and monitoring fees charged by bankruptcy attorneys. All of these tasks were formerly performed by the court. The court still plays a role in approving attorney's fees, however. The U.S. trustee is also given the right to move for dismissal of a case under chapter 7 for substantial abuse of the provisions of the Code and for dismissal of cases under all chapters for undue delay in filing required documents. (Dismissal of cases is discussed in Chapter 12.) The U.S. trustee's role in a bankruptcy case beyond the duties enumerated in the statute remains unclear. However, the U.S. trustee is prohibited from *ex parte* contracts with the judge (private contacts without the presence of other parties) concerning particular cases.

Chapter 2

CHAPTER 7 BANKRUPTCY (STRAIGHT BANKRUPTCY): THE BASIC STEPS

When most people think of bankruptcy, they think of the type of bankruptcy provided for in chapter 7 of the Bankruptcy Code, a liquidation proceeding that is usually called *straight bankruptcy*. This type of bankruptcy has, by far, been the most popular type of proceeding for individuals. Although the percentage of debtors choosing chapter 7 has diminished somewhat because of the advantages that chapter 13 offers, it continues to be the chapter most frequently used, and it remains an important option for consumer debtors.

This chapter describes the routine steps in a typical liquidation case, from beginning to end, with emphasis on the procedures in no-asset cases. (In a no-asset case, none of the debtor's assets are available to unsecured creditors because all are exempt or subject to liens to the full extent of their value.) Chapters 4 through 7 provide the details of how a bankruptcy case is prepared and handled.

In a liquidation case, all of the debtor's nonexempt assets are distributed to creditors, and at the end of the proceedings, the debtor receives a bankruptcy discharge eliminating most debts. From the beginning of the case until its conclusion, each step in the process is directed toward one or both of these ends.

COMMENCEMENT OF THE CASE

Who May File?

Any individual residing, domiciled, or having property or a place of business in the United States may file a chapter 7 bankruptcy. The individual need not be insolvent, and no other test must be met. (However, in limited circumstances a chapter 7 case may be dismissed by the court for "substantial abuse," as discussed in Chapter 12.)

Although a debtor may file on his or her own behalf, an individual generally may not file a bankruptcy case as trustee on behalf of some other person. This may cause occasional problems in cases in which parents have title to liened property in trust for their children. However, the child may be able to file, claiming as exempt the interest as beneficiary of the trust. It may also be possible for the trustee, by filing a chapter 13 case, to secure the benefits of the automatic stay and to prevent the loss of property, but adequate protection must be provided to the creditors. A legally incompetent person may be qualified to file under the Code. In that case, a guardian may be appointed by a court, or an attorney may be able to file the petition as "next friend" to the debtor.

One limitation exists on the broad right to file under chapter 7. An individual is not eligible to file a case if, within the preceding 180 days, (1) he or she was the debtor in a bankruptcy case dismissed for willful failure to abide by orders of the court or to appear before the court in proper prosecution of the case or (2) he or she requested and obtained voluntary dismissal of a bankruptcy case following the filing of a creditor's request for relief from the automatic stay. (The automatic stay is discussed in Chapter 8.)

In interpreting this section, it is important to note that a petition within 180 days of an involuntary dismissal is not improper unless the failure to abide by court orders or to appear was willful. Because the clerk cannot normally make this determination when the later case is filed, it should occur only if, after a motion to dismiss by some party in interest, the court finds the requisite willfulness as a matter of fact.

Simply failing to make payments of filing fees or payments under a prior confirmed chapter 13 plan should not, by itself, preclude a successive filing for 180 days. Nor should failure to appear at the meeting of creditors in a prior case, by itself, be grounds for dismissal of a subsequent filing. A new petition may even be proper while a prior petition is still pending, if the only reason that the prior case is pending in the court's inefficiency in closing it.

There is also some doubt as to the provision concerning voluntary dismissals following requests for relief from the automatic stay. The obvious purpose of this provision is to prevent debtors from repeatedly filing new bankruptcy cases and obtaining new automatic stays after relief was requested or granted in previous cases. With this purpose in mind, it is not unreasonable to read the word *following* to imply some causal connection between the request for relief and the new filing, and some courts have adopted this reading of the law. The provision was surely not meant to apply where there is a voluntary dismissal and a new case after a request for relief from the stay is denied, withdrawn, or settled favorably to the debtor. Congress was not legislating for this type of situation. Similarly, the provision should not apply when the voluntary dismissal and new case are remote in time from the request for relief from the stay, for example, where a request for relief was filed several years earlier and has nothing to do with the new case. Moreover, the existence in the Code of specific limitations on refiling strongly suggests that courts are prohibited from issuing more general orders precluding future filings, although some courts nonetheless continue to issue such orders.

Apart from eligibility to file a chapter 7 case, there are certain requirements for obtaining a chapter 7 discharge. Because the discharge is usually the main goal of filing, few people who do not meet these requirements should voluntarily start a chapter 7 case. The various bars to discharge are listed in the Bankruptcy Code. (Most are discussed at greater length in Chapter 13.) Problems commonly occur when the debtor has received a bankruptcy discharge in a case filed less than six years earlier, with some exceptions for chapter 13 cases, and when the debtor has committed certain acts with an intent to hinder, delay, or defraud a creditor.

The Initial Forms

Although the bankruptcy filing process may seem intimidating at first, a voluntary case actually starts when the debtor files a simple, two-page petition. (A copy of that form can be found in Appendix B.) If no schedule of liabilities is filed with the petition, a list of creditors must also be submitted.

The fee for filing the petition is currently $130. This sum, along with a $30 noticing fee, is normally paid at the time of filing. The fee for a husband and wife filing together as a joint case is the same as for an individual filing alone. The court will accept the petition without the fee if it is accompanied by an application to pay the fee in installments over the next 120 days. The noticing fee presumably cannot be paid in installments. Unfortunately, the law specifically provides that the filing fee may not be waived for debtors who cannot afford it. It is not clear whether this prohibition also applies to the noticing fee. If the fees are never paid or if the required forms are not filed, the case will normally be dismissed.

Debtors must also file a number of other forms either concurrently with the petition or shortly thereafter. These include the debtor's statement of affairs and schedules. (Copies of these forms appear in Appendix B.) A disclosure of attorney's fees and a statement of intentions with respect to property securing consumer debts must also be filed. In many districts, local rules may prescribe another form or two, such as a matrix of creditors' names and addresses for use in preparing mailing labels.

FIRST STEPS AFTER FILING

The filing of a voluntary chapter 7 petition "constitutes an order for relief" under that chapter. This means that the process of granting the relief requested is automatically set in motion.

An interim trustee, chosen from the panel of trustees established in the district, is immediately appointed. The interim trustee normally becomes the permanent trustee. Creditors may elect a different trustee, but this rarely happens in consumer cases. This trustee usually has little to do until later in the case except, perhaps, to peruse the papers filed.

If the debtor has filed an application to pay the filing fee in installments, the court issues an order setting the dates for those payments.

The filing of the petition puts into effect the automatic stay provided for by the Code. (The automatic stay is discussed in Chapter 8.) With a few limited exceptions, the stay prevents further proceedings or acts against the debtor or the debtor's property by anyone, except in the bankruptcy court, with respect to any claims arising before commencement of the case. The stay freezes the debtor's property so that it may be examined and administered in the bankruptcy case. The law also requires any entity holding property that the trustee may use, sell, or lease to make money for the benefit of creditors, or that the debtor may exempt, to deliver that property to the trustee immediately.

Within a few weeks after filing, the court normally mails to all creditors, the debtor, and the debtor's attorney, a notice of the stay and of the date and place set for the meeting of creditors. The notice also contains deadlines for creditors who wish to file claims or lawsuits raising objections to discharge or to the dischargeability of a particular debt. Under the rules, the deadline for complaints objecting to discharge or requesting determination of certain dischargeability issues is 60 days after the first date set for the meeting of creditors. If the case appears to be a no-asset case, the court may notify creditors that claims need not be filed unless they later receive notice that there are assets.

THE MEETING OF CREDITORS

The debtor's first, and often only, appearance at a hearing usually occurs at the meeting of creditors. This meeting is sometimes known as the *section 341(a) meeting* because it is required by section 341(a) of the Bankruptcy Code. It is normally scheduled 20 to 40 days after the debtor files the bankruptcy case, and it must be held at least 20 days after the court's notice. It may be held at the court or at any other place that the court deems to be convenient to the parties. This proceeding is intended to give the various parties a chance to question the debtor and to examine his or her affairs. In practice the meeting allows the trustee to learn whatever he or she feels is necessary to perform the required duties.

Despite the name, creditors rarely appear at the meeting of creditors in a consumer bankruptcy. Some of those who do attend are there only because they are unsophisticated and believe that the notice they received compels their attendance. Others may occasionally come to ask questions if they think they need information for a lawsuit they might file objecting to discharge or dischargeability of a debt.

The meeting itself is usually conducted by the interim trustee or the U.S. trustee at the place where the court holds its sessions. It may last from three to 30 minutes. The interim trustee generally asks the debtor a series of routine questions covering most of the information in the statement of affairs and schedules.

The bankruptcy judge is not permitted to attend the meeting, so that he or she is not influenced by any information brought out there. It is somewhat unclear whether court evidentiary rules apply, and it is doubtful that the trustee (who is, in essence, another party to the case) has the authority to resolve any disputes that arise. Disputes should presumably be brought before the judge for resolution if any party feels strongly enough about it to do so. Although creditors new to bankruptcy may not realize it, it is clear that the trustee has no power to rule on any question concerning the stay, the discharge, or any other dispute between a creditor and the debtor.

AFTER THE MEETING OF CREDITORS

What happens after the meeting of creditors depends to some extent on whether the debtor has assets that are neither exempt nor fully subject to liens and are thus available for creditors. Unless some party objects, the debtor always retains property that is claimed as exempt. The trustee generally abandons property that has no significant nonexempt equity. When the property is abandoned, the trustee in effect disclaims interest in it, and the property reverts to the debtor. Ordinarily, once property is abandoned by the trustee, that decision is irrevocable.

In cases where there is property securing a consumer debt—that is, there is a lien on property—and where the debtor has filed a statement of intention to redeem the property, surrender it, or reaffirm the debt, that intention must be performed. (These options are discussed in detail in Chapter 10.) The normal deadline for the debtor's performance is 45 days after the statement is filed, but the court may extend that deadline for cause if the debtor so requests before it expires. In any case, the debtor's rights with regard to the property should not be affected by the debtor's failure to meet the deadline, which serves only as a guideline to when the required events should occur.

In cases where property remains in the estate, it is normally administered by the trustee, except where the property has little value. In such cases, called *nominal-asset cases*, the debtor may request that the property be abandoned on the grounds that it would not provide any meaningful distribution to creditors after the costs of administration were paid. Any sale of estate assets involves some administrative expense to the trustee, and these costs must be paid before creditors receive anything. If only a small amount of property can be sold, all of the proceeds would likely go to the trustee and none to the creditors, thus defeating the purpose of the sale, which is to benefit the creditors. The amount of assets considered to be nominal varies from district to district, and ranges from under $500 to about $2,500.

If the estate has more than nominal assets, they must be turned over to the trustee at or after the meeting of creditors. The debtor is usually offered the option of paying their value to the trustee instead. The trustee then collects any other property of the estate that is neither exempt nor abandoned and liquidates the estate (converts it to cash). The trustee must normally give 20 days notice of intent to sell the property, and any party, including the debtor, may object to the proposed sale, within specified time limits. The property may be liquidated through a private sale or a public auction.

While the nonexempt assets of the estate are being liquidated, the trustee receives and evaluates all claims filed by creditors, objecting to them if they are improper. Unless an objection is filed, a proof of claim in proper form is deemed allowed, which means it is considered valid. This does not necessarily mean that the claim will be paid in full, or even at all. Payment of a claim depends on whether there are sufficient assets to pay it. The distribution scheme is described below.

Any objections to claims that are filed are ruled on by the court. Once the status of the claims is determined and the deadline for filing claims is past, the trustee distributes the assets to creditors.

If any property is partially subject to liens, the claims of secured creditors (those who hold the liens) are paid before distribution to unsecured creditors (those who do not hold liens). If an asset is partially exempt, the debtor's exemption should be paid in cash generated from the sale of the asset before distribution.

The distribution is carried out according to priority rules in the Bankruptcy Code. The rules put into effect various policy decisions of the drafters regarding who should be paid first. Payments to creditors whose claims are allowed for this distribution are generally called *dividends*. Briefly, the order of distribution is as follows (many of these categories being rarely applicable, even in the consumer cases in which a distribution occurs):

1. Senior liens granted to secure credit obtained by the trustee or the debtor during the case (normally for operation of the debtor's business)

2. Secured creditors, in order of lien priority (usually based on which creditor obtained a lien on the property first), from property not abandoned (where there is a nonexempt interest in the property that the trustee can liquidate)

3. Junior liens granted to secure credit for the operation of the debtor's business during bankruptcy

4. "Super priority" unsecured claims granted to creditors who have been harmed by failure of the debtor or trustee to provide adequate protection of their interests in property during the case (the concept of adequate protection is discussed in Chapter 8)

5. Administrative expenses of conducting the bankruptcy case—including costs of preserving the estate; taxes incurred by the estate; payments to the trustee, attorneys, accountants, and so forth—and certain specified expenses of creditors helping the estate

6. Certain unsecured claims, in involuntary cases only

7. Allowed unsecured claims for wages, salaries, or vacation, severance, or sick pay earned from the debtor within 90 days before the filing of the petition or the cessation of the debtor's business, whichever occurred first, up to $2,000 per claimant

8. Allowed unsecured claims for contributions to employee pension or benefit plans, arising from services furnished to the debtor within 180 days before the filing of the petition or the cessation of business, whichever occurred first, up to $2,000 times the number of employees, minus the amount paid under (7) above

9. Allowed unsecured claims of persons engaged in the production or raising of grain, for grain or its proceeds, against debtors who own or operate grain storage facilities, or of U.S. fishermen, up to $2,000, against debtors operating fish produce storage or processing facilities

10. Certain allowed unsecured claims from the deposit of money by consumers for the purchase, lease, or rental of property or services not provided, up to $900 per individual

11. Certain allowed unsecured claims of government bodies—for example, taxes—specified in the law

12. Certain allowed unsecured claims based on responsibilities to the government related to its oversight of the banking industry

13. General unsecured claims filed on time

14. General unsecured claims filed after the deadline for filing claims

15. Allowed claims for fines, penalties, forfeitures, or multiple, exemplary, or punitive damages

16. Interest at the legal rate on all claims paid, from the date of filing

17. The debtor receives any property that is left after all of the above are paid in full.

If there is not enough money to pay every one of these categories, as is almost always the case, the distribution stops, and the lowest category that is reached is paid *pro rata* (the same percentage for each creditor) on its claims.

If the debtor has certain types of community property, which in some states includes property owned by a spouse who has not filed a bankruptcy case, distribution follows a somewhat different order. The community property is segregated from other property of the estate and the estate is distributed in several stages. Within all but the first two stages, the order set forth above is applied. The stages are as follows:

1. The claims set out in (1) through (4) above, in that order, from property to which they are applicable

2. Claims for administrative expenses, which can also be paid from other property of the estate, as justice requires

3. Community claims (generally, claims for which the community property may be taken by creditors outside of bankruptcy) against the debtor or the debtor's spouse, from community property in the estate, except to the extent that the community property could only be taken for separate debts of the debtor

4. Community claims against the debtor not paid under (3) above, from community property in the estate that could only be taken for debts of the debtor

5. Claims against the debtor, including community claims not paid under (3) and (4) above, from property of the estate other than the community property involved

6. Community claims against the debtor or the debtor's spouse not already paid, from all remaining property of the estate

After distribution, the trustee makes a final report and accounting to the court. This concludes the case.

In most cases involving consumer debtors, of course, no distribution is made to any of the parties listed above because there are no assets to distribute. In such cases, depending on local practice, the trustee may make a report to the court, setting forth any objections to the discharge or the claim of exemption.

THE DISCHARGE AND THE DISCHARGE HEARING

The final step in a straight bankruptcy is usually the granting of the debtor's discharge. The discharge applies to all debts except certain taxes, debts not listed by the debtor in the schedules, some debts for alimony and spousal and child support, most fines and penalties owed to government bodies, some student loans, debts that were or could have been listed in a prior bankruptcy as to which discharge was denied or waived, certain debts incurred through driving while intoxicated, certain debts of individuals involved in the banking or savings and loan industry, and debts that have been ruled nondischargeable during the case. (A detailed discussion of these exceptions to discharge is found in Chapter 13.) Also, to the extent that a secured creditor's lien has not been disallowed, nullified, or satisfied during the case, the creditor will most likely retain the right to bring a lawsuit to enforce its lien after the bankruptcy if the debtor does not pay the debt according to its terms.

In cases in which the debtor desires to reaffirm a debt (enter into a new and binding promise to repay) and in such other cases as the court deems appropriate, the court schedules a discharge hearing. Few courts, if any, regularly conduct discharge hearings in cases in which there is no reaffirmation. The discharge hearing is the last opportunity for the reaffirmation of most discharged debts. Because of a strong policy against reaffirmation agreements, which were greatly abused by creditors under the prior law, the Code requires that the judge carefully explain reaffirmation to the debtor at the discharge hearing. The reaffirmation agreement must then be reviewed by the court unless (1) the creditor has a lien on the debtor's real estate, or (2) the debtor's attorney files a written declaration that the reaffirmation agreement is a fully informed and voluntary act that does not impose undue hardship on the debtor or the debtor's dependents. The court may only approve the agreement if it does not impose undue hardship on the debtor or the debtor's dependents and is in the debtor's best interest.

Once the discharge has been entered, a no-asset chapter 7 case is complete, except for a notice of discharge, which the court sends to the debtor and the creditors. Unless new property comes into the estate within 180 days of the filing of the original petition, the court has nothing further to do, and the case is closed.

Chapter 3

CHAPTER 13 BANKRUPTCY: THE BASIC STEPS

A chapter 13 bankruptcy gives the debtor the opportunity to adjust his or her financial affairs without having to give up or liquidate current assets. Rather than being designed to pay debts out of those assets, a chapter 13 case usually involves payment of debts out of future income, although the debtor may also decide on some payment out of current assets. The debtor is allowed to keep and use all property, whether exempt or not, and to pay some or all debts according to a plan approved by the court. At the completion of this plan (or, in some cases, earlier) the debtor receives a discharge, eliminating further responsibility for most debts. With several significant exceptions, this discharge is similar to the discharge received in a chapter 7 case.

This chapter describes the sequence of events in a typical chapter 13 bankruptcy. Many of these events are quite similar to those in a chapter 7 bankruptcy. Chapters 4 through 7 of this book provide a detailed guide to the steps that are normally taken in preparing and handling the case.

COMMENCEMENT OF THE CASE

Who May File?

Chapter 13 is available to "individual[s] with regular income" who reside, are domiciled, or have property or a place of business in the United States. As discussed in Chapter 2, an incompetent person may be eligible to file a bankruptcy case, including a case under chapter 13. To be an "individual with regular income," one must be "any individual whose income is sufficiently stable and regular to enable such individual to make payments under a plan under chapter 13." This definition was clearly intended to encompass not only wage earners, but also recipients of government benefits, alimony or support payments, or any other regular type of income. The question of how regular the income must be is left to the courts, but since such types of income as commissions are meant to be included, it is clear that the debtor need not receive payments at particular or rigid intervals. A spouse or other living partner of a person with regular income, who has no independent source of income, may be able to file a petition without the other spouse or partner. The definition focuses on whether the debtor will have funds available for a plan. Thus, if a person can show a regular allowance from a living partner for expenses, he or she should be eligible for chapter 13. An unemployed spouse may clearly file jointly with the other spouse. (The regular income requirement is discussed further in Chapter 11.)

Besides regular income, a second limitation on eligibility for chapter 13 is the amount of debt. Although the limits do not pose problems for most consumer debtors, chapter 13 is not available to debtors (or debtor couples) with more than $100,000 of noncontingent, liquidated, unsecured debts or more than $350,000 of noncontingent, liquidated, secured debts. (This requirement is discussed further in Chapter 11.) As in chapter 7, though, the debtor need not be insolvent.

As in chapter 7 bankruptcies, an individual whose prior bankruptcy was dismissed within the previous 180 days may not be eligible for chapter 13 relief. The Code bars the debtor from filing a new case if the prior case was (1) dismissed for willful failure of the debtor to abide by orders of the court or to appear before the court in proper prosecution of the case or (2) voluntarily dismissed following a request for relief from the automatic stay of the Code. (See Chapter 2 for further discussion of these provisions.)

A major advantage of chapter 13 is the absence of the bars to discharge found in chapter 7. A chapter 13 discharge may be obtained by a debtor who has received a chapter 7 discharge within six years before filing or who would not be granted a discharge due to some other provision in chapter 7. The only impediments to discharge in a chapter 13 case are the requirements for a plan, discussed below, and the possibility that the discharge could, in some cases, be revoked on the grounds that it was obtained fraudulently.

The Initial Forms

The debtor begins a chapter 13 bankruptcy case by filing a two-page petition, which is identical to a chapter 7 petition but is filled in somewhat differently. (A copy of the petition can be found in Appendix B.) As in chapter 7, the petition must be accompanied by a $130 filing fee (whether the petition is individual or joint) or an application to pay the fee in installments, plus a $30 noticing fee. If an application to pay in installments is filed, the debtor need not pay the filing fee at the time of filing but must usually still pay the noticing fee; the filing fee may be paid over a period of up to 180 days. No waiver of the filing fee is permitted, and it is unclear whether the noticing fee may be waived for debtors who cannot afford to pay it. If the debtor is not prepared to file schedules with the petition, he or she must supply a list of creditors and their addresses.

In addition to the petition, the debtor must file schedules and a statement of financial affairs. (Copies of these forms are found in Appendix B.) A disclosure of attorney's fees and a chapter 13 plan (the debtor's description of which creditors will be paid when, how, and how much) are also required. If these documents are not filed with the petition, they must be filed within 15 days afterward. The schedules and statement of financial affairs for a chapter 13 filing are identical to those required in chapter 7. There are only two significant differences in the filing required under the two chapters. First, chapter 13 filers can omit a statement of intent with regard to property securing consumer debts. Second, a chapter 13 plan is required. Local rules or practice may require certain other papers to be filed, either with the petition or shortly thereafter.

The debtor is given great leeway in formulating the chapter 13 plan, subject to only a few requirements. The most important of the provisions that are usually required are listed below:

1. All claims that are made "priority claims" by the Bankruptcy Code must be paid in full. (These claims are those grouped in categories [4] through [12] under "After the Meeting of Creditors" in Chapter 2.)

2. The present value of payments to unsecured claims must be at least equal to what would be paid in a chapter 7 liquidation. (The term *present value* means that if the claims are paid over time, the creditor may request interest to compensate for the delay in payment. This provision is discussed in detail in Chapter 11.)

3. With respect to each allowed secured claim (generally, a claim of a creditor holding a lien on the debtor's property) provided for by the plan, either (a) the holder of the claim accepts the plan, (b) the plan provides for payments with a present value in the amount of the claim and continuance of the lien, or (c) the debtor surrenders the property securing the claim to the creditor. (This provision is discussed in detail in Chapter 10.)

4. If a party in interest objects to the plan, the plan must either commit all of the debtor's disposable income (income not necessary for the reasonable expenses of supporting the debtor and the

debtor's dependents) for three years or pay unsecured claims in full. (This provision is discussed in detail in Chapter 11.)

Conversion from Chapter 7 Proceedings

Another way of obtaining chapter 13 relief is through conversion from a chapter 7 case. Any debtor who has begun a chapter 7 case may convert it to a chapter 13 case at any time provided that the debtor is eligible for relief under chapter 13. The court's determination that debts are nondischargeable in chapter 7 does not preclude conversion, and in fact, conversion may be the best strategy in such a situation, given the broader discharge available in chapter 13. (The comparative discharges are discussed in detail in Chapter 13 of this guide.) Similarly, any person who has commenced a chapter 13 case may elect to convert it to a chapter 7 case. A debtor may convert a case from chapter 7 to chapter 13 without obtaining the court's permission only if the case was commenced as a chapter 7 case; if the case had previously been converted to chapter 7, a second or third conversion may occur only with the court's permission.

FIRST STEPS AFTER FILING

As in a chapter 7 case, the filing of a petition operates as an order for relief and sets the bankruptcy process in motion. A trustee, usually the standing trustee for the district, is appointed, and if the debtor has applied for it, an order is entered for payment of the filing fee in installments.

The filing of a petition immediately puts into effect the automatic stay, which prevents any further creditor actions against the debtor or the debtor's property with respect to claims arising before the case began. The filing of a chapter 13 case also puts into effect a stay of actions against most nonfiling codebtors who are obligated to pay claims against the debtor, such as cosigners on loans or other debts. (These automatic stays are discussed in detail in Chapter 8.) Creditors must obtain the permission of the bankruptcy court before proceeding with any of the acts prohibited by either stay. In the case of the stay of actions against codebtors, this permission may be granted to the extent that one of the following is true:

1. The codebtor was the principal debtor who received the money or property on which the claim is based (that is, the debtor was the cosigner).
2. The debtor's plan proposes not to pay the claim.
3. The creditor would be irreparably harmed by the stay.

The Bankruptcy Code requires that, as of the commencement of the case, any entity holding property that the trustee or the chapter 13 debtor may use, sell, or lease or that the debtor may exempt must deliver that property to the trustee. (This requirement is discussed further in Chapter 8.) Because the debtor in a chapter 13 case generally has a right to possess all property of the estate, the trustee presumably then delivers the property to the debtor.

The debtor must begin making plan payments within 30 days after filing the plan, unless the court orders otherwise. These payments are retained by the trustee pending confirmation (court approval of the plan). If the plan is not confirmed, they are returned to the debtor after administrative costs are deducted.

This provision permits quicker payment to creditors and also gives the court some evidence of the debtor's ability to pay, a consideration in confirming the plan. Failure to commence payments as required may be grounds for dismissal of the case.

Within a relatively short time, the clerk issues the notice of the meeting of creditors (which is also called the section 341(a) meeting because it is required by section 341(a) of the Code). This form also notifies creditors of the automatic stay and of the deadlines for filing their claims with the court.

THE MEETING OF CREDITORS

The meeting of creditors, required in each case, is normally scheduled between 20 and 50 days after the bankruptcy petition is filed. As in a chapter 7 case, the primary purpose for the meeting of creditors is to give the trustee and the creditors the opportunity to question the debtor and to determine whether there are any grounds for objecting to the plan. The trustee generally inquires into the information presented in the schedules, statement of financial affairs, and plan, including the debtor's ability to make the proposed payments. Despite the popular name for the proceedings, creditors rarely appear in most judicial districts. The bankruptcy judge is not permitted to attend.

The meeting is likely to last between five and 30 minutes and it generally follows the pattern of routine questions asked in a chapter 7 case. In some districts, the proceeding serves as an opportunity for the debtor to negotiate with the creditors or the trustee to obviate any objections to the plan.

The debtor may wish to file claims on behalf of certain creditors who have not filed themselves, in order to protect the purposes of the plan. For example, a debtor who wants a secured or nondischargeable claim to be paid through the plan would file a claim on behalf of that creditor if the creditor does not file its own claim. This may be done at the meeting of creditors or within 120 days thereafter.

During or after the meeting, the trustee must decide whether to object to any of the claims filed. The debtor may also object to the amount, validity, lien status, or any other aspect of a claim. Ultimately, all disputes on these matters must be resolved by the bankruptcy judge, who sometimes considers them in conjunction with the confirmation hearing.

THE CONFIRMATION HEARING

The confirmation hearing may occur on the same day as the meeting of creditors or sometime within the next several months, depending on local practice. In either case, the court must give at least 25 days' notice of the date of the hearing. Its purpose is to provide a basis for ruling on whether the plan will be confirmed, to inquire into whether the requirements of chapter 13 are met, and to hear any objections to confirmation and any evidence or argument that is necessary. Although the court often rules on confirmation at the hearing, there is no requirement that it do so. If confirmation is denied, the debtor is normally allowed an opportunity to modify the plan to meet the court's objections.

The confirmation order binds the debtor and all creditors to the terms of the plan. Normally, the trustee then begins distributing payments to creditors under the plan. Confirmation also "revests" title to all property of the estate in the debtor, free and clear of any creditor's claim, except as otherwise provided in the plan. This means that, unless the plan provides otherwise, the debtor has title to his or her property free of the bankruptcy. If the plan is completed successfully, there are normally no impediments to the debtor's discharge. However, in limited circumstances, the court may revoke an order of confirmation if a party in interest can show that the confirmation order was procured by fraud.

MODIFICATION OF THE PLAN AND TRANSACTIONS AFTER BANKRUPTCY IS FILED

The debtor may wish to modify the plan he or she originally submitted for various reasons. This can generally be accomplished with little difficulty. Before confirmation, the plan may be modified as a matter of course, as long as the modified plan meets the requirements of chapter 13. If a claim holder has filed an acceptance of the plan, the acceptance is deemed to apply to the modified plan unless the holder's rights are modified and the holder withdraws acceptance.

After confirmation, the procedure is slightly different. The debtor may modify the plan unless, after notice and a hearing, the modification is disapproved. Given the Code's definition of "notice and a hearing" as simply the giving of notice and the opportunity to request a hearing, it is possible that disapproval could occur without a hearing unless the debtor or some other party requests one. In addition, a hearing might not occur if the court feels it is not necessary. In most cases, though, the court resolves any objection to a postconfirmation modification after a hearing. Although the debtor need not establish good cause for modification, the modified plan must, of course, meet the requirements of the Code.

A common reason for modification is to cure postbankruptcy mortgage defaults by adding the defaulted amounts to the plan. The debtor may also wish to provide for postpetition transactions that arise from an unforeseen emergency or change in the debtor's circumstances. Postpetition claims may generally be provided for in the initial plan but will be disallowed if the claimant knew or should have known that the trustee's prior approval of the debtor's incurring the obligation was practicable and such approval was not obtained. Postpetition obligations may also be incurred with the trustee's permission and paid outside the plan, that is, with payments not being made through the trustee. Unless a postpetition claim is provided for by the plan, it survives the chapter 13 discharge at the end of the case.

The trustee or the holder of an unsecured claim may also move for modification of the plan. The principal reason for such a motion would be a change in the debtor's income or expenses that would allow the debtor to make larger payments. Normally, a modification of the plan at a creditor's request is not granted without a hearing unless the debtor consents. Because the Bankruptcy Rules are not fully clear on the procedure for postconfirmation modification, local practice may vary. Debtors should oppose any plan to which they do not fully consent. (Motions for modification of a plan after confirmation are discussed further in Chapter 11.)

RESULTS OF A DEBTOR'S FAILURE TO COMPLETE THE PLAN

In some cases, usually due to loss of income, the debtor is unable to complete the plan as proposed. In such situations, four options are available, each of which has somewhat different consequences.

Hardship Discharge

The Bankruptcy Code provides for a hardship discharge if the debtor's problems are caused by circumstances for which the debtor is not justly accountable. Such circumstances may include the debtor's death or a serious deterioration of the debtor's financial circumstances. A hardship discharge may be granted at any time after confirmation, provided that unsecured creditors have received as much as they would have received in a chapter 7 liquidation. Thus, there need not have been the full payment of priority claims normally required in a chapter 13 case.

It is unclear what happens to holders of liens on the debtor's property after a hardship discharge. If they have retained their liens under the plan, they presumably still have liens in the amounts of their allowed secured claims left unpaid. (As discussed in Chapter 10, the allowed secured claim is normally the lesser of the claim or the value of the collateral at the beginning of the bankruptcy case.) If a creditor did not retain a lien, its claim would presumably be discharged, and no lien would remain. As to other claims, the debtor receives a discharge equivalent to that granted in a chapter 7 case, and not the broader chapter 13 discharge that the debtor would have received on completion of the plan. (A discussion of the difference between the discharge in chapter 7 cases and the discharge in chapter 13 cases where the plan is completed may be found in Chapter 13 of this book.)

A hardship discharge is granted only when modification of the plan is not practicable. The Code seems to prefer modification whenever possible. The debtor, too, often has good reason to prefer that remedy.

Modification of the Plan

It is often possible to modify the plan, under the provisions discussed above, to accommodate new problems as they arise. The payments under the plan may be reduced or even terminated if the modified plan still complies with the requirements of chapter 13.

The advantages of modification are that the broader chapter 13 discharge is preserved and the hardship discharge tests need not be met. However, the priority claims and allowed secured claims (claims in which there are liens that cannot be eliminated) provided for in the plan must normally still be paid. If they cannot be paid, modification may be impracticable.

Conversion to Chapter 7

The chapter 13 debtor always has the right to convert a case to chapter 7 without showing hardship, and in most cases such a conversion provides the same relief as the hardship discharge. A new set of schedules generally need not be filed; however, a statement of intention concerning consumer debts in which there are liens, if not previously filed, must be submitted within 30 days after the order of conversion is entered or before the date set for the meeting of creditors, whichever is earlier.

The debtor must also file a supplemental schedule of debts arising since the chapter 13 case was initially filed. These debts will be treated as if they arose before commencement of the case. Thus, where applicable, the automatic stay prevents creditor action on these debts, and they may be discharged. After the conversion, the debtor's nonexempt property, if any, is liquidated, and the debtor receives a chapter 7 discharge as described in Chapter 2.

Unlike the case in which a hardship discharge is granted, the court looks to the full value of the debtor's estate in a case converted to chapter 7, and some courts have held the estate to include all property acquired since the chapter 13 petition was filed. On conversion, however, the debtor should be entitled to receive postpetition earnings held by the trustee, even if a plan has been confirmed, at least to the extent of applicable exemptions. In addition, a postpetition increase in the value of property acquired prepetition should not be included in the estate.

Any nonexempt property in the estate is liquidated, regardless of what the creditors have already received under the plan (at least to the extent necessary to pay all creditors in full). In cases in which the debtor has nonexempt assets and can meet the requirements to obtain a hardship discharge, that course of action is often preferable to conversion.

On the other hand, an advantage of conversion is that it allows postpetition debts arising before conversion to be treated as if they arose prepetition. These debts may thus be discharged if they are dischargeable under chapter 7. This may make conversion an attractive option for the debtor who has significant unsecured postpetition debts. Conversion of the case does not create a new automatic stay when stay relief has been previously granted, for example to a mortgage holder trying to foreclose. It may sometimes be possible, however, to move to have a stay reimposed if the debtor can ensure that the creditor's rights will be protected.

The debtor may wish to convert if the reasons for the initial choice of chapter 13 no longer apply. For example, the debtor may have chosen chapter 13 to protect property, such as an automobile, from repossession. If that property is later destroyed or is no longer of value to the debtor, chapter 13 may no longer be necessary.

Conversion may also be advantageous when the debtor is unable to complete his or her plan, is ineligible for a hardship discharge, and yet wishes to obtain a discharge of unsecured debts or to preserve the effect of lien avoidance or other orders obtained under chapter 13. (The ability of a debtor to avoid, or nullify, certain liens is discussed in Chapters 9 and 10.) If a case is voluntarily or involuntarily dismissed, rather than converted, liens avoided in the bankruptcy are reinstated.

Conversion to chapter 7 can also be ordered against the debtor's will on request of a party in interest, such as a creditor. The court may order conversion only "for cause," such as unreasonable delay to the prejudice of creditors, failure to file a timely plan, failure to commence plan payments, denial of confirmation along with denial of time to file a modified plan, a material default by the debtor in performance of a plan, revocation of confirmation, or termination of a plan according to its own terms. However, if the debtor is a farmer, the Code provides that the court may not convert the case to chapter 7 unless the debtor so requests.

Dismissal

Dismissal may occasionally be preferable to any of the other options. The debtor has the right to obtain dismissal of a chapter 13 case at any time unless the case was previously converted from another chapter. This route may be particularly attractive if it appears that the case may be converted to chapter 7 against the debtor's will and if the debtor has nonexempt property that he or she does not wish to see liquidated. Whether the right to a dismissal continues after the case has been converted is unclear.

A dismissal places the debtor and the creditors where they were before the case began. Unless the court orders otherwise, a dismissal vacates most bankruptcy orders and returns the parties as much as possible to the status quo before the petition. In some cases, this may be preferable to the other alternatives, leaving the debtor to deal with creditors as best he or she can. The debtor is obviously entitled to the benefit of any payments made before the case is dismissed. Some debts may have been completely or partially paid, and the debtor may be able to work out an agreement directly with the creditor on the balance due.

Dismissal, like conversion, can also be ordered against the debtor's will, for cause, at the request of any party. In addition to the reasons that might justify conversion, the court may also dismiss the case for failure to pay required fees and charges or for failure to file required documents.

DISCHARGE

The final step in a successfully completed chapter 13 case or in one ended under the hardship provisions is the discharge order, which wipes out most debts. A discharge must be granted by the court "as soon as practicable" after the debtor completes all payments under a confirmed plan. There can be no further objection to discharge at this point. Thereafter, the discharge is revocable only if it was obtained by fraud and only if the fraud first came to an objector's attention after the discharge. Revocation of a discharge must be sought within a year of the discharge.

The discharge hearing provisions of the Bankruptcy Code, discussed in Chapter 2, apply to chapter 13 as well as to chapter 7. Thus, the debtor must seek court approval for any reaffirmation agreement on consumer debts that are neither secured by real estate nor negotiated by an attorney who certifies that they are fully informed, voluntary, and do not pose any hardship. The debtor must also be warned about the consequences of reaffirmation at the discharge hearing whenever there is reaffirmation.

The discharge received in a chapter 13 bankruptcy is often broader than that received in a chapter 7 case. It includes all debts provided for by the plan except most support and alimony payments, drunk driving debts, many unpaid student loan debts, restitution debts ordered in connection with a criminal sentence and long-term debts with final payments due after the completion of the plan that are cured in the plan (as discussed in Chapter 10). Thus, the chapter 13 discharge may eliminate liability on many debts not dischargeable in a chapter 7 case, including those incurred through fraud or false pretenses, willful and malicious injuries, and fines or penalties. (The chapter 13 discharge is discussed in detail in Chapter 13 of this guide.) However, as in chapter 7, to the extent that a secured creditor's lien has not been disallowed, avoided, or satisfied, that creditor will most likely retain the right to bring a lawsuit to enforce its lien if the underlying debt is not paid according to its terms.

A notice of discharge is mailed to all creditors and the trustee soon after the discharge. The debtor and the debtor's attorney also receive a copy of this notice, which normally marks the end of the case. However, even after the case is closed, the debtor may have a case reopened if additional relief is necessary.

Part II

BANKRUPTCY STEP BY STEP

Chapter 4

KNOWING ALL THE FACTS ABOUT YOUR FINANCIAL PICTURE

Unlike the first three chapters, Chapters 4 through 7 are intended primarily to be a guide to the specific details involved in filing consumer bankruptcy cases. To put these details into a meaningful context, the reader should have a general grasp of the basic concepts of bankruptcy set out in Chapters 1 through 3. These next chapters describe all of the necessary steps involved in consumer bankruptcy cases. It is hoped that they will serve as a road map for those who are considering embarking on the process and as a useful self-checkup for those who have decided on or perhaps have already begun their bankruptcy cases. Because most of the steps involved in chapter 7 and chapter 13 cases are identical or at least similar, both types of proceedings are considered together.

THE IMPORTANCE OF KNOWING ALL THE FACTS

Before a bankruptcy case can be filed, the debtor must decide whether bankruptcy is, in fact, the best vehicle for dealing with the problems that the debtor faces. In a typical consumer bankruptcy case, most of the attorney's analysis involves comparing bankruptcy with other possible avenues of handling financial problems.

A necessary prerequisite to such comparison is a knowledge of all the relevant facts. Although it may sometimes be possible to rule out bankruptcy based on knowledge of only a few facts (for example, that a debtor does not wish to lose certain property that cannot be saved in bankruptcy), it is never possible to decide safely to pursue bankruptcy without a thorough knowledge of the facts. Without such knowledge, unknown property (such as the right to a tax refund) may be lost in bankruptcy; major debts may turn out to be unaffected because they cannot be discharged or because there are liens on property; or property might be incorrectly valued and, as a result, lost to creditors.

Equally important is that, without complete information, an attorney may not be able to use the bankruptcy for the debtor's maximum benefit. The protection of the automatic stay may be lost, for example, if a creditor is not notified before repossessing the debtor's car because no one checked to see if the debtor was behind in payments. The debtor's right to eliminate or modify a lien may be lost because the existence of the lien is not discovered in the fact-gathering stage of the case. Moreover, debts not listed in the bankruptcy papers might survive a bankruptcy discharge. Even if they are discovered during the pendency of the case and can be included, they may lead to additional fees for the debtor and more work for the debtor's attorney.

Therefore, it is essential for anyone planning to see an attorney about a bankruptcy case to gather as much of the information discussed below as possible. Having done so will make the consultation more productive and will ensure that the maximum benefit is obtained if a bankruptcy case is filed.

Finally, much of the information that should be gathered early on is necessary for the proper completion of the bankruptcy forms. It makes sense, then, to review this information before, rather than after, committing to pursue a bankruptcy instead of other possible strategies.

TYPES OF DEBTS

In considering bankruptcy and its possible effects, it is crucial to understand the different types of debts that can exist, as classified by state and bankruptcy laws. Bankruptcy's effect on a particular debt depends largely on what type of debt it is.

Secured Debts

All secured debts have one characteristic in common. The person or entity to whom they are owed has a *lien* on some piece, or perhaps many pieces, of the debtor's property. A lien gives the creditor special rights to that particular property if the creditor's debt is not paid. These rights allow the creditor to go after the property to pay the debt before the property can be used to pay creditors who do not have liens on it.

There are several types of liens. With a mortgage, for example, a borrower agrees that the creditor can foreclose on real estate if the debt is not paid. Security interests in property, such as cars or appliances, represent another type of lien. The borrower signs an agreement giving the creditor the right to repossess the property if the debt is not paid. If the home, car, or appliance was purchased with the money from the transaction in which the debtor agreed to the lien, it is called a *purchase-money security interest*. If the underlying debt did not finance the purchase of the collateral, for example in the case of a second mortgage securing a home equity loan, a lien agreed to by the debtor is called a *nonpurchase-money security interest*. The right of a pawnbroker to hold property until a loan is repaid is one type of security interest. Unlike the others mentioned above, though, it is a *possessory* rather than a *nonpossessory* security interest because the creditor has possession of the liened property.

The law may create a lien that arises without an agreement in certain circumstances; this is called a *statutory lien*. Examples include a tax lien, which the Internal Revenue Service or a state or local government may obtain if a tax is not paid, and a garageman's lien, which in many places gives someone who has repaired an automobile the right to hold onto it until the repair costs are paid.

Finally, some liens arise as the result of court proceedings; these are called *judicial liens*. In many states, when a civil judgment determining that someone owes a debt is entered in the court records, a lien is automatically placed on all real estate owned by the person who was sued, at least if the real estate is in the county in which the judgment is filed. A creditor may also ask a sheriff or other judicial officer to put a lien on other types of property after a court judgment against a debtor. The sheriff then *attaches*, or *levies* on, the property, which could be a car, furniture, stock, a bank account, or almost anything other than real estate. The lien that results, called a *levy*, is also a judicial lien.

Two or more creditors may sometimes have liens on the same property. In such cases, there are legal rules regarding who has first dibs, or *lien priority*, on that property. Priority usually, but not always, depends on who obtained the first lien. The creditor that has the highest priority is sometimes called the *senior lienholder*, and the others are called *junior lienholders*.

The total amount of liens on a property determines the debtor's *equity* in the property. Equity is generally computed by subtracting the total amount of liens from the total fair market value of the property. For example, if a house is worth $100,000 and on it are a first mortgage of $50,000, a second mortgage of $10,000, and a judgment lien of $5,000, the equity in the house is $35,000. The liens on a property occasionally add up to as much as or more than the property is worth. In this case, the owner has no equity or perhaps "negative equity" in the property.

The liens held by many secured creditors cannot be eliminated in bankruptcy. If the debtor wants to keep the liened property, these debts must be paid during or after bankruptcy. However, bankruptcy does offer various ways of solving problems with secured debts and sometimes offers ways of eliminating liens. (Liens are discussed in Chapters 8 through 10.)

Unsecured Debts

Most debts are unsecured debts, which are, in a sense, ordinary debts. They may be owed to individuals or to businesses and may result from loans, purchases, and even liability for an accident or a wrong done to another person. The distinguishing feature of an unsecured debt is that the creditor does not have a lien on any of the debtor's property. This means that the creditor has no special rights above those of other creditors to obtain repayment from any particular piece of property owned by the debtor.

Generally, unsecured debts may be discharged, or eliminated, in bankruptcy. However, certain types of unsecured debts are exceptions to this rule and are nondischargeable. (These exceptions to discharge are discussed in detail in Chapter 13.)

Priority Debts

In passing the bankruptcy laws, Congress decided that a few categories of unsecured debts should receive better treatment than others in the distribution of the debtor's assets. These debts are called *priority debts*. If, after liens on the debtor's property have been paid, additional assets can be made available to creditors (assets that the debtor cannot save using exemption laws), the priority creditors are paid first from those assets. Only after the priority claims are paid in full are the other unsecured creditors paid.

The most common priority claims include various kinds of taxes owed to government bodies, claims of employees for wages and benefits (up to a certain amount), and deposits made by consumers for goods and services never delivered (up to certain amounts). In addition, the administrative costs necessary to file the bankruptcy case and keep it going—including the fees of lawyers, trustees, and other professionals—called *administrative claims*, receive first priority treatment. All of the priority claims are listed in Chapter 2, categories (4) through (12).

It is important to distinguish priority debts from nondischargeable debts. Most priority debts are dischargeable in bankruptcy, in both chapters 7 and 13. Priority status means only that, if there are assets in the bankruptcy estate to be distributed, creditors with priority status are satisfied before most other creditors. As discussed later in Chapter 11, it also means that the debt must usually be paid in full in a chapter 13 plan. On the other hand, most nondischargeable debts (other than some taxes) do not receive any special treatment in the distribution of assets in bankruptcy. The creditors to whom those debts are owed simply retain the right to try to collect them from the debtor after bankruptcy.

TYPES OF PROPERTY

Just as it is important to understand the different types of debts a person may have, it is also important to be familiar with different types of interests in property. Many of the rights of debtors under the Bankruptcy Code—such as rights to exempt property, discussed in Chapter 9, or rights to modify or eliminate liens, discussed in Chapters 9 and 10—depend on what type of property is involved and what type of an ownership interest the debtor has in the property.

Real Property

In legal parlance, the term *real property* refers to real estate. It includes any types of real estate owned by a debtor, including residential and commercial land and buildings. Real property also includes any other rights a debtor might have with respect to real estate. A lease for an apartment is considered an interest in real property, as is an easement, that is, the right to use a particular piece of ground for some purpose.

In most states, a mobile home is not considered to be real property, although if it is permanently affixed to land, it might be considered real property in some places. The ownership or leasing of the land under a mobile home is always considered real property.

Property can sometimes become real property if it is permanently attached to a building. Items such as cabinets or plumbing are called *fixtures* once they become a part of a building and are then considered to be part of the real estate.

Personal Property

All other property is considered to be personal property, sometimes called *personalty*. Personal property includes vehicles, furniture, appliances, jewelry, household goods, and every other item that is an object in and of itself. These types of property are called *tangible personal property*.

Personal property also includes rights that a person may own, at least if the rights have some monetary value, such as bank accounts (the right to get your money from the bank), stocks and bonds, rights to pensions, rights to sue people or corporations, and even rights to obtain season tickets to a popular team. These types of property are called *intangible personal property*.

TYPES OF PROPERTY OWNERSHIP

Real property and personal property may be owned in one of several different ways. The type of ownership sometimes affects whether a particular creditor may go after that property under the laws of a state or in bankruptcy. Following are some common types of ownership and a somewhat simplified discussion of each.

Sole Ownership

Property may be solely owned by a single individual. This is generally the simplest situation, and the creditors can normally seek to collect their debts from that property if it cannot be protected through exemption or bankruptcy laws. However, the creditors of another individual, even the spouse of the property owner, cannot normally pursue the property of an individual who does not owe them a debt. For this reason, some financial counselors occasionally recommend that individuals who are likely to be sued "go bare," making sure they do not own any property. However, state and bankruptcy laws generally consider it fraudulent for someone who owes money or is likely to incur debts to simply give away property to protect it from creditors.

Tenants in Common

There are several forms of joint ownership of property. The most basic is called a *tenancy in common*. Each co-owner, or cotenant, owns a share of the property; the shares may or may not be equal. Each cotenant is free to sell his or her share without the consent of the others, and if a cotenant dies, his or her heirs get the deceased's share. Creditors who are trying to collect debts can pursue the share of a tenant in common and obtain ownership of it. They (or any cotenant) may then be able to force a sale of the whole property if they wish.

Joint Ownership with Right of Survivorship

A different type of joint ownership is joint ownership with the right of survivorship. Depending on state law, joint owners, sometimes called *joint tenants*, do not always have the right to sell or give away their individual shares, and creditors of only one joint owner may not always be able to pursue the property interest. The main distinguishing feature is that each joint owner has a stake in the property owned by the other joint owners; that is, a joint owner has the right to receive that property share if the other joint owner dies first.

Tenancy by the Entireties

A somewhat archaic type of ownership, tenancy by the entireties, still exists in 15 to 20 states in varying forms. This type of joint ownership with right of survivorship can exist only between a husband and wife, and it ends when either spouse dies or when they are divorced. In most states in which it exists, the property, called *entireties property*, can never be taken for payment of a debt unless it is a joint debt of both husband and wife.

Community Property

In nine states (Arizona, California, Idaho, Louisiana, Nevada, New Mexico, Texas, Washington, and Wisconsin), another form of ownership exists, for married people only, called *community property*. Generally, all property acquired during a marriage by either spouse automatically becomes the community property of both. These states have varying rules about whether creditors of only one spouse can go after this property for payment of debts. If one spouse dies or the couple is divorced, the property is no longer community property.

Other Forms of Property Ownership

There are several other forms of property ownership, but they do not arise in the cases of most ordinary consumers. For example, property may be owned in trust. If the trust is a valid trust, meeting various requirements of state law, it is a separate legal entity that owns its own property. There is usually a trustee, someone who makes decisions about the property, and one or more beneficiaries, people or other entities who may receive money or property from the trust in accordance with the dictates of the person who established it (the settlor of the trust).

Property may also be owned by corporations or by partnerships. These legal entities are separate from the individuals involved. In other words, if a corporation owns property, the owners or shareholders of the corporation do not own that property themselves. The corporation is like another person with its own ownership rights. Similarly, a partnership may own property. The partners own shares of the partnership and have the right to act on behalf of that entity, but they do not own the partnership's property. Corporations and partnerships are prevalent mainly in business situations, and the complex rules governing them are beyond the scope of this book.

BUDGET ANALYSIS

A final ingredient in the financial picture of family or individual is a complete analysis of ongoing expenses and income. Only with this information in hand can the likely outcome of a bankruptcy be projected, for the family will continue to have its usual expenses, even if most or all debts are discharged, and will have to pay them with the anticipated available income.

A family or individual that is considering bankruptcy must therefore put together a budget of ongoing anticipated expenses and income. Once this is done, it may become apparent that bankruptcy by itself will do little to solve the financial problem because, even with the elimination of most or all debts, ongoing expenses still significantly exceed anticipated income. In such cases, at least part of the solution will be to pare expenses or to raise income.

Cutting expenses is never easy. Families must look at such major items as housing expenses. Is cheaper housing available? Other items, such as restaurant meals, fancy automobiles, vacations, expensive clothes, and other luxuries must sometimes be given up. Smaller savings can be made by conserving energy, cutting out extra phone service options, reducing or eliminating cable television bills, and cost-conscious shopping at thrift stores, garage sales, and supermarkets.

The alternative, of course, is to increase income. This can sometimes be achieved by a spouse working outside the home, though these gains may be offset by expenses for child care and transportation. A lower income family may be eligible for government benefits such as food stamps, energy assistance payments, or public assistance.

In any case, budget information is important for analyzing whether bankruptcy makes sense. It is also critical for determining whether a chapter 13 case is feasible, and it is required on the schedules filed in every bankruptcy case. Creditors and the court are permitted to examine this information if they wish, though most do not.

ASSEMBLING INFORMATION

The steps necessary to gather complete information about a family or individual's financial picture vary somewhat from case to case. For example, if no real estate is involved, a title search might not be necessary. If a debtor has kept organized and complete records, little more may need to be done.

Frequently Overlooked Property and Debts

Certain types of information are frequently overlooked in bankruptcy cases. The Bankruptcy Code defines property and claims very broadly, so it is important to consider even nontraditional types of assets and debts that most people do not consider to be directly involved in their financial situation. Some of the most commonly missed items in the cases of consumer debtors are described below.

Property

Among the types of property that people often forget in reporting their assets are long-dormant accounts with savings institutions such as banks and credit unions. Especially in the case of the latter, the debtor may not have access to a share balance (deposit) that was required to secure a loan. Nonetheless, such a balance belongs to the depositor and may be important to the case. Similarly, debtors often do not consider pledged goods, such as those in the hands of pawnbrokers, to be their own. As much property as possible should be withdrawn from the hands of others before bankruptcy. Not only can this property be converted to exempt assets, if necessary, but the return of the property will avoid later difficulties. After the bankruptcy, the holding party may be reluctant to relinquish the property. (Exemption planning is discussed in Chapter 5.)

Other types of property that debtors may not recognize include entitlement to tax refunds or credits; security deposits given to landlords or utilities; accrued vacation pay; future commissions from sales; salary or pension rights; causes of action (rights to sue for money); leasehold interests that are of value; shares in housing, shopping, agricultural, or other cooperatives; and entitlements to government grants such as energy assistance grants. It is crucial to know about all of these interests, both to ensure that they will not be lost and to take full advantage of them. Often, a bankruptcy petition should be postponed until a tax refund is received or vacation pay or other entitlements are exhausted.

Finally, debtors often overlook insurance interests. Individuals may have life insurance with a cash value or credit insurance that can be terminated and "cashed in" at the time of bankruptcy. On the other hand, whether a debtor has fire or automobile insurance may be an important factor in providing "adequate protection" to creditors who might otherwise be entitled to possession of their security. (The concept of adequate protection is discussed in Chapter 8.)

Local practice usually determines the extent to which the trustee or court will inquire into such nontraditional assets. However, there is no excuse for the debtor and the debtor's attorney to be less than fully informed and prepared for all possible problems that might arise.

Debts

Naturally, the opportunity for discharge of debts in bankruptcy should be used to its fullest, and every conceivable liability should be searched out and considered in weighing the advantages of a bankruptcy petition. Debtors do not always realize that they have certain types of debts, especially if payment has not been demanded for them. For example, just as a right to sue someone may be a form of property, so too may it give rise to a debt if the debtor is the potential defendant. The terms of a lease or land installment-sales contract may be important; it is sometimes possible to modify them in a chapter 13 case or if an unfair rent-to-own contract is found. (These matters are discussed in Chapters 10 and 11.) Debts of others for whom a person has cosigned are not usually considered by the cosigner as his or her own liability, nor are amounts that remain due after property is repossessed in satisfaction of secured debts.

In many states, a person is automatically liable for "necessaries" (food, clothing, shelter, medical care, and so on) provided by a third party to an individual's dependents or for welfare payments provided; few people are aware of these liabilities. A debtor may omit utility bills that are paid regularly because they are not perceived as comparable to a loan or other long-term debt. A debtor may not realize that bankruptcy can restore a driver's license that was revoked because of an old tort judgment or fine that is dischargeable. (Regaining a driver's license is discussed in Chapter 13.) If public benefit overpayments are being deducted from current benefits, the recipient should list these overpayments as debts because doing so could end the deductions.

Special care must be taken to consider how debts are likely to be treated in bankruptcy. Are there large liabilities for student loans, child support, or alimony that might not be discharged? Has there been recent, improvident use of credit cards in excess of the credit limits imposed? If so, a creditor could challenge discharge of that debt. Debtors should consider, at the same time, the possible loss of their credit cards due to a bankruptcy. Most creditors will automatically revoke them when their claims are discharged.

Other Aspects of Financial Affairs

Finally, careful scrutiny must be made into other areas of a debtor's affairs:

1. Are there any payroll deductions, such as those for a credit union, that the debtor can terminate? This step usually prevents later complications of trying to recover money deducted after a bankruptcy is filed. It also increases the debtor's available income.

2. Has the debtor made any prebankruptcy transfer or disposition of collateral for a secured debt or other property that could cause problems because the trustee or a creditor will claim it was improper? (Such claims of fraudulent transfers and "willful and malicious" injuries to creditors are discussed in Chapters 9 and 13.)

3. Did the debtor give a financial statement to any creditor that was not completely true? If so, the creditor might claim that the debt was obtained fraudulently. (Such claims are discussed in Chapter 13.)

Other Sources of Information

Depending on the complexity of the financial situation and the completeness of the information already gathered, it may be necessary to seek further information elsewhere. One source that should not be overlooked is the creditor to whom a debt is or may be owed. Creditors are usually quick to respond to inquiries regarding the balance due and the security interests they have, especially if they think it may be to their benefit, as in a chapter 13 case.

In addition, a credit report, which can be used to check or to supplement previous information, may be obtained for a small fee from any of several national credit reporting agencies. Similarly, past appraisals, lien or title searches, and previous years' tax returns may be necessary or helpful. A lien search on real estate may indicate other liens that the debtor does not remember or does not know about and that may be eliminated or otherwise dealt with in the bankruptcy. If the value of property is of significant importance, a current formal or informal appraisal may be required to get a full picture of the case.

THE IMPORTANCE OF FULL DISCLOSURE

No matter what method is used to inquire into the debtor's financial situation, it is important to provide the attorney with every detail requested. Serious consequences can result from less than full disclosure to the attorney, and debtors can rest assured that they are protected by the confidentiality of the attorney-client relationship.

Property not listed as exempt on the bankruptcy schedules may be lost, and debts that are not reported will not normally be discharged. In addition, there is often a court filing fee—not to mention likely attorney's fees—for amending the papers (adding information later). By giving incomplete or false information under oath on the bankruptcy forms, the debtor risks not only losing the discharge, but also criminal prosecution.

More than anything else, though, an attorney's ability to provide the best possible representation for the debtor may suffer if the attorney has less than the whole story. The real loser, if this happens, is the debtor. Most informed debtors realize the importance of a real effort on their part to help develop the facts of the case.

Chapter 5

DOES BANKRUPTCY PROVIDE THE BEST SOLUTION?

Whether, how, and when to file a bankruptcy petition are probably the most important decisions made in a bankruptcy case. Like many questions of legal strategy, the decision to file is rarely simple. It involves the interplay of a number of factors. Many of these are unique to each individual or family; others turn on state law, custom or practice in a community, or the provisions of the Bankruptcy Code. This chapter describes the considerations and alternatives that consumer debtors and their attorneys should explore when making their decision. The chapter also describes some prebankruptcy steps that could improve the debtor's position if a bankruptcy case is filed.

OVERCOMING THE PERCEIVED STIGMA OF BANKRUPTCY

In the United States, like most societies, the moral overtones of not paying one's debts are substantial. We all learn how important it is to keep our promises, to pay for what we have purchased, and to repay what we have borrowed, not simply as a matter of law, but as a matter of ethics and morality. Naturally, businesses constantly reinforce the idea that failing to pay our debts is very wrong. Thus, the idea of bankruptcy, which represents a declaration of sorts that the debtor does not intend to pay, may be difficult for debtors to accept at first, especially if they have sincerely insisted to creditors that they intend to make good on their obligations.

It is important to remember that the right to file a bankruptcy case is given by laws, provided for in the Constitution, that are intended to provide a fresh start for those in financial trouble. Big corporations—like Texaco, TWA, and Penn Central—and famous people—such as Jerry Lewis, Mickey Rooney, Tammy Wynette, and even former Treasury Secretary John Connally—have not hesitated to use this right. When a business makes a loan or allows a customer to purchase goods or services on credit, it recognizes that a certain percentage of customers will not be able to repay. Businesses charge more to their customers to compensate for that risk.

Legally, the right to file a bankruptcy and discharge a debt is considered an "implied term" of the contract between a consumer and a business. This means that it is part of every consumer credit agreement that if the consumer qualifies for bankruptcy relief the creditor will receive only what it is entitled to receive in bankruptcy. Therefore, when a debtor who is in financial trouble files a bankruptcy case, he or she does not violate the real agreement between the parties.

The Bible itself provides for periodic release from debts:

> At the end of every seven years thou shalt make a release. And this is the manner of the release: every creditor shall release that which he has lent unto his neighbor and his brother; because the Lord's release hath been proclaimed. (Deut. 15:1–2)

The "stigma" of bankruptcy is largely a creation of creditors, who have every reason to make bankruptcy appear unattractive, and they spend large amounts on advertising and public relations to do so. In fact, people rarely learn about most individual bankruptcy cases. Consumer bankruptcies are not generally publicized in newspapers or elsewhere, although they are a matter of public record. Other than the creditors who receive notice of a bankruptcy case, few other people are likely to know about it.

DISPELLING COMMON MYTHS ABOUT BANKRUPTCY

Either because they are perpetuated by creditors or for some other reason, certain myths about bankruptcy have persisted over the years. Perhaps most common is the belief of many consumers that they are not permitted to obtain credit for a number of years after bankruptcy. This is simply untrue. Although a bankruptcy case may make it more difficult to obtain credit, as discussed below, there is no law that prohibits it. In some cases, it may actually be easier to obtain credit after bankruptcy than before.

Some debtors believe that they will be prohibited from owning property after bankruptcy. Again, there is no basis for this belief. In fact, there are no limitations on property that may be owned by a person after a bankruptcy case is filed. However, as discussed in Chapter 1, property acquired during or very shortly after a bankruptcy case must sometimes be used to pay creditors.

Finally, some people believe that they will lose all of their property in bankruptcy. This, too, is incorrect. Debtors are permitted to keep most or all of their property in bankruptcy cases. Depending on the laws of a particular state, certain amounts of property are protected from creditors. (Such exempt property is discussed in Chapter 9.) In chapter 13 and occasionally in chapter 7 cases, there are also ways of keeping property that is not classified as exempt.

ADVANTAGES OF BANKRUPTCY

In a sense, most of this book is devoted to describing the advantages of bankruptcy for consumer debtors and showing how to make the most of those advantages. Before a consumer can intelligently select a course of action, the advantages and the disadvantages, if any, applicable to the case must be considered.

Discharge of Most Debts

The principal goal of most bankruptcies is to have most unsecured debts discharged. The bankruptcy discharge totally eliminates any personal obligation to pay many types of debts. (A few types of debts are not dischargeable, as discussed later in Chapter 13. Also, if a creditor has a lien on property taken as collateral, the debt owed to that creditor may still have to be dealt with after bankruptcy because the lien will, in some cases, survive.) For most debtors, bankruptcy is a relatively quick and easy way to end the creditor harassment, hardship, anxiety, and marital stress normally associated with debt overload. The discharge of debts is usually the primary component of bankruptcy's fresh start.

Protection of Property and Income from Unsecured Creditors

Bankruptcy is often the only sure way to protect a debtor's property from unsecured creditors (those who did not take a lien on property as collateral at the time of the transaction). Bankruptcy may provide total protection for a home, car, or other vital property.

The amount of property that debtors can protect from creditors through exemptions in bankruptcy is, in many states, far greater than the amount that they can protect under the state law execution processes through which creditors attempt to seize debtors' property or income. Even where state execution exemptions are similar to or better than the federal bankruptcy exemptions or where the federal exemptions are not available, bankruptcy allows the debtor to avoid having to assert the exemptions repeatedly in response to the execution attempts of different creditors. (The federal bankruptcy exemptions are discussed in Chapter 9.)

Normally, bankruptcy also serves to prevent any garnishment (attachment or seizure) of wages or other income after the petition is filed. This, in turn, may protect a client's job if the employer does not favor multiple wage garnishments. Even attempts to reduce Social Security or other public benefit payments to get back previous overpayments should be preventable by a timely bankruptcy petition, as discussed in Chapter 13.

Tools for Eliminating or Modifying Secured Debts

A bankruptcy discharge does not, by itself, eliminate the liens on a debtor's property that secured creditors have obtained before bankruptcy. However, other provisions in the Bankruptcy Code do give debtors mechanisms to deal with most secured creditors. Many types of liens may be eliminated, either because they impair exemptions, as discussed in Chapter 9, or because they are on property that is worth less than the liens, as discussed in Chapter 10. In a chapter 13 case, payments on most other secured debts can be lowered, and a reasonable time can be gained to cure almost any defaulted secured debt. Often, one or more of these aspects of bankruptcy enable a debtor to retain a home, car, or furniture that would otherwise be lost.

Automatic Stay

The most valuable feature of a bankruptcy is sometimes the automatic stay, which the debtor gains instantaneously on filing a petition. The stay is an automatic court order that prohibits all sorts of collection attempts by creditors, allowing the bankruptcy to proceed in an orderly fashion. It forces an abrupt halt of most creditor actions against the debtor, including repossessions, garnishments or attachments, utility shutoffs, foreclosures, and evictions. Many of these can thereafter be permanently prevented. The stay is also an effective way (though hardly the only way) to end creditor collection efforts. Creditors who violate the stay risk contempt of court, money damages, and attorney's fees. Beyond all this, the stay gives the debtor a breathing spell, time to sort things out. (The stay is discussed in detail in Chapter 8.)

Other Protections Available through Bankruptcy

As discussed more fully later in Chapter 13, bankruptcy offers other protections with respect to discharged debts. Bankruptcy may offer the only possible way for a client to keep or regain a driver's license that is subject to revocation because of an unpaid debt arising from a motor vehicle accident. This, in turn, may mean employment and income for the client's family. In some cases, bankruptcy may mean freedom for a debtor who might otherwise be incarcerated for failure to pay support obligations or as a result of a contempt proceeding involving some other debt. The Bankruptcy Code also protects the debtor from many types of discriminatory action by government bodies and private employers on the basis of unpaid debts discharged in bankruptcy. Nor can any private party take any action intended to coerce payment of such debts.

Litigation Advantages of the Bankruptcy Forum

An important factor to consider in opting for bankruptcy is the opportunity to litigate disputes with creditors in a federal court, which has at least initial jurisdiction over such disputes after a case has been filed. If there is a substantial dispute concerning whether the debtor owes or is owed money, the bankruptcy court may provide a more sympathetic forum than the local state court, and it may be more familiar with the applicable consumer or commercial laws. A debtor's lawyer may find that the bankruptcy court provides other advantages; federal courts are often better places to litigate certain types of cases than most state courts. Other rights, such as statutes of limitations or the ability to assert claims against the government, may also be affected to the client's advantage.

In sum, then, bankruptcy may be the best way, if not the only way, for a debtor to save a home, a job, a car, or thousands of dollars. It may even mean the debtor's freedom, literally as well as figuratively.

DISADVANTAGES OF BANKRUPTCY

Despite all of the advantages that bankruptcy may provide, there are many valid reasons for choosing not to file a petition. Some of these concern problems in the cases of particular debtors; others relate simply to the fact that bankruptcy is not the only means to address the debtor's legal problems and may not be necessary.

Loss of Property

One consequence of a chapter 7 bankruptcy is the loss of nonexempt property or its value in cash. This is not a problem for many debtors because consumer debtors rarely have any nonexempt property. Except in those few states that have low exemptions and have passed laws making the federal bankruptcy exemptions unavailable to their residents, the amount of property a debtor is allowed to keep is generous enough to protect the property of most nonhomeowners and many homeowners. Only debtors with equity of substantially more than $7,900 per debtor in a home, $1,200 in a car, or $4,000 in household goods and certain other property are likely to have problems under the federal exemptions. Even in those cases, a chapter 13 bankruptcy often presents a viable alternative through which debtors may retain all of their possessions.

Effect on Credit and Reputation

A bankruptcy will be part of a debtor's credit history for as long as the law allows, that is, ten years under the Fair Credit Reporting Act. This means that anyone who requests a credit report will be informed of the bankruptcy filing. The effect this will have on future credit cannot be predicted, but it is an understandable concern of many people who are considering bankruptcy.

There is no definite response to this concern. However, debtors who owe substantial amounts, especially if they are in default, already have poor credit ratings. In the eyes of some creditors, a bankruptcy that wipes the slate clean will be an improvement. Not only will the potential customer be free of other financial obligations, but he or she will also be unable to obtain a chapter 7 discharge for another six years in most cases. For these reasons, some creditors have been known to actively solicit recent bankruptcy debtors.

As bankruptcy has become more prevalent in the United States, creditors have increasingly considered it only one factor in their decision about granting credit, and most have chosen not to automatically exclude the ever-growing number of people who have filed a bankruptcy case. Even mortgage lenders are often willing to disregard a bankruptcy that is more than a few years old.

In any case, the available research on the subject is inconclusive. It seems fair to say, though, that each credit decision turns on the bias of the individual creditor, and most creditors look more to a potential customer's current income and its stability than to anything else. Debtors should also remember that they always have the option of voluntarily paying a favored creditor with whom they wish to maintain a line of credit, either before the bankruptcy or afterward. (However, payments of more than $600 to a single creditor within 90 days before the bankruptcy should be avoided, if possible, because a bankruptcy trustee may try to get them back as "preference," as discussed in Chapter 9.) It is often possible for a debtor to pay off a low balance on at least one credit card before bankruptcy, so that the creditor need not be listed on the schedules. In most cases, the creditor will then permit continued use of the credit card after bankruptcy.

As discussed earlier, bankruptcy's effect on a debtor's reputation in the community is almost always imperceptible. In a small town, however, especially if debts are owed to local people, the stigma of bankruptcy cannot be entirely discounted. The potential harm can only be evaluated locally, on a case-by-case basis, and weighed against the advantages that bankruptcy offers. Again, the possibility of voluntarily paying selected debts should not be overlooked if it would ameliorate the problem.

Possible Discrimination after Bankruptcy

Closely related to the problem of reputation is that of discrimination against debtors who have filed bankruptcy cases. To a large extent, the Bankruptcy Code alleviates this problem.

The Available Protections

Government bodies generally may not discriminate on the basis of a bankruptcy or because of a debt discharged in bankruptcy. Thus, as discussed later in Chapter 13, a housing authority or grantor of government assistance benefits cannot deny benefits to a person based on previously discharged debts. Similarly, utilities may not deny service based on a bankruptcy or discharged debts, though they may demand a security deposit for continued service. Private employers may not discriminate with respect to employment or terminate employment based on bankruptcy or discharged debts. Debtors can rest assured that the law protects them in this regard and that they will be able to enforce their rights in court, if necessary.

However, the distinction between discrimination based on bankruptcy or discharged debts and discrimination based on future financial responsibility should be clearly understood. That is, even creditors who are precluded from discrimination based on bankruptcy may refuse new credit or other services if the refusal is properly based on other considerations.

The law regarding discrimination by other private entities, such as creditors who provide essential services, is not as clear. It should be pointed out that this type of discrimination is extremely rare, especially in urban areas where many providers of goods and services are available. It would be most likely to occur in a small town, where only one merchant offered a particular product or service. In that case, if it could be shown that later discrimination was a prohibited attempt to coerce payment of the debt, the debtor could go to court to seek damages because the creditor violated the bankruptcy laws.

Again, the situation can best be assessed locally, on a case-by-case basis. Discrimination against debtors who have filed bankruptcy cases is normally not a problem, but if a debtor is in doubt, he or she should consult an experienced bankruptcy attorney.

Medical Debts

Medical debts to doctors or hospitals with whom a patient would like to continue a relationship are often a concern. Particularly in small communities that have few health-care providers, debtors may worry that a discharge will leave them with few options for future care.

In fact, if the debtor cannot pay past debts anyway, the doctor or hospital involved may have little concern about a bankruptcy discharge. Often a frank discussion with a sympathetic doctor about inability to pay will allay any concern about future refusal to provide service.

A second option is for the debtor to agree to make voluntary payments after the bankruptcy. In extreme cases, reaffirmation of a particular debt may be appropriate. (Reaffirmation of debts is discussed in Chapter 13.) Before taking such drastic action, however, the debtor should remember that the ethical obligations of doctors and hospitals preclude them from refusing to serve patients who are in extreme need. Moreover, even the most recalcitrant doctor will generally provide care if cash payments or medical coverage is offered, and many hospitals have a legal obligation under state or federal law to provide free medical care.

In summary, there is no completely satisfactory answer to questions about future health care because a doctor has no legally enforceable obligation to provide care to a debtor who has discharged prior medical debts. However, this should rarely affect access to needed care.

Feelings of Moral Obligation

Another factor mitigating against bankruptcy may be the debtor's own feelings on the subject. With regard to such feelings, it is best to remember other values that must also be considered. Besides the fact that bankruptcy is a right guaranteed by law and provided for in the Constitution and even the Bible, a debtor should consider the hardship it may avoid for his or her family. It may be the only way to provide the family with food, clothing, and shelter in hard times. Debtors often decide that the moral obligation to provide for loved ones outweighs the obligation to pay their creditors.

Debtors who wish to pay some or all of their debts should consider chapter 13. If the debtor has sufficient income, a chapter 13 bankruptcy may provide a viable mechanism for repaying creditors and solving other problems. Finally, debtors should remember that filing for bankruptcy does not prevent them from voluntarily paying their debts at a later time if they wish. This realization provides comfort to those who cannot come to terms with the idea of turning their backs on their creditors forever.

Cost of Filing a Petition

Besides any attorney's fee, bankruptcy carries an out-of-pocket cost of at least $160 for the court fees. Other fees may raise this figure somewhat. In a chapter 13 case, for example, the trustee is usually entitled to a commission of up to 10 percent of the payments made through the plan. In some cases, various utilities may require security deposits to ensure continued service.

These costs, like the less tangible costs, must be weighed when deciding whether to file a bankruptcy case. Usually, the other factors discussed in this chapter are considerably more important. However, where the debts are not large or troublesome, it may simply not be worthwhile to spend the amount necessary to eliminate them.

Failure to Solve the Underlying Problem

In some cases, bankruptcy is simply the wrong tool to use, and none of the advantages listed earlier will be realized. One such situation is that of the debtor whose debts are fully secured by security interests or other liens on property that cannot be impaired through bankruptcy and who does not have sufficient income to remedy a default even with all of the help bankruptcy provides. Unless there is some advantage to litigating in bankruptcy court, bankruptcy will not solve this debtor's basic problems. At most, it may discharge the debtor's personal liability for the debts and gain the advantage of the automatic stay for a month or more. Although in some cases this could be worthwhile, in most it will not ultimately benefit the debtor.

The problem of debtors in this predicament is often that their current expenses exceed their income. Because bankruptcy (except for chapter 13's ability to stretch out or reduce certain types of short-term expenses) basically deals with assets and liabilities, it does not address this problem directly in most cases.

The opposite situation can also sometimes cause problems. If a debtor has substantial and valuable nonliened property that cannot be exempted, a premature bankruptcy will generally hasten property loss rather than prevent it. Because unsecured creditors must sue the debtor to obtain judgment liens or levies on the debtor's property, loss of the property outside bankruptcy may be quite slow. On the other hand, liquidation of nonexempt property generally occurs quickly in the bankruptcy process. And, because unsecured creditors are entitled to the present value of nonexempt property in chapter 13, a case under that chapter would be quite costly. In this situation, the best option is probably to wait at least until execution on the property appears imminent, unless the debtor can afford the necessary chapter 13 case.

Another potentially difficult situation arises when a debtor holds property in trust for children or other relatives. Because a trust may not file a bankruptcy petition, it may be difficult to gain the protection of bankruptcy for such property. However, relief may be possible if the beneficiaries of the trust file cases on their own behalf, which could protect their beneficial interests in the property. Alternatively, the debtor's bare legal title as trustee of the property may be sufficient to invoke the automatic stay while a creditor secured by the property in question is paid through a chapter 13 plan.

Some debtors may be barred altogether from filing a bankruptcy for some period of time. An individual cannot file if he or she had a previous bankruptcy case dismissed in the past 180 days and the dismissal was (1) for willful failure to abide by court orders or to appear in court in proper prosecution of the case or (2) a voluntary dismissal following a request for relief from the automatic stay of section 362 of the Code.

Finally, some debtors may stand to gain little from a chapter 7 bankruptcy because they cannot receive a discharge due to a prior bankruptcy. For these people, the prospect is somewhat brighter. In most cases, a chapter 13 case can still provide significant relief.

ALTERNATIVES TO BANKRUPTCY

Obviously, when deciding about whether to file a bankruptcy case, the debtor must consider the alternatives available for dealing with his or her financial difficulties. Some debtors may find alternatives that are better than bankruptcy.

Consequences of Doing Nothing

Some debtors, either because they are paralyzed by the stress of their situation or because they simply do not know what to do, do nothing at all to deal with their financial problems. This course of action (or inaction) can lead to various consequences, depending on the type of debt involved and the business practices of the particular creditor.

Collection Letters and Telephone Calls

The first step of virtually all creditors is to send one or more letters in an attempt to collect the debt. The first of these letters is typically quite friendly ("Have you overlooked this payment?"), but the letters get progressively nastier after that. Some creditors will also telephone debtors to try to convince them to make payments. Again, these calls can become quite unpleasant.

After a few collection attempts, creditors often contract out this task to collection agencies. Collection agencies are businesses that send letters and make phone calls on behalf of creditors who are trying to collect debts. They are usually paid a percentage of the amount collected. A primary tactic of collection agents is to play on consumers' feelings of guilt and moral obligation and to obtain new promises to pay so that consumers will pay rather than feel they have lied to the collector. Lawyers sometimes act as collection agents—usually sending letters seeking collection of debts, but sometimes calling as well—in the hopes that the legal letterhead will scare the debtor into paying.

There is a long history of creditors and collection agents becoming abusive and harassing in these efforts. Debtors are under no obligation to talk to collectors on the phone or in person. A surprising number of consumers do not seem to realize that they can simply hang up or, if the collector calls right back, leave the phone off the hook and walk away. Once they realize that they are getting no response to their calls and letters, collection agencies eventually give up because they are not able to take more drastic action, such as filing a lawsuit.

As a result of widespread abuses, state and federal laws have been enacted that prohibit a variety of collection practices. These include making repeated calls during a short period of time, calling at inconvenient times, contacting employers or other third parties about debts, making deceptive statements, being verbally abusive, soliciting postdated checks, and making threats that cannot or will not be carried out. However, because few government resources are devoted to enforcing these laws, they are frequently ignored. The only effective remedy against abusive and harassing collection tactics may be a lawsuit filed by the debtor.

The federal law regulating collection agencies, the Fair Debt Collection Practices Act, and some state laws regulating creditors contain another useful provision. If a consumer notifies a collection agency (or sometimes a creditor) that he or she does not wish to be contacted further about the debt, the contacts are supposed to cease. Usually, if not always, a letter to this effect, stating the consumer's knowledge that further contacts are prohibited, will end collection calls and letters. The consumer should send the letter certified mail, return receipt requested, and should keep a copy of the letter in case proof is later needed that the collector violated the law.

Sending a letter of this type does not prevent creditors from taking other action—such as filing a lawsuit, repossessing, or foreclosing—if the creditor is willing and able to do so. However, creditors, particularly those with relatively small claims or claims on credit cards, rarely go any further in trying to collect. Indeed, the fact that a creditor has chosen to use a collection agency may well mean that it will not file a lawsuit or take any further action.

The worst thing to do in response to collection calls or letters is to send a small payment in hopes of relieving the pressure. Making such payments only encourages more calls and letters because the collectors have reason to believe that their strategy is working. Moreover, small payments rarely even keep up with the mounting interest and do not reduce the debt. The creditors who most actively contact a debtor are usually those that can or will do little else to harm the debtor. They should therefore be the lowest priority for the debtor to pay. If the debtor is contemplating bankruptcy, the money may be needed for attorney and court fees.

Consumers in financial trouble should make payments to creditors only as part of a complete strategy for dealing with all of the debts involved, as discussed below under "Budgeting and Payment Agreements." Even then, it is often better to offer creditors a lump sum (perhaps half of the total due) to wipe out the entire debt, rather than make small payments that go in large part to pay additional interest and late charges.

Foreclosure, Eviction, and Repossession

Far more serious than collection calls and letters are the possibilities of repossession and foreclosure by creditors with liens on the debtor's property. A creditor that holds a mortgage on the debtor's home can, and usually will, begin foreclosure proceedings after a default of several months, unless mutually satisfactory arrangements are made to catch up on the payments. If nothing is done to stop them, such proceedings will lead to the loss of the debtor's home within a period of two months to a year, depending on state and local laws and procedures.

Similarly, a landlord who is not paid will commence eviction proceedings, usually after two to three months of nonpayment, but sometimes earlier. Eviction can occur within weeks after the proceedings are started.

A creditor that holds a security interest (lien) in personal property may simply repossess that property, without going to court at all, if the repossession can take place without a breach of the peace. Lenders on almost all car loans take such security interests, and they will usually attempt to repossess a vehicle once a debtor is two or more payments behind, though repossession is usually permitted legally after the debtor misses a single payment. If the car is in a garage and the debtor refuses to surrender it, the lender may have to seek a court order or wait until the car is on the street. The lender cannot enter the debtor's home without permission. For the same reason, a creditor usually cannot repossess household furniture or appliances unless the debtor allows the creditor into the home. The debtor has no obligation to do so without a court order. Many creditors do not bother to seek an order if they cannot peaceably repossess furniture or appliances. Nonetheless, the possibility of repossession must be taken very seriously, especially if a car is needed for work or other important purposes.

Utility Shutoffs

Providers of utilities—such as electricity, water, gas, and phone service—have a potent weapon to assist in the collection of their claims. They can terminate service. Because the utility normally has a monopoly for a particular geographic area, the termination of service may leave the debtor without lights, water, heat, or telephone service.

Because they do have a monopoly and are regulated, the ability of utilities to terminate service is limited. They must normally give notice of their intent to terminate service and must permit debtors to work out reasonable payment arrangements. In many states, public utility regulators are available to resolve disputes about bills and payment arrangements if the debtor seeks their intervention.

Lawsuits

A creditor who has not been paid sometimes decides to file a lawsuit against the debtor. This action has several purposes. First, it often scares a debtor into paying. Many debtors do not understand the difference between a civil suit and a criminal action. They are afraid that they will have to go to court or even that they can go to jail for not paying. In fact, when a civil suit is filed, the defendant (the person sued) is not required to go to court.

However, if the defendant does not respond to the suit, he or she loses automatically for the full amount claimed. This is called a *default judgment*, and it is simply a court order deciding that the debtor owes the money claimed and perhaps some attorney's fees to the creditor for bringing the suit. Except in a very few places where a debtor may actually be called to court to make a payment agreement and may be jailed for not making the payments that the court thinks he or she can make, no debtors go to jail for not paying their debts.

Creditors also bring lawsuits for a second reason. Once a judgment is obtained in a lawsuit, the creditor can try to execute, that is, to obtain some of the debtor's property to pay the debt. In some places, the judgment is automatically a judicial lien on the debtor's real estate, though a creditor will rarely attempt to force a sale of real estate unless the judgment is many thousands of dollars. It is more likely that the creditor will wait until the property is sold, at which time all liens are normally paid, with interest.

The most common method of execution in consumer cases is wage garnishment. In most states, a creditor with a judgment may obtain a court order requiring that the debtor's employer pay some of the debtor's wages to the creditor. Limits on how much of the debtor's wages can be taken vary from state to state. Some types of income, such as Social Security, unemployment compensation, and pension benefits cannot be garnished. Because of the effect that garnishment can have on a family's budget and living situation, garnishment is one of the main events triggering a bankruptcy filing. Bankruptcy ends the garnishment immediately.

Creditors may also seek to execute on other property. The easiest types of property to execute on are bank accounts and other liquid assets, such as investment accounts and the like. A bank account execution is called an *attachment* or a *garnishment*, and it "freezes" the account. This may cause the debtor's checks to bounce and may lead to a series of problems with landlords, utilities, friends, and others, in addition to charges for bounced checks. Unless a bankruptcy is filed or the funds in the account can be claimed as exempt from execution, the creditor ultimately receives them.

Although creditors can theoretically execute on other personal property, such as household goods or vehicles, they rarely do so. Property such as used furniture or appliances has little monetary value and can usually be claimed as exempt, so it is rarely worth the creditor's time and legal fees to pursue it. However, a few creditors may threaten execution on household goods to scare debtors into paying. If such threats are made without any intent to carry them out, they are unfair collection practices.

In some states, there are debtors who are totally judgment-proof. This means that creditors can do virtually nothing to take property or income away from these individuals because they have no property or income that can be executed on. All of their property may be exempt from execution or, in the case of a home or car, subject to other creditors' liens that equal or exceed the value of the property. The secured creditors would have to be paid first if the property were sold.

People sometimes attempt to render themselves judgment-proof either in anticipation of debts or after they have incurred debts. For example, doctors and other individuals who fear possible malpractice judgments are sometimes advised to "go bare" by putting all property in the name of a spouse or other relative. Others who are engaged in illegal or questionable activities for which they might be sued attempt similar strategies. These actions are usually deemed fraudulent as a matter of law. Every state has "fraudulent transfer" or "fraudulent conveyance" laws that allow creditors or a bankruptcy trustee acting on their behalf to go after property that a debtor has given away either in anticipation of debts or after becoming indebted.

Budgeting and Payment Agreements

For debtors who have few and relatively small debts or only a short-term payment problem, it may be possible to work out a new family budget that permits repayment of debts in an orderly fashion without a bankruptcy case. Sometimes, by cutting back on less necessary expenses, a family may be able to free up sufficient income to catch up on past debts.

Such arrangements usually require creditors to enter into payment agreements that allow the debtor to catch up over a period of months. If not all creditors cooperate, the plan may fail. It is essential to have the cooperation of at least those creditors who can take the most serious action against the debtor, such as landlords, mortgage companies, utilities, and creditors with liens on property. If these creditors do not cooperate, bankruptcy may be the only way to hold them off.

Credit Counseling Agencies

Many communities have nonprofit agencies that offer consumer credit counseling. These agencies help consumers establish new budgets that will allow them to repay creditors through payment agreements similar to those described above. They may occasionally be able to get creditors to reduce their claims or to stop running interest. Creditors may be somewhat more willing to cooperate with consumers when they work through counseling agencies.

However, most counseling agencies are funded by creditors, and they see their primary mission as facilitating the repayment of debts. Therefore, they may be reluctant to recommend a bankruptcy case, even when there is no other reasonable solution. Counselors may instead advise that the debtor take a second or even a third job to pay back debts. In such cases, attempting to work through a counseling agency may be a waste of time and money that could be better spent getting a fresh start through a bankruptcy case. Working through a counseling agency might also make it more difficult or even impossible to complete a successful bankruptcy later.

In dealing with a consumer credit counseling agency, it is probably wise to ask early about its attitude toward bankruptcy and about how often it recommends that solution. If the agency does not recognize bankruptcy as a legitimate means of dealing with debts or if it strongly recommends against it in almost all cases, that is a good sign that the agency has the interests of creditors more at heart than the interests of its debtor clients.

Debtors should always steer clear of for-profit credit counselors. These agencies are almost always involved in consumer fraud, offering for a fee services that consumers can usually receive elsewhere for free, such as referral to a bankruptcy attorney. They also often give legal advice about bankruptcy, which they are not qualified to give and which is frequently incorrect.

Refinancing Debts

In some cases, refinancing debts can be a legitimate and useful tool for solving financial problems. In many others, however, it can lead to disastrous results, making a debtor's situation far worse than it was before.

Refinancing often takes the form of a debt-consolidation loan. This type of loan makes sense if (1) it converts high-interest debts to lower-interest debts and (2) it lowers payments to a level that the debtor is sure is affordable, usually by lengthening the term of the loan as well as by lowering the interest rate. Consolidation loans offered by finance companies, therefore, are rarely a good idea because they usually charge interest rates that are among the highest in the market. Also, it makes little sense to include in any consolidation loan a debt with a low interest rate or no interest rate or a creditor who is willing to wait to be paid.

Refinancing has several potentially serious pitfalls. First, it often costs money in the form of points and application fees if the loan is secured, such as a home equity loan secured by a mortgage. More important, a debt-consolidation loan may transform unsecured debts, which can easily be discharged in a bankruptcy case, into a mortgage loan that survives a bankruptcy and jeopardizes the debtor's home if it is not paid. Although most other creditors never go after a debtor's home if they are not paid, a mortgage lender is almost certain to do so. Therefore, a debtor should refinance through a mortgage or home equity loan only after carefully considering all other options, including bankruptcy, and only if the debtor is absolutely certain that he or she can make all of the payments on the loan.

Finally, debtors may see numerous advertisements for mortgage brokers and loan companies who do not have their best interests at heart. The second-mortgage business is rife with lenders who not only charge exorbitant interest and fees, but also enter into loans hoping to foreclose and obtain the debtor's home inexpensively at a foreclosure sale.

Other Assistance

Several other sources of financial assistance may be available for individuals and families with debt problems. Every state has programs to help lower-income people who cannot afford to pay their utility bills. These programs may offer hundreds of dollars of assistance toward those expenses, weatherization services to reduce future bills, or even limitation of the bills to a percentage of the customer's income. Information about such programs can be obtained from utility companies or social service providers in the community.

Several states and cities also offer programs to assist homeowners or renters with their payments to avoid foreclosure or eviction. In addition, homeowners with Federal Housing Administration (FHA) insured mortgages are eligible to participate in the Department of Housing and Urban Development (HUD) assignment program if they fell behind on a mortgage for circumstances beyond their control and have a reasonable prospect of resuming payments within three years. Information on how to apply for the program is sent to borrowers before a foreclosure on an FHA mortgage. Those who qualify are permitted to defer all or part of their mortgage payments for up to three years. It is important to pursue these benefits persistently. They can be extremely valuable, but they are usually granted only after a homeowner appeals from an initial rejection. The Veterans Administration (VA) theoretically has a similar program for VA mortgages, but unfortunately homeowners are not informed about it, and assistance is granted only rarely.

Defending against Disputed Debts

There may sometimes be a real dispute about whether a debt is owed. For example, a home improvement contractor may arrange a mortgage loan to pay for the job but then do shoddy work or not complete the job. Similarly, there may be misrepresentations in a transaction to buy a car or to finance some other major purchase.

In such cases, the solution may be to fight the debt in court. Of course, unless free legal counsel is available, the costs of such a lawsuit may be considerable. If the debt is large enough, though, it may be worth the investment to obtain a fair settlement. In many cases where a consumer protection statute is violated, the creditor may be required to pay the debtor's attorney if the debtor ultimately wins the case or obtains a favorable settlement.

OTHER FACTORS TO CONSIDER

In deciding whether to file a bankruptcy case, several other factors must be considered. Is the debtor likely to fall further into debt? For some the answer is no; their debts arose before they lost a job because of layoff, disability, or retirement. For many, though, there is the prospect of medical bills or other continuing financial problems that will result in greater debt. For most, there is also a slight possibility of a motor vehicle accident or other incident creating a large liability.

Some debtors have only a few debts and have strong defenses against them. For those debtors, the best avenue might be either litigation or settlement outside of bankruptcy court. This decision may also depend on whether resources are available to make the alternative of vigorous litigation a possibility.

In all of these cases, a debtor should bear in mind that the same relief in bankruptcy will almost always be available later but that filing a bankruptcy case now will impair the right to file another in years to come. Thus, unless a judgment-proof debtor expects to acquire nonexempt property soon, he or she may wish to wait.

Ultimately, the debtor must make a decision. Do the advantages of bankruptcy outweigh the disadvantages? Will bankruptcy have a positive effect on the debtor's life? For many consumers who face real threats that can be dealt with in bankruptcy, the answer is yes. But even those who are not in danger of sustaining a tangible loss may value the peace of mind that comes from having their burden of debt lifted. Whether debtors hope to someday make it out of a life of poverty or simply seek relief from the constant pressure to pay what is owed, these feelings should not be discounted.

SELECTING THE TYPE OF BANKRUPTCY CASE

Tied to the decision of whether to file a bankruptcy case is the question of which type of bankruptcy offers the greatest advantage. Although this decision may be changed after the case is filed, it is nonetheless important to ultimately settle on the chapter that offers the greatest advantages.

Considerations Favoring Chapter 7

For many consumer debtors, straight bankruptcy, now provided for in chapter 7 of the Bankruptcy Code, has traditionally been the remedy chosen. There are a number of reasons why chapter 7 usually meets the needs of the low-income debtor in particular.

One of the main factors leading to a chapter 13 case—the desire to protect nonexempt property—is rarely present. In most states, a low-income debtor or a debtor who does not own a home rarely has any nonexempt property. Nor is the debtor likely to have any excess income with which to pay unsecured creditors through a chapter 13 plan.

Thus, unless a chapter 13 petition is necessary for some specific reason, such as those discussed below, many consumer debtors will not desire it. They can obtain a quick and easy fresh start through a chapter 7 case that will discharge most of their debts. Even if the debtor has one or two secured creditors to deal with, a chapter 13 plan may not be necessary. Debtors can handle some secured creditors as well, or better, in a chapter 7 case by reducing or eliminating their liens or by defending against their claims outside the bankruptcy court.

A small number of consumer debtors have a different problem. Their debts exceed the limitations for eligibility to file a chapter 13 case. If a debtor's secured debts exceed $350,000 or unsecured debts exceed $100,000, the Code denies the debtor access to chapter 13. These limits are not doubled for a husband and wife filing together. The debt limits may dictate that only one spouse file a chapter 13 case if that spouse's debts alone are within the statutory limits.

Moreover, a chapter 13 case may be filed at any time after a chapter 7 case. Thus, if a chapter 13 case is not necessary when the debtor wants to file, it may still be filed later if circumstances change. There is no chapter 13 counterpart to the rule barring a new chapter 7 discharge after a prior bankruptcy case.

Considerations Favoring Chapter 13

Probably the most common reason for filing a chapter 13 case is the presence of one or more secured creditors who cannot be satisfactorily handled any other way. One frequent example is a bank or finance company that is about to repossess the debtor's car. Few legal steps prevent repossession as quickly and effectively as a chapter 13 petition and plan. A chapter 13 case can usually lower the monthly payments and perhaps the balance due. Similarly, chapter 13 can be used to halt a mortgage foreclosure, giving the client time to cure a default and perhaps a chance to lower the payments or principal due. (See Chapter 10).

As mentioned above, other reasons to file a chapter 13 case spring from deficiencies in the relief available under chapter 7. If the debtor has nonexempt property, it is protected in chapter 13, though its present value must usually be paid to unsecured creditors over the course of the plan. If the debtor has obtained a chapter 7 discharge in a case filed within the previous six years, the only real option in bankruptcy is chapter 13.

Another feature of chapter 13 that may sometimes be important is the broader discharge that it provides. Many debts that are not dischargeable in chapter 7 may be discharged in chapter 13. These include some taxes; debts incurred by use of false financial statements, false pretenses, or fraud; willful and malicious torts; fraud in a fiduciary capacity; certain restitution obligations; and debts that could not be discharged in a previous bankruptcy case.

Even though some nondischargeable debts, such as taxes, must be paid in a chapter 13 case because they are priority debts, a chapter 13 plan may still benefit the debtor by allowing him or her to stretch out the payments over a longer period than would otherwise be possible and perhaps avoid interest and penalties. In addition, most of the possible objections to a chapter 7 discharge—such as fraudulent transfer, concealment of property, or inability to explain loss of assets—may not be raised in a chapter 13 case; however, the issue of the debtor's good faith may be raised as an objection to chapter 13 plan confirmation.

A decision to file under chapter 13 sometimes depends on how likely it is that these questions will arise. Some debts are dischargeable in chapter 7 unless a creditor files a complaint seeking a declaration of their nondischargeability, as discussed later in Chapter 13. When an objection to discharge or dischargeability is not predictable, it may be preferable to commence a chapter 7 case and later convert to chapter 13, if necessary.

Another reason to file a chapter 13 case is to help debtors who want to pay their debts but need the protection of the bankruptcy court and, perhaps, the discipline of a chapter 13 plan. In addition, chapter 13 usually offers an end to finance charges and late charges on unsecured claims and possibly less detriment (where there is any) to the debtor's credit rating and reputation. However, debtors should remember that most of these advantages are available without a chapter 13 case. They may pay all or part of any debt voluntarily after a chapter 7 case, without the deadlines and extra costs of a chapter 13 plan.

Some debtors are required to file a chapter 13 case because they cannot afford to pay their bankruptcy attorney's fee except by installments as part of a chapter 13 plan, as discussed in Chapter 14. However, this device is sometimes subject to abuse by attorneys; the bankruptcy courts are giving greater scrutiny to chapter 13 cases that seem to have been filed primarily so that the debtor's attorney could "use the chapter 13 trustee as his collection agent."

Finally, if the debtor is uncertain as to whether any bankruptcy is the right solution but for some reason must file a petition before that doubt can be resolved, chapter 13 usually offers a safer course than chapter 7. The debtor may voluntarily dismiss a case commenced under chapter 13 at any time without obtaining court permission. The same is not true of a case commenced under chapter 7 or later converted to chapter 7. In a chapter 7 case, the dismissal may occur only with leave of the court and may be refused if it appears to prejudice the rights of creditors.

Use of Chapter 11 by Consumer Debtors

In *Toibb v. Radloff*, the Supreme Court held that individual debtors may file under the reorganization provisions of chapter 11 of the Bankruptcy

Code. Although even a cursory review of the chapter 11 process is beyond the scope of this guide, some basic information about chapter 11 from the perspective of consumer creditors is available in Chapter 15.

For the great majority of consumer debtors, chapter 11 is not the right choice. Most of the relief available in chapter 11 is available for individuals in chapter 13 at a much lower cost in time and money. However, a limited number of debtors might prefer chapter 11 over chapter 13 in the following situations: (1) the debtor is ineligible to file under chapter 13 because of noncontingent, liquidated, secured debt in excess of $350,000 or noncontingent, liquidated, unsecured debt in excess of $100,000; (2) the debtor cannot pay priority tax claims within the five-year period permitted under chapter 13 but could do so within the six-year period permitted under chapter 11; (3) the debtor seeks to avoid chapter 13's prohibition on modifying home mortgage obligations (discussed later in Chapter 10); or (4) the debtor has a high income and yet hopes to avoid the ability-to-pay test of chapter 13 (discussed later in Chapter 11).

Chapter 11 cases tend to be expensive and complicated. Unlike chapter 13, a chapter 11 case may not be dismissed without court permission; a plan may be proposed by creditors, rather than the debtor, over the debtor's objection; creditors generally must vote on the plan; there is no codebtor stay; and the same exceptions to discharge found in chapter 7 apply. For this reason, it is advisable to make certain that chapter 11 is necessary before filing under that chapter.

SHOULD BOTH SPOUSES FILE?

In cases in which both a husband and wife are involved, an additional question presents itself: Should both spouses file, or only one of them? The answer is that it is usually preferable for both to file. The same $160 initial court fee can provide both spouses the advantages of a bankruptcy discharge. Debts are often jointly owed; a spouse who does not file remains liable as a codebtor and may continue to be pursued by creditors after the case.

The decision to file jointly, if appropriate, must be made at the outset of the case; numerous courts have held that a spouse cannot be added later to an existing bankruptcy petition. If a debtor's spouse seeks to file after the initial petition, the best option might be to file separately under the same chapter and request joint administration of the two cases.

There are several exceptions to the general rule that both spouses should file. The most obvious is the situation in which one spouse does not wish to participate. Most of the advantages of bankruptcy can still be obtained by filing a petition on behalf of the willing spouse.

A second exception is the case in which one spouse is barred from filing by a prior bankruptcy or, if the case proposed is a chapter 7 case, some likely objection to discharge. Similarly, some debt of the nonfiling spouse—for example, a very large priority debt that must be paid or a debt above the debt limitations—might make a viable chapter 13 case impossible.

Probably the most important exception occurs when filing for only one spouse would protect property. This sometimes means not filing for a spouse with nonexempt property. However, creditors can usually continue to proceed against that property. The more likely reason is the presence of substantial amounts of entireties property or other jointly owned property in excess of the applicable exemption levels, which under state law are not reachable by a creditor of only one spouse. In such cases, if only one spouse files and the state, rather than federal, exemptions are chosen, all of that spouse's interest in such property may be exemptible, at least as to creditors of only the filing spouse, as discussed later in Chapter 9. After the bankruptcy, creditors will be unable to reach any of the debtor's property because their claims will have been discharged. The advantages of one spouse filing in such situations, then, are obvious.

Finally, debtors must consider the effects of the bankruptcy on community debts and property in community property states. Although the considerations involved vary from one state to the next, most community property generally becomes a part of the estate, and most community claims are usually discharged even if only one spouse files. Thus, most or all of a spouse's property and debts may be affected by the bankruptcy regardless of whether he or she joins in the petition. This factor may bring either advantages (discharge) or disadvantages (loss of property) to a nonfiling spouse and should be considered carefully.

TIMING THE PETITION

A final factor to consider in deciding on a course of action is the timing of the petition. Even after the debtor decides that a bankruptcy should be filed, it is sometimes advisable to wait before filing.

In some cases, a debtor has no choice but to file immediately. Prompt action may be necessary to forestall a repossession, eviction, execution sale, or utility shutoff. It may also be the only way to stay a state court proceeding and thereby avoid much unnecessary litigation. Another reason for a quick bankruptcy is an expectation of soon acquiring nonexempt property. Such property does not usually become part of the estate after filing. (An entitlement to receive property in the future usually does become property of the estate, however.) In all of these cases, a bankruptcy can be filed almost instantaneously, if necessary, under the current rules.

Effects of Prebankruptcy Transfers or Other Actions

One of the prime reasons for a delay in filing stems from the possible effects, both negative and positive, of prebankruptcy transfers of property. Transfers that have already been made may dictate a delay in filing, or it may be advisable to make other transfers before filing to gain maximum advantage from the case.

Fraudulent Acts, Transfers of Property, and Preferences

Several types of acts fall into the class of transfers that dictate delays; some of these may affect a discharge in chapter 7 proceedings. If the debtor, with intent to hinder, delay, or defraud creditors, has transferred, removed, destroyed, mutilated, or concealed his or her property within one year before filing a petition, a successful objection to a chapter 7 discharge may be brought, as discussed later in chapter 13. This definition may include the transfer of specific property subject to a security interest in favor of a creditor, but only if the requisite intent existed. If it seems likely that such an objection will be raised, it may be prudent to delay filing a chapter 7 case, if possible, until a year has passed since the transfer. Even then, a trustee may still seek to recover a fraudulent transfer, and a secured creditor may still claim willful and malicious conversion of the collateral but only to seek an exception to the discharge of that creditor's claim in a chapter 7 case.

Usually less serious are two other types of transfers: (1) avoidable preferences and (2) fraudulent transfers made without intent to defraud creditors. The worst possible result of these actions is a reversal of the transfer by the bankruptcy trustee. An *avoidable preference* can be defined as a transfer of property worth more than $600 from an insolvent debtor to a creditor to pay a prior debt if the transfer allows the creditor to receive more than it would otherwise receive in a chapter 7 liquidation case. The transfer must have been made within 90 days before filing (or one year before filing if the creditor is an "insider," a relative or close associate of the debtor). Thus, large payments to some creditors before bankruptcy may be set aside by the trustee if made within the stated time periods. If this is a concern—for example, if the payment was made to a friend or relative—it may be better to delay filing until after the applicable preference period has passed. It should be stressed that there is nothing improper or illegal about making a preferential payment. The only possible negative consequence is avoidance, or reversal, of the transfer by the trustee.

A fraudulent transfer of property may also be set aside by the trustee. As discussed in Chapter 9, a *fraudulent transfer* is a transfer or obligation made within one year before filing, either (1) for the purpose of hindering, defrauding, or delaying creditors or (2) for which the debtor did not receive reasonably equivalent value at a time when the debtor was insolvent or was about to incur debts beyond his or her ability to pay. In addition, a transfer that can be set aside under a state fraudulent transfer or fraudulent conveyance statute can usually be set aside by the trustee at any time within the period allowed by that statute (usually longer than one year). Generally, these provisions prevent a debtor from giving away property to shield it from creditors. This may be of no concern to the debtor, but if it is, it may be advisable to wait, if possible, before filing.

On the other hand, some preferences and fraudulent conveyances may be set aside by the debtor within the same time periods allowed the trustee. If the transfer was involuntary, the debtor did not conceal the property, and the debtor could have exempted the property involved, then the debtor may set aside the transfer. If the debtor plans to make use of this power, it may be crucial to file the petition before the time period runs out.

Exemption Planning

A debtor can sometimes take steps to improve his or her legal position before filing. Most of these come under the general rubric of exemption planning. Basically, exemption planning means arranging the debtor's affairs so that a maximum amount of property can be claimed under the exemption provisions and a minimum amount is lost to creditors in the bankruptcy. It is akin to tax planning, which is the way people arrange their affairs to take maximum advantage of the tax laws. In the opinion of most experts, exemption planning is perfectly legal under the present law, at least if not done to excess.

A debtor has a number of ways to take advantage of the exemption provisions. For example, some states require the debtor to file a homestead deed to claim the state homestead exemption. Assets that are not exempt, such as cash above the amounts allowed, can be spent on household goods and clothing (each item must be worth less than $200), life insurance, or other items in categories in which the debtor has unused exemptions (assuming the federal exemptions or similar state exemptions are available). If there is nonexempt equity in the debtor's home, the possibility of obtaining a second mortgage (again using the money to purchase exempt assets) should be weighed against loss of that equity (or against paying that amount in a chapter 13 case). All of these steps are nothing more than a rearrangement of a debtor's assets. Unless decisions in the courts that would decide the debtor's case have found them not permissible, these steps should be relatively free from risk.

It is also important to consider property owed to the debtor. Tax refunds due are always considered part of the estate and are claimed by the trustee if they are not exempt. If the refund due is greater than the debtor's unused exemptions, it may be better to wait until it arrives and spend it on exempt assets before filing the bankruptcy petition. In some areas, exemption planning may even come down to waiting until the debtor's payday to file; careful trustees may seek out any nonexempt wages or vacation pay owed the debtor for the previous few days. If no unused exemptions remain, prepaid rent could also pose a problem; in a few areas, trustees and judges may consider the remaining portion of a month's prepaid rent, as well as any security deposits to landlords or utilities, to be assets. Arrangements for a temporary refund may be worked out if no money is presently owed to the utility companies. Trustees have even been known to claim bank deposits as assets because checks that were written have not yet cleared by the date of filing. Local practice regarding these items varies greatly and should be investigated. In most areas, trustees do not inquire into these small amounts due the debtor, and if the debtor has significant unused exemptions to cover these amounts, there is no cause for concern.

A debtor may also take steps to ensure that no new nonexempt property comes into the bankruptcy estate after filing. Property might come into the estate, for example, if the debtor receives or becomes entitled to acquire it by bequest, devise, or inheritance, as a result of a marital property settlement or divorce decree, or as a beneficiary of a life insurance policy or death benefit plan. If the situation warrants, it may be advisable to change temporarily a will or insurance policy that gives rise to a possible entitlement and to arrange marital settlements accordingly. Because most of these steps involve acts of people other than the debtor (that is, the person who writes a will or owns an insurance policy), there is little likelihood that they could adversely affect the debtor's case.

Finally, exemption planning should be distinguished from a process by which debtors transfer property completely out of their estate. It is not permissible, for example, for a debtor to give valuable property to a spouse or other relative shortly before bankruptcy, without return of fair payment or exchange, in order to keep it from coming into the estate. Such conduct may be considered an effort to defraud the estate and may give rise to a challenge to discharge, avoidance of the transfer as fraudulent, or even, in serious cases, to criminal prosecution.

Other Reasons for Delaying a Petition

Anticipating Further Debts

It is sometimes said that a bankruptcy should not be filed until the debtor's debt load has peaked. If the debtor anticipates further unavoidable liabilities, such as medical bills, the bankruptcy should be delayed until after these are incurred, if possible. The object is to gain maximum benefit from the discharge. This delay must be carefully distinguished from another type of behavior: obtaining goods or services under false pretenses with no intent of paying for them. Debts incurred in this manner may be declared nondischargeable in a chapter 7 case, as discussed later in Chapter 13. Fortunately, the line between these two courses of action is not as difficult to draw as it might at first seem. The courts have found nondischargeable only the most obvious examples of debts incurred with no intent to pay, for example, prebankruptcy vacation trips and credit card shopping sprees. Expenses for medical bills and other necessities are rarely challenged.

Paying Favored Creditors

Debtors may wish to delay a bankruptcy until after they have paid a creditor whose claim they do not want to see discharged, for example, a friend or the grantor of a credit card they hope to keep. As noted above, a payment of more than $600 within the applicable preference period could be set aside by the bankruptcy trustee. If a debtor wants to pursue this course of action and ensure that the creditor retains the payment, the petition must be delayed until after the preference period has run out. It is usually preferable not to delay a bankruptcy for this purpose, but rather to pay the creditor after the petition is filed, using either exempt assets or postpetition income. There is no impediment to this course of action in a chapter 7 case, and it will usually not be questioned in a chapter 13 case.

Forestalling Harm

Finally, there are occasions when a bankruptcy petition should be delayed for purposes of litigation strategy. For example, a debtor facing an eviction or mortgage foreclosure may also desire a bankruptcy. By waiting to file the petition until eviction or foreclosure can no longer be delayed in state court litigation, the debtor can take advantage of the automatic stay arising from the bankruptcy to gain additional time to remain in his or her residence. This additional time can be invaluable because the debtor may later be able to settle the housing problem, either outside the bankruptcy or in chapter 13; at the least, the debtor will have more time to find another place to live. It is entirely appropriate to time a legitimate and necessary bankruptcy to obtain the maximum advantage for the debtor. However, filing a bankruptcy petition solely for the purpose of delay is quite a different matter. It would likely be found improper or cause for court discipline of the debtor, the attorney, or both.

HOW COMMON PROBLEMS CAN BE REMEDIED IN BANKRUPTCY

Unsecured Credit Card Debts and Other Bills

Unsecured debts are generally discharged in both chapter 7 and chapter 13 bankruptcy cases. This means, in essence, that they are simply wiped out. The price for this in chapter 7 is that unsecured creditors receive the debtor's nonexempt property, if any. However, in most chapter 7 cases the debtor has no nonexempt property. (Exceptions to the discharge are discussed later in Chapter 13.)

In a chapter 13 bankruptcy, the debtor must usually pay unsecured creditors the greater of (1) the present value of what the creditors would receive in chapter 7 (usually the value of the nonexempt property) or (2) the amount that the debtor can afford after reasonable living expenses over a three-year period. (See Chapter 11 for details.)

Utility Bills

Because utility bills are almost always unsecured debts, they are discharged in both chapters 7 and 13 like other unsecured debts, and the debtor may resume or continue service with a zero balance. However, in addition to the rights of unsecured creditors, utilities are entitled to demand a security deposit, payable within 20 days after the bankruptcy is filed, as a condition of future service. The amount and terms of the deposit are usually similar to those required of the utility's new customers. (See Chapter 8 for details.)

Wage Garnishments and Other Court Seizures of Property

Except, perhaps, in the case of a wage garnishment for payment of family support in a chapter 7 case, a bankruptcy petition brings an immediate halt to all wage garnishments, sheriff's levies or attachments on property, and other court seizures of property. As soon as the executing creditor or court officer is notified of the bankruptcy, these activities should cease. It is then usually possible to discharge (or, occasionally in a chapter 13 case, pay) the debt that brought about the seizure or garnishment, which prevents it from occurring again with respect to that debt after bankruptcy.

Automobile Loan Defaults and Repossessions

A bankruptcy petition prevents the repossession of an automobile or other motor vehicle once the creditor has knowledge of the petition. If property has already been repossessed but not yet sold by the creditor, the creditor must ordinarily return it, as discussed in Chapter 8.

The debtor then must usually provide for payment of the debt because the creditor's security interest normally cannot be eliminated. This is typically done through a chapter 13 plan, which often also reduces the interest rate and the amount of payments and stretches out the number of payments.

Mortgage Delinquencies and Foreclosures

One of the principal uses of bankruptcy—chapter 13 in particular—is to prevent mortgage foreclosures. The bankruptcy petition brings foreclosure proceedings to a halt. The debtor may then propose a chapter 13 plan that usually either pays off the full mortgage (if it has a relatively low balance, such as a second mortgage) or cures the delinquency. In the latter situation, the debtor usually begins making regular mortgage payments each month while paying off the delinquent amount through payments over several years in the chapter 13 plan. (See Chapter 10 for more information.)

Tax Debts

Most tax debts are not dischargeable in bankruptcy, as discussed later in Chapter 13. However, a bankruptcy filing can stop Internal Revenue Service (IRS) collection activity and can permit a debtor to pay the debts in a chapter 13 plan. If the debts are not secured, this strategy often prevents the accrual of additional interest and penalties. Even if the debts are secured, the interest rate may be lowered, and the debtor may not have to pay penalties.

Chapter 6

THE BANKRUPTCY FORMS

Once it has been decided that bankruptcy is appropriate in a particular case, most of the remaining work is relatively routine. Much of it involves preparing the necessary papers for the initial filing. This chapter describes the forms used in typical bankruptcy cases and discusses their purpose.

FORMS REQUIRED TO START A BANKRUPTCY CASE

A debtor normally starts a bankruptcy case by filing several documents at once. In a chapter 7 case, the documents are the petition, the debtor's statement of financial affairs and schedules, a statement of intentions with respect to property securing consumer debts, and a disclosure of attorney's fees paid or promised.

In a chapter 13 case, the documents are quite similar; they are the petition, the statement of financial affairs and schedules, the chapter 13 plan, and the attorney's fee disclosure.

Local rules may require one or two other papers. Many bankruptcy courts require the debtor to provide, either at the time of filing or shortly thereafter, a form (commonly called a *matrix*) for mailing labels to be used by the court. Also commonly mandated is a form that summarizes the plan in a chapter 13 case.

The initial filing must be accompanied by a filing fee of $130. An additional noticing fee of $30 is charged in connection with all chapter 7 and chapter 13 filings, effectively raising the initial fee to $160. If the debtor cannot pay the entire fee when filing and has not paid any money to an attorney, he or she may instead file an application requesting that the filing fee be paid in installments. This application is generally granted.

Emergency Bankruptcy Filings

It is sometimes necessary to file a bankruptcy immediately in order to use the automatic stay to stop some imminent harm from befalling the debtor. In such cases, it is often impossible to gather the necessary information and prepare all of the required papers quickly enough.

The Bankruptcy Rules provide a solution for this problem. They allow a debtor to commence a case by filing only the two-page bankruptcy petition and a list of the debtor's creditors and their addresses. The filing must also include the filing fee (or an application to pay the fee in installments) and the noticing fee.

The remainder of the usual forms must be filed within 15 days. The court may extend the deadline for these forms if the debtor presents a good reason why he or she needs more time.

If the remaining forms are not filed, the case is usually dismissed. This may be acceptable to the debtor if bankruptcy later proves to be the wrong course of action, since the dismissal is normally without prejudice. (Of course, a case should not be filed if the debtor has no intention of pursuing it; filing solely for purposes of delay is improper and could be punished by the court.) It cannot be assumed that the case will always be dismissed, however. A chapter 13 case may be converted to chapter 7, and if the creditors or the trustee object to dismissal of a chapter 7 case, the court may allow the case to proceed. This might give creditors the right to obtain some of the debtor's property in payment of their debts more easily than without a bankruptcy case.

THE BANKRUPTCY PETITION

The bankruptcy petition, which is the pleading that officially begins a case, is a two-page form that the debtor must fill out appropriately. Like most of the initial forms, the content of the petition must conform to the Official Bankruptcy Forms promulgated by the U.S. Courts. (Copies of the most important of these forms, including the petition, are included in Appendix B.)

The bankruptcy petition must include the debtor's Social Security number, and all names, including fictitious or trade names, that the debtor has used over the previous six years. The petition requests basic information about the type of case being filed (individual, joint, partnership, corporate, or otherwise), the number of creditors, the debtor's assets and liabilities, cases by the same debtor within the prior six years, and pending related cases. The petition also states that the debtor meets the basic requirements for filing the case under the chapter selected in the court in which the case is filed.

The petition in every consumer chapter 7 case must also contain a statement by the debtor that he or she is aware of and understands the choice available between relief under chapters 7, 11, 12, and 13 of the Code. This means that, in a chapter 7 case, the debtor must sign the petition twice. In addition, to reinforce the importance of an informed choice between chapters, every consumer chapter 7 bankruptcy petition must contain a declaration by the debtor's attorney that he or she has explained the relief available under chapters 7, 11, 12, and 13.

The petition must be filed with the bankruptcy clerk, who transmits a copy to the U.S. trustee. The petition itself rarely gives rise to any problems in a case. The exceptions are occasional problems concerning whether the case is filed in the proper bankruptcy court or whether a particular debtor may use chapter 13. Even in regard to the latter problem, the court normally refers to the schedules and statement of financial affairs rather than the petition in deciding the issue.

THE BANKRUPTCY SCHEDULES

The main purpose of the bankruptcy schedules (Official Form 6) is to give an exact picture of the debtor's assets, liabilities, and budget, as of the date of filing, in a standard form that facilitates administration of the case. This section describes generally the content and purpose of the schedules, but local rules may impose additional requirements, such as a requirement to alphabetize the creditors.

Schedules A, B, and C: The Debtor's Property

Schedule A is the list of the debtor's real property. In this schedule, the debtor must list all legal, equitable, and future ownership interests in real property, specifying the types of interests he or she posses. Property that the debtor is leasing must be listed separately in Schedule G.

If the debtor is married, the schedule must indicate whether the property is owned by the husband, the wife, jointly, or as community property, regardless of whether the petition is filed jointly. If the property is owned jointly, whether or not by spouses, the box describing the nature of the debtor's interest must indicate this. The debtor must state the value of the property interest without deducting for any secured debts, such as mortgages, which are listed in the last column and described more fully in Schedule D. However, if the debtor shares ownership of the property, the value assigned should account for the limited nature of the debtor's ownership interest.

Schedule B is a list of the debtor's personal property. In this schedule, the debtor must list all of his or her interests in personal property, along with a description and the location of the property. In addition to tangible possessions, all other types of interests should be set out in this schedule. This includes any right to sue others for damages and any eligibility for government grants, such as energy assistance, earned income tax credits, retroactive Social Security awards, and so on. Property that the debtor is purchasing under a rent-to-own agreement should also be listed if the debtor wants to treat the rent-to-own agreement as a credit sale rather than a rental agreement, as discussed in Chapter 10. For married debtors, the property may be listed as that of the husband or the wife or as joint or community property.

Courts require varying degrees of specificity in descriptions of property. Some allow debtors to group low-value items of property broadly in categories, such as "used clothing" or "assorted household goods all worth under $200." Others require much more specific lists.

Courts usually give quite a bit of leeway in terms of valuation. Normally, the value takes into account the proposed method of liquidation by distress sale, without deduction for liens or exemptions. Debtors should estimate the "garage-sale value" of specific items of property. It is important to bear in mind the low sale value of most used furniture and appliances. Because of this low value, trustees have little interest in the debtor's personal property, except perhaps for a few big items. Some categories of property present trickier problems of valuation. The value of the right to bring a lawsuit, for example, must be discounted for the possibility of losing the case or being unable to collect damages.

In every case, the trustee and the creditors have an opportunity to demand more detail later. Therefore, the consequences of an innocently imperfect description of assets are not grave.

Schedule C is the list of property that the debtor claims as exempt. In this schedule the debtor must first state whether he or she is using the state or the federal bankruptcy exemptions. (There is no choice if the state has precluded the latter.) Because a detailed explanation of this and other exemption issues can be found in Chapter 9, only a few points need be made here in regard to this schedule.

Obviously, the debtor's goal is to exempt as much property as possible—preferably all of it. For many consumer debtors, this is not difficult. If all property cannot be exempted, the debtor should consider exemption planning before filing the petition, as discussed in Chapter 5.

For each item listed in Schedule C, the debtor must cite the specific applicable exemption law. The value given in Schedule C for the exemption usually equals the value given in Schedules A and B, except that lien amounts should be deducted. When the federal exemptions are available, property that would not normally appear to be exempt may be exempted under the wild-card exemption, discussed in Chapter 9. Some state statutes also provide for wild-card exemptions. When exemptions contain monetary limits, two or more different exemptions that are applicable to the same property can be combined.

Debtors need not use exemptions on property that the trustee cannot reach, for example, to the extent that property is subject to a nonavoidable lien. Only equity in the property over and above the lien need be exempted. For example, if a debtor owns a $50,000 home subject to a $46,000 mortgage, only the debtor's interest—the $4,000 equity above the mortgage—need be claimed as exempt.

A debtor must pay careful attention to Schedule C. This is underscored by provisions in the Bankruptcy Code that provide property listed as exempt is exempt unless a party in interest objects. Because there is a strictly enforced deadline for objecting to exemptions, it is to the debtor's advantage to be certain that all good faith exemptions are listed. This shifts the burden to the trustee and the creditors to raise timely objections, if they can. It may also be important, in light of several recent court decisions, to specify that the debtor is exempting the debtor's entire interest in the property listed. Some courts have held, erroneously, that listing an item and an amount means only that the debtor has reserved that amount out of the item's total value as exempt. Although in most cases a fair reading of the other schedules listing the same amount as the total value of the debtor's interest in the property should make clear that the debtor intends to claim as exempt the total value of his or her interest, it may be safest to specify this fact on Schedule C itself.

Schedule C (and all the debtor's schedules) may be amended without special court permission at any time before the close of the case; thus, mistakes and oversights are easily corrected. The amended schedules are then subject to objection for a limited period of time.

Schedules D, E, and F: Creditors

Schedules D, E, and F divide all of the debtor's debts into three categories: those to secured creditors, those to creditors with priority, and those to unsecured creditors without priority.

These schedules must list the correct name and address of each creditor. If this is not done and, consequently, a creditor fails to receive notice of the case, the dischargeability of a debt may be affected, as discussed later in Chapter 13.

The other information—regarding the account number, the amount of the debt, the date it was incurred, whether there are codebtors, and the consideration for the claim—is usually less crucial but should of course be answered as accurately as possible. When accurate information is unavailable, the debtor's best estimate is usually sufficient as long as it is made in good faith. In most consumer cases, the amount listed in the schedules has little relevance; if assets are available, they are paid according to the proof of claim filed by the creditor, rather than according to the debtor's schedules.

For joint petitions only, the debtor must list whether the debt is owed by the husband or the wife or as a joint or community debt. The debtor must note the existence of a co-obligor (other than a spouse with whom the debtor has filed jointly) by checking the appropriate box labeled "codebtor" and providing the necessary information in Schedule H.

If there is any chance that a debt will continue to be relevant after bankruptcy (as with secured or nondischargeable debts), the debtor should not admit to a debt larger than the debtor will later maintain to be due. If the amount of the debt is contingent, unliquidated, or in dispute, that should be noted in the appropriate place. A debt is usually considered to be *contingent* if payment is not yet due and will not become due unless a particular event occurs in the future. An example of a contingent debt is an auto accident claim against the debtor in which the debtor denies any responsibility. (Such a debt would also be unliquidated and disputed.) A debt is *unliquidated* when the debtor has a legal obligation to pay some amount of money, but the amount has not yet been fixed. An example of an unliquidated debt is an auto accident claim in which the debtor acknowledges liability but the amount of the liability has not yet been fixed. By listing such debts and having them discharged, the debtor can often avoid having to fight over the details concerning the validity or amount of the debt.

Because debts that are not listed will generally not be discharged, it is obviously important to list every conceivable claim against the debtor so that the discharge may be used to maximum advantage. As discussed earlier in Chapter 4, this may necessitate careful investigation into the various types of debts that are frequently overlooked.

Schedule D lists all secured creditors. In this schedule the debtor must include all creditors that hold liens, even if the debtor or trustee can later eliminate their liens during the bankruptcy. Creditors that hold security deposits must also be listed here. Banks and other savings institutions with a right of setoff against the debtor's accounts (the right to collect a debt from the money in an account) should be considered secured for the amount in such accounts. (With good planning, however, all money will normally be withdrawn before bankruptcy, and these creditors will therefore be unsecured.) Again, if the debtor intends to treat a rent-to-own contract as a credit sale of property subject to a security interest, the rent-to-own debt should be included in this schedule. There is a box in the Official Form for the debtor to check if there are no secured creditors at all.

If the debtor wishes to dispute whether a claim is secured, it must be listed in Schedule D, along with the fact that the security interest is disputed. As with all of the forms, the goal is clarity in depicting the debtor's affairs. As long as this is achieved, even errors as to placement in the proper schedule are not of great importance.

Schedule E lists the different categories of debt that may have priority under the Bankruptcy Code. The Official Form has boxes to designate the types of priority debt or to note that the debtor has no priority obligations.

By far the most common type of priority debt owed by consumer debtors is taxes. Not all tax claims are entitled to priority, however, and only those that are both priority claims and unsecured are listed in Schedule E. This is especially important because priority tax claims must be paid in full in chapter 13, and they are nondischargeable in chapter 7. In a chapter 7 case in which there are assets in the estate, it is important to make sure that nondischargeable tax debts are listed as priority claims so that they will be paid first. Other types of priority debts occasionally found in consumer cases are those for wages or consumer deposits, which sometimes exist if the debtor had a small business.

All of the debtor's remaining debts are included on Schedule F. The general principles stated above apply here with equal force, and all possible claims should be listed. Debtors often forget the contingent subrogation claims (claims for reimbursement) that may be available to codebtors who later pay off a claim, including those on mortgages guaranteed by the VA or FHA and those on guaranteed student loans. If these claims are listed, codebtors will be notified of the case, and any possible claims they have will be extinguished. Another frequently overlooked category of debt is a continuing obligation to pay prorated amounts on a prepetition contract for services, such as condominium assessments, which may be dischargeable.

Schedule G: Unexpired Leases and Executory Contracts

Schedule G, the schedule of unexpired leases and executory contracts, is required for all cases. An *executory contract* is broadly defined as one for which significant aspects of performance remain due on both sides. An *unexpired lease* is one that has not yet terminated by its terms. Schedule G is designed primarily to notify the trustee of leases or other executory contracts that might be assumed or rejected because of their potential benefit or cost to the bankruptcy estate. Although the issues that might be raised by the schedule are rarely of great importance in consumer cases, this information is not difficult to provide. If, as is common, the debtor has no unexpired leases or executory contracts, the debtor must check the box on the form marked "none." (Executory contracts are discussed later in Chapter 11.)

For most consumer debtors, a residential apartment lease is the only entry on this form. It must be listed even if the lease is only a month-to-month oral agreement. Some debtors have an ongoing employment contract or a pending sale agreement for goods or real estate. These should be listed as well.

An issue that occasionally arises is how to treat a rent-to-own contract for consumer goods. For the reasons discussed in Chapter 10, there is a significant advantage and considerable precedent for treating these contracts as security agreements rather than executory contracts. Consequently, a rent-to-own obligation should generally be listed in Schedule D as a secured debt.

Schedule H: Codebtors

The debtor must list any codebtors, other than a spouse in a joint case, in Schedule H. The instructions for the Official Form provide that, in community property states, a married debtor not filing a joint case should always report the name and address of the nondebtor spouse, together with any other names that the nondebtor spouse has used within the previous six years. As discussed above, codebtors should also be listed as creditors in Schedule F to discharge any potential subrogation claims if the codebtors later pay off the obligation.

Schedules I and J: Income and Expenses

The last two parts of Official Form 6 are Schedules I and J, which require a complete disclosure of the debtor's income and expenses. In chapter 7 cases, these schedules are intended to provide information that could help a bankruptcy court to determine whether a chapter 7 case might be a "substantial abuse" and therefore subject to dismissal, as discussed in Chapter 12. In chapter 13, Schedules I and J allow the trustee and interested creditors to determine whether the debtor's plan is feasible, whether it is in compliance with plan requirements, and whether the debtor has the ability to pay unsecured creditors. The court may also look to these schedules to decide whether the plan is the debtor's best effort and whether there is cause for extending the plan beyond the usual three years. If an objection to confirmation is filed, the debtor's budget will be relevant to whether the debtor meets the ability-to-pay test, which is discussed in Chapter 11.

Schedule I must include income for both spouses in a joint case and when one spouse files individually, unless the spouses are separated and a joint petition is not filed. Income contributions to the debtor by a nonspouse must generally be listed separately in the schedule as "other monthly income." This is of particular importance in chapter 13 cases in which the income contributions are necessary to meet the regular income eligibility requirement or to make the plan feasible.

When income from a business or farm is included, a detailed statement must be attached. When it is unlikely that possible income will be received, such as alimony or support payments that have historically not been paid, this should be noted to present a realistic picture. Although food stamps and certain other public benefits are not legally treated as income for many purposes, they should nevertheless be considered income for the purpose of the bankruptcy filing. The existence of food stamps in Schedule I, for example, will be offset by the debtor's food expense in Schedule J.

The form requires information about anticipated increases or decreases in income of more than 10 percent in the year after the filing of the case, and any nonspeculative expected changes must be listed. For example, if unemployment benefits are due to terminate during the first year of the case, the date of termination should be given.

Schedule J requires information about the expenses of the debtor and the debtor's family. A box is provided in the Official Form to be checked by spouses who have filed a joint case but keep separate households. Such debtors are instructed to file separate schedules of expenditures; the second schedule is labeled "spouse." When the debtor has regular expenses from the operation of a farm or business, a detailed statement must be attached.

For chapter 13 cases, the debtor must work out the plan before finishing the Schedule J questions on the amount to be paid into the plan.

Declaration Concerning Debtor's Schedules

The Official Form schedules include a separate declaration page. This contains an oath under penalty of perjury that the debtor has read the schedules and that they are true and correct to the best of his or her knowledge, information, and belief. Joint debtors must each sign the declaration page.

Summary of Schedules

After completing all of these schedules, the debtor must complete a form summarizing debts, property, income, and expenses. The form is self-explanatory. After the summary is filled out, it must be inserted in the schedules for filing, sometimes at the front if required by local practice.

STATEMENT OF FINANCIAL AFFAIRS

The statement of financial affairs (Official Form 7) is required in both chapter 7 and chapter 13 cases. Every debtor must answer questions 1 to 15; boxes may be marked "none" if that is the appropriate response to a given question. Questions 16 to 21 are required only for debtors who have been engaged in business within the two years preceding bankruptcy.

Spouses filing a joint petition may file a single statement. In cases under chapters 12 and 13, married debtors must provide information for both spouses whether or not a joint petition is filed, unless the spouses are separated and a joint petition is not filed. Debtors who are engaged in business must provide the requested information for all unincorporated businesses as well as for their personal affairs.

The first two questions on the statement of financial affairs address the debtor's income history. The information required for these questions goes back two years and may therefore be different from the expected future income included in Schedule I. The income figures provided must be in terms of gross income, not take-home pay. Although income is usually not relevant in a chapter 7 case, which deals primarily with assets and liabilities, a statement of high income or one that does not fit with other information provided may prompt further investigation. It may also trigger an inquiry by the court as to whether the filing of a chapter 7 case would be a "substantial abuse" of that chapter, as discussed in Chapter 12.

The next eight questions concern recent transfers or losses of property by the debtor. Using the responses to these questions, the trustee can often avoid transfers or seek proceeds due the debtor. Because debtors themselves may exercise avoiding powers, as discussed in Chapter 9, especially with respect to executions on their property, accurate information here is important to protect these rights. Finally, the answers to these questions could point out possible impediments to discharge, such as transfers to hinder or defraud creditors, which are discussed further in Chapter 13.

The first part of question 3 requests information about loans and other debts on which more than $600 was repaid within the 90 days before the bankruptcy. The second part deals with payments of any amount made to or for the benefit of insiders (relatives or close associates of the debtor) within the year before the bankruptcy. The trustee may be able to recover these payments as preferences, as discussed in Chapter 9. Again, in most cases, the trustee is not interested in pursuing small amounts of money. Local practice varies as to the specificity required in answering this question. In some places it may be sufficient to state that "monthly payments" or "several payments" of a particular amount were made to some or all creditors. An interested trustee may then inquire further.

Question 4 seeks information about all lawsuits involving the debtor that are pending or that were terminated within the previous year. It also seeks the details of any execution, seizure, or garnishment in the previous year. The information required is minimal; the debtor need only provide the caption, case number, nature of proceeding, court, and status of the case. Such information may help uncover creditor actions that the trustee or the debtor can set aside. It may also lead to further information about the debtor's affairs. In addition, property seized or levied on may still belong to the debtor and may come into the estate if it has not been sold. The question also recognizes that lawsuits brought by the debtor may, in fact, be assets of the debtor that can benefit the estate. When such claims are listed, they should also be included in Schedule B as property of the debtor and in Schedule C as exempt, if possible.

Question 5 requests information about repossessions, foreclosures, deeds in lieu of foreclosure, and returns of property. These may also give the trustee an opportunity to recover property for the estate.

Question 6, concerning assignments and receiverships, is rarely applicable to consumer cases, but it sometimes identifies property that might be recovered by the trustee.

Question 7 seeks information about large gifts or charitable contributions in the year before the bankruptcy. Because gifts, by definition, are transfers for which the debtor received nothing in return, the trustee reviews the answer to this question to determine whether recoverable property may have been lost to the estate. The debtor need not list ordinary and usual gifts to family members (such as birthday or holiday gifts) if they total less than $200 per recipient. Similarly, charitable contributions totaling $100 or less to a single recipient need not be listed.

Question 8, covering gambling, theft, or fire losses, is designed to explain lost assets. It is also sometimes used to smoke out dishonest debtors who use this section to account for the sudden disappearance of large amounts of property. In some cases, this question helps the trustee discover the availability of a claim to insurance proceeds that might substitute for the lost property.

Question 9 seeks disclosure of payments made for debt counseling or bankruptcy within one year of the case by or on behalf of the debtor. In addition to payments made to third-party counselors and prior attorneys, the debtor must also include payments made in connection with the existing case. Payments made by parties other than the debtor must also be disclosed. The question's purpose is to assist in court supervision of attorney's fees paid to the debtor's counsel and, occasionally, to turn up exploitative debt counseling or other bankruptcy-related scams.

The next question, number 10, again looks for transfers that can be set aside, including fraudulent transfers. Any transfers that were not in the ordinary course of the business or financial affairs of the debtor (such as payments for normal household expenses) and that are not listed elsewhere in the statement must be listed in response to question 10. The granting of a security interest, such as a mortgage, is a transfer within the meaning of this question. Also included are payments to any entity that are not listed elsewhere and involuntary transfers other than repossessions and returns.

Questions 11 and 12, concerning closed financial accounts and safe-deposit boxes, are designed to determine if the debtor has hidden or transferred any assets that could benefit the estate. These questions are sometimes used to trace the debtor's assets. Closed financial accounts must be listed, whether they are in the debtor's name or are for the debtor's benefit. They may include bank accounts, certificates of deposit, credit union accounts, pension funds, brokerage accounts, and other types of financial accounts. Safe-deposit boxes must be listed only if they contained cash, securities, or other valuables within the year before the bankruptcy. In some jurisdictions, trustees routinely request additional information about the contents of safe-deposit boxes or the statements from closed accounts.

Question 13 requests information about setoffs by a bank or any other entity within the 90 days preceding the case. The trustee or debtor may have the option to recover the setoff, as discussed in Chapter 9.

Question 14 deals with property that is held by the debtor but belongs to another person. The trustee might inquire into this further, especially if large amounts of such property exist or if the property seems to encompass things that most people would own themselves, such as household goods or clothing. Property held in trust for another should also be listed here.

The final question that is applicable to debtors who are not engaged in business, number 15, requests the debtor's prior addresses for the previous two years. The answer to this question sometimes helps the trustee or a suspicious creditor to find additional interests of the debtor in real estate or to begin an investigation of potential hidden assets.

Questions 16 to 21 are applicable to debtors who have owned or operated businesses—including family farms, partnerships, and sole proprietorships—within the two years preceding the case. The debtor must provide information about the business, the business books and records, inventories, present and former business partners, officers, directors, and shareholders, as well as withdrawals or distributions made to insiders.

Like the schedules, the debtor must sign the statement of financial affairs under penalty of perjury. For almost all consumer debtors, the responses to the questions in the statement of financial affairs are routine. It is likely that the trustee will engage in little more than a cursory review of the statement and that it will have little impact on the case. Obviously, though, thorough answers are appropriate because any attempt to obfuscate is likely to lead to problems and perhaps a claim that the debtor is seeking to hide assets.

STATEMENT OF INTENTION WITH REGARD TO PROPERTY SECURING CONSUMER DEBTS

Another document required in chapter 7 cases is the statement of intention regarding property securing consumer debts. In this document, the debtor must state his or her intentions, as of the filing date, with regard to any property, real or personal, that serves as collateral for a consumer debt. The document must be filed within 30 days after the debtor files a petition under chapter 7, or on or before the date of the meeting of creditors, whichever is earlier, unless the court extends the filing deadline for cause. As a practical matter, the document is normally filed with the statement of affairs and schedules in a chapter 7 case.

The Bankruptcy Rules require that the statement of intention be prepared as prescribed by Official Form 8. That form requires (1) a specific list of all property securing consumer debts and (2) the names of the creditors holding liens on the property. The rules also require that the statement be served on the trustee and each creditor named in the statement on or before the date on which the statement is filed. Although it is not clear whether any negative consequences will result from failing to act in accordance with the statement, it is normally advisable to file amendments when the debtor's plans change and to serve them, as required, on the trustee and any affected creditors.

It is important to note what this section does and does not require. It requires only that the debtor state (1) whether the property will be surrendered or retained, (2) whether it will be claimed as exempt, (3) whether the debtor intends to redeem the property, and (4) whether the debtor intends to reaffirm the debt secured by the property. If the property is to be retained, the Official Form appears to require a choice between one of three options: (1) reaffirmation, discussed later in Chapter 13, (2) exemption and redemption of the security, discussed in Chapter 10, or (3) exemption and avoidance of the lien, discussed in Chapter 9.

However, the debtor need not choose one of the options provided under the Code or in the Official Form. A debtor may choose to retain the property subject to the creditor's security interest and state law rights, whatever they may be. When this option is chosen, none of the three applicable boxes should be checked. In such cases, it may be advisable to include a note that makes the debtor's intentions clear.

There is no provision in the Bankruptcy Code stating that a debtor may not change his or her intentions. In fact, the debtor may amend the statement of intention at any time before the period for performance of the intention expires. Although the debtor is normally required to follow through on the stated intentions within 45 days, that deadline should be seen only as a guideline for when redemption or reaffirmation should occur, if they are going to occur. The Code also makes it clear that the statement of intention does not alter any of the debtor's substantive rights as they previously existed.

In most chapter 7 cases, completion of the statement of intention is quite simple. Chapter 7 debtors generally retain all of their property because they claim their interests in all of it as exempt. (A debtor who has significant nonexempt property usually chooses chapter 13 rather than chapter 7.) The fact that the property is encumbered by a secured creditor's lien does not prevent the debtor from claiming his or her interest, subject to the lien, as exempt. In many cases, the lien may be partially or totally avoidable in bankruptcy. Few debtors reaffirm their debts or redeem more than one or two items.

In any case, the function this statement is simply one of notice. It is intended to meet creditors' complaints at congressional hearings that they could not get through to debtors' attorneys and were not permitted to contact *pro se* (unrepresented) debtors at all.

CHAPTER 13 PLAN

The most important document filed in a chapter 13 case is usually the debtor's proposed plan. This plan, which only the debtor can propose, describes how the debtor wishes to reorganize his or her financial situation. Its purpose is to clarify how the debtor desires payments and distributions to be made in the case. The plan may be modified without special court permission before court confirmation and, with the court's permission, after confirmation in certain circumstances, as described in Chapter 11.

The form of the plan is not prescribed by the rules or the statute. Most attorneys draft a standard plan that may be modified to suit the needs of each case. As long as the plan meets all of the requirements of the statute and clearly describes how creditors will be paid, its form should be acceptable.

The Bankruptcy Code requires only a few plan provisions. First, the plan must provide for full payment of all claims entitled to priority under section 507 of the Code, unless the claim holder agrees otherwise. These claims must be paid, even if they would have been discharged in a chapter 7 case. Most important among them are usually for administrative expenses, which include the trustee's commission and —in cases handled by private attorneys—the debtor's attorney's fee. The trustee's commission, to cover both compensation and expenses, is usually around

9 or 10 percent of the payments, although it may be reduced in unusual cases and is lower in some parts of the country. The law sets a minimum trustee's commission of $5 per month, unless the court orders otherwise.

A second requirement is that the plan provide for submission of all or such portion of the debtor's future income as is necessary for the execution of the plan. In an exceptional case, a debtor might conceivably propose to make no payments through the trustee and therefore submit no income. Whether such a plan would be deemed to meet this requirement is unclear.

Third, if the plan classifies claims in order to treat different types of claims differently, it must provide the same treatment for each claim in a particular class. This provision is intended to prevent unfair discrimination against disfavored creditors. As discussed later in Chapter 11, the courts have not yet agreed as to which classifications are fair. Although it is clear that secured claims, priority claims, claims with codebtors, and probably claims that are nondischargeable may be treated separately, there is considerable difference of opinion as to discrimination among other groups of unsecured claims.

With the exception of these requirements, chapter 13 generally provides total flexibility as to the order of distribution. No particular scheme is required, although most plans call for payment of priority and secured debts before other debts. Some debtors may wish to have priority administrative expenses paid first so that the debtor's attorney can be paid. It might sometimes be advisable to pay some priority claims later in the event that the case is converted to a chapter 7 proceeding in which those claims would be discharged. In this case, it would be to the debtor's advantage to pay first secured creditors holding nonavoidable liens that would remain in existence after a chapter 7 case, rather than unsecured dischargeable priority claims.

However, such a plan would likely meet with objections from the trustee, at least if his or her claim for administrative expenses is deferred. Generally, however, priority status does not entitle a claim to payment before all others, but merely to full payment sometime during the plan.

Payments and distributions need not be equal. The plan may provide for graduated payments over time, annual payments, or even a lump-sum payment from the debtor's property. However, the court may disapprove such a plan if it finds it to be not in good faith or not feasible. The plan may provide for payments over any period of time up to five years, although specific court approval is needed for plans that last longer than three years and the debtor must show good cause.

The court may also disapprove a plan if it does not meet certain standards regarding secured claims provided for in the plan. Unless the holder of such a claim has accepted the plan, the court may require that the debtor either surrender the property securing the debt or propose to make payments that have a present value of at least the amount of the allowed secured claim, with the creditor retaining its lien, as discussed in Chapter 10. To achieve the latter, unless the full amount of the allowed secured claim is paid immediately, the plan should provide for interest on the outstanding amounts. The courts have not yet agreed on an appropriate rate of interest.

Similarly, the court may refuse to confirm a plan if it does not meet two tests that require payments in some circumstances to unsecured creditors. The first is the best-interests-of-creditors test. This test requires the property that will be distributed under the plan to unsecured creditors to have a present value of not less than the amount those creditors would receive in a chapter 7 liquidation. Put another way, the present value of payments to unsecured creditors under the plan must be at least equal to the value of the debtor's nonexempt property, minus hypothetical costs of administration in a chapter 7 case in order to satisfy the test. The second test is based on the debtor's ability to pay. It requires that unsecured creditors receive all of the debtor's disposable income. *Disposable income* is defined as all income not committed by the debtor for maintenance and support of the debtor and the debtor's dependents or otherwise committed to pay claims under the plan, as discussed further in Chapter 11.

In addition to the criteria set forth above, the Code offers some guidance as to what the plan may do, but few limitations. The plan may classify claims, as long as it does not unfairly discriminate; modify the rights of holders of secured claims, except those secured only by a security interest in real property that is the debtor's principal residence; provide for curing or waiving any default; provide for payments on unsecured claims to be concurrent with those on secured claims; provide for curing defaults on long-term debts; provide for postpetition claims, provide for payment of claims through the sale of property; and provide for assumption or rejection of any executory contract or unexpired lease. Moreover, the plan may include any other appropriate provision not inconsistent with title 11.

As a practical matter when formulating a chapter 13 plan, the debtor should keep several broad principles in mind. A strategy must be designed for priority, secured, and unsecured debts that meets the debtor's objectives and is consistent with the Code and the debtor's available income. Legitimate priority debts must generally be paid in full. Secured debts may be treated in one of four ways: (1) pay them in full in the plan, (2) cure the default, (3) treat them outside the plan and let the lien ride through unaffected by bankruptcy, or (4) avoid the lien and treat the debt as unsecured. Unsecured creditors are entitled to at least what they would receive if the debtor's estate were liquidated in chapter 7 (the best-interests-of-creditors test). All of these options and requirements of the Code are discussed elsewhere in this book.

The debtor must have sufficient income to pay at least the amounts necessary to meet these standards for secured, priority, and unsecured debts, plus the trustee's commission. There is no need to accept any creditor's proof of claim as a given. It is possible to object to a creditor's characterization of a claim as priority or secured, to the amount that the creditor is claiming, or to the creditor's right to a claim at all. Once the amounts listed above are committed to the plan, it is necessary to return to the debtor's budget to check whether the debtor has additional disposable income. If so, it normally must be paid to the unsecured creditors under the ability-to-pay test.

Unless there are only one or two debts, it is usually impossible to specify the precise amounts that will be paid to different creditors under the plan. The ultimate distribution typically depends on a number of events that occur only after formulation of the plan. For example, the amount of a secured claim may be disputed. If the plan provides for a certain level of payments to the trustee, the amount to be distributed to claims paid after the disputed claim can be calculated only after the amount of the disputed claim has been determined. Moreover, not all creditors file claims; nationally, 40 percent do not. Thus, the amount each unsecured creditor receives from the total allocated to unsecured claims depends on how many unsecured creditors file claims.

For these reasons, the plan need not specify how much each creditor will receive; it may simply describe the order of distribution in sufficient detail so that the trustee will know how to proceed once the amounts of all allowed claims are known. As long as the amounts paid into the plan by the debtor appear to be sufficient to meet the requirements outlined above, the plan should be confirmed. In any case, as mentioned earlier, modifications are freely allowed if a problem does arise.

OTHER FORMS

Aside from the papers already described, one or two other forms must usually be filed. In every case, the debtor must file a disclosure of fees paid to his or her attorney. The purpose of this form is to allow the court and the U.S. trustee, who must also receive a copy, to monitor fees to be sure they are reasonable.

If the filing fee is not paid in full at filing, the debtor must file an application to pay it in installments. The form for this application is provided in Official Form 3. It also contains a proposed order for payments in installments. This application may not be filed if the debtor has paid anything to his or her attorney in connection with the bankruptcy.

If the debtor cannot file the schedules, statements, or a plan within 15 days of the petition, a motion for additional time may be filed. This motion must show cause for the extension and must be served on the bankruptcy trustee, if any, and the U.S. trustee. Most courts routinely grant an extension of time.

Finally, local practice may require other papers and may dictate the size of the paper to be used, whether backers are needed, and so forth. Most districts now require a form to be used in preparing mailing labels, to be filed either with the petition or shortly thereafter. The debtor should consult local rules or the clerk's office for these and any other requirements.

SIGNING, VERIFYING, AND FILING

After all of the forms have been prepared and reviewed, they must be verified by the debtor and signed by the attorney of record and the debtor. In exceptional circumstances, a petition may be signed and filed by another on behalf of the debtor pursuant to a power of attorney. It is always an excellent idea to review the documents carefully before signing. This serves as a final check on their correctness and also prevents any later misunderstanding about whether the forms were properly prepared.

The debtor's attorney normally signs two documents: the petition (including Exhibit B to the petition in chapter 7 cases) and the disclosure of attorney's fees. The debtor signs the petition (in two places in chapter 7 cases) and the statement of intention and verifies the schedules and statement of financial affairs. Either the attorney or the debtor may sign the chapter 13 plan. Under federal law, a notarized signature to a verification is not necessary if the signer certifies its truth under penalty of perjury.

Once the papers have been signed and verified, they are ready for filing. With the filing of these documents, or just the petition, the bankruptcy case is ready to proceed.

Chapter 7

AFTER THE PAPERS ARE FILED

Once a debtor decides to pursue a bankruptcy and files the documents to commence the case, the remainder of many routine bankruptcy cases seem anticlimactic. Although numerous complications can occur and significant steps must sometimes be taken on the debtor's behalf, quite often only a few formalities are left after filing the initial papers. This chapter describes the events that occur in every case and also some of the other proceedings that may arise during the pendency of the case.

CONSIDERATIONS AFTER FILING

It is important that debtors be aware of what will occur after the case is filed. The debtor should expect to receive the notices that will be issued by the court. These usually include the Notice of Appointment of a Trustee and the Notice of the Meeting of Creditors, which can be combined with other notices of deadlines. Debtors must advise their attorneys of a change of address. The court must also be advised, otherwise all notices will go to the debtor's old address.

The debtor should also understand any obligations to make payments, including installment payments of the filing fee, payments under a chapter 13 plan, payments outside the plan, and security deposits for utility service. In most cases, these payments are due within a month or two after the case is filed. Chapter 13 plan payments must begin within 30 days after the plan is filed, unless the court orders otherwise.

Debtors should also know their rights under the automatic stay provisions, which are discussed in detail in Chapter 8. They should know that creditors are not permitted to seek payment of any debts, that any creditor that does take any action should be advised of the bankruptcy, and that the creditor's action should be reported to the person handling the case.

In general, debtors should not pay any prebankruptcy debt (except in cases in which debts will remain after bankruptcy or in which they are being paid outside a chapter 13 plan). Debtors should not enter into new credit transactions without consulting with their attorney, especially in chapter 13, in which the trustee's permission is usually needed.

Any property that the debtor acquires that would become a part of the estate—for example, inheritances, marital property settlements, and life insurance proceeds—must be reported on supplemental schedules filed with the court. And, of course, a chapter 7 debtor should not dispose of any property that is not exempt because the trustee can and probably will demand that it be turned over. Local practice may sometimes require the trustee's permission even to use property of the estate, although this practice is questionable and may be challenged successfully if a chapter 13 case has been filed or if the property is exempt.

BEFORE THE MEETING OF CREDITORS

Notice of the Automatic Stay and Turnover Requirement

Although all creditors should receive a notice of the automatic stay as part of the notice of the meeting of creditors, that notice may not be sufficient to protect the debtor's rights. It may not be mailed until weeks or even months after the petition is filed; in the meantime, creditors without notice might take action harmful to the debtor. Creditors without notice of the case are normally not found in contempt of a stay they knew nothing about.

Thus, if there is any chance that a creditor might act to the debtor's detriment soon after the case is commenced, notice should be given that the stay is in effect. This notice is usually given by the debtor's attorney—by certified mail, if possible, and preceded by a phone call, if necessary—to forestall any threatened repossession, execution, or utility shutoff. Notice might be appropriate in other cases involving creditors that are prone to harassing collection efforts and those that are filing legal proceedings in state courts. It might also be appropriate to notify the courts in which actions against the debtor are pending. In chapter 13 cases, the attorney's letter should mention the stay of actions against codebtors, if applicable.

If, after notice, a creditor or judicial officer acts in violation of the stay, the debtor's counsel may file a motion to have that party held in contempt of court as well as an action for damages and attorney's fees. It is well established that the stay is automatic, that no further court order is necessary to restrain a creditor, and that actual notice of the bankruptcy, even without official notice from the court, is sufficient. Appropriate sanctions that can be sought from the bankruptcy court include actual damages, punitive damages, orders to pay the attorney's fees of the party enforcing the stay, and orders to undo the action that violated the stay.

The filing of a bankruptcy case puts into effect the automatic turn-over provisions of sections 542 and 543 of the Code. Under these sections, which are discussed in Chapter 8, any entity holding property that the trustee might use, sell, or lease (powers exercised by the debtor in chapter 13 cases) or that the debtor may exempt must turn over the property to the trustee. Because the debtor may exempt equity in property subject to a lien or even an interest in property when there is no measurable equity, this should include property held by creditors that has been repossessed or is subject to a possessory lien, such as that held by a pawnbroker or a warehouse that claims storage fees. Notice by certified mail of the property holder's obligation is appropriate, followed up by court action, if necessary.

Amendments to Statement or Schedules

Amendments are often not necessary in a well-prepared case, but if they are, the procedure is quite simple. Under the current Bankruptcy Rules, the debtor may amend the initial papers without special court permission at any time before the case is closed. The procedure requires the filing of an amended document signed by the debtor under oath.

The rules also provide that "[t]he debtor shall give notice of the amendment to the trustee and to any entity affected thereby." Principally, this notice is intended for creditors added by amendment so that they may protect their rights. In certain cases, the late filing of an amendment adding a creditor could prejudice the right to discharge a debt. Therefore, the debtor should make sure that the creditor receives notice of the amendment and a copy of the notice of the meeting of creditors as soon as possible. Because the court sends out notices when a creditor is added, there is a $20 fee for filing such an amendment. However, this fee can be waived on application to the court for good cause. For all other amendments, there is no fee.

Avoidance of Transfers of Exempt Property

As discussed in Chapters 9 and 10, the Code gives debtors a wide range of powers to avoid transfers, including various liens on property. Many of these powers are intended to protect the debtor's full use of the exemptions provided by the Code or by state and federal nonbankruptcy law.

In most cases in which a transfer, such as a lien, may be avoided by the debtor, the debtor seeks avoidance of the transfer by the court before discharge. The language of the Code indicates that lien avoidance is not self-executing and must be initiated by the debtor. The Bankruptcy Rules set out the procedure for lien avoidance. When a debtor seeks to avoid a judicial lien or certain nonpurchase-money security interests, a motion must be filed. For all other types of lien avoidance or other exercises of avoiding powers, an adversary proceeding, which is essentially a lawsuit within the bankruptcy case, is required.

Regardless of the method chosen, it is good practice to follow through once an order has been obtained. The order proposed to the court should include a provision requiring the lienholder or transferee to take all steps necessary to terminate the lien. Once it has been signed, it may be forwarded to the lienholder accompanied by a request that termination of the lien be recorded in all necessary records offices and that evidence of this action be sent to the debtor's counsel. However, it may sometimes be more expeditious simply to file the bankruptcy court order in the appropriate records offices. The later procedure ensures that the debtor's rights are fully protected.

Redemption of Property

Another important right that the debtor may exercise against secured creditors in a chapter 7 case is the right to redeem certain personal property by paying the lienholder the value of that property. (This right is discussed in detail in Chapter 10.) As with lien avoidance, it is probably easiest to attempt a stipulated settlement regarding redemption before filing for judicial enforcement. Of course, such a settlement must involve the lienholder's agreement on the value of the property. It could also involve the lienholder's agreement not to seek to enforce the lien as long as the stipulated amount is paid in agreed-on installments, either with or without reaffirmation of the debtor's personal liability.

If an agreement cannot be reached, the debtor's counsel must seek judicial enforcement of the right to redeem. It is unclear whether the rules require that this be done by complaint or by motion. If the value is contested, the debtor must provide proof of value in court. The debtor should file the application before the discharge is granted, and the application should normally be initiated within 45 days after the filing of the statement of intentions, unless the court extends that deadline.

Complaints on Dischargeability

It may sometimes be advisable for strategic reasons for the debtor to seek a determination by the bankruptcy court as to the dischargeability of a particular debt. This action can resolve a dispute about whether a debt is discharged once and for all, in the forum of the debtor's choice, and the debtor may obtain specific injunctive relief as well. For example, if a particular tax is to be discharged, having the bankruptcy court specifically order the taxing authority to cease collection attempts may be preferable to raising the discharge as a defense later in some other forum. Similarly, it is almost always a good idea to obtain a determination in bankruptcy court on the dischargeability of a student loan when undue hardship is an issue, as discussed later in Chapter 13.

The procedure for seeking a determination of dischargeability is governed by the adversary proceeding rules. A complaint stating the relief sought must be filed and served. Unlike complaints of creditors raising the nondischargeability of certain debts, this complaint may be filed at any time.

Objections to Claims of Creditors

When creditors do file claims and particularly when they file secured or priority claims, an objection to a claim may be crucial to the debtor's case. This objection may mean the difference between the success and failure of a chapter 13 plan or the reduction of a secured debt by thousands of dollars. The objection may allege that the claim has not been filed on time or is improper for some other reason.

The objection to a claim may raise any defense the debtor has against the creditor. It may also seek a determination that the claim is only partially secured or not secured at all because the value of the property encumbered by a lien is less than the amount of the claim or less than the amount of liens having higher priority right to the property.

Under current rules, there is no fixed deadline for filing an objection, but because the claim is allowed unless an objection is filed, the debtor should file the objection before distribution of dividends begins in a chapter 13 case or before the case is closed in a chapter 7 case. The rules stipulate that the objection must be in writing and must be mailed or delivered to the claimant, the trustee, and the debtor at least 30 days before a hearing on the objection. If necessary, discovery (the right to pretrial information from an opponent) should be available, and the matter can be treated as a fully contested lawsuit between the debtor and the creditor.

Other Disputes That May Arise

Various other types of disputes may occur between the debtor and the creditors before or after the meeting of creditors. Perhaps the most common dispute that puts the debtor on the defensive is a creditor's motion for relief from the automatic stay. Strategies for defense of these proceedings are discussed in Chapter 8. Such motions usually bring to a head early in the case disputes regarding secured claims. Creditors sometimes file a complaint objecting to discharge or seeking a determination that a particular debt is nondischargeable, as discussed later in Chapter 13. It is also possible that a motion to dismiss will be filed if there has been some procedural defect. The court may hold a hearing on whether a chapter 7 case constitutes a "substantial abuse" of the Code. (These issues are discussed in Chapter 12.)

There may also be issues that the debtor should bring to the court's attention. One method of doing this is by filing a complaint seeking a determination from the court regarding the issue in dispute. (Further discussion of such litigation is contained in Chapter 12.)

Retaining Nonexempt Property in Chapter 7 Cases

In consumer chapter 7 bankruptcies, although the trustee clearly has a right to take possession of nonexempt property before the meeting of creditors, this rarely occurs. All parties involved usually recognize that, when nonexempt property is of limited value, the simplest method of disposition is to sell it back to the debtor, who may purchase it with exempt assets or postpetition income. For example, the debtor's automobile may be worth $2000 more than can be exempted. Terms can usually be arranged for payment of the $2000 to the trustee in lieu of turning over the car for a sale in which the debtor would receive the exempted amount in cash. As long as the case will not be delayed, the trustee is usually willing to accept the payment in installments. If difficulties do arise, the case can be converted to chapter 13, in which the debtor has the absolute right, in essence, to do the same thing—to pay the value of the nonexempt property over time.

If the total value of the nonexempt property in a chapter 7 case is small—for example, less than $1000—it should also be possible to argue that the property should not be sold because the proceeds would be largely or totally consumed by administrative expenses and thus would be of little or no benefit to creditors, especially if the assets are not liquid assets, such as a bank account. In many cases, even when the debtor does not pursue this argument, the trustee either neglects to administer (that is, sell) such property or formally abandons it (gives up the estate's claim to it). Under the prior Bankruptcy Act, many courts dealt with other nominal-asset cases by ordering abandonment of the property back to the debtor, and Congress made clear its desire that this should occur under the Code. The Executive Office of the U.S. trustees also has policies discouraging the administration of low-value assets.

Commencement of Payments in Chapter 13 Cases

In accordance with the provisions of chapter 13, the debtor must commence making payments pursuant to his or her plan within 30 days after filing the plan. Payments to the trustee must be retained by the trustee until the plan is confirmed or until confirmation is denied. If the plan is confirmed, the trustee then distributes the payments in accordance with the plan. If confirmation is denied, the trustee returns the payments to the debtor after deducting the allowed administrative expenses.

If the plan proposes to cure a default on a secured claim, the debtor must make regular payments to the secured creditor as they come due in addition to the trustee payments for the arrears. In most jurisdictions, this can be accomplished by payments directly to the secured creditor, thereby avoiding a trustee's commission.

The first months of a chapter 13 plan create a significant hardship for some debtors because of the confluence of required utility deposits, installment payments on the filing fee, and the need to commence plan payments. One potential solution is a plan featuring graduated payments to the trustee, with lower payments in the first several months and higher payments thereafter. As long as the total to be paid over the life of the plan meets the requirements of the Code and the payments in each month commit the debtor's full disposable income, a graduated payment plan should be confirmed without a problem.

THE MEETING OF CREDITORS

In many routine consumer bankruptcies, the only real event of any importance between filing and discharge is the meeting of creditors, sometimes colloquially called the *first meeting of creditors* or the *section 341(a) meeting* in honor of the relevant statutory provision. Although it may pose occasional problems, this proceeding is usually routine and uneventful.

Preparation

Most debtors cannot believe that the meeting of creditors is rarely anything to worry about; they expect their creditors to turn out in force to grill them about why they are not paying their just obligations. The debtor must therefore have a good understanding of the procedure and the questions that are likely to be asked.

Most trustees tend to ask the same questions in every case. Because the questions center on the schedules and statements that the debtor has already filed, it is essential to review these carefully, paying particular attention to the items claimed as exempt and the values given them.

It is also necessary to assemble whatever documents that local practice requires the debtor to bring to the meeting. In some jurisdictions, no documents need be produced in a chapter 7 case. In others, the trustee may wish to see deeds, titles to motor vehicles, tax returns, rent receipts, bank statements, and so on. These requests are often stated in a notice sent to the debtor before the meeting.

The meeting of creditors is a good time to check on which creditors have filed proofs of claim. Because generally the only creditors that will be paid in a chapter 13 plan (or in those few chapter 7 cases where there are dividends) are those for whom proofs of claim are filed, the debtor's counsel should file claims on behalf of any creditors that have not filed and whom the debtor wants to pay. The debtor may file such claims at any time during the 120 days after the first date set for the meeting of creditors. It is also useful to check the claims filed at this time, as well as shortly after the deadline for filing claims, to determine whether there are any claims to which the debtor wishes to object.

Procedure

The debtor must attend the meeting of creditors. In exceptional cases of hardship, including illness or incarceration, this requirement might be waived on a motion filed by the debtor, and the debtor would be examined by telephone or by written questions and answers.

The proceeding is likely to be short and informal for most consumer debtors. Despite its popular name, it is rarely graced by the presence of any creditors. Indeed, neither trustees nor creditors show much interest in most consumer cases. There are several reasons for this lack of interest. Probably paramount is the belief that such debtors rarely have any assets worth pursuing and that the cost in time and effort required of the trustee and creditors is not justified by the benefits achieved. Unless the trustee can obtain property for the estate worth many hundreds of dollars, his or her fee will not be significantly increased in a chapter 7 case. Most creditors realize that there is little they can accomplish at the meeting other than perhaps obtaining some information. Creditors occasionally appear to find out the location of their collateral and to attempt to negotiate its future disposition. Usually, though, the only ones to show up are unsophisticated creditors who are under the misimpression that they are required to attend.

Local practice varies from jurisdiction to jurisdiction, however. In a few localities, for example, it is relatively common for creditors to appear in chapter 13 cases to negotiate with the debtor's counsel and the trustee concerning various provisions of the plan. When this occurs, it is important to remember that the trustee has no power to make a final decision on whether a particular plan will be confirmed. When issues are contested, the trustee or a creditor may file an objection; the debtor may present opposition, if necessary, and let the court resolve the issue. As often as not, even when issues are raised at the meeting of creditors, neither the trustee nor any creditor will go to the effort necessary to formally raise the appropriate objection.

The primary purpose of the meeting is to obtain further information about the debtor's case, particularly regarding the debtor's assets and liabilities. This is accomplished through a set of routine questions propounded usually by the presiding officer, who may be the bankruptcy trustee or the U.S. trustee, depending on local rules. In a few jurisdictions, the debtor's attorney may pose the questions.

The questions typically seek to check the accuracy of the debtor's schedules and statement and, in a chapter 13 case, the debtor's ability to perform under the plan. It is not uncommon that the meeting brings out information that is somewhat inconsistent with the previously filed documents, but it is rare that any serious problems arise. Any discrepancies in the documents can usually be cured by amendment.

The questions may also concern the right to a discharge. These questions will rarely be very detailed unless a particular creditor has appeared to seek information on a debt that it claims is nondischargeable. The proceeding may then become, for all practical purposes, a deposition in which the creditor asks most of the questions.

By and large, though, the questions parallel those in the Official Forms that the debtor has already answered, and they have similar purposes. They seek information concerning fraudulent transfers, preferences, former bankruptcies, and, usually, how the debtor fell into financial difficulty. Unless an answer arouses suspicion, the questions are rarely followed up. In many districts, though, trustees are careful to ask about types of property that are frequently not listed by debtors, such as tax refunds, security deposits, and the like. Even if new property is uncovered, however, it can usually still be claimed as exempt by amendment of the schedules.

Because the bankruptcy judge is not present at the meeting of creditors, disputes may occasionally arise either between the debtor and the creditors or between the debtor and the trustee. For example, the debtor's counsel may need to object to certain questions for various reasons, such as privilege, the Fifth Amendment, relevance, or repetitiousness. Although neither the statute nor the rules address how such disputes are to be resolved, it does seem clear that neither the bankruptcy trustee nor the U.S. trustee can issue enforceable orders. Presumably, then, the debtor's attorney should instruct the debtor not to answer, if necessary, to reserve the dispute for the court's decision.

Debtors are sometimes confused about how much they may consult counsel during the examination. In most jurisdictions, the practice is quite liberal; the debtor is allowed to confer with counsel before answering a question, and counsel is allowed to interject clarifying remarks when necessary.

Some bankruptcy trustees require that debtors surrender all credit cards still in their possession at the time of the meeting of creditors. Although most debtors are quite willing to relinquish the cards, if they have not already done so, some may have legitimate objections to this procedure, especially regarding necessary accounts that may not even be in default. If the debtor wishes to retain the cards, the request for their surrender should be opposed. Most judges and trustees admit that, because they lack specific authority for the turnover of the cards absent a request by the creditors involved, they will not pursue the issue, especially if the debtor has shown good reason for retaining the cards.

Another issue that crops up frequently in some jurisdictions involves creditors who attend meetings seeking to pressure debtors into consenting to enter into reaffirmation agreements. These creditors often threaten the debtor with repossession of personal property pursuant to questionable or nonexistent security interests. For the reasons discussed more fully later in Chapter 13, reaffirmation of debts is rarely a good idea. In most cases, repossession is unlikely because the creditor cannot repossess without breaching the peace if the debtor simply refuses to allow the creditor into the home, and the creditor would need to obtain a court order permitting repossession. Few creditors ever take the trouble to pursue the matter that far. In the unusual instance in which it does occur, issues concerning the validity of the security interest can be addressed in that proceeding.

Finally, at this time the debtor in a chapter 13 case may wish to file any priority or secured claims that creditors have not already filed and that the debtor wants to pay under the plan. The reason for this filing, as discussed above, is to ensure that the money the debtor is paying into the plan to deal with these creditors does not go instead to pay general unsecured claims. It is probably good practice also to file at this time any other claims that the debtor wishes to pay, even though these claims may also be filed later. These claims may include nondischargeable debts and claims on which friends or relatives have cosigned (so that they are paid, at least in part, by any distribution). The time limits provided for in the rules for filing claims are outlined in the notice of the meeting of creditors.

AFTER THE MEETING OF CREDITORS IN CHAPTER 7 CASES

In the typical no-asset bankruptcy, there is little to be done between the meeting of creditors and the discharge. Proceedings that have already been started, such as for lien avoidance or redemption, may continue. Amendments to the schedules or statement of affairs may be necessary. However, amendments that add creditors may not always be of value after the deadline for filing a nondischargeability complaint has passed, as discussed later in Chapter 13.

If the debtor has more then nominal nonexempt assets, of course, they are turned over or their value is paid to the trustee, who liquidates them. This rarely happens because consumer debtors with nonexempt assets usually opt for chapter 13.

In some districts, the trustee files a report to the court concerning whether he or she objects to the exemptions claimed or to the debtor's discharge. This report is not required; under the Code, the exemptions are self-executing if no objection is filed.

The trustee or any creditor who wishes to object to the exemptions claimed must file the objections in writing and serve them within 30 days after the conclusion of the meeting of creditors (or, if later, the date of any amendment to the exemptions claimed). Thereafter, as discussed in Chapter 9, there will be a court hearing on the objections. The objecting party has the burden of proving that the exemptions are not properly claimed.

CONFIRMATION HEARING IN CHAPTER 13 CASES

In a chapter 13 case, the next step after the meeting of creditors is normally the confirmation hearing, which may be held on the same day or anytime up to several months later. It is sometimes not possible to conclude the confirmation hearing until many months after the meeting of creditors, pending the court's decision on objections to priority or secured claims. Without this decision, there is no way to determine whether the plan pays such claims in full, as is usually required for confirmation.

The procedures followed at the confirmation hearing vary widely, due to the great changes in chapter 13 under the Code. If neither the trustee nor any creditor objects to confirmation, the hearing may take only a few minutes. The court simply enters an order of confirmation, finding that the plan complies with all of the provisions of chapter 13. The debtor's attendance may not be necessary. In fact, some bankruptcy judges actively discourage counsel from bringing their clients to the confirmation hearing, so that the debtors will not lose another day's pay. Other judges do not even require that counsel be present when there is no objection; they simply sign the confirmation order in their chambers.

If there are objections or if the court has questions of its own, testimony and argument may be taken regarding the debtor's income, ability to pay, and other matters. Normally, objections are filed before the hearing. Creditors who have not filed a proof of claim are generally not permitted to object to the plan. (The issues likely to be raised by objections are discussed in Chapters 10 and 11.)

The day of the confirmation hearing is a good time to determine which claims have been filed because the deadline for filing claims will usually have expired. If only a few claims have been filed, the plan may provide more than enough payments to pay all filed claims in full. If that is the case, it is obviously in the debtor's interest to modify the plan to lower either the amount or the number of payments. Otherwise, because of the way some trustees' computers are programmed, the debtor may continue to make payments to the trustee even after all claims have been paid.

ADMINISTRATION OF THE CHAPTER 13 PLAN

Trustee Payments to Creditors

Once the chapter 13 plan has been approved, the trustee usually takes over the administrative details. Although the debtor may have been making payments for some time, no funds are distributed to creditors until after confirmation. If the time for filing claims has not yet elapsed, there may be further delays before all claims are determined and allowed. In the interim, objections to other claims, as well as other disputes that arise, may be litigated.

It is a good idea for the debtor's counsel to monitor the trustee's payments periodically once distribution has begun. Most trustees allow convenient access to their records, and some trustees mail computer printouts to debtors or their counsel. It is not uncommon for computer-ordered payments from a trustee's office to deviate from either the plan or the claims actually filed. In this event, it is important to bring the problem to the trustee's attention before incorrect amounts have been paid. An occasional check on the progress of the plan can also reveal any other budding problems, such as a delinquency in the debtor's payments.

Postpetition Claims

Once distribution has begun, events normally flow smoothly for the duration of the plan, with the debtor or the debtor's employer sending payments regularly to the trustee for distribution. The Code allows certain postpetition claims (debts incurred after the petition) to be incorporated into the plan; such debts may also be paid outside the plan. Allowable postpetition claims may include postpetition tax debts and consumer debts for property or services necessary for the debtor's performance under the plan. Regardless of whether the postpetition claims are to be paid through the plan or outside it, creditors often require the trustee's approval before any significant obligation is incurred. Approval is rarely difficult to obtain, though local practices may vary.

When the debtor, trustee, and creditor do not agree that a postpetition claim should be paid through the plan, there may be different results. It has been held that only a creditor may file a postpetition claim; a debtor may not force a postpetition creditor into the plan involuntarily. If a creditor does not choose to file a claim, the postpetition claim will survive the bankruptcy and be enforced in nonbankruptcy courts to the extent that it is not paid.

If a creditor does want the claim to be treated under the plan and the claim is filed and allowed by the court, a modification of the plan may be necessary to accommodate the claim. This may be accomplished by increasing the payments or the length of the plan and perhaps by classifying the claim separately so that it is paid in full. At least one court has held that, if the debtor refuses to apply for the necessary modification, the claim cannot be allowed and will be retained by the creditor for enforcement outside the bankruptcy.

Postpetition claims that are filed and allowed are normally discharged by a chapter 13 discharge. However, if the trustee's approval of a postpetition debt could have been obtained by the debtor but was not, that debt survives the discharge to the extent that it has not been paid.

Modification of the Plan

Debtors often need to modify the plan after confirmation, either to raise payments to accommodate a postpetition claim or to lower payments because the debtor has had a change of circumstances. The trustee or a holder of an unsecured claim may also seek modification if they believe the debtor's financial circumstances have improved since confirmation. The debtor probably need not prove changed circumstances to establish grounds for modification. The modified plan must meet all of the tests for confirmation of the original plan. The procedure requires the filing of a motion and notice by the court to appropriate affected parties. If a modification sought by the debtor is unopposed, no hearing is normally held, and the modification is approved. Once approved, it binds all parties.

Usually, a hearing is held on any request for modification by a party other than the debtor, unless the debtor expressly agrees to it. However, as with many issues that affect a debtor's rights, it is best to file an objection to the relief requested because a response guarantees that the debtor will obtain a hearing.

Inability to Complete the Plan

Many debtors encounter difficulties of various sorts in completing their chapter 13 plans as originally confirmed. These difficulties may arise from loss of income, unexpected expenses, marital problems, or other causes.

Financial problems sometimes prevent debtors from making the required plan payments as they come due. When this occurs, the debtor should attempt to catch up, if possible. Most trustees are willing to accept delinquent plan payments as long as the debtor does not fall too far behind. In serious cases, though, the trustee may request dismissal due to the debtor's failure to comply with the plan.

Some debtors are unable to keep up with mortgage payments that must be made outside the plan. This problem generally gives rise to a motion by the secured creditor for relief from the stay to commence or continue foreclosure proceedings. The best response, if possible, is for the debtor to catch up before the motion is heard. Most secured creditors will allow the debtor to catch up because they know that, if the debtor brings the delinquent payments to a hearing on a motion for relief from stay, the bankruptcy judge will probably deny relief. Other creditors will agree not to foreclose immediately, allowing the debtor an opportunity to catch up on payments if the debtor agrees to future relief from the stay if he or she fails to catch up. It is generally a good idea to avoid such agreements, except as a last resort when no modification of the plan or defense to relief from stay is possible.

When these issues come to a head, either by motion to dismiss or motion for relief from stay, the debtor has several options to consider. Often, if not always, the debtor can still obtain full or partial bankruptcy relief by one of the strategies discussed below.

The most preferable option is often modification, the procedure for which is described above. Modification may allow the chapter 13 plan to proceed to conclusion by lowering the payments to an amount that the debtor can afford or by extending the payments. It may also be possible to modify the plan to terminate earlier than originally proposed. As long as all the chapter 13 requirements are met, including full payment of priority debts, this type of modification should be allowed. However, if the claims of secured creditors have not yet been satisfied, the termination of the plan may pose difficulties unless the debtor can make arrangements with those creditors. In either type of modification, the debtor preserves the right to the broader chapter 13 discharge. This is important for debtors who have unsecured debts that are not dischargeable in chapter 7.

A second possibility is to apply for a hardship discharge. This discharge will be granted when the failure to complete payments is "due to circumstances for which the debtor should not justly be held accountable," but only if modification is impracticable and the present value of payments to unsecured creditors is not less than the amount they would have received had the case originally proceeded as a chapter 7 liquidation. In most consumer cases, these tests should not be difficult to meet. The debtor need not pay all priority claims to obtain a hardship discharge; however, secured creditors that have not yet been fully paid normally retain their liens for the unpaid amounts of their allowed secured claims, thus possibly posing problems that must be resolved after the bankruptcy case is over. Finally, the hardship discharge is not as broad as the normal chapter 13 discharge, but rather is coextensive with the chapter 7 discharge. This may mean that some debts are not discharged. However, unlike the chapter 7 discharge, if 70 percent of the unsecured claims have been paid, the hardship discharge will not bar a subsequent chapter 7 discharge within six years.

A third choice is conversion of the case to chapter 7. The debtor may do this without obtaining any special court permission. Creditors may also request conversion for various reasons. In some cases, conversion offers no advantage over the hardship discharge and could pose problems. Some courts have held that all property acquired after filing may become property of the chapter 7 estate. In those jurisdictions, newly acquired property that the debtor cannot claim as exempt could be lost. Many other courts, however, have held that the property of the estate and the exemptions in a case converted from chapter 13 to chapter 7 should be based on property held when the original chapter 13 petition was filed.

In any case, postpetition debts are included in the ultimate chapter 7 discharge, which could be a major advantage if the debtor has incurred significant new debts after filing. These debts would be included in the hardship discharge only if the debtor had obtained the trustee's approval and had incorporated the debts into the plan. Again, although priority claims would be discharged to the extent allowed in chapter 7, secured claims and claims that are nondischargeable in chapter 7 would remain to be dealt with after discharge. If objections to a discharge are possible in chapter 7, this route may not be advantageous to the debtor. (Objections to discharge are discussed later in Chapter 13.)

If the debtor cannot obtain approval of a modified plan, is ineligible for a hardship discharge, and yet still wishes to obtain some bankruptcy relief, conversion may be the only option. Because voluntary or involuntary dismissal reinstates not only all prepetition debts but also all avoided liens, conversion may be necessary in such cases to retain the benefit of successful litigation under chapter 13.

A final option is dismissal, which is available in any chapter 13 case that was not previously converted from another chapter. Dismissal may be preferable if the debtor cannot meet the hardship test or best-interests test for a hardship discharge and if the debtor stands to lose significant nonexempt property in a conversion to chapter 7. To the extent possible, dismissal returns the parties to the status quo before the bankruptcy, negating many benefits that the debtor might already have obtained, such as the avoidance of liens. Nonetheless, the debtor might find it preferable to deal with creditors outside of bankruptcy rather than subject nonexempt assets to immediate liquidation. If the case is dismissed, all trustee payments to creditors immediately cease, and property in the hands of the chapter 13 trustee should be promptly returned to the debtor.

Once the case is dismissed, the debtor has the option to file again under either chapter 13 or chapter 7. If this option is in the debtor's interest, care should be taken that the anticipated subsequent case does not violate the restrictions on refiling within 180 days of a dismissal. (These restrictions are discussed in Chapter 2.)

Both the absolute right to dismiss and the right to convert may be lost by the debtor who does not exercise them in a timely manner. Once the case is converted to chapter 7, perhaps on request of creditors, the chapter 13 right to dismiss the case presumably ceases to exist. Similarly, once a case is dismissed over the debtor's objection, no further right to convert exists. Thus, it is important to exercise these rights before an involuntary conversion or dismissal. Although a new chapter 7 petition can usually be filed after a chapter 13 case is dismissed, it would entail needless effort and a new filing fee. The consequences of an involuntary conversion may include the loss of nonexempt property that is critical to the debtor's affairs.

THE DISCHARGE AND THE DISCHARGE HEARING

The final step in most bankruptcy cases is the court's order of discharge. The court is required to hold a hearing concerning the discharge in any case in which the debtor desires to reaffirm a debt, in order to warn the debtor about the dangers of reaffirmation. Otherwise, such a hearing occurs only at the court's discretion, and few courts hold discharge hearings when there is no reaffirmation.

When a discharge hearing is held, the Code clearly requires the debtor to attend. Although there is no apparent need for the debtor's presence when debts are not being reaffirmed but the court still schedules a discharge hearing, the mandatory appearance provision was probably intended, in part, to impress the debtor with the solemnity and importance of the bankruptcy. It is the first and only time that most debtors see a judge in their bankruptcy cases. In view of the questionable importance of such a ritual, it may be possible to convince the court to waive the required appearance of the debtor when attendance at the hearing would cause real hardship. Indeed, several courts have held that Congress did not really mean what it said and that the debtor need not attend in all cases.

Whether or not a discharge hearing is held, the debtor ultimately receives a discharge order from the court. The debtor should keep a copy of the discharge order and a list of creditors scheduled in the bankruptcy in a safe place in case issues arise later about the disposition of the case.

Reaffirmation of Debts

The principal stated purpose of the discharge hearing is to advise debtors of their rights, especially with regard to the reaffirmation of debts. In a well-handled case, the debtor's counsel should already have done this. Without doubt, reaffirmation is rarely a good idea. Reaffirmation, which in essence is a promise to pay a debt despite its discharge, effectively waives the benefits of discharge for that particular debt and should be considered only in exceptional circumstances. If a debtor is in economic default—that is, behind in payments on a secured debt—and does not wish to pursue chapter 13 to handle the problem, reaffirmation might be appropriate in exchange for a creditor's forbearance. Similarly, if it is unlikely that any lawsuit for additional money would be brought after foreclosure on a mortgage, either because the value of the collateral far exceeds the debt or because such lawsuits are barred in the debtor's state, then little harm can be done by reaffirming that debt. In either case, the debt should not be reaffirmed in an amount exceeding the value of the collateral; there may also be ways to save the debtor's property without reaffirmation, as discussed later in chapter 13.

Many debtors (and attorneys) are under the misimpression that no payment may be made to a creditor after bankruptcy unless the debt is reaffirmed. This is simply not correct. The results sought by reaffirmation of a debt can usually be obtained just as well by simply continuing to make regular voluntary payments on a debt. For example, creditors rarely foreclose on security or pursue a cosigner if payments on a debt are current. Although it is reassuring for the debtor to have a promise from the creditor that it will not exercise the right to foreclose given it by the common bankruptcy clause in consumer contracts, this agreement can often be negotiated without a reaffirmation which again obligates the debtor personally. The debtor usually has some leverage in negotiating such an agreement because the debtor may be able to defend against a claim or dispute the value of the security.

In any case, if a creditor does threaten adverse action, it can usually be prevented by a new chapter 13 case, if necessary. Because chapter 13 provides that a plan may waive a default and that a prior bankruptcy is no bar to filing, debtors are fully within their rights to use a new chapter 13 case to prevent such creditor abuses.

Despite its clear disadvantages for the debtor, many agree to reaffirmation on advice of counsel. In most cases, their attorneys are lazy, unaware of the alternatives to reaffirmation, or both. It is in these situations that the discharge hearings can serve an important purpose. The judge's main duty is to advise debtors of the dangers of reaffirmation, of the fact that reaffirmation is not required, and of the debtor's right to rescind the reaffirmation within 60 days after it is filed with the court or, if later, up to the date of the discharge.

An attorney who represents a debtor in negotiating a reaffirmation agreement on a consumer debt must also counsel the debtor about the advisability of reaffirmation. The attorney must then file a declaration with the court that the reaffirmation is a fully informed and voluntary agreement that does not impose an undue hardship on the debtor or the debtor's dependents.

In all other reaffirmations of consumer debts, except those secured by real property, the court must decide whether to approve the reaffirmation agreement. Agreements may be approved only if they do not impose an undue hardship on the debtor or the debtor's dependents and only if they are in the debtor's best interests.

Procedure at the Discharge Hearing

If the court decides to have a discharge hearing even though there will be no reaffirmation of debt, the hearing is usually a very brief affair, with nothing to be said by the debtor or the debtor's counsel. In fact, in many jurisdictions, the debtor's counsel need not attend the hearing. The court usually warns the debtor about creditors trying to collect their debts or obtain reaffirmations in the future and lets the debtor know that bankruptcy is a serious business. The court then advises prudence in future credit transactions and wishes the debtor good luck. Given the potential for mind-numbing repetition, some judges give this message simultaneously to all the debtors scheduled on a particular day. Others give it to the first debtor to appear and then simply ask the debtors appearing later whether they heard what was said earlier, noting that the same applies to them. Some judges repeat the message, with slight variations, for each debtor who appears.

If a reaffirmation is proposed for approval, most courts require a motion and a proposed order to be filed before or at the hearing. The court may then examine the debtor closely to determine if he or she understands what reaffirmation means and to discover whether reaffirmation is really in the debtor's best interest. If it is not, the reaffirmation should not be approved.

AFTER DISCHARGE

Once the discharge has been granted and all related litigation has ended, one or two steps normally remain. These final details may be quite important in particular cases and should not be neglected.

Public records must often be modified to reflect what has occurred in the bankruptcy. For example, if liens no longer exist or have been modified, the debtor's counsel should verify that any record of the liens has been corrected. This is normally done as part of the lien avoidance process, but it is important to check the records when closing a case.

In some jurisdictions, it is good practice to notify courts in which legal proceedings have been pending that the discharge has been granted or that certain judgments are void. Technically, this is not necessary because the effect of the discharge is automatic, but local practice or the dictates of court etiquette may make it advisable in particular areas.

Finally, debtors should be fully aware of the meaning of their discharge so that they are not misled into paying discharged debts. They should report any contacts by creditors to their attorneys to obtain advice and to initiate steps against those creditors, if necessary. Debtors should also be aware of the other protections arising from their discharge, particularly against government and employer discrimination.

Most importantly, debtors must not ignore legal actions brought against them after bankruptcy. Many debtors are under the impression that the bankruptcy makes any further action to protect their interests unnecessary. This may be technically true with respect to some debts, but as a general rule it is advisable to seek the advice of counsel if sued by a creditor after discharge. Some creditors may wrongfully institute legal actions to collect a discharged debt, and although this type of action can usually be rectified, early intervention and assertion of the bankruptcy discharge can prevent later complications, such as harm caused by a wrongful execution. Other creditors may seek to foreclose on a valid lien or to collect a debt that was not discharged, such as a student loan. In these cases, the debtor needs counsel as much as ever. The solution may be a new chapter 13 bankruptcy or any one of numerous other defensive strategies, such as reopening the bankruptcy case to schedule a creditor that was not previously listed.

Part III

LEGAL ISSUES IN BANKRUPTCY

Chapter 8

AUTOMATIC STAYS AND TURNOVER OF PROPERTY

By simply filing a bankruptcy petition, the debtor brings to his or her aid an instrument of awesome breadth and power: the automatic stay of the Bankruptcy Code. Few other legal steps that may be taken on behalf of a consumer can bring about relief so simply, so effectively, and so dramatically. The stay provisions of the Code, along with the other related provisions that are discussed in this chapter, take effect the instant a case is filed. From that moment, they place the debtor and the debtor's property under the protection of the bankruptcy court.

The power of these provisions extends to many sorts of actions that may be taken against consumers, including some that, at first glance, do not appear to be related to debt. These actions are stopped, totally and immediately, by filing the two-page bankruptcy petition. Indeed, the certainty of obtaining such relief is often a prime factor in the debtor's decision to file a case. In some situations, no other remedy may be as effective, and often none will be as simple. For debtors who have waited to deal with their problems until the last minute before some serious adverse action, the automatic stay may provide the only practical solution. For debtors for whom all other legal steps have failed, it may provide a way of at least postponing a crisis while the debtor seeks relief in the bankruptcy court.

THE AUTOMATIC STAY

Purpose

The basic purpose of the stay is to protect the debtor and his or her property. As stated in a congressional explanation of the Bankruptcy Code:

> [t]he automatic stay is one of the fundamental debtor protections provided by the bankruptcy laws. It gives the debtor a breathing

spell from his creditors. It stops all collection efforts, all harassment, and all foreclosure actions. It permits the debtor to attempt a repayment or reorganization, or simply to be relieved of the financial pressures that drove him into bankruptcy.

The stay freezes the debtor's assets as of the date of filing, preventing individual creditors from picking away at them for their own benefit to the detriment of the ultimate goals of the bankruptcy. In chapter 7 liquidation cases, this guarantees the protection of the debtor's property, or equity therein, so it can be exempted to provide a fresh start and so nonexempt property can be fairly distributed to creditors. In chapter 13, the stay ensures protection of property that may be necessary not only for the debtor's fresh start, but also for the success of the debtor's plan.

Along with other provisions governing property of the estate, the stay permits the bankruptcy court to handle all aspects of the debtor's situation in an orderly manner. It prevents other courts and parties from interfering with or complicating the bankruptcy process, at least until the bankruptcy court allows. Virtually all activity concerning the debtor and the debtor's property thus comes into a single forum to be handled in accordance with the (usually) overriding purposes of the bankruptcy.

Duration

The duration of the automatic stay can vary significantly, depending on the circumstances. Theoretically, it can be ended almost immediately if circumstances require that the court grant relief to affected parties. These circumstances, usually dealing with perishable property, are almost never present in cases involving consumer debtors. As a practical matter, the stay is usually not lifted by the court at a creditor's request in much less than 30 days; and it may last for the duration of the case, a matter of three to six months in chapter 7 and up to five years in chapter 13.

Scope

The acts prohibited by the automatic stay are set out in a series of overlapping provisions of the law. This section discusses those provisions.

Legal Proceedings

The stay bars "the commencement or continuation, including the issuance or employment of process, of a judicial administrative, or other action or proceeding against the debtor that was or could have been commenced before the commencement of the case . . . or to recover a claim against the debtor that arose before the commencement of the case." Thus, almost all forms of civil legal actions are brought to an abrupt halt. The only possible exceptions to this provision are actions that did not arise out of circumstances existing before the case and that do not pertain to a claim that existed before the case. These actions may still be barred by a different provision, however.

One issue arising with increasing frequency is how to treat injury claims in cases in which the acts giving rise to liability occur prepetition, but no injury is discovered until after the commencement of the responsible party's bankruptcy case. Many courts have held that the victim has a prepetition claim that is subject to the automatic stay.

Among the many types of legal proceedings affected by the automatic stay are attachments, garnishments and executions, evictions, and almost all family-related court proceedings, including custody, divorce, and some support cases. Also prohibited are administrative proceedings, such as those to revoke a driver's license, to intercept a tax refund, or to determine and collect an overpayment of public benefits, as well as arbitrations and other less formal proceedings. Even proceedings against the debtor in which the debtor is sued solely as a trustee for someone else and proceedings based on admittedly nondischargeable debts are prohibited unless the court lifts the stay. Appeals of all proceedings against the debtor are also stayed. No further steps may be taken in stayed proceedings without the permission of the bankruptcy court. However, the stay is subject to several limited exceptions, which are discussed later in this chapter.

It is important to note that the stay bars only actions against the debtor, not those brought by the debtor. The debtor's actions may be continued after commencement of the case, although the trustee may acquire an interest in an action and a party may be able to remove (transfer) the action to the bankruptcy court. It is also quite clear that the stay does not affect acts against codebtors who are jointly liable with the debtor on particular debts, except as provided in the codebtor stay of chapter 13, which is discussed below.

Acts Directed against the Debtor's Property

Several provisions protect the property owned by the debtor at the time of filing. They prohibit the following:

1. The enforcement, against the debtor or against property of the estate, of a judgment obtained before the commencement of the case under the Bankruptcy Code

2. Any act to obtain possession of property of the estate or property from the estate or to exercise control over property of the estate

3. Any act to create, perfect (file in public records), or enforce any lien against property of the estate

4. Any act to create, perfect, or enforce any lien to the extent that the lien secures a claim that arose before the commencement of the case under the Code

These provisions have slightly different effects, depending on whether a judgment or a lien is involved. A judgment obtained before filing cannot be enforced against either the debtor or property of the estate.

The provisions prohibiting acts to obtain possession or to utilize liens against property of the estate apply regardless of when the claim arose because property of the estate is essentially frozen, to be administered only by the bankruptcy court. In a chapter 13 case, this can be very important because all property that the debtor acquires while the case is pending generally becomes property of the estate. The prohibition of acts to obtain possession also applies to property not owned by, but in possession of, the estate, such as leased property, even if the lease was terminated before the case. It also applies to any other property in which the debtor has any property interest and to intangible property rights— such as rights to enforce a contract and rights to insurance coverage or proceeds—as well as to tangible property.

Finally, these provisions generally prevent the creation, perfection, or enforcement of any lien against property of the debtor that is not part of the estate, when the debtor has such property—for example, property abandoned in a chapter 7 case—if the lien secures a prepetition claim. Thus, repossessions or sales of repossessed property are clearly enjoined.

The applicability of the stay to acts against property of the estate often turns on difficult questions as to whether the debtor had a property interest when the case was filed. Generally, even limited rights in property bring a stay into effect. Thus, the stay may halt even evictions, foreclosures, or other transactions that are nearly complete, depending on state law regarding the debtor's property rights.

Other Acts Prohibited by the Stay

The automatic stay also prohibits the following:

1. Any act to collect, assess, or recover a claim against the debtor that arose before the commencement of the case

2. The setoff of any debt owed to the debtor that arose before the commencement of the case against any claim against the debtor

3. The commencement or continuation of a proceeding before the U.S. Tax Court concerning the debtor

These provisions round out the stay's protections.

Creditors may not engage in any collection activity nor in any other acts to try to force the debtor to pay a prepetition claim. As noted earlier, the word *claim* is broadly defined to include not only rights to payment, regardless of whether they are liquidated, contingent, matured, disputed, or secured, but also many rights to other court remedies. Administrative reductions of public benefits—that is, Social Security, unemployment compensation, or welfare—that are based on a claim of overpayment or fraud are not allowed. If a collection motivation is shown, the withholding of a student's transcript or other benefits normally provided to nondebtors is also prohibited. Similarly, creditors may not exercise a right of setoff (paying themselves with money they owe to the debtor) against the debtor's property, such as bank accounts, without violating the stay, nor may they garnish the debtor's wages or collect their debts from property of the debtor that comes into their hands, such as energy assistance payments. Even the acceptance of payroll deductions that the debtor authorized before the bankruptcy as payment for a prepetition debt constitutes an act to collect that debt and is thus a violation of the stay.

The IRS has been one of the most frequent adversaries in litigation regarding these issues. The IRS now appears to recognize the necessity that it seek court relief from the stay before it can set off a tax refund against a prebankruptcy tax debt. This may be because, in several instances, the IRS was held in contempt for setting off tax refunds without getting relief from the stay. However, despite these cases, it is often difficult to have tax refunds released to a debtor because the IRS claims a right to "retain" them.

The Automatic Stay Protecting Codebtors in Chapter 13

In chapter 13 cases, another type of automatic stay also goes into effect. This stay prohibits any act or civil legal action to collect all or part of a consumer debt from a codebtor. Congress found this provision to be necessary because, in many instances under the old Chapter XIII, codebtors were pursued by creditors as soon as a debtor filed a case, leading ultimately to the failure of the Chapter XIII plan.

There are several limitations on this stay. It applies only to consumer debts; it does not apply to codebtors who became obligated in the ordinary course of their business. It ends automatically if a chapter 13 case is closed, dismissed, or converted to a chapter other than chapter 12.

In several other situations, the codebtor stay is effective as of the filing of the bankruptcy case, but it may be lifted by the court on request of a creditor or other party in interest. Such a request could be grounded on the fact that the chapter 13 debtor was really the cosigner and the nonfiling individual received the goods, services, or money that were the basis for the claim. The request could also be based on irreparable harm to the creditor caused by the stay. The stay will also be lifted to the extent that the debtor's proposed chapter 13 plan does not provide for full payment of the claim. Thus, if a plan proposes to pay 10 percent of a claim, the stay may be lifted for the remaining 90 percent. On the other hand the fact that a creditor will be paid late through the plan does not justify relief from the stay if payment will be made in full. However, some courts have held that a codebtor may be pursued for postbankruptcy interest to the extent that it is not paid in the plan.

The procedure by which creditors may obtain relief from the codebtor stay is similar to that followed for relief for the automatic stay, discussed below, except in a few respects. A creditor that files a motion for relief from the codebtor stay based on allegations that the plan will not pay its claim in full need not obtain a default judgment or other court order terminating the stay if the motion is not opposed. If the debtor or codebtor does not file a response to the motion and serve it on the creditor within 20 days, the codebtor stay is terminated to the extent that the creditor requested. It is important to note that this exception applies to only one of the grounds for relief from the codebtor stay (failure to propose payment in full) and it has no effect if a response to the creditor's motion is filed and served before the deadline.

Exceptions to the Automatic Stay

The breadth of the automatic stay is narrowed slightly by 16 exceptions that are listed in the Bankruptcy Code. Many of these exceptions—such as those concerning commodity futures or HUD foreclosures on multiple-family dwellings—have little bearing in consumer cases. Some, though, are occasionally relevant.

The stay does not automatically prohibit commencement or continuation of criminal proceedings. Thus, a criminal case based on a bad check can continue without violation of the stay. This exception does not permit the collection of a monetary liability imposed as part of a probation program or as restitution in a criminal case, however. It is less clear whether the court can substitute jail time for the unpaid restitution as an element of the punishment for the crime. And if the debtor does not pay restitution and then fails to obtain a discharge, the consequences may be severe.

It is unclear whether contempt of court proceedings are stayed. If the contempt proceeding is intended to coerce payment of a debt, as opposed to upholding the dignity of the court, the stay almost certainly applies.

Other exceptions to the automatic stay are acts to collect alimony, maintenance, or support from property that is not property of the estate. In a chapter 7 case, postpetition income can be pursued for this purpose, but property of the estate cannot (at least until it has gone out of the estate because it is exempt or abandoned). In a chapter 13 case, on the other hand, because all property acquired by the debtor is property of the estate, all actions to collect alimony, support, or maintenance are usually stayed, at least until confirmation of the debtor's plan.

Another exception allows proceedings and enforcement of some nonmonetary judgments pursuant to government regulatory powers. Even with a government regulatory action, the court looks carefully to determine whether the real goal of the proceeding is to collect money from the debtor, which is prohibited. Another exception to the automatic stay allows checks that are delivered prepetition to be cashed. Similarly, taxing authorities may issue notices of tax deficiency.

Finally, proceedings and actions pursued by the debtor against others are not stayed. Although this occasionally becomes complicated when there are claims and counterclaims in one action or when there are multiple parties, the distinction can and should be made; the debtor's action should be permitted to proceed.

Nonautomatic Stays

None of the inclusions or exceptions to the automatic stay in any way limits the power of the bankruptcy court to stay other actions. Thus, if the automatic stay is found to be not applicable to a criminal proceeding based on a bad check, the court may nonetheless be persuaded that the purpose of the action is really to collect the liability and thus to circumvent the bankruptcy. Some bankruptcy courts have held that the prosecution of criminal actions can be enjoined from proceeding when restitution is a likely result. However, several appellate decisions have not looked favorably on such injunctions, holding them violative of the principles of federal-state court relationships.

Furthermore, the court may use its powers under the Code to reinstitute the automatic stay if it has previously been terminated. Thus, if the stay was allowed to terminate inadvertently or if circumstances have changed substantially since a court order lifting the stay, the court may renew all or some of its protections.

Notice of the Automatic Stay

Creditors are notified officially of the automatic stay in the notice of the meeting of creditors. This notice is not always adequate for several reasons. First, the notice is not mailed until weeks or occasionally months after the petition is filed. Second, it is sent only to the creditors that are listed in the schedules or statement. Landlords and other entities to whom no debt is owed are not included in these lists. Finally, the notice that is part of the current official forms is not a model of clarity, especially for chapter 7 cases. Few unsophisticated creditors that receive it have any understanding of which actions are prohibited.

The only solution to this problem is for the debtor or the debtor's attorney to give additional notice of the stay to creditors and others who might violate the stay without prompt, clear notice. The notice should be sent by certified mail, return receipt requested, immediately after the petition is filed. If time is a critical factor, a telephone call preceding the mailed notification may be appropriate. The debtor's notice can be more specific than the official notice; it can be tailored to the action that the recipient is likely to take. Copies of the notice should be sent to both the party stayed and the party's attorney so that no excuse of communication problems is possible. To suspend or forestall IRS collection actions, such as a wage levy, notice should be given to the revenue officer on the case and to the IRS Special Procedures Staff in the district office collection branch for the relevant jurisdiction. Finally if appropriate, the notice can advise that the debtor will seek to have violators of the stay held in contempt and held liable for unfair practices, with damages and attorney's fees assessed against them.

Enforcement of the Stay

Most courts have held that actions in violation of the stay are void. This means that any actions taken after the bankruptcy filing—including foreclosure sales, repossessions, and judgments—are without effect. This is true whether or not the violator acted with knowledge of the stay, though there are limited exceptions to this general rule.

Courts have the power to undo violations of the stay by injunction, by nullifying postpetition transfers, and by entering other types of orders, if appropriate. For example, numerous courts have held that postpetition credit union deductions or repossessed automobiles must be returned.

The Bankruptcy Code contains specific penalties against a creditor who causes injury to an individual by a willful violation of the automatic stay. A *willful violation* is one committed knowingly; no malice need be shown. Even when a violation begins innocently, refusal to rectify it after notice of the case renders it willful. A willful violation also occurs when a creditor fails to act affirmatively to prevent an action prohibited by the stay—for example, by failing to prevent the selling of property at a sheriff's sale that was originally scheduled before the bankruptcy petition was filed. In such cases, the Code provides for actual damages, costs and attorney's fees, and punitive damages, if appropriate, to be awarded to the debtor.

An issue in some cases is whether the creditor has received notice. For damages to be available, the debtor must show notice of the stay to the party enjoined. A telephone call to a creditor or its counsel provides such notice, but problems of proof could arise when the notice is not in writing. Similarly, if the filing occurs at the last minute to prevent a foreclosure sale, repossession, or utility termination, the debtor should inform the creditor or the creditor's agent directly at the location of the threatened action. Even posting a copy of the petition on property that is likely to be repossessed should be sufficient notice to the creditor and the repossessing agent.

In addition to the specific penalties in the Code, the debtor also has remedies for violation of the automatic stay as contempt of a court order. The punishment for contempt may be more extensive than that available under the Bankruptcy Code. It may include fines and attorney's fees against both the violator and any attorney who advised the violation. Many courts have held that damages may also be awarded for contempt.

Another issue that often arises concerns the remedies available against government entities for violation of the stay. In light of recent Supreme Court cases taking a narrow view of when the government may be sued under the Bankruptcy Code, there is some doubt about whether damages are available against state and federal government entities for violating the automatic stay. Even if remedies are precluded under specific Code provisions based on Supreme Court decisions, contempt remedies should still be available. However, punitive damages may not be authorized.

Contempt sanctions can be imposed regardless of whether the violation is in willful disregard of the stay. As long as the violating party knows of the stay, it is responsible for the consequences. The duty is on creditors, especially those regularly involved with bankruptcy cases, to establish procedures that ensure compliance with the stay so that bankruptcy cases proceed smoothly. Indeed, if either a creditor or its collection agent has knowledge of the case, the creditor may be held in contempt for any post-petition collection attempts by its agent. Creditors may not base their defense on their reliance in good faith on the advice of an attorney that actions are not barred by the stay. Nor is computer error a valid defense.

Proceedings Seeking Relief from the Stay

Although the scope of the stay is broad and the sanctions to enforce it are powerful, its protections may be short-lived. A common creditor response to the bankruptcy petition is to file a proceeding seeking relief from the automatic stay. Creditors initiate this proceeding by filing a motion for relief in the bankruptcy court. Local court practices vary as to whether the debtor must file a written response to the motion.

The Code sets out strict time limits for litigation involving stays of acts against property. At least a preliminary hearing must be held in the bankruptcy court on a request for relief from the stay within 30 days. If the hearing is not held, the stay is terminated automatically. If the court finds at the preliminary hearing that there is a "reasonable likelihood that the party opposing relief" from the stay will prevail in the stay litigation, the stay can be continued until the conclusion of a final hearing. The final hearing must be commenced within 30 days after the preliminary hearing.

These time limits were meant to prevent a bankruptcy judge from simply ignoring a motion to lift the stay and thus denying the party bringing the motion an appealable order through which to seek review. The time limits may be waived by the party seeking relief, either explicitly or implicitly.

In presenting a motion for relief from the stay, the creditor always carries an initial burden of showing some cause for the court to lift the stay. The creditor's failure to show cause should result in a decision for the debtor. If the creditor does produce some evidence showing cause for relief from the stay, it is then up to the debtor to produce evidence or to convince the court that relief should not be granted.

Grounds for Relief from the Stay

Cause

The Bankruptcy Code provides that the stay may be lifted "for cause." Although it is clear that a lack of adequate protection is one such cause, the provision is meant to allow courts considerable discretion to grant relief for other reasons. Thus, legal proceedings against the debtor that have nothing to do with bankruptcy, such as child custody cases, would ordinarily be allowed to go forward. Similarly, the court may lift the stay with respect to other activities that have no effect on the bankruptcy. As a catchall provision, this ground for relief is also used to remedy a variety of other situations in which the stay is not deemed necessary by the court.

One situation in which creditors sometimes allege that there is cause for relief involves a debtor who had previously filed a bankruptcy case that was dismissed and who has refiled to again get the benefit of the automatic stay. In some cases, there may be nothing improper about refiling, although the Bankruptcy Code contains limitations on refiling within 180 days after a prior case is dismissed voluntarily or for willful failure to pursue the case or to obey court orders. The courts are also quite hostile to debtors who repeatedly file bankruptcy cases solely to receive the benefit of the stay and who have no intention of pursuing them to their conclusion.

Another type of cause averred in a number of cases is the debtor's failure to make current payments on a mortgage or other secured obligation. If the failure to pay is prolonged or if the collateral is depreciating and there is no prospect for cure, a court may decide that there is no reason to maintain the stay. The court often articulates the ground for relief from stay in cases under chapters 12 or 13 as "failure to comply with the plan."

Lack of Adequate Protection

By far, the greatest number of motions seeking relief from the stay are based on the grounds that the debtor has failed to provide the creditor with "adequate protection" of the creditor's interest in property. The provision of adequate protection is a basic concern of the Code, and thus the definition of the term is of critical importance. Yet *adequate protection* is not defined in the provisions of the Code. Adequate protection is probably best described by the Code's language stating that it must insure the protected party realization of the "indubitable equivalent" of that party's interest in the property in question. Although *indubitable equivalent* is not defined either, the concept is apparent. In a situation involving the automatic stay, adequate protection has been provided if there is no reasonably foreseeable way that the protected party's interest in the property can be economically harmed by continuation of the stay. Ultimately, whether adequate protection has been provided is a question of fact to be decided by the bankruptcy court.

The Code contemplates that the debtor will propose methods of providing adequate protection that are intended to satisfy a party that might seek relief from the stay. These methods might include a cash security deposit, procurement of a guarantor, insurance, or anything else that protects the interests of the other party.

One of the most common and important examples of adequate protection for a secured debt is the existence of an equity "cushion." For example, in the case of a $40,000 mortgage on a $60,000 house, the existence of $20,000 in equity protects the creditor. Even if the stay is continued for quite a while, the creditor should easily be able to fully satisfy its claim, by foreclosure if necessary, when the stay is lifted. In other words, unless the collateral is worth less than the claim or will depreciate so much that it might not fully satisfy the claim, adequate protection is normally provided by an equity cushion. If the possibility of destruction is eliminated, usually through insurance, real estate collateral values will generally remain high enough to provide adequate protection.

With depreciating collateral, such as motor vehicles, the debtor may need to make periodic cash payments that reduce the claim at least as fast as the value of the collateral decreases. Payments might be provided through a chapter 13 plan or by agreement with the creditor. The court may monitor or reconsider the situation at later dates to ensure that the creditor is protected.

Because the debtor often has little or no equity in the property at issue, perhaps the most useful concept of adequate protection in the foreclosure or repossession context is the concept of cash payments to compensate the creditor for the collateral's depreciation. This provision of the Code allows the debtor to propose a plan in a chapter 13 case that, in effect, cures or pays off the debt on a car or home. As long as the debtor makes plan payments, the creditor is adequately protected within the meaning of the Code.

In opposing a creditor's claim that adequate protection has not been provided, it is necessary to show that the creditor will not be economically harmed by continuation of the stay. Even if no equity can be shown, the stay may be continued if the creditor's then-current interest is protected. For example, a tenant may offer to make payments on a lease equivalent to what the lessor would receive by renting the property at that time to another tenant, or a debtor may make payments on an automobile loan that protect the creditor against depreciation.

Finally, the Code does not require termination of the stay when there is no adequate protection. The stay may be modified to provide a time limit for some action. It may also be conditioned, for example, on monthly payments being made or other risks to the property being eliminated.

Lack of Equity and Lack of Need for Effective Reorganization

The final ground for relief from the automatic stay is limited to acts against property, and it requires proof of two coexisting facts:

1. That the debtor does not have an equity interest in the property
2. That such property is not necessary for an effective reorganization

The purpose of this provision is to allow creditors to proceed against property that is of no value to either the debtor or the estate insofar as the bankruptcy case is concerned. If there is no equity in property that can be exempted by the debtor or sold by the estate and if the property is not needed in a reorganization of the debtor's affairs, the property is not needed for bankruptcy purposes.

The stay should not be lifted if it protects some interest in property that the debtor may exempt. Allowing a creditor to proceed outside the bankruptcy court could jeopardize the exemption and thus the debtor's fresh start. If there is equity in property that is not exempt, the court usually prefers that it be disposed of in the normal bankruptcy liquidation process. And if the property is necessary for an effective reorganization, the purposes of the bankruptcy reorganization provisions are protected by the continuation of the stay even when the debtor has no equity.

Because of the poor drafting of the law, a question has arisen over whether these provisions are even applicable to consumer cases. The term *reorganization* is usually applied only to cases under chapter 11 of the Code, which is generally used for business reorganization. Most courts have found that chapter 13 cases, at least, were meant to be included within the term *reorganization*. In regard to the purpose of the stay, it is just as necessary to protect completion of a chapter 13 plan as it is to protect completion of a corporate reorganization, and the term *reorganization* should be deemed to include such cases.

In cases in which relief is sought under these provisions, questions of how property is to be valued necessarily become crucial. There are a variety of legal issues on which courts differ. Should the property be given a liquidation value, a wholesale value, or a replacement-cost value? As of what date should the property be valued? The answers to these questions often determine whether relief from the stay is granted. In any case, the debtor may need to bring in an appraiser to testify or to provide other evidence of property values and to show how loss of the property would adversely affect the debtor's case.

Leases

Special problems are posed under the stay provisions in cases that involve leases. It may be quite possible for a debtor to give a landlord adequate protection, perhaps in the form of a security deposit. However, it is usually difficult to argue that the debtor has equity in the leased premises unless he or she holds a long-term lease at a rate below current market values or receives other benefits from remaining in possession, such as might exist with public housing or in a rent-control jurisdiction. Also, in regard to the necessity for an effective reorganization, it is usually somewhat harder to argue that moving to other leased premises is as great a hardship as losing a home owned by the debtor, because the lease usually guarantees only a short term of residency in any case. If rent-control laws include eviction controls, stronger arguments can be made.

The greatest problems arise because, through the stay, the debtor could, in effect, extend a lease beyond the term to which he or she was otherwise entitled. In some cases, the debtor could retain possession of property in which he or she otherwise had no rights whatsoever still in existence.

The most difficult cases are those in which the debtor's tenancy and right of possession, but not actual possession, are validly terminated under the lease or by a court order before the bankruptcy is filed. In such cases, many bankruptcy courts have been loathe to continue the stay because the debtor has no legal interest in the property without a lease that the debtor or trustee may assume. (Assumption of leases is discussed in Chapter 11.) According to these courts, if the debtor and the estate have no legal interest in the property, then cause exists for lifting the stay just as it would if the debtor were simply a squatter who had moved in after the commencement of the bankruptcy. They have held that if the debtor cannot assume the lease, perhaps because it is impossible to cure a default promptly, there is no reason to allow the stay to continue.

Despite these holdings, there are several reasons why the stay may be continued for a leased property, even if the tenancy has ended or will soon end. These arguments are most convincing in cases in which the debtor provides adequate protection and the continuation of the stay is necessary to an effective reorganization. At least one court has held that the effect of the stay is to nullify a prior judgment for possession and termination of tenancy. The stay's provisions are meant to allow the debtor to use property, such as collateral that would otherwise be repossessed, including property that the debtor does not technically "own."

Even if this argument is not accepted, as long as adequate protection is provided, there is no economic harm to the landlord compared to what could otherwise be realized by renting the property. In addition, the substitution of money for the right of possession is in accord with a long line of recent court cases that have held that residential rental real estate is a consumer good and not a unique interest for which money is no substitute. This is an especially compelling argument in the bankruptcy court, which, as a court of equity, must consider the "balance of hurt." When a landlord cannot show any real harm resulting from the stay and protests only the continued occupancy of people to whom he or she does not choose to rent, the bankruptcy court may not feel compelled to lift the stay preventing eviction of the debtors.

Thus, although the early court decisions have not been encouraging, there are strong arguments for the continuation of the stay with respect to leased property even after the lease terminates.

UTILITY SERVICES IN BANKRUPTCY CASES

Closely akin to the automatic stay provisions of the Code are the provisions regarding refusal to provide utility service. Although the general purpose of these provisions closely parallels that of the automatic stay, their operation and effect are somewhat different.

The Debtor's Right to Utility Service

The first part of the relevant section of the law sets forth a general rule that applies for at least the first 20 days after the petition is filed. It states that no utility may "alter, refuse, or discontinue service or discriminate against" the debtor solely on the basis of an unpaid prepetition debt or the filing of a bankruptcy case during this period.

This clearly prohibits a utility from shutting off the debtor's service in the first 20 days after the bankruptcy. Thus, what was said earlier in this chapter about giving notice to creditors and about court sanctions for violations of the stay applies equally in this context. Swift court relief, as well as possible fines and attorney's fees, should be available for illegal shutoffs.

One problem that occasionally arises concerns shutoffs that are ostensibly based not merely on the unpaid debt, but rather on defective equipment, an illegal hookup by the customer, or some other reason. Naturally, situations of this type boil down to a problem of proof, and special attention should be given to why the utility happened to terminate service immediately after the bankruptcy.

More complicated is the question of obtaining service if it was discontinued before the bankruptcy. Some courts have held that the Code requires that the utility service be reinstated because it cannot be "refused" solely on the basis of the unpaid debt. If service is refused due to an unpaid debt, the Code is violated.

The Utility's Right to Discontinue Service If Adequate Assurance of Payment Is Not Provided

These protections are significantly limited by another provision of the Code, which provides that a utility may "alter, refuse, or discontinue service" if the debtor does not furnish adequate assurance of future payment within 20 days of filing a voluntary bankruptcy petition. The language quoted above reads, as first glance, as if it is self-executing. Most courts have read it to mean that the utility may terminate service after 20 days without special permission from the court if it does not believe adequate assurance has been provided. If this is the case, then it behooves the debtor to come to some agreement with the utility as to what it considers to be adequate assurance before the 20 days has run out or, in cases in which there is a dispute, to seek the court's intervention along with a court order if the utility will not agree to continue service.

The term *adequate assurance* is not defined in the Code, except to the extent that examples are given. Those examples are a "deposit or other security." Certainly, a deposit is most common in consumer cases, and typically the utility requests a specific deposit from the debtor. At least one court has suggested that the deposit terms permitted by state utility regulations set the maximum that a utility can demand without court modification.

It is clear that, in most places, service cannot be terminated if the bill is fully current when the bankruptcy petition is filed. The mere filing of a bankruptcy petition does not give the utility the right to terminate service. This conclusion is also supported by statements in the original Report of the Bankruptcy Commission that the term *adequate assurance*, in a slightly different context, is not intended to give the nondebtor party greater rights in a case than it would otherwise have. Thus, if the state regulations do not require any deposit for continuance of service to someone who pays a prior utility bill before termination, it can be argued that it would be discrimination to require a deposit from a debtor in bankruptcy whose utility bills are current. Alternatively, the debtor's past record of prompt payments could be considered, in itself, adequate assurance. A 1984 amendment to the Bankruptcy Code clarified these principles by adding an explicit prohibition of discrimination with respect to service based merely on the filing of a bankruptcy.

The amount of the security deposit necessary is usually standardized in a particular court and is not contested. When disputes have occurred, the guidelines to be used in determining the amount necessary for adequate assurance have slowly emerged from case law. Although the precise amount varies from case to case, the courts have tended to look to "all of the circumstances" including the prebankruptcy history of the debtor, the nature of the debtor, how much was owed, the previous course of dealing and conduct on the part of the utility, the stability of the debtor's present circumstances, the speed with which the utility may terminate service, the frequency of payments, and the likely usage of the utility in the months to come. Other factors that might be considered include the time of year (a deposit of one average monthly payment could pay for six months' heating service in nonwinter months), the possibility of sureties, and the likely availability of energy assistance for some consumers. One reported case considered most of these factors and finally set a deposit approximately equal to one upcoming winter month's bill, payable in three monthly installments by the debtor, with the utility to refund half of the deposit, with interest, a year later, and the other half according to its normal practice. The court also provided for speedy termination in the event of nonpayment.

Once the debtor has provided adequate assurance to the utility, the involvement of the bankruptcy court normally ends. Absent a contrary procedure specifically ordered by the court or agreed to by the debtor as part of the adequate assurance, state law will govern the treatment of postpetition debts. Thus, any termination procedures and any consumer rights provided by state law are applicable to debts arising after adequate assurance has been provided.

TURNOVER OF PROPERTY TO THE TRUSTEE

In addition to the automatic stay, the commencement of the case also activates two other automatic provisions relating to the debtor's property. These provisions require the turnover to the trustee of property in which the debtor has an interest. These provisions are similar; one applies to "custodians," such as sheriffs or receivers legally appointed to take charge of the debtor's property, and the other applies to all other entities.

The General Rule

Very simply, the Code requires that any entity, other than a custodian, in possession, custody, or control of property that the trustee (or a chapter 13 debtor) may use, sell, or lease or that the debtor may exempt must immediately deliver to the trustee the property or the value of the property, unless the property is of inconsequential value or benefit to the estate. The purpose of the turnover provisions is to assist the trustee in gathering up all property of the estate for the liquidation or reorganization that will take place in bankruptcy, as well as to put into effect the debtor's right to claim exemptions.

This general rule has a few exceptions, which are not often applicable in consumer cases. Except for these, the rule normally applies to all property of the estate, since an individual debtor usually might choose to exempt any property of the estate, that is, any property in which the debtor has any legal or equitable interest. (See Chapter 10 for a discussion of which property a debtor may exempt.) It applies no matter where the property is located and no matter how it was acquired by the entity in possession. The rule also applies to recorded information, such as records held by an attorney.

Procedure

Theoretically, a party obligated to turn over property should do so immediately on notice of the case. Occasionally this happens. Thus, the first step that the debtor's attorney should take is to give the creditor or other party in possession notice of the case, both informal and formal, in a manner similar to that used to give notice of the automatic stay.

In practice, however, most holders refuse to turn over property. Many simply do not believe that they are required to do so, because these provisions are not nearly as clear as those setting out the automatic stay. In such cases, the debtor has no alternative but to obtain a court order for turnover, seeking immediate relief if necessary. The debtor may also seek a contempt of court order, damages, and attorney's fees.

Other holders refuse to turn over property on the grounds that they are entitled to adequate protection. In these cases, it is best to negotiate such adequate protection, if possible, because as a practical matter the court will require it before issuing a turnover order. If the property sought is to be used, sold, or leased, then the creditor has a right to demand that this be done only if adequate protection is provided.

Finally, it is important to give notice of the case promptly to any holder of property, not only to obtain a turnover, but also to prevent the complications that could arise if a holder without notice transfers the property to a third party. It is clear that, without notice, the holder cannot be held responsible for such a transfer, and thereafter the property may not be recoverable.

Issues of Possession after Turnover

The Code requires turnover of property to the trustee, not to the debtor. Nowhere does the Code clearly spell out the procedure that should be used to transfer property from the trustee to the debtor in cases in which it seems clear that the debtor should have it. For example, if property that the debtor may exempt in a chapter 7 case is turned over to the trustee, the trustee may not feel free to relinquish it to the debtor before the exemptions are finalized.

It seems fairly obvious that the intent of the Code is that debtors should have possession of exempt property during the case; they are not expected to relinquish their household goods pending approval of the exemptions they have claimed. In fact, the exemptions are approved automatically if there is no objection to them. Moreover, such goods are rarely of any use to the trustee, who would incur needless expense in storing and preserving them. In view of all this, plus the general purpose of the exemptions—which is to allow the debtor to maintain a modest standard of living—there can be little doubt that property claimed as exempt should be immediately relinquished to the debtor by a trustee to whom it is turned over, at least absent a serious dispute about the exemption claim.

Until this issue is definitively resolved, however, it is best to avoid potential problems. As much exempt property as possible should be in the debtor's possession on the date that the case is commenced. All monies should be withdrawn from bank accounts so that access to them is not prevented because they were turned over to the trustee or frozen. If possible, the filing should be delayed until after receipt of a tax refund because the IRS frequently pays such refunds to the trustee rather than to the debtor.

In chapter 13 cases, the situation is somewhat more clear. Because the Code provides that the debtor is to remain in possession of all property of the estate, there seems to be no reason for the trustee to retain any property turned over to him or her. Such property should be promptly delivered to the debtor. Indeed, it is unfortunate that there is no provision requiring turnover directly to the debtor to obviate the necessity for trustee involvement because in most cases, the right to use, sell, or lease property belongs to the debtor, not the trustee.

Finally, it should be noted that much of what was said above applies equally to property obtained by the trustee through the use of other powers. The trustee has a wide range of ways to gather property into the estate and to avoid prebankruptcy transfers of property. Many of these are discussed in the context of the debtor's exemptions in the next chapter.

Chapter 9

EXEMPTIONS

INTRODUCTION TO THE EXEMPTION PROVISIONS

For most consumer debtors, no section of the Bankruptcy Code is more important than the one that governs the debtor's rights in regard to exempt property. This section makes enormous advances in debtors' rights. On the whole, the exemption provisions in the Code make bankruptcy much more attractive to consumers than under the previous law, and they give better protection to debtor's property than is available under most state laws governing execution.

Indeed, the availability of exemptions is usually key to the debtor's decision about whether to file a bankruptcy, and which type of case to file. If the debtor has significant amounts of property that are not exempt and would thus be lost in a chapter 7 liquidation, a chapter 13 case is usually preferable. In a chapter 13 case, the amount of nonexempt property may determine the minimum that must be paid to unsecured creditors; if that amount cannot be paid through the plan, then a chapter 13 case may not be feasible.

The exemption provisions are closely related to other parts of the Code. For example, they give the debtor many of the trustee's powers to avoid prepetition transfers of property as well as some additional powers over and above those of the trustee. These powers are all discussed in this chapter. The turnover provisions of the Code, discussed in Chapter 8, specifically require that property that is in the possession of a third party and that the debtor can exempt be turned over to the trustee. Similarly, the right to redeem certain types of property from liens, discussed in Chapter 10, applies only to exempt or abandoned property. Finally, many of the protections after discharge bear a direct relationship to what property has been exempted.

Definition of Exempt Property

The Code contains no formal definition of the terms *exemption* or *exempt property*. Fundamentally, these are the designations given to the property that the debtor is permitted to retain in a chapter 7 liquidation. Other than the exempt property, virtually all of the debtor's property interests that have value are transferred to the trustee for the benefit of creditors.

With some exceptions, exemptions do not affect valid security interests or other liens on property of the debtor. A debtor must usually pay the secured creditor the amount of its secured claim to eliminate a lien. Because the lien can be thought of as diminishing the debtor's interest in the liened property, only the value of the interest remaining after subtracting the amount of the lien need be claimed as exempt.

The procedure for claiming exemptions is not fully spelled out in the Code. Although the Code states that the debtor shall "file a list" of property claimed as exempt, the questions of when, where, and how this list is to be filed are left to the Rules of Bankruptcy Procedure. The rules require the debtor to file the claim of exemption with the schedules at the outset of a case.

Purposes of Exemptions

Historically, the purpose of exemption laws has always been to allow debtors to keep those items of property that are deemed essential to daily life. Without this bare grubstake, it was feared that debtors could not retain the minimum of dignity and self-respect to which all members of society are entitled. Perhaps more importantly, it was feared that stripping debtors of all of their property would increase their chances of becoming charges of the public, unable to maintain themselves without assistance.

In the bankruptcy context, exemptions serve the overriding purpose of helping the debtor to obtain a fresh start. They allow the debtor to come out of the process with not only a minimum amount of dignity, but also the essentials on which to build a new life. They leave at least a basic vestige of the possessions that the debtor has acquired, so that the debtor may proceed to move forward, rather than spend time struggling simply to exist.

These policies have been judged by state legislatures and by Congress to be more important than satisfying the claims of unsecured creditors (and, in bankruptcy, some secured creditors) with certain items of the debtor's property. The Bankruptcy Code gave new strength and protection to these principles, eliminating many of the creditor practices that, over the years, had come to undermine them.

WHAT PROPERTY IS EXEMPT?

State versus Federal Exemptions

In many states, a debtor may choose from two sets of exemptions. As under the prior law, a debtor in any state may choose to use the exemptions provided by state law and by federal nonbankruptcy law—for example, laws protecting Social Security benefits and veteran's benefits. If the debtor chooses the state exemptions, then certain other property of the estate not normally subject to process under state law may also be claimed as exempt.

The Code also provides a comprehensive list of special federal exemptions that are applicable only in bankruptcy cases. Debtors may choose these exemptions as an alternative to the traditionally available exemptions, as long as their state of domicile has not "opted out" of the federal exemption scheme. The opt-out provision, adopted as a last-minute compromise to secure passage of the Code, allows any state to pass a law prohibiting the use of the special federal bankruptcy exemptions. Although this concept is unusual, it has not been successfully challenged. To date, 36 states have passed such a law, and in those states, debtors may use only the state and federal nonbankruptcy exemptions. A chart listing the states that have opted out, as well as the major exemptions available in each state, appears in Appendix A. (A state may also opt out of the federal bankruptcy exemptions and pass its own bankruptcy exemptions, which may be different from its normal exemptions from execution.)

By repealing their opt-out laws, of course, those states can opt back into the federal exemptions. In any case, even when a state has opted out of the federal bankruptcy exemptions, the remaining provisions of the Code are still applicable to enhance the exemptions that are available to the debtor; a state may not opt out of those provisions.

Assuming that the debtor's state has not opted out, the debtor must choose the applicable exemptions. In a joint filing of a husband and wife, both spouses must choose the same exemption scheme. If the spouses cannot agree on which exemptions to choose, they are deemed to have chosen the federal exemptions. They also, however, have the option of filing two separate petitions, with each spouse electing the exemptions of his or her choice.

The Federal Bankruptcy Exemptions

The property that can be claimed as exempt under the federal bankruptcy exemptions (in states that have not opted out) is listed specifically in the Code.

Because the exemptions may be claimed by each debtor individually, a husband and wife filing a joint case are each entitled to the full exemption amounts specified for each category of property listed, effectively doubling those amounts for jointly held property. (In many states, there is a legal presumption that property acquired during the marriage is owned jointly.) However, the same provisions probably prevent the application of one spouse's unused exemption amount to the separate property of the other spouse.

As a result, problems may occasionally arise from the wording of some of the exemptions. For example, if there are two jointly held motor vehicles, each worth $1,200, each joint debtor could only exempt one-half of the value of one car because the $1,200 motor vehicle exemption applies to the debtor's interest in one motor vehicle. This would leave the equivalent of one vehicle not exempted under that subsection. A simple solution to this problem would be a prebankruptcy trading of interests so that each spouse owned one car in full. Then each could exempt the full $1,200 value of his or her car. Thus, prebankruptcy exemption planning may be especially important in joint filings.

The authors of the Code expected that all of the exemption amounts would be adjusted regularly for inflation. For this reason, the Code provides for a recommendation from the Judicial Conference to Congress regarding adjustments of all dollar amounts in the Code. However, the only adjustments that have occurred to date were downward.

Homestead

The largest specific dollar amount applicable to particular property is the $7,500 that each debtor may claim as a homestead exemption. This exemption, like all of the others, applies only to the debtor's interest in property—that is, the equity over and above liens and security interests. Hence, a single debtor with a one-half interest in a $40,000 jointly owned home encumbered by a $30,000 mortgage, has a $5,000 interest in that home (1/2 x [$40,000 – $30,000]). Because it is worth less than the $7,500 exemption, the debtor's interest would be fully exempt. However, it is important to remember that in subtracting liens to determine equity, precomputed but as yet unearned interest should not be included. Only the current "payoff figure" due on the lien can properly be considered owed.

As discussed earlier, two joint owners may exempt an interest of $15,000 under this exemption. In fact, they may add an additional $800 to that figure (or to any other exemption) because the wild-card exemption, discussed below, permits each to exempt an interest of $400 in any property.

The homestead exemption is applicable to interests in either real or personal property, and therefore it clearly includes mobile homes, houseboats, and so on. It also clearly includes nonownership interests, such as leases. The property must be a residence of the debtor or a dependent of the debtor, though it apparently need not be the principal residence. A burial plot may also be included under this subsection.

Unlike some state exemption schemes, the federal bankruptcy homestead exemption does not explicitly apply to proceeds of the sale of a homestead. However, when a home is sold after bankruptcy is filed, the exemption is preserved because the Code explicitly states that exemptions are to be determined as of the date that the bankruptcy petition was filed. It is less clear whether a debtor may use the federal homestead exemption to exempt proceeds of a sale of a home that occurred before filing. This uncertainty can frequently be avoided with careful prebankruptcy exemption planning.

Motor Vehicle

A debtor may exempt an interest of up to $1,200 in one motor vehicle. It is important to note the limitation in this provision to one vehicle per debtor. Again, the exemption need be applied only to the debtor's interest over and above any security interest. An interest in excess of $1,200 may sometimes be picked up using another exemption, such as the wild-card exemption for any property or, in some cases, the exemption for tools of a trade.

Household Goods and Similar Items

The Code allows a debtor to exempt an interest of up to $200 in any item of household furnishings, household goods, wearing apparel, appliances, books, animals, crops, or musical instruments held primarily for the personal, family, or household use of the debtor or the debtor's dependents. Like the other exemptions, this may be doubled in a joint case to include items of up to $400 in value if jointly owned by the debtors. There is an aggregate dollar limit of $4,000 per debtor on the property that may be exempted under this subsection. Still, many thousands of dollars worth of property may be saved for debtors under this provision, especially in joint cases in which the exemption is doubled.

One question that occasionally arises concerns the definition of the term *item*. When several related pieces of property may be considered to be a set worth more than $200, disputes could occur as to whether that set is "an item." For example, it is not clear whether each chair in a dining room set, each spoon in a set of silver, or each speaker in a stereo system should be considered to be an item apart from the set as a whole. Common sense should prevail in dealing with these issues.

The scope of the subsection may also raise questions. It does not generally include motor vehicles, though a lawn tractor might be an exception. Similarly, most items specifically listed elsewhere in the exemption provisions, such as jewelry, are not usually included. Although the provision is not specifically limited to personalty, it may be hard to use the provision to have real property exempted (except possibly for some fixtures and the like). Finally, items used primarily for business purposes are not meant to be included.

Except for debtors who conduct a business in their home, this exemption should be applicable to just about all of the personal property normally kept at the debtor's residence that is not specifically mentioned in other exemptions. The scope of the exemption clearly extends beyond necessities; unlike other exemptions, it does not include only amounts "reasonably necessary for the support of the debtor." The household goods exemption is concerned only with how the property is used, not whether it might be considered a luxury.

Jewelry

Each debtor is allowed to exempt up to $500 worth of jewelry, as long as it is held primarily for the personal, family, or household use of the debtor or a dependent. As with the household goods exemption, the wild-card exemption applicable to "any property" may be used to increase this amount. For example, a jewelry item worth $700 may be exempted using the $500 jewelry exemption plus $200 worth of the wild-card exemption.

Questions may arise under this provision concerning whether a particular item is classified as jewelry or wearing apparel. If the item is worth less than $200, it is usually to the debtor's benefit to classify it as the latter because a larger total exemption is available for wearing apparel worth less than $200 per item. On the other hand, if the debtor has items worth more than $200, the debtor's use of other exemptions will determine which interpretation is more favorable. If none of the wild-card exemption has been used and all of the jewelry exemption has, it is preferable to argue that the items are wearing apparel so that on each item any value in excess of the $200 available for wearing apparel may be exempted (until the wild-card exemption is exhausted). However, if the jewelry exemption has not yet been used, it will be preferable to argue that the item is jewelry so that the amount available only for jewelry can be used and the wild-card exemption can be saved for some other property. In any case, case law developed under the various state exemption laws pertaining to jewelry and wearing apparel will be relevant to the argument.

Any Property

Probably the most important of the federal exemptions is the one that can be applied to "any property" and is sometimes called the *wild-card exemption*. The amount of this exemption is $400 per debtor, plus any unused amount of the homestead exemption, up to $3,750 per debtor. The applicability of the unused homestead exemption to any property, sometimes called the *homestead pourover*, was originally intended to equalize homeowners and renters but was significantly reduced when the $3,750 limit was added in 1984. It still gives tremendous flexibility to both homeowners and renters, however, because many homeowners do not choose to or need to use the entire homestead exemption for their residence.

As noted above, the wild-card exemption can be used in conjunction with any other specific exemption to pick up value in excess of the exemption—for example, the remaining $600 on an $1,800 car. It can also be applied to any possible property interest, including intangibles, nonliquid property, causes of action, tax refunds, cash, and public benefits already received.

Tools of Trade

Each debtor may exempt up to $750 worth of implements, professional books, or tools of trade that belong to the debtor or to a dependent of the debtor. This exemption, too, may overlap with some of the others. For example, a motor vehicle might be claimed as exempt under this subsection as well as the subsection for motor vehicles if it is used by the debtor in his or her trade (beyond normal commuting.) Thus, a vehicle worth $1,950 per debtor could be claimed by combining these sections. As with jewelry, it may be preferable to argue that a particular item falls within the household goods exemption—that is, that it is held primarily for personal, nonbusiness use—if its value is less than $200 or if the tools of trade exemption has been exhausted on other property.

Unmatured Life Insurance

The subsection providing for an exemption for unmatured life insurance, as distinguished from the subsection following it, covers those interests in life insurance owned by the debtor that do not have a cash or loan value. Thus, any interest in term insurance can be included. Policies that do have a cash or loan value are, in effect, divided into two property interests: (1) the interest in receiving proceeds and (2) the cash or loan value. The former may be exempted in full under this subsection. Credit life insurance is specifically excluded from the coverage of this subsection.

If the debtor is merely the beneficiary of a policy that insures the life of a living person and is owned by someone other than the debtor, no exemption need be used because the debtor generally has no ownership interest in that policy. (However, if the insured dies within 180 days after the bankruptcy petition is filed, the debtor's right to the proceeds does become property of the estate, though it may be exemptible, as discussed below.) The debtor need not be the person insured by the life insurance contract for this exemption to apply.

Accrued Dividend, Interest, or Loan Value of Life Insurance

Interests in life insurance policies that have a cash value of up to $4,000 per debtor may also be exempted. From this amount must be subtracted any amounts that the insurance company uses to continue premium payments under a contract that provides for automatic payments out of the accrued value.

Unlike the exemption provided by the previous subsection, this exemption may only be applied to policies insuring the life of the debtor or someone of whom the debtor is a dependent. Nonetheless, because life insurance can be a relatively liquid type of property, if a debtor has excess liquid assets before filing a case that cannot be otherwise exempted, this exemption provides a way to exempt a substantial additional amount through a prebankruptcy purchase of life insurance.

Health Aids

A debtor may exempt an unlimited amount of professionally prescribed health aids for the debtor or a dependent of the debtor. This exemption clearly covers such items as wheelchairs and artificial limbs. Arguably, it is much broader and could include specially equipped automobiles or even normal automobiles essential to receiving medical treatments. It is also possible that property prescribed for therapy, such as swimming pools, could be included.

Disability, Retirement, and other Benefits Replacing Wages

Because of the Code's broad definition of property that comes into the bankruptcy estate, a debtor's entitlement to receive various benefits in the future has for the first time become subject to the claims of creditors.

Rights to such entitlement must therefore be exempted if they are to be saved for the debtor's future use. Thus, the Code exempts the right to receive Social Security, unemployment, welfare, disability, and illness benefits in the future. Alimony and support payments are also exempt but only to the extent reasonably necessary for the support of the debtor and any dependents of the debtor.

Similarly, payments under most pension plans and many employee benefit plans are exempt to the extent reasonably necessary for the support of the debtor and the debtor's dependents. The determination of whether a pension is reasonably necessary for the support of the debtor and any dependents requires an examination of the debtor's age, earning capacity, present and future financial needs, and ability to reestablish a retirement fund.

The Supreme Court recently concluded that pension and employee benefit plans that qualify under the Employee Retirement Income Security Act do not come into a debtor's bankruptcy estate at all. When plans are not in the estate, the debtor need not claim them as exempt. In addition, when a plan does not qualify under ERISA, regardless of whether it is exemptible under the Code, applicable state law restrictions on transfer or exemptions may nevertheless protect the funds.

Except in the case of Social Security and Supplemental Security Income (SSI) benefits, property traceable to benefits already received may have to be exempted under other provisions of the federal exemptions. If so, this is a departure from some of the federal nonbankruptcy laws protecting income benefits, such as veteran's benefits, under which accrued benefits were also exempt from execution. Thus, a debtor who has saved from such benefits a substantial amount of money that it may not be possible to claim as exempt, perhaps because of a large retroactive payment, may be better off choosing the alternative of the state and federal nonbankruptcy exemptions.

As noted above, some types of property covered by this provision—for example, alimony, child support, and private retirement plans—are exempt only to the extent reasonably necessary for the support of the debtor and the debtor's dependents. This limitation was included primarily to prevent wealthy people with enormous amounts of income from such sources from protecting all of that income in bankruptcy. With this in mind, the courts are relatively liberal in deciding what amounts are reasonably necessary for support. Although the statute gives no guidance, judges who see mostly middle-class debtors usually approve a standard at least as high as the Bureau of Labor Statistics' intermediate living standard.

Another question that is likely to arise concerns the definition of the term *public assistance*. Welfare cash payments are obviously included. It also seems clear that supplements such as food stamps and energy assistance should come within this category. The question becomes slightly more difficult with housing subsidies. Payments under Section 8, which reduce a family's rent to a certain percentage of income, are presumably analogous to food stamps, which reduce food costs to a certain percentage of income. From there it should not be difficult to extend the principle to mortgage interest subsidies and the subsidy inherent in living in public housing, where rent is limited to a certain percentage of income. Similar issues arise with regard to the federal earned income tax credit.

It is often not necessary to specifically claim all of these benefits as exempt. It is not generally done at present in most parts of the country. In any case, trustees are unlikely to show much interest in public assistance benefits because they are probably not transferable and may therefore be abandoned as of no value to the estate. If a trustee does show interest, the schedules and claim of exemption can be amended at that time.

If the rights are listed, problems arise with respect to the appropriate value to assign to them and how far to extend the principle. Should the right to receive welfare be valued as the right to receive welfare forever—for example, the total of payments for a person's life expectancy discounted for passage of time? Or is its value only nominal because it is not really transferable and may end the next day if other income appears? Must all workers who have paid Social Security taxes list a vested or nonvested contingent right to receive Social Security benefits when they retire or become disabled? Local practice, which usually does not require the listing of such assets, generally provides a guide regarding such questions.

Rights to Compensation for Injury or Losses

The last category listed among the federal bankruptcy exemptions covers the right to receive payments and property traceable to payments for various types of injury or loss. These include crime-victim reparations awards and payments, not to exceed $7,500, on account of bodily injury of the debtor or a person upon whom the debtor is dependent (but not including pain and suffering or pecuniary loss). They also cover wrongful death awards based on the death of someone of whom the debtor was a dependent, payments on life insurance that insured the life of someone on whom the debtor was a dependent, and payments in compensation for loss of future earnings of the debtor or someone of whom the debtor was a dependent. In each case, the exemption is limited to the amount necessary to support the debtor and the debtor's dependents.

It is important to note, first, that this exemption category includes property that can be traced to the listed benefits as well as the benefits themselves. This may pose difficult problems of tracing past payments. Second, some but not all of the payments listed are limited to amounts reasonably necessary to the support of the debtor and the debtor's dependents. The comments made in the section above in respect to this limitation are equally applicable here.

One category has a specific dollar limit: $7,500 on account of personal bodily injury. This category not only explicitly excludes pain and suffering and compensation for pecuniary loss (the latter being covered by a separate provision), but also implicitly seems to exclude punitive damages. It is unclear how the bankruptcy court will be able to divide lump-sum awards or settlements into these component parts. Because the burden of proof when objecting to exemptions is on the objecting party, the exemption should be allowed unless the objector can demonstrate that a specific portion of the award is not exempt. It is also unclear to what extent damage recoveries, or the right thereto, for nonbodily injuries—such as discrimination or invasion of privacy—may be protected. Although these may not be covered by the subsection of the Code that is limited to personal bodily injuries, some portions of them may be deemed compensation for loss of future earnings and thus exempt under the subsection protecting such compensation.

State and Federal Nonbankruptcy Exemptions

Federal Bankruptcy Modifications of These Exemptions

In cases in which the federal bankruptcy exemptions are either not chosen or not available, debtors have available to them the exemptions provided for by state or local law or by federal nonbankruptcy law. (For convenience, this collection of exemptions is referred to simply as the *state exemptions*.)

The types and amounts of property that the debtor may exempt under state laws vary significantly from state to state. A summary of the major exemptions for each state appears in Appendix A.

The property that the debtor may exempt in bankruptcy under a state exemption scheme probably includes any property that is not subject to process under state law, such as the right to sue on injury claims. And state exemption rights are significantly enhanced by the Bankruptcy Code in several ways.

First, debtors have access to all of the other protections of the Bankruptcy Code. Any waiver of exemptions is unenforceable, regardless of whether exemptions could be waived under state law. The extensive powers to avoid prebankruptcy transfers of exempt property are all applicable to the state as well as the federal exemptions. And exempt property is permanently protected after the bankruptcy under the Code, as discussed later in this chapter. Finally, debtors have the right to redeem property claimed as exempt. As discussed in Chapter 10, this right can be extremely important in dealing with purchase-money or possessory security interests in chapter 7 cases.

However, debtors may still have to comply with state procedural requirements for claims of exemptions. For example, in states that require debtors to file a declaration of homestead before the use of that exemption, courts have not all agreed on the question of whether that requirement is also a prerequisite to claiming a state homestead exemption in bankruptcy.

Exemption of Property Not Subject to Process

Debtors who claim the state exemptions in bankruptcy may be able to take advantage of a special provision that protects certain joint property. This provision allows the debtor to claim as exempt "any interest in property in which the debtor had, immediately before the commencement of the case, an interest as a tenant by the entirety or joint tenant to the extent such interest as a tenant by the entirety or joint tenant is exempt from process under applicable nonbankruptcy law."

The intent of this provision is to protect the property that a creditor of only the debtor (and not of both joint tenants) could not have levied on as of the date that the bankruptcy was filed. One example is property owned as tenants by the entireties, in states in which such property can be seized only by a joint creditor of the cotenants. If one cotenant files a bankruptcy and claims the state exemptions, such an interest in entireties property may be claimed as exempt, at least from creditors that hold claims against only that cotenant.

It is important to note several other aspects of this subsection:

1. It applies to both real and personal property.
2. It is unlimited in value.
3. It is applicable to any interest.

Thus, debtors with a significant amount of property that falls within these provisions may be far better off choosing the state rather than the federal exemptions, at least when few if any of their debts are owed to creditors who could pursue the joint property.

The purpose of this subsection is to preserve the protection given under nonbankruptcy law to property that could not be seized by creditors under state law. Without this subsection, debtors who use the state exemptions, either by choice or because their state has opted out, would have been worse off than before the Code was enacted. Their interests in entireties or other property that is not subject to state law creditors' seizure would have, for the first time, been brought into the bankruptcy estate under the broadened definition of property of the estate. Such property, then, would have been available to their creditors, even though it had not been available under state law, unless it could be exempted. Because it had never been available to creditors under state law, state exemption laws did not take such property into account, and state exemption provisions were insufficient to protect it. The Code's drafters intended to fill this breach.

The primary use of this provision is in cases in which all or almost all of the debts involved are debts of only one spouse. In such cases, at least, the entireties property is protected from liquidation, or if there are small joint debts, only a small portion of it will probably be deemed to be nonexempt.

Thus, the state exemptions, as enhanced by the Code, may have a great deal to offer to debtors, even in states in which they have relatively low dollar limits. Debtors in states that have opted out of the federal bankruptcy exemptions list have no choice but to make the most of the state provisions. But all other debtors should carefully consider that option as well because it may sometimes provide greater benefits than the federal exemption provisions.

PROCEDURE FOR CLAIMING EXEMPTIONS

The Initial Claim

The Bankruptcy Code itself says little regarding the procedure for claiming exemptions, other than that the debtor or a dependent must "file a list" of property claimed as exempt. If the debtor does not file this list, a dependent may do so. As discussed in Chapter 6, the Bankruptcy Rules require this list to be filed as part of the bankruptcy schedules. The property must be at least somewhat specifically described. If it is not, the debtor may later encounter problems in protecting property that was not specifically listed or the proceeds of such property.

Amending the Claim of Exemption

Under the rules, the debtor may amend any part of the schedules, including the exemption claim, without special court permission before the case is closed. This right presumably includes a change from the state to the federal exemption scheme or vice versa. A debtor may sometimes even be allowed to reopen the case after discharge to amend the exemptions. Courts have ruled, however, that a debtor may not exempt property that he or she has knowingly concealed from the trustee. And after the case is filed, a debtor may not convert nonexempt property into exempt property to claim it as exempt.

The Bankruptcy Rules require all parties affected by an amendment to be notified of the change; in the case of amended exemptions, notice should presumably be given to all creditors, at least when the amendment is significant. Failure to give notice may extend the deadline for objections.

Objections to Exemptions

The Code allows objections to claims of exemption by "a party in interest," again specifying no procedure. The procedure is provided instead by the Bankruptcy Rules. The party that is most likely to object is the trustee. However, the rules make it clear that any creditor has the right to file objections to exemptions.

Trustees in some districts still file reports of any objections to exemptions as well as a recommendation concerning discharge. In any case, all objections to exemptions must be filed within 30 days after the conclusion of the meeting of creditors or the filing of any amendment to the exemption list, unless, within that period, the court grants an extension. Objections to exemptions that are not filed on time cannot be considered.

Copies of the objections must be provided to the trustee, the person filing the exemption claim (usually the debtor), and that person's attorney. At the hearing on the objections, the objecting party must prove to the court that the exemptions are improper.

As in other areas of bankruptcy procedure, questions of value may be critical. The debtor usually wants to argue that, for exemption purposes, the "fair market value" of the property is its liquidation value (what could be obtained at a forced sale) because the purpose of the valuation is to see if liquidation of the property will produce more than the exemption amount. The value should be determined as of the date that the petition was filed, and any appreciation since then should be considered to be property acquired postpetition that is not part of the estate.

Of course, if the property is sold during the bankruptcy case, the sale price is normally the best evidence of its value. When property is sold by the bankruptcy trustee during the bankruptcy case and unexpected proceeds are realized, the debtor should be allowed at a minimum to amend the exemption claim and thereby obtain the exempt share of the funds raised.

Allowance of Exemptions

If no timely and successful objection is made to the debtor's exemptions, they are automatically allowed. Untimely objections cannot be entertained by the court, regardless of whether the original exemption was proper.

This means that the trustee or a creditor can dispute an exemption only by filing a timely objection. In practice, as often as not, the trustee never files the necessary objection. In those instances in which an objection is filed on time, the debtor can then argue the question of whether the property is actually exempt.

Given the burden on the trustee and the creditors to raise timely objections, the debtor should be careful to make all appropriate exemption claims at the outset of the case, when possible. It is to the debtor's advantage to describe the property fully, including any features that would decrease its value if it were sold, and then to list the basis for the exemption. Obviously, the limit on this principle is one of good faith. Bad-faith exemption claims that are not honestly made not only create the risk of a successful objection, but also expose debtors and their counsel to the risk of court sanctions as punishment.

Once property is exempt by virtue of the expiration of the deadline for objections, nothing prevents the debtors from using or otherwise disposing of their exempt interest. When a single piece of property is only partially exempt, the debtor may retain the entire property until the trustee pays the value of the exemption to the debtor in cash. This means that the debtor can continue to reside in property that the trustee may liquidate without having to make rent or other payments to the trustee.

MAKING THE MOST OF EXEMPTIONS

The Bankruptcy Code provides many protections and powers in connection with debtors' exemption rights. The exemptions, whether state or federal, cannot be waived for bankruptcy purposes, even if state law would normally allow a waiver of exemptions. The debtor's powers to enhance the exemptions, as discussed below, also cannot be waived. In essence, the Code's exemption provisions govern all laws applying to bankruptcy exemptions, except for the actual items that a debtor can claim as exempt by using the state exemptions. Under this uniform bankruptcy system, dependents of the debtor may claim exemptions if the debtor does not, and the exemptions are automatically allowed if no objection is filed.

Exemption Planning

As discussed in Chapter 5, the amount of property that may be claimed as exempt can be greatly increased, if necessary, by careful exemption planning. For example, cash in a nonexemptible bank account can be applied toward a mortgage to create exemptible home equity. Although there was some question as to the propriety of exemption planning under the prior Act, the federalization of most bankruptcy exemption law should somewhat ease those doubts. However, some courts have found the movement of very large amounts of money into exempt types of property to be fraudulent.

The Debtor's Avoiding Powers

One of the most far-reaching and exciting changes of the Bankruptcy Reform Act was its grant to the debtor of the power to avoid (nullify) many types of prebankruptcy transfers of exempt property. This set of powers opened up an entirely new area in which debtors can greatly expand on the exemption rights given to them by state or federal law.

General Principles

The power to avoid transfers is expansive due in part to the broad definition of the word *transfer*. The Code includes within this term any lien, execution sale, setoff, or other mode of disposing of or parting with an interest in property, whether voluntarily or involuntarily, including foreclosure of the debtor's equity of redemption.

With certain limitations, the debtor may thus invalidate numerous types of transfers and recover valuable interests in property as long as those interests can be claimed as exempt. Put another way, if the interest in property involved fits within the exemption scheme used by the debtor and if the interest is impaired by a transfer of a type covered by the avoiding powers, that transfer may be avoided. But if only a portion of the transferred property may be claimed as exempt, the transfer may be avoided only to that extent.

The avoiding powers may be invoked even if the debtor has no equity in a particular property as long as the debtor has some rights to that property that can be claimed as exempt, even a mere right to possession or to redemption. It is not necessary to show that the debt on which a transfer is based is a dischargeable debt before the transfer can be avoided. The statute seems clear that nondischargeability of an underlying debt is no defense to an otherwise proper action to avoid a transfer that impairs an exemption. The avoiding powers are equally available in chapters 7 and 13.

Procedure

The Bankruptcy Rules prescribe the procedure that the debtor must follow for lien avoidance. For judicial liens (judgments, sheriff's levies, attachments) and liens on household goods, lien avoidance is accomplished by filing a motion in the bankruptcy court. However, more complicated types of transfer or lien avoidance require an adversary proceeding (a lawsuit within the bankruptcy case). And at least some avoidance actions may carry with them a right to trial by jury. The Supreme Court has made clear that a defendant to a fraudulent transfer action that has not filed a proof of claim in the bankruptcy case has a right to jury trial that is protected by the Seventh Amendment to the Constitution.

It is the debtor's burden to file a lien avoidance proceeding; if none is filed, all liens on the debtor's property, including otherwise exempt property, will normally survive the bankruptcy.

Power to Avoid Judicial Liens

The Bankruptcy Code gives the debtor an almost unqualified right to avoid any judicial lien that impairs an exemption. Because the term *judicial lien* is defined broadly to include levies, judgment liens (including confessed judgments), and liens obtained by sequestration or any other legal or equitable proceeding, this right gives the debtor a powerful tool.

A dispute occasionally arises concerning whether a particular lien is a judicial lien. These disputes sometimes involve liens granted in divorce proceedings. In such cases, careful legal analysis of the Code's definition is required.

The power to avoid judicial liens extends to every type of exempt property without limitation. Unlike some other avoiding powers, it may be used regardless of when the lien was obtained. Even if the lien caused the property to be removed from the debtor's possession, it can be avoided, forcing the return of the property.

Like the other avoiding powers, if the lien only partially impairs the exemption, only that part may be avoided. Thus, if a $3,000 judgment lien encumbers a house worth $9,000, in which an interest of $7,500 can be claimed as exempt, only $1,500 worth of the lien can be avoided; the other $1,500 is deemed an encumbrance on that interest in the house that was not exemptible. On the other hand, when the total value of the liened property can be claimed as exempt, then any amount of liens can be avoided because even if only a few dollars worth of liens remained, they would impair the exemption. Hence, if a house worth $7,500 is totally claimed as exempt, judgment liens of $100,000 may be totally avoided under this section. When only some liens may be avoided, the avoidable liens that are lowest in priority are the ones that impair the debtor's exemption. (The lowest-priority liens are usually those that were most recently filed—that is, a second mortgage has lower priority than a first mortgage.)

The Supreme Court has held that these provisions can only be used to avoid the fixing of a lien on a debtor's preexisting interest in property. Unless the debtor had an interest in the property before the lien attached to the property, the lien cannot be avoided. In applying this principle to a lien granted in a divorce decree, the Court found that the divorce decree had extinguished the debtor's preexisting one-half interest in the marital home and granted him a new interest. The Court therefore concluded that the simultaneously created lien for the benefit of the debtor's former spouse did not attach to a preexisting interest of the debtor in property and that the avoiding power was not available. The Court left open the possibility that when it is attached to property that had previously been titled only in the name of the debtor spouse, a divorce decree lien could be avoided.

Power to Avoid Nonpossessory, Nonpurchase-Money Security Interests in Certain Items

One of the most potent of the avoiding powers given to debtors is the power to avoid nonpossessory, nonpurchase-money security interests in the following items:

1. Household furnishings, household goods, wearing apparel, appliances, books, animals, crops, musical instruments, and jewelry that are held primarily for the personal, family, or household use of the debtor or a dependent of the debtor
2. Implements, professional books, or tools of the trade of the debtor or the trade of a dependent of the debtor
3. Professionally prescribed health aids for the debtor or a dependent of the debtor

A *nonpossessory lien* is a lien in which the creditor does not have possession of the property. (For example, a pawnbroker has a possessory lien when he or she holds the debtor's property.) A *nonpurchase-money security agreement* is an agreement between the debtor and a creditor that gives the creditor a lien in a transaction that did not finance the purchase of the liened property. Such liens are often taken by finance companies. To be avoidable, the creditor's lien must be both a nonpurchase-money security interest and nonpossessory.

As the previous list illustrates, this avoiding power extends to most but not quite all of the debtor's exempt tangible personal property that is not in the creditor's possession. These items need not be within the $200 value limitation set forth in the federal exemption for household items as long as they have been validly claimed as exempt under either the federal exemptions or other applicable exemption law. Thus, if a motor vehicle is claimed as exempt using the motor vehicle exemption but is also used as a tool of the debtor's trade, a nonpossessory, nonpurchase-money lien on that vehicle may be avoided. The dispute in such cases often centers on the definition of *tools of trade* under state or federal law because many states have an exemption for tools of trade that is large or unlimited in amount.

Power to Exempt Property Recovered by the Trustee

A power of the debtor somewhat less likely to be used allows the debtor to exempt any property that the trustee recovers using the various trustee powers to recover property. If such property comes into the trustee's hands, the debtor may claim it as exempt as long as the prebankruptcy transfer of the property from the debtor was not voluntary and the debtor did not conceal the property. The debtor may also exempt the property if the debtor could have avoided the transfer because the transfer was pursuant to a nonpossessory, nonpurchase-money security interest.

In some cases under this and certain other debtor avoiding powers, an issue may arise concerning whether the transfer that was avoided was a voluntary transfer. For example, there is no question that a debtor who pays money to a creditor holding a gun to the debtor's head has made an involuntary transfer. Would it be much different if the debtor paid a large utility arrearage on the threat of a shutoff of heating or water service to a home in which the debtor's children live? What about a debtor threatened with lesser evils—for example, repossession of property necessary for daily existence, such as a refrigerator?

In any case, it is unlikely that such disputes will arise when the trustee avoids a transfer because trustees rarely bother to avoid a transfer of property that the debtor may claim as exempt. Indeed, it is unusual for trustees to avoid the small transfers involved in consumer cases at all; when the only result will be more exempt property for the debtor rather than proceeds for the creditors, trustees have little incentive to do so. Except in cases in which the trustee would recover a substantial amount of nonexempt property along with the exempt property, the trustee is not likely to use the avoiding powers often in consumer cases.

When the trustee does move to avoid a lien on a car or other property, however, it may cause problems for the debtor by creating nonexemptible equity in the property. The debtor may not be able to exempt the property because the transfer of the lien was voluntary. In such cases, the trustee may attempt to liquidate the property if the debtor does not pay the trustee its value.

The Debtor's Right to Use the Trustee's Avoiding Powers

More likely to be used are the provisions of the Code that give the debtor the wide panoply of avoiding powers available to the trustee in cases in which the trustee does not choose to use those powers to avoid a transfer.

The use of these powers is subject to the same limitations that exist when the trustee does exercise his or her powers; the transfer to be avoided cannot have been a voluntary transfer, and the debtor may not use these powers for property that the debtor concealed. The discussion above on voluntariness applies equally to these powers.

The debtor's powers under these provisions are otherwise the same as those of the trustee. To use them, it is first necessary to understand what powers the trustee has. The discussion below describes each of the trustee's powers only briefly because each has given rise to innumerable disputed court decisions. The debtor's possible use of these powers is also discussed.

The "Strong-Arm" Clause

Through the use of the "strong-arm" powers, the trustee (and thus the debtor in many instances) can avoid a wide variety of transfers. The "strong-arm" provisions of the Code allow the trustee to avoid any transfer or obligation incurred by the debtor that is voidable by

1. A creditor that extends credit to the debtor at the time of commencement of the case and that obtains at that time and with respect to such credit a judicial lien on all property on which a creditor on a simple contract could have obtained such a judicial lien, whether or not such a creditor exists
2. A creditor that extends credit to the debtor at the time of the commencement of the case and obtains, at such time and with respect to such credit, an execution against the debtor that is returned unsatisfied at such time, whether or not such a creditor exists
3. A bona fide purchaser of real property other than fixtures from the debtor against whom applicable law permits such transfer to be perfected, that obtains the status of a bona fide purchaser and has perfected such transfer at the time of the commencement of the case, whether or not such a purchaser exists

In addition, these provisions bestow the power to avoid any transfer or obligation that is avoidable under applicable law by an existing creditor that holds an unsecured claim. All of these rights depend on the powers given to creditors or purchasers under state or local law, which can vary widely and can raise complicated legal issues.

The most frequent use of these powers in the past has been the avoidance of security interests and other liens that were not properly recorded in public records. The law of almost every state gives an executing lien creditor priority over the holder of any such security interests in personal property. A close examination of the nature and manner of perfection of a creditor's security interest may reveal avoidable transfers. Trustees have often successfully asserted these rights when financing statements were incorrectly filed in public records, thus rendering the security interest unperfected, or when a transaction denominated as a lease was found to be a disguised security interest with no financing statement filed. Similarly, the law in most states gives judicial lien creditors and bona fide purchasers priority over unfiled or improperly filed mortgages and many other unrecorded liens on real estate.

Certain other transfers may also be totally avoided under these provisions if they could have been avoided, even in part, by an existing unsecured creditor outside of bankruptcy. This provision allows the trustee to make use of applicable state laws to avoid fraudulent transfers and other types of transfers that are avoidable under state law by existing creditors.

The debtor's rights to use these powers are somewhat limited by the language excluding voluntary transfers. Because many security interests and transfers of property are voluntary, the debtor cannot avoid them even if by the trustee can.

The debtor can use these powers to avoid various types of unperfected or improperly perfected involuntary liens, such as mechanic's or repairman's liens and tax liens, if they are subordinate to judicial liens or the rights of bona fide purchasers under state law. These powers can also be used to cut off various rights in real property if the debtor did not create those rights voluntarily.

These powers will likely be used most by debtors to attempt avoidance through incorporation of state fraudulent transfer laws. In some 12 states, this means the Uniform Fraudulent Conveyance Act (UFCA). Approximately 24 other states have adopted the Uniform Fraudulent Transfer Act (UFTA). Still others have varying case law derived from the old English Statute of 13 Elizabeth.

Statutory Liens

Certain statutory liens may be avoided under a different provision of the Code. *Statutory liens* are liens that arise automatically due to a state or federal law, without the property owner's agreement and without a court proceeding. These include any lien that first becomes effective upon insolvency or insolvency proceedings of various types, liens that could be defeated by a bona fide purchaser of the liened property on the date of commencement of the bankruptcy case, and liens for rent. These liens may be avoided even if they have already been enforced by a sale before the filing of the bankruptcy case.

Among the liens avoidable under this section are unfiled federal tax liens and possibly even certain recorded tax liens. Debtors are also likely to use these provisions in states in which landlord's liens for rent are common and in cases involving mechanic's liens, innkeeper's liens, and other statutory liens that are subject to the rights of bona fide purchasers under state law.

Preferences

By far the most frequently used trustee avoiding power is the power to avoid preferences. With certain exceptions, set forth in the Code, the trustee may avoid any transfer of property of the debtor

1. To or for the benefit of a creditor
2. For or on account of an antecedent (prior) debt owed by the debtor before the transfer was made
3. Made while the debtor was insolvent
4. Made (a) on or within 90 days before the date of filing of the petition or (b) between 90 days and one year before the date of filing of the petition, if the creditor was an insider (a relative or close associate of the debtor) at the time of the transfer
5. That enables the creditor to receive more than the creditor would receive (a) if the case were under chapter 7 of the Code, (b) if the transfer had not been made, and (c) if the creditor received payment of the debt to the extent provided by the provisions of the Code

The basic purpose of this section is to promote equality among creditors by invalidating prebankruptcy seizures or transfers of the debtor's property that would give particular creditors more than they would receive in chapter 7 liquidation. It also serves to deter creditors from engaging in a race to get at the debtor's property before bankruptcy; creditors know that if they do obtain the property and perhaps hasten a bankruptcy, they will only have to surrender the property to the trustee.

Certain major exceptions to the preference avoidance powers exist. The first is for exchanges that are intended to be and are in fact "substantially contemporaneous" exchanges for new value—for example, cash purchases, purchases paid for immediately by check, or security interests securing new value. The Code does not define *substantially contemporaneous*. Also excepted are transfers made before the debtor's receipt of new value, as long as no other nonavoidable security for the new value was received. Similarly, payments on debts that the debtor incurred in the ordinary course of business or financial affairs are excepted. This includes most payments for current utility services, goods bought with payment due in 30 days, and most charge accounts. Unusually late payments are not excepted, however.

Payments made pursuant to settlement agreements have been found to be outside the ordinary course of a debtor's business. Nor are payments following a special or unusual request by a creditor for payment considered to be within the ordinary course of business. It is not clear whether a major loan of a type obtained only once or a few times over a debtor's lifetime would be considered to be in the ordinary course of the debtor's financial affairs. The term *ordinary course* may open the door to challenges of fraudulent or unfair transactions when security interests are taken in the debtor's property or loans and refinancings are prompted by extraordinary factors in the debtor's situation.

Certain liens created within 90 days are also excluded from the preference category:

1. Security interests that secure new value given by the secured party to enable the debtor to acquire property and that the debtor used for that purpose, if properly filed within 10 days after the debtor receives possession of the property
2. Security interests in inventory or receivables, to some extent
3. Statutory liens that are not otherwise avoidable

The debtor's use of the preference avoiding power can be quite varied. Levies and execution sales by otherwise unsecured creditors are clearly avoidable, including wage garnishments within 90 days before the bankruptcy filing. A payment made pursuant to a criminal restitution order can be recovered, even if it was made through a third party, such as a court clerk. Payments made to and retained by collection agencies can be recovered directly from the agency. These types of transfers normally meet all of the required tests for preferences and are definitely considered involuntary.

The fact that a debt is nondischargeable should not affect the use of this power. Thus, a debtor may also set aside a garnishment for a child support arrearage or a tax levy and perhaps other tax payments. However, if the debt was being collected as it fell due through the garnishment, such as current support payments, the antecedent debt element would not be present, and a preference would not exist.

Repossessions pursuant to valid security interests that could not otherwise be avoided generally do not constitute preferences. However, if the security interest was extracted within the preference period in exchange for forbearance on a preexisting debt or if new security during that period for a refinancing exceeds the new value given, then the security interest and any enforcement of it would constitute preferences. Also, if property of greater value than the debt has been repossessed and not sold by the creditor, either because the sale has not yet been scheduled or because the creditor has chosen to exercise a right of strict foreclosure and keep the property, then the creditor has received a preference by recovering property of greater value than it would receive in a liquidation.

Security interests in general, though, raise the thorny problems of voluntariness. Security interests are almost voluntary by definition. The Code defines *security interest* as a "lien created by agreement." But what of the security interest granted only under threat of dire consequences—for example, foreclosure or eviction? Like the payment of utility arrearages under a threat of midwinter cutoff, rent arrearages under threat of eviction, or support arrearages under threat of imprisonment, such a transfer can arguably be considered involuntary and made under duress. Other transfers that might be considered involuntary include those pursuant to contractual terms that the debtor does not understand. Because it is widely accepted that many of the terms used in consumer credit contracts are neither bargained for nor understood by consumers, this could mean setting aside wage assignments and other security arrangements.

One additional limitation is placed on the avoidance of preferences. Neither the trustee nor the debtor in a consumer bankruptcy may avoid a preference or preferences totaling less than $600 to a single creditor. This new provision, which is undoubtedly directed at consumer debtor preference actions against loan companies and utilities, will greatly reduce the number of preferences that debtors can avoid. It is important to note, however, that it applies only to preferences and not to any of the other avoiding powers.

Fraudulent Transfers

Besides the trustee's power to avoid transfers that are fraudulent under state law, the Code contains its own fraudulent transfer avoidance power. Under the Code's definition, the trustee may avoid a transfer or obligation if the transfer or obligation was made or incurred within one year before the case was filed and

1. The transfer or obligation was made or incurred with actual intent to hinder, delay, or defraud any entity to which the debtor was or became indebted, on or after the date that the transfer occurred or the obligation was incurred, or

2. (a) The debtor received less than a reasonably equivalent value for the transfer or obligation, and
   (b) (i) the debtor was insolvent on the date of the transfer or obligation or became insolvent as a result of the transfer or obligation, or
   (ii) the debtor was engaged in a business or was about to engage in a business or transaction with unreasonably small capital, or
   (iii) the debtor intended to incur or believed that he or she would incur debts beyond his or her ability to pay

For consumer debtors, by far the most important of these provisions is the provision that classifies as fraudulent any transfer for less than reasonably equivalent value that occurred within one year preceding the petition while the debtor was insolvent. Because most consumer debtors are insolvent under the Code's definition, which excludes consideration of exempt property, this section allows the debtor to avoid any transfer (as *transfer* is broadly defined by the Code) within the previous year that was for less than reasonably equivalent value as long as the transfer was not voluntary and the debtor did not conceal the property.

The debtor's most likely use of this power would be to avoid transfers—such as mortgage foreclosures, repossessions, or execution sales—in which the property that the debtor lost was worth significantly more than the value received. Due to the imperfections of the procedures through which debtors' property is seized or sold to satisfy their debts—procedures that often involve inside deals or auctions attended only by speculators—such cases are relatively common. Although there has been some doubt about whether involuntary, judicially authorized or conducted sales can be considered to be avoidable fraudulent transfers, most courts have found that the avoiding power is indeed applicable to such transfers.

In the leading court decision on the subject, the debtor's real property had been conveyed by a public sale to satisfy a defaulted deed of trust. The amount bid and paid by the purchaser was $115,400, which was the amount outstanding on the deed of trust. The property had a value of $200,000, however, and the court held that the payment of 57.7 percent of this value was not a "fair equivalent value" of the transfer. Therefore, the transfer was avoided. The court noted that it had found no cases in which payment of less than 70 percent was considered to be a fair equivalent value.

With regard to the transferee's argument that the public sale was not a transfer made by the debtor, the court looked to the broad definition of *transfer* and found the transfer by foreclosure sale to be clearly within that definition. Reasoning that the estate had lost an equity of $84,600 through the transfer, the court also found that the purposes of the fraudulent conveyance provisions to prevent depletion of the estate were served by setting aside a transfer for far less than the fair value of the property. The case has since been followed by several Circuit Courts of Appeals and other courts, though some courts have held to the contrary.

Most courts that have permitted foreclosure sales to be avoided have concluded that a flexible approach to the concept of reasonably equivalent value must be taken, based on the evidence presented in each case. When junior lienholders are paid from the proceeds of the sale, their payment probably constitutes an element of the value received by the debtor. However, when junior liens are not paid, they should not be taken into account in calculating what the debtor received because the junior lienholders retain unsecured claims against the debtor.

A major limitation on the use of these provisions should be noted, however. If a transfer is avoidable only under these provisions, any transferee who has paid value and acted in good faith is given a lien on the interest transferred or may enforce the obligation incurred to the extent of the value given to the debtor. Because *value* is defined to include satisfaction of an antecedent debt, the transferee in the case discussed above, for example, would retain a lien for $115,400. If the creditor had executed on a previously unsecured debt, this lien might not be avoidable under any of the debtor's other avoiding powers. However, it could presumably be paid in installments in a chapter 13 plan.

Postpetition Transfers

In line with the general principle that filing a bankruptcy freezes the debtor's property for administration by the bankruptcy court, the Code generally allows the trustee to avoid most postpetition transfers of the debtor's property. Like the other avoiding powers, the debtor may exercise this power if the property was not concealed and the transfer was not voluntary.

There are a number of exceptions to this general rule. One of the most important protects transfers of the debtor's property by third parties who have received no notice of the bankruptcy case. A typical example is a bank that transfers funds in a debtor's bank account to honor a check drawn by the debtor. In addition, any transfer authorized by a specific Code provision or by the bankruptcy court is not avoidable. There are also several less common exceptions.

The debtor may use this power in conjunction with the automatic stay provisions to invalidate involuntary postpetition transfers. One example of a case in which the stay might need to be supplemented is a repossession ordered by a creditor that had no notice of the bankruptcy. Although the creditor would probably not be held in contempt because it had no notice of the case, the repossession could clearly be reversed. A setoff after the bankruptcy could be similarly undone. In chapter 13 cases, in which the debtor's postpetition income is property of the estate, any deduction by a credit union from wages is avoidable. To prevent any problems in effecting this last type of avoidance, it is advisable to withdraw before the bankruptcy any prior authorization for such deductions that might muddy the issue of voluntariness.

Setoff

The Code gives the trustee the power to avoid some, but not all, setoffs of mutual debts in the 90 days before the petition is filed. A *setoff* occurs when a creditor pays itself with money belonging to the debtor that it is holding or by canceling a debt that it owes to the debtor. The most common setoff occurs when a bank or other financial institution pays a debt that the debtor owes to it by seizing the funds in the debtor's account.

If a setoff is permissible under nonbankruptcy law, the Code provides certain tests that must be met before the setoff can be avoided. First, a setoff may be avoided if it is not for a mutual debt. If the debtor owes the debt in a capacity other than that in which a debt is owed to the debtor, no mutuality exists, and no setoff is permitted. For example, if the debtor has deposited money in his or her individual account, a setoff of that deposit against the debtor's obligation as a trustee for another person by the bank may be avoided because it is against the debtor in a different capacity. This principle is frequently applied to setoffs involving debtors' IRA accounts. Similarly, a creditor may not set off a prepetition claim against a postpetition claim because of the express wording of the Code and because the debts are not considered to be "mutual." However, it is not always easy to determine whether mutual debts exist.

Second, a setoff may be avoided if it is exercised to satisfy a claim against the debtor other than an allowable claim. Thus, if defenses to the claim's allowability, including defenses to the claim itself, are successfully asserted, a setoff may be avoided.

Third, if a creditor exercising a setoff acquires its claim from another entity, either after the filing of the petition or within 90 days before filing while the debtor was insolvent, the setoff may be avoided.

Fourth, if a creditor exercising a setoff has caused the debtor to increase the amount owed by the creditor to the debtor—for example, by pressuring the debtor to build up a bank deposit—while the debtor was insolvent in order to obtain a setoff, the setoff may be avoided.

Finally, a setoff may be avoided to the extent that it results in the creditor's improving its position over what it was either (1) 90 days before the filing of the petition or (2) if no "insufficiency" existed on that date, on the first date that an insufficiency existed. The Code defines *insufficiency* as the "amount, if any, by which a claim against the debtor exceeds a mutual debt owing to the debtor by the holder of such claim."

For example, if a debtor owed $5,000 to a bank and 90 days before filing the case had a deposit balance of $200, there would be an insufficiency on that date of $4,800 ($5,000 – $200). If, 40 days before the filing, the bank was then owed $3,000 and the debtor had a deposit of $2,000, there would be an insufficiency on that date of only $1,000 ($3,000 – $2,000). If the bank then set off against the entire deposit, that setoff could be avoided in its entirety because on the date of setoff, the bank's insufficiency position had improved to the extent of $3,800 ($4,800 – $1,000), an amount greater than the amount of setoff. If, instead of $200, there had been $2,500 on deposit 90 days before filing, then the improvement in position would have been $1,500, and that amount of the $2,000 setoff would be avoidable. Finally, if the amount on deposit 90 days before the filing had been $6,000 and then, three days before filing, the debtor withdrew $3,500, then the first insufficiency would be $1,500. A setoff after that date would be avoidable to the extent that the insufficiency on the date of setoff exceeded $1,500.

It is important to note that the avoiding powers address only setoffs before the filing of the petition. The improvement-in-position test described above apparently does not apply at all to setoffs after filing if the automatic stay is no longer in effect.

Liens Securing Fines, Penalties, and Forfeitures

The final type of transfer that is avoidable by the trustee and sometimes by the debtor applies only in cases under chapter 7. This provision allows avoidance of liens for penalties, fines, punitive damages, multiple damages, and the like, to the extent that the amount secured by the lien does not represent compensation for actual pecuniary loss. Under this section of the Code, a tax lien can be avoided to the extent that it secures penalties for late payment, for example.

Other Limitations on the Debtor's Use of the Trustee's Avoiding Powers

In addition to the overriding limitations that the debtor may not avoid any voluntary transfer or any transfer in which the debtor concealed property, there are a number of other limitations on the debtor's avoiding powers. Naturally, the avoiding powers are limited by the extent of the debtor's available exemptions. The Code permits exemption of particular property only to the extent that the exemption for that type of property is still available.

More importantly, the avoiding powers are subject to the limitations that the Code places on the trustee. One such limitation sets a statute of limitations for avoidance actions at the earlier of (1) two years after appointment of the trustee or (2) the date that the case is closed.

When a transfer is avoided, the Code generally allows recovery of the transferred property (or its value in some cases) from both the initial transferee and a subsequent transferee. There are several major exceptions to this general rule. The debtor may not recover from any transferee subsequent to the initial transferee if that transferee has either (1) paid money or property in good faith without knowledge of the voidability of the transfer or (2) taken from a prior transferee who has paid money or property in good faith and without knowledge. In such cases, the only recovery can be the value of the property from the initial transferee. And if an initial transferee acted in good faith, the transferee must return the property but retains a lien for the cost or the increase in value due to any improvements on the property, whichever is less.

Finally, a lawsuit to recover property after the avoidance of a transfer must be commenced either within one year after the avoidance or before the case is closed, whichever comes first.

Preservation of Avoided Transfers or Recovered Property

An important but often overlooked addition to the avoiding powers is the right to preserve avoided transfers for the debtor's benefit. The Code provides that a transfer avoided or property recovered by the debtor or the trustee may be preserved for the debtor's benefit to the extent that the debtor may exempt that property.

This means that the debtor, in effect, steps into the shoes of the holder of the avoided transfer vis-à-vis any other entity with rights junior to that holder and thereby obtains rights superior to junior lienholders. For example, if two joint debtors have a $10,000 home that has an $8,000 judicial lien and a $10,000 mortgage junior to the judicial lien, the debtors, if they can exempt their $10,000 interest (as they could under the federal exemptions), may avoid the judicial lien. Without preservation of that lien, however, this would not benefit the debtors because it would merely move the mortgage up in priority, from being secured for $2,000 and unsecured for $8,000 to being fully secured for $10,000. By allowing the debtors to preserve the avoided judicial lien for their own benefit, the Code keeps the mortgage in its previous position—that is, secured only to the extent of $2,000 and unsecured for the remaining $8,000. Needless to say, this power can be of great importance in cases in which there are multiple liens on a particular property.

PROTECTION OF EXEMPT PROPERTY AFTER DISCHARGE

Another important feature of the new bankruptcy exemption scheme is the continuing protection given to exempt property after the discharge. The Code provides that, with a few exceptions, no creditor holding a prebankruptcy claim may ever execute against the property that is claimed as exempt.

The principal significance of this subsection is that even creditors that hold claims for which a bankruptcy discharge was denied may not reach exempt property to execute on their still-valid claims. Thus, if a discharge is denied because of a false financial statement, because a debt was not listed, because of fraud or willful and malicious injury, or because the debt was a student loan, the debtor may nevertheless be fully protected from execution on these debts if he or she has only property exempted in the bankruptcy case. The only exceptions to this general rule are debts for nondischargeable taxes, support or alimony, and liens that are not avoided during the bankruptcy.

This provision serves the obvious purpose of ensuring that the debtor's fresh start is not frustrated by preexisting debts. It makes the exemptions permanent, protecting the minimum grubstake afforded by the exemption provisions from almost every attack arising out of the debtor's prebankruptcy circumstances.

Chapter 10

DEALING WITH SECURED CREDITORS

One of the greatest advances for consumers under the Bankruptcy Code came in the powers they were given with respect to secured debts. Under the prior Bankruptcy Act, relatively little could be done to protect consumer debtors from the holders of secured claims. A straight bankruptcy generally did not affect the status of otherwise valid liens or security interests, and as a practical matter, few Chapter XIII plans could get very far with respect to secured claims unless the holders of those claims agreed to the plan or were not affected by it. Now, in contrast, almost every conceivable type of security interest can be altered in some way through bankruptcy, often to a tremendous degree and with very significant benefits for the debtor.

Some of the ways that the rights of secured creditors can be affected are covered in previous chapters of this guide, and those discussions are not repeated here. Chapter 8 dealt at length with two of these areas: the automatic stay, which, among other things, generally prevents lien creation, perfection, and enforcement once the petition is filed; and the turnover provisions, through which the debtor may recover property from a secured party who obtained possession of it before the case. Chapter 9 discusses the debtor's various powers to avoid transfers, including some liens and security interests that impair the debtor's exemptions. Through use of these powers, the debtor can often entirely eliminate security interests in household goods, judicial liens, execution sales, garnishments, repossessions, setoffs, and other transfers of property that occurred before the debtor filed the bankruptcy.

All of the powers discussed in previous chapters can enormously improve a debtor's position with respect to many secured claims. This chapter is devoted to several additional ways in which the problems of secured claims may be lessened or removed. These methods may be used either in conjunction with the options already discussed or when those other remedies are not available.

THE ALLOWED SECURED CLAIM

Concept of the Allowed Secured Claim

Critical to an understanding of most of the provisions dealing with secured claims is a familiarity with a key concept in the Bankruptcy Code: the allowed secured claim. The term is applicable to cases under all chapters of the Code.

The Code provides that a secured claim cannot be an allowed secured claim in an amount greater than the value of the creditor's collateral. An undersecured claim (one that is secured by collateral worth less than the claim) that is filed and allowed is therefore bifurcated, or divided, into two parts: (1) an allowed secured claim in an amount equal to the value of the collateral and (2) an allowed unsecured claim for any excess of the total claim over the value of the collateral.

One simple example is a debt, not otherwise subject to defenses or setoffs, in the amount of $2,000 that is secured by an automobile worth $500. With respect to the creditor's claim, the debtor could request a determination that the claim be divided into an allowed secured claim of $500 and an allowed unsecured claim of $1,500. Similarly, if, during the entire 90 days before the filing of the petition, a debtor had a bank account of $500 that was subject to setoff by a bank to which the debtor owed $2,000, the court would determine that the bank had an allowed secured claim of $500 and an allowed unsecured claim of $1,500.

The purpose of the allowed secured claim concept is quite apparent. In accord with the general bankruptcy scheme, it looks to the actual property interests that exist at the time of the bankruptcy to determine the rights of the parties. A secured creditor's interest is measured by what it would receive at that time through enforcement of its security interest, and that amount, of course, would be the value of the collateral. The Code therefore gives that secured creditor a better position than the unsecured creditors in bankruptcy only to that extent, even if the secured creditor's total claim is much greater than the value of the collateral, because in a practical sense, the secured creditor can realize only that value due to its secured status. Its rights to property other than the collateral are no greater than those of other creditors. By treating the amount of the claim in excess of the value of the collateral as an unsecured claim, the Code prevents the secured creditor from exercising undue power or getting an unfair advantage over the unsecured creditors out of proportion to the true value of its security interest.

Unfortunately, the Supreme Court has somewhat limited the application of the allowed secured claim concept. Despite clear statutory language in the Code stating that a lien securing a claim that is not an allowed secured claim is void, the Court held that a chapter 7 debtor could not have a lien declared void on the basis of that language, even though the lien did not secure a claim that was an allowed secured claim. This decision will probably affect neither debtors' rights under chapter 13 nor the right to redeem property, which is discussed later in this chapter. In fact, in *Nobelman v. American Savings Bank*, the Supreme Court recently recognized implicitly that most liens could be reduced to the value of their collateral ("stripped down") through a chapter 13 plan. In that case, the Court held that a claim secured only by a home mortgage could not be stripped down in chapter 13, but only because the Code provides special protection to the holders of such claims, as discussed later in this chapter.

Procedure for Determining the Allowed Secured Claim

Any dispute concerning the amount of the allowed secured claim usually arises as an objection filed by the debtor after the creditor has filed its claim. If the secured creditor fails to file a proof of claim, the debtor may file a claim on behalf of the creditor in the amounts that the debtor believes to be secured or unsecured. Provided that the deadline for filing claims has not passed, the creditor then has an opportunity to file its own claim, which would supersede the one filed by the debtor. In either case, the debtor may then initiate a court proceeding against the creditor, seeking a court order determining the amount of the claim.

If there is any dispute about the claim, it is essential that the debtor file a complaint or motion objecting to a secured claim and have the claim determined. Absent such a proceeding, the claim is presumed valid. If the court does not affirmatively decide that the claim is not allowable for some particular reason, the claim may be allowed as filed, notwithstanding contrary provisions in the debtor's chapter 13 plan.

The methods of contesting and proving value in this context are generally the same as in determining value in proceedings for relief from the automatic stay. Therefore, the discussion of that question in Chapter 8 may be helpful. Ultimately, the debtor may have to be prepared to prove a value different from that testified to by the creditor's witnesses, which may require retention of an appraiser or another expert.

There is an important difference, however. In proceedings for relief from the stay, the debtor often tries to prove that the value of the property is high so that there is equity in it. In claim litigation, the debtor's goal is to prove that the value of the property is as low as possible.

Date of Valuation

The first relevant issue is the date as of which value should be determined. Depending on whether the property is increasing or decreasing in value, it may be in the debtor's interest to argue for an earlier date or a later one, whichever will produce a lower value. Although there is little difference in most cases, the issue can be significant in cases of rapidly depreciating new automobiles, rapidly appreciating real estate, or property that has been damaged since the filing of the case.

Perhaps in the interests of simplicity, some courts have chosen the filing date of the petition or plan for valuation in all cases, on the theory that the parties' rights are frozen as of that date in most other respects. A number of other courts have used the date of the valuation proceeding as the critical date for valuation; others have selected the date of the chapter 13 plan confirmation hearing, looking to the value of the property as of that date.

Method of Valuation

More controversial has been the issue of which method to use to determine value, an issue that has monetary significance in virtually every case. It is not surprising that many courts have addressed this issue.

Perhaps the easiest case occurs when property has been purchased quite recently in relation to the date of valuation. In such cases, courts have often taken the price paid by a willing buyer to a willing seller and adjusted it for any clear changes in the condition of the property.

The more typical situation concerns property of changing value that was purchased substantially in advance of the valuation date. In such cases, particularly when a car is involved, courts have tended to look to industry guides when possible, but in somewhat varying ways. Some courts presume that the value is that set forth in industry guides, rebuttable by evidence that the condition of the property was better or worse than average.

The most frequent question in regard to automobile values has been whether to use the wholesale, loan (trade-in), or retail value listed in the different industry guides. Not surprisingly, debtors have usually argued for the lowest of these values, the wholesale value, on the theory that the vehicle would usually be auctioned for that price if repossessed. This argument is strongest in cases in which the creditor is not an automobile dealer and would clearly dispose of the vehicle on the wholesale market. Moreover, as one leading court decision noted, the interest being valued is the creditor's interest, the right to foreclose on the collateral, and the replacement value of the vehicle is irrelevant. Creditors, of course, argue that the court should set the allowed secured claim at an amount equal to the replacement cost of the property, its retail value, or even higher. Although few courts have accepted this argument, some have compromised on the issue for various reasons, choosing the trade-in value or some other figure between the wholesale and retail values.

For household goods and other items without established industry guides to value, the problem of valuation is more difficult. The court decisions refusing to use retail value for automobiles should clearly prevent purchase price from becoming the standard. The best guideline is probably the used-furniture market in the area, which may consist primarily of auctions and garage sales. In many rural areas, auctioneers are called to testify about the value of different items in that market.

When there are prior liens on property ahead of the lien that is to be valued, the amount of those liens must first be subtracted to determine if there is value over and above the prior liens. If the prior liens equal or exceed the value of the property, then the allowed secured claim of the creditor with the lower-priority lien is equal to zero. It is always appropriate to deduct the costs of a hypothetical sale because a creditor could not realize anything from its lien without a commercially reasonable disposition of the property. However, some courts refuse to deduct those costs when the debtor proposes to keep the property.

HOLDING OF CASH COLLATERAL BY CREDITORS

One way in which debtors may be deprived of certain property after bankruptcy pursuant to a lien or security interest must also be mentioned in the context of secured claims. After filing a bankruptcy case, a debtor may suddenly find that a bank or credit union to which the debtor owes money refuses to allow withdrawals from the debtor's bank or share account. This occurs because the bank or credit union, if it has a right of setoff (a right to pay a debt owed to it with the funds it is holding), is considered to be a holder of cash collateral.

If a bank retains a right of setoff, it may not exercise that setoff without first obtaining relief from the automatic stay, as discussed in Chapter 8. However, it is not automatically required to turn over the property to the trustee or the debtor because the Code requires turnover only of property the trustee may use, sell, or lease or that the debtor may exempt. The trustee may not use, sell, or lease cash collateral without the creditor's consent unless the court, after notice and a hearing, finds that there is adequate protection and approves such use. Moreover, the debtor's exemption rights may also be defeated by a right of setoff, just as they may be by a valid nonavoidable lien.

However, the debtor does have some arguments against such a freeze on a bank account. In chapter 13, the debtor is entitled to possession of all property of the estate, and under the laws of some states, a freeze on an account may be considered the first step to a setoff, which is prohibited by the automatic stay. Several courts have therefore prohibited banks from freezing debtors' accounts after they file bankruptcy cases.

The problem of a bank account freeze can generally be prevented simply by making sure that the debtor has no money in the account as of the date of the bankruptcy petition. If a debtor has not depleted the account before bankruptcy, the account, or a part of it, may in effect be seized by the bank or credit union creditor. Once this has occurred, there may be little that can be done to recover the debtor's funds, assuming that a valid right of setoff exists and unless the debtor has defenses to the underlying claim or adequate protection.

STATEMENT OF INTENTION

The Code requires a chapter 7 debtor to file a statement of intention with respect to property securing consumer debts. The debtor need not state all of his or her plans on this statement. All that is required is a statement of whether the debtor intends to retain or surrender the collateral, whether it is claimed as exempt, whether the debtor intends to avoid the lien, and whether the debtor intends to reaffirm the debt. Although the Official Form for this statement that is appended to the Bankruptcy Rules appears to require a choice between several options if the debtor retains the collateral, the debtor may choose none of them if desired. The debtor may choose other options besides those listed on the form. In most jurisdictions, for example, a debtor may choose to simply continue paying an automobile loan without either redeeming or reaffirming the debt.

The statement of intention must be filed within 30 days after the filing of a chapter 7 petition or on or before the date of the meeting of the creditors, whichever is earlier. The court can also extend the deadline within that period. The statement must be mailed to the trustee and to all creditors named in the statement on or before the date it is filed. Thereafter, the debtor may amend it without court permission at any time up to when performance is to take place.

The Code also requires that the debtor "shall perform his intention" within 45 days after the statement is filed or such additional time as the court allows for cause. In most cases, this is quite simple because if the debtor stated an intent to retain or exempt property, that has long since been accomplished. These Code provisions can be seen as a guideline for when redemption or reaffirmation should be accomplished, if that is the debtor's intent. However, because the pertinent Code section expressly provides that it does not affect substantive rights, it should not be a bar to redemptions, even if they are not accomplished by the deadline.

Although the chapter 7 trustee is supposed to "ensure that the debtor shall perform" the stated intention, the Code gives the trustee no mechanism to use. As a practical matter, trustees generally become involved if asked by a secured creditor, and that is likely only when the stated intention is redemption or reaffirmation. The trustee could presumably then bring the matter to the attention of the court for resolution, something that the secured creditor could do just as easily on its own.

The statement of intention thus seems designed primarily as a way for secured creditors to obtain notice of what the debtor plans to do and as a guideline to when redemption and reaffirmation should occur. However, because substantive legal rights are expressly left unaffected, the debtor may change his or her intentions and apparently need not file a new statement. Also, there appears to be no penalty provided for failing to carry through on the stated intentions. At worst, that conduct would give a secured creditor an additional argument in seeking relief from the automatic stay.

THE RIGHT OF REDEMPTION IN CHAPTER 7 CASES

One of the new provisions enacted in the Bankruptcy Code provides for a limited right of redemption in chapter 7 cases. In essence, it provides that, for certain secured consumer debts, the security interest may be eliminated on payment to the creditor of the value of its collateral—that is, the amount of its allowed secured claim.

Purpose

The purpose of the redemption provisions is to prevent secured creditors from getting an unfair advantage out of proportion to the value of their security. Under prior law, a secured creditor had the right to demand full payment or to obtain a reaffirmation of a secured debt after bankruptcy and to repossess or otherwise recover the collateral if the payment or reaffirmation did not occur. This often allowed the creditor to collect far more than the market value of the collateral due to the fact that the debtor could not easily replace the property securing the debt. Congress believed that it was unfair for a creditor holding a security interest in some necessity, such as a refrigerator, to demand payment of a debt of several hundred dollars when the collateral was worth only $50 on the market, simply because the item was irreplaceable for the indigent debtor.

Limitations on the Right to Redeem

The redemption provision provides a simple procedure for the chapter 7 debtor to remove the creditor's lien by paying the creditor the real value of the property. There are several limitations on that right, however. It is available only to individual debtors and only with respect to certain property and certain debts. Specifically, it can only be used in cases of dischargeable consumer debts that are secured by tangible personal property that either the debtor has exempted or the trustee has abandoned. It is not available with respect to real estate or intangible liquid assets.

Questions may arise concerning whether property has been or can be claimed as exempt. Unless the property is exempted or abandoned, redemption cannot be used. (These questions are discussed in Chapters 2 and 9.)

Redemption by Payment in Installments

A final issue with respect to redemption is whether the Code gives the debtor the right to pay the amount of the allowed secured claim in installments. Most courts have decided that, unless the creditor agrees otherwise, the debtor must redeem through cash payment of the redemption amount and that neither the debtor nor the court can impose an installment arrangement on the creditor.

These decisions sometimes present a problem to the debtor who cannot afford to pay the entire allowed secured claim in cash and is unwilling or unable to negotiate a reaffirmation agreement. Two possible solutions are to handle the debt under chapter 13 or simply to continue the payments on the entire debt without reaffirming. The latter solution would not permit the reduction of the debt to the value of the collateral. (Both of these options are discussed later in this chapter.)

Secured Creditors Who Refuse to Agree to Continued Installment Payments

The secured creditor who refuses installment payments may also present a problem to the chapter 7 debtor who is current on payments for a secured debt, such as an automobile loan or a mortgage. Secured creditors that the debtor does not propose to affect in the bankruptcy almost always continue to accept payments and rarely attempt to enforce their security interests as long as payments are current. Occasionally, however, a creditor will try to foreclose on the basis of a contract clause that makes the bankruptcy itself a default on the obligation.

Many courts have stated that, although a debtor has not reaffirmed a secured claim, a creditor holding that claim has no right to exercise its rights under such a clause as long as payments are current. However, if a debtor cannot otherwise prevent the creditor from taking action, the debtor can usually obtain relief by converting the case to chapter 13, if it is still pending, or by commencing a new chapter 13 case after the chapter 7 case is closed. Chapter 13 imposes effective restraints on secured creditors, as discussed later in this chapter.

Indeed, the threat of conversion to chapter 13, in which the creditor can be forced to accept installments and possibly reduced payments as well, or of other litigation, is usually sufficient to force a creditor to accept a redemption in which the allowed secured claim is reaffirmed and paid in installments. The threat may be so effective that the creditor may even agree to an arrangement more advantageous to the debtor—for example, that the creditor will not enforce its security interest as long as certain payments on an amount reduced to the value of the collateral are made—without the debtor reaffirming the debt. Nothing in the Code precludes such an arrangement, which has the significant advantage of eliminating any possible liability of the debtor for a later court judgment based on a reaffirmed debt.

Uses in Practice

The right to redeem is used most often to reduce the amount payable on purchase-money or possessory security interests in household goods, such as appliances, and on both purchase-money and nonpurchase-money (or possessory) security interests in motor vehicles. The former, unlike nonpossessory nonpurchase-money security interests in household goods and certain other items, are not avoidable under the exemption lien avoidance powers discussed in Chapter 9. Similarly, security interests in motor vehicles are not normally avoidable unless they are nonpurchase-money and nonpossessory and the vehicle is a tool of trade of the debtor or a dependent.

Except when the creditor agrees to installment payments or the court permits them, consumer debtors use redemption mainly to redeem items of low value because the total value of the item must be paid in cash. (As discussed above, in cases in which there is collateral of higher value and the creditor cannot be forced to accept installments, the debtor must use one of the other remedies discussed in this chapter.) When redemption for a cash payment is possible, it provides a simple procedure by which the debtor may eliminate the security interest as well as the debt, which is discharged, once and for all. In cases in which the property is subject to more than one lien, a secured creditor's interest may be totally eliminated under the redemption provisions if the liens ahead of that creditor are greater than the value of the property.

The only factual issue that usually arises is the value of the property. The remarks earlier in this chapter and in preceding chapters are equally applicable here. As in cases involving the automatic stay or exemptions, the date of valuation may be critical. Because the type of property subject to redemption usually depreciates in value over time, it is normally to the debtor's advantage to have the valuation date be the date of redemption rather than the filing date of the bankruptcy petition.

Redemption is apparently meant to be used without resort to the court in the first instance. When the parties agree to value and terms, redemption is accomplished by simply paying the creditor. Of course, without this agreement, the court's intervention is necessary to determine that an amount tendered is, in fact, the amount of the allowed secured claim.

USING CHAPTER 13 TO HANDLE SECURED CREDITORS: THE CHAPTER 13 CRAMDOWN

Perhaps the greatest powers to affect the rights of secured creditors are found in the provisions of chapter 13. The Bankruptcy Code provides that the debtor's plan may "modify the rights of holders of secured claims, other than a claim secured only by a security interest in real property that is the debtor's principal residence." For long-term claims, including those secured only by a mortgage on the debtor's principal residence, the plan may provide for the curing of any default over a reasonable period of time.

Modification of Secured Creditors' Rights to Claims Not Secured Only by Real Estate That Is the Debtor's Principal Residence

Most of the flexibility given to the debtor in chapter 13 comes from the broad right to modify the rights of secured creditors. In bankruptcy parlance, this right to limit the enforceability or change the terms of a creditor's contract over the creditor's objection is called a *cramdown*.

The Code does not define the term *modify*, so it may presumably be given its broadest possible meaning—that is, that any term of the contract is subject to change. Thus, except as limited by other Code provisions, the debtor might propose to pay a lower total amount than originally agreed, to lower the amount of payments, to pay the debt over a longer period of time, to defer payments until after other debts are paid, to eliminate various oppressive terms, or even to eliminate totally the creditor's lien.

Limitations on Debts Secured Only by Real Estate That Is the Debtor's Principal Residence

The debtor's rights to modify are subject to several major limitations. First, except to the extent of curing a default over a reasonable period of time, the right to modify does not extend to debts secured only by a security interest in real property that is the debtor's principal residence. This limitation, although important, is not as broad as it first appears. It does not apply if the creditor has other security besides the mortgage. Except in cases of some conventional first mortgages, many claims secured by real estate are also secured by household goods or at least by the possible refund of proceeds from credit insurance. Even in first mortgages, often clauses give creditors security interests in appliances, rents, or escrow accounts established for payment of taxes and insurance. And many banks have the right of setoff against a debtor's bank account, either by law or by way of a deposit agreement. A creditor may not release security interests in such other property to gain protection from the limitation on modification.

In addition, the limitation does not appear to apply to the debtor's right to waive or cure a default on any secured claim. Several courts have held that, when the plan otherwise conforms to the Code, a plan may cure or waive a default even on a claim secured only by real property that is the debtor's principal residence because a cure is not a "modification." Using this reasoning, courts have held that chapter 13 plans that propose to pay such claims in full may effectuate a cure that is not a prohibited modification. Thus, for example, a debtor may be able to eliminate the effects of a due-on-sale clause that is asserted by a creditor as grounds for foreclosure.

By its terms, the limitation applies only when the claim is secured solely by a "security interest" in the residence. As defined by the Code, a *security interest* must be a lien created by agreement, and the limitation is thus not applicable when the claim is secured by a judicial lien or a statutory lien. Nor does the limitation apply to property that is the debtor's principal residence if it is not real property, as in the case of a mobile home that is not considered to be realty.

Because of the special protection provision, a chapter 13 plan may not alter the interest rate, payment amount, or other terms of such a mortgage. In *Nobelman v. American Savings Bank*, the Supreme Court held that this provision also prevents claims secured only by a mortgage on the debtor's principal residence from being bifurcated and stripped down to the value of the collateral. The Court held that, even if a plan modified only the unsecured portion of a mortgage claim, the plan would still contravene the prohibition against modifying the rights of the holder of such a claim.

Requirement of Adequate Protection

A second limitation on the rights of chapter 13 debtors to deal with secured creditors is the requirement of adequate protection to creditors that have liens on property used, sold, or leased by the debtor. At least until a plan is confirmed, it is clear that a creditor may request relief from the automatic stay if adequate protection has not been provided, as discussed in Chapter 8. It is not clear whether this right continues after a plan is confirmed because the Code states that the provisions of a confirmed plan bind each creditor. A number of courts have held that confirmation of a chapter 13 plan in effect overrides the creditor's preexisting right to adequate protection and eliminates the creditor's right to relief as long as the debtor is in compliance with a confirmed plan.

Provisions Dealing with Allowed Secured Claims Provided for by the Plan

A third important factor in determining whether the court will approve the modification of a secured creditor's rights is compliance with the Code's plan confirmation standards. One of these standards is that one of the following conditions should be met for each allowed secured claim that is provided for:

1. The holder of the claim has accepted the plan.
2. (a) The plan provides that the holder of the claim retain the lien securing such claim, and (b) the value, as of the effective date of the plan, of property to be distributed under the plan on account of the claim is not less than the allowed amount of the claim.
3. The debtor surrenders the property securing the claim to the holder.

The first and third of these options are fairly simple. If the creditor consents to modification of its rights, by negotiated settlement or otherwise, the court need not be concerned. A number of courts have held that a secured creditor that does not object to a plan may be deemed to have accepted it. In addition, if the debtor surrenders the collateral to the creditor, that creditor, in effect, is no longer a secured creditor, only an unsecured creditor with respect to whatever debt remains.

The most complicated provision is the second, which deals with retention of the property over the creditor's objection. To meet this standard, the plan must specifically provide that the creditor retains a lien—that is, that the creditor will continue to have priority rights to the property subject to the lien. However, some of the rights usually associated with the lien are necessarily limited by chapter 13, such as the right to repossess. The main purpose of the lien retention is to preserve the creditor's rights in the property if the plan ends in failure before the creditor receives the amount to which it is entitled on its allowed secured claim. Once the debtor has paid the allowed secured claim, the lien may be eliminated, and the plan may so provide.

To meet this confirmation standard, the plan must also provide that the present value of the payments to be made to the creditor under the plan equals the amount of the allowed secured claim. This means that, if payments are to be made over time, the creditor must receive interest on the amount of the allowed secured claim so that the amount it ultimately receives is equivalent economically to what it would have received if the allowed secured claim had been immediately paid in cash.

If the debtor seeks to deal with a secured claim through the plan, there must first be an allowed secured claim. If the creditor does not file a claim, the debtor may have to file on the creditor's behalf. The Bankruptcy Rules provide that the debtor may do so at anytime between the first date set for the meeting of creditors and 120 days thereafter.

For this reason, it is generally a good idea to check the claims docket for the case shortly after the meeting of creditors. If a secured creditor whom the debtor proposes to pay in the plan has not filed a proof of claim, one should be filed on behalf of that creditor within the deadline in an amount consistent with the debtor's schedules and plan.

On the other hand, the debtor may sometimes not wish to provide for a secured claim in the plan because he or she is unable or unwilling to pay that creditor through the plan. For example, the debtor may owe a large mortgage to a relative who is not likely to foreclose, or the debtor may be current on an automobile loan and may wish to continue payments outside the plan to avoid the trustee's charges. Nothing in the Code requires that all secured claims be provided for in a chapter 13 plan.

Assuming that a secured claim is filed, it will be allowed in the amount requested unless an objection is raised. If an objection is raised, the claim must then be determined and allowed. As discussed earlier in this chapter, if such a determination is sought, the allowed secured claim cannot be greater than the value of the collateral. It may also be reduced to the extent that it is subject to defenses that the debtor may raise as objections to the claim. However, if the value of the collateral is greater than the amount claimed, the allowed secured claim can include interest earned, plus any reasonable fees, costs, and charges under the original agreement. In determining what fees are reasonable and thus may be allowed as part of the allowed secured claim, the bankruptcy court need not award as much as the contract or state law might allow.

Once the allowed secured claim has been determined, it is then necessary to determine what payments will equal the present value of that claim. To do this, it is also necessary to know the amount of the trustee's fees and expenses, if the claim is to be paid through the plan, and also the interest rate to be applied.

The former can easily be learned from the trustee, but the latter has been a matter of considerable dispute. Creditors have naturally argued for high interest rates, usually the contract rates, while debtors have attempted to secure lower rates, such as the legal rate of interest provided by state law. Although some courts have opted for each of the extremes, most have come down somewhere between them, often invoking the vague concept of the market rate of interest. The court often calculates this market rate by adding a small "risk factor" to the risk-free cost of money—that is, the rate for treasury bills or the prime rate. The same approach is used for secured IRS claims, despite the interest rate set forth in the Internal Revenue Code. In any case, if a creditor or trustee does not object to the interest to be paid, the plan may be confirmed, notwithstanding the fact that it does not meet all of the standards in the Code.

Once the interest and trustee commission figures are all known, it is possible to compute what payments, over what period of time, will be sufficient to pay the allowed secured claim plus the necessary interest and the trustee's fees. This can be done most easily by first applying the annual percentage rate to the allowed secured claim for the number of payments and the time period desired. After these payments are calculated, the trustee's percentage fee may simply be added to each payment.

Right to Cure Defaults on Long-Term Debts

There are certain claims that the debtor cannot pay within the time period of the proposed plan, which can never exceed five years, simply because they are large, long-term obligations that have many years of payments remaining before they will be fully satisfied. The Code allows the debtor to cure a default on such an obligation within a reasonable period of time without having to pay the entire debt balance within the time period of the plan. This procedure can be utilized to cure both prebankruptcy and postbankruptcy defaults. In addition, courts have generally ruled that land installment sales contracts, sometimes called *lease-purchase agreements*, are secured debts, and so they too should be subject to the cure provisions of the Code.

Cure of Mortgages after Acceleration or Foreclosure Judgment

Although a few courts originally held otherwise, it is now well established in most jurisdictions that defaults on long-term debts, such as mortgages, may be cured in chapter 13 even if there has already been an acceleration of the debt payments or a judgment that caused the entire balance to become due. A cure may also be effected even though the debtor has no personal liability on the underlying obligation due to its discharge in a prior bankruptcy, because the creditor continues to have a claim against the debtor's property.

Similarly, a debtor who took over payments on a mortgage when a property was transferred to him or her may cure despite the absence of personal liability on the original obligation. Some courts have allowed the period for the cure to extend beyond the last scheduled payment date, but others have held that the cure must be completed by the scheduled maturity date of the loan.

Finally, appellate courts have decided that there is no right to cure a default once a foreclosure sale has taken place, though there may be a 60-day extension of any right to redeem. However, if a foreclosure can be avoided as a fraudulent transfer, as discussed in Chapter 9, the right to cure may be reinstated.

Length of Time Permitted for Cure

The Code does not define what period of time is "reasonable" for the purpose of curing a default. The period necessarily depends to some extent on the facts and circumstances of each case. It is not safe to assume that the court will find a cure over the entire length of the plan to be reasonable, although in some cases that long a time period has been allowed. Many bankruptcy courts routinely permit three to five years to cure a mortgage default, if necessary.

Method of Maintaining Current Payments on Debts Being Cured

Most bankruptcy courts permit current payments on long-term obligations that are being cured to be paid outside the plan, directly to the mortgage holder. Because the payments on long-term obligations are often higher than on any others, it is a common practice to make them outside the plan to avoid the substantial cost of the trustee's percentage fees and expenses (usually 9 to 10 percent).

Amount Necessary to Effectuate Cure

Another question arising under the cure provisions is the extent to which creditors may collect attorney's fees and costs as part of the amount needed to cure. The answer usually turns on the precise language of the contract and on state law. The Code allows the collection of these charges only if the parties' agreement provides for it. In addition, many state statutes place significant limitations on fee arrangements or prohibit them entirely. These state laws are usually read into any contract to which they are applicable as implied terms.

Fees may be allowed in a cure situation only to the extent that they are reasonable and necessary. When a creditor's litigation is unsuccessful or unnecessary, it should not be rewarded by the assessment of attorney's fees against the debtor. Similarly, if the creditor does not provide adequate records to establish that its attorney's fees are fair and reasonable, the fees should be denied. The filing of a claim does not require an attorney, and thus no attorney's fees may be charged for that task.

Another important question is how interest is to be computed when a long-term obligation is cured in chapter 13. Unfortunately, the Supreme Court, in *Rake v. Wade*, recently rejected the holdings of most lower courts and held that a creditor may demand that interest be paid on arrears being cured through a chapter 13 plan. The Court reached this result by holding that the arrearages constitute a separate and distinct allowed secured claim.

The Court then held that interest on the arrears for the period preceding plan confirmation could be required with respect to an oversecured mortgage because the Code permits creditors to demand preconfirmation interest on any oversecured claim. For the period after confirmation, the Court found the secured creditor confirmation standards applicable to the "arrearage claim" and thus held that a creditor could demand present value interest on the arrears as a condition of plan confirmation.

The effect of a cure under chapter 13 is to nullify all consequences of the default. Thus, in the case of a long-term mortgage, the debtor would normally be returned to the original amortization schedule once the default has been cured. Unfortunately, holders of long-term mortgages do not always comply with this principle, and debtors may have to bring proceedings at the end of a chapter 13 plan to ensure that the cure is fully effectuated and not subverted by a mortgage holder's contrary bookkeeping practices.

The cure provisions, then, are particularly useful when the debtor is behind on a mortgage and the creditor refuses to allow the debtor to bring the payments up to date gradually. In essence, they provide a method of forcing the creditor to be reasonable by giving the debtor a right to cure over a reasonable time, at least when the creditor has adequate protection and cannot obtain relief from the automatic stay.

RENT-TO-OWN TRANSACTIONS IN BANKRUPTCY

So-called rent-to-own transactions, in which a consumer pays a weekly or monthly payment as "rent" for an appliance or furniture and eventually obtains ownership of it, have become common in many parts of the country, even though they are incredibly expensive and unfair to consumers. A comprehensive discussion of the myriad legal issues arising in rent-to-own transactions is beyond the scope of this guide. However, even though little bankruptcy precedent directly addresses the status of rent-to-own agreements in bankruptcy, bankruptcy court may be an excellent forum for consumers who seek a remedy for some of the worst abuses of the rent-to-own industry.

Most importantly, the automatic stay provides probably the fastest and surest way to prevent the continued harassment of delinquent debtors by rent-to-own companies. Because rent-to-own property in the debtor's possession becomes property of the estate when the debtor files for bankruptcy, the automatic stay immediately enjoins continued efforts by a rent-to-own creditor to collect delinquent payments or to recover the property. If a rent-to-own creditor continues to seek payment or repossession, it will be liable for damages. The full range of stay remedies, including punitive damages, may be appropriate, considering some of the industry's outrageous collection practices.

Numerous potential issues arise in addressing how rent-to-own contracts should be treated in bankruptcy. Most creditors argue that the contract is a lease agreement representing an executory contract and that the debtor's options are limited to assuming or rejecting the contract, as discussed in Chapter 11. The debtor should argue instead that the contract creates a secured debt, giving rise to the full panoply of remedies discussed in this chapter. In fact there is ample precedent for treating installment sales contracts for real property and leases with purchase options as security agreements. Most cases that have addressed the property interests created by rent-to-own contracts support the view that they should be treated as credit sales in bankruptcy cases. This treatment gives rise to such rights as the debtor's right to redeem, to modify the creditor's rights, or to cure any default and the right to limit the creditor's secured claim to the value of the collateral.

Whether the contract is treated as executory, as a security agreement, or otherwise, the debtor should not forego the opportunity to litigate the amount of the rent-to-own company's proof of claim, if any, and to lodge against the company any claims or counterclaims that the debtor may possess. Such claims may include usury, unfair trade practices, debt collection claims, and truth-in-lending or consumer leasing claims. The bankruptcy court is often the most sympathetic forum for debtors who seek to address rent-to-own abuses.

Chapter 11

ISSUES ARISING IN CHAPTER 13 CASES

No part of the Bankruptcy Code caused more controversy or confusion in its early days than the greatly revised chapter 13. In drafting that chapter, Congress made an explicit effort to encourage greater use of its provisions, which had been rarely employed in most parts of the country under the prior act. Even where it had been used, practices under the old Chapter XIII varied widely among judicial districts, with substantial deviations from the strict terms of the Act.

The current chapter 13 contains many provisions that make it more attractive to debtors, for the first time providing consumers with the flexibility to rearrange their affairs in plans that parallel the types of plans that corporations have long been able to devise. Chapter 13 plans must meet only a few basic requirements in order to provide some protections to creditors. Beyond these requirements, the debtor has enormous freedom to create a plan that best suits his or her circumstances.

Unfortunately, because chapter 13 was so new and so different, creditors and some judges initially resisted its liberality. Because little relevant case law existed under the old Act and because the legislative history was relatively scant, widely divergent opinions arose concerning the use of chapter 13. Some judges tried to apply concepts developed under prior law and failed to take adequately into account the congressional intent to liberalize the law. Of course, many other decisions applied the statute more faithfully, but the result was a tremendous disparity in the extent to which chapter 13 was viable for low-income debtors in different judicial districts.

As experience under chapter 13 grew and cases reached the appellate courts, most of these problems disappeared. Further clarification came from Congress in 1984, when new amendments addressed some of the most litigated issues. Hence, there is now a large body of law to turn to in interpreting chapter 13, and both knowledge and use of its liberal provisions have increased considerably.

ELIGIBILITY FOR CHAPTER 13

A threshold issue that has occasionally been troublesome and that has been aggravated by inflation concerns eligibility to file under chapter 13. The Code provides that, to be a chapter 13 debtor, the debtor must:

1. Be an individual with regular income or an individual with regular income and that individual's spouse
2. Owe noncontingent, liquidated, unsecured debts of less than $100,000 on the date of filing
3. Owe noncontingent, liquidated, secured debts of less than $350,000 on that date

Regular Income

In consumer cases, issues may arise concerning any of these requirements, which could preclude the filing of a chapter 13 case. Probably the most common issue for low-income debtors is whether the debtor is an "individual with regular income." The Code defines this phrase as an "individual whose income is sufficiently stable and regular to enable such individual to make payments under a plan under chapter 13." Some courts had held that the previous Chapter XIII was limited to wage earners, but the congressional reports make clear that the intent of the new statute is to expand eligibility to recipients of public benefits, such as welfare and Social Security, small-business proprietors, and those supported by other income, such as alimony or pensions.

The Code is somewhat unclear on whether a spouse who is not separated or divorced is eligible to file alone if only the nonfiling spouse brings income into the family. A nonworking spouse who receives a regular amount of income for expenses from the income-earning spouse could arguably file alone. Indeed, a schedule of regular payments from the nonfiling spouse to the trustee could even be ordered by the court as part of the plan. Similarly, payments from other friends or relatives can sometimes satisfy the regular income requirement as long as there is a reasonable assurance that the payments will continue.

Regardless of its source, the amount of the debtor's income must be sufficient to allow the debtor to make payments under a plan. This presumably means that it must be sufficient for the plan proposed by the debtor as long as that plan complies with the Code.

The case law defining an individual with regular income has so far been relatively scarce. Some creditors have argued that a husband and wife who operate a business should be considered partners and thus not be eligible for chapter 13. The resolution of that challenge turned on a finding that the requisites for establishing a partnership under state law had not been met. Even if an individual is a member of a partnership or a husband and wife are considered partners, the individuals who are partners should not be precluded from filing under chapter 13. Although a partnership cannot file a chapter 13 case, an individual who happens to be a partner is clearly eligible, provided that the other eligibility requirements are met.

More often, courts are concerned about whether asserted regular income really exists. One debtor who provided the court with no factual evidence that he was earning enough regular income as a cabinetmaker to meet the payments proposed was found ineligible to file a chapter 13 case. Similarly, when a debtor with no past income merely anticipates future income, the case may be dismissed or converted to chapter 7 unless the debtor provides clear evidence that the income will be forthcoming. Even when the debtor's income appears on paper to be sufficient, the court may deem evidence of inability to make similar payments under a previous plan to cast doubt on the debtor's stated budget. When the debtor's schedules do not show sufficient income to make the necessary level of payments, it is likely that the court will find the debtor to be ineligible for chapter 13. On the other hand, the income need not be absolutely assured; a farmer whose income is dependent on good weather and fair prices for crops should not be denied access to chapter 13 merely because future income is somewhat speculative.

In view of these cases, the debtor would be wise to begin regularly setting aside an amount equal to the plan payments as soon as he or she files the bankruptcy petition, if not earlier. Under the Code, plan payments to the trustee must begin within 30 days after filing the plan, which is usually before the meeting of creditors and confirmation of the plan, unless the court orders otherwise. If such payments are regularly made or set aside, there can be little doubt as to the debtor's ability to perform under the plan. Conversely, the failure to make preconfirmation payments often leads to dismissal of the case unless the debtor has a valid explanation or can modify the plan to abate or lower the payments.

Debt Limitations

Other issues may arise concerning the dollar-amount limitations on claims against debtors who file chapter 13 cases—limitations designed to exclude large businesses from evading the requirements of chapter 11. For these limits to be met, it may be critical whether an undersecured debt is considered a secured or an unsecured debt. Depending on the facts of a particular case, the debtor may wish to argue that the entire amount of a secured debt should be considered against the $350,000 limit on secured debts or that only the amount of the allowed secured claim (equal to the value of the collateral) should be measured against that limit, with the unsecured portion of the claim secured against the $100,000 limit on unsecured debts.

One early case that considered this question illustrates the problem. It involved debtors who owed secured creditors more than $350,000 but whose property securing that debt was worth less than $350,000. The creditor asserted that the debtors were ineligible for chapter 13 because their secured debts were too high. It argued that claims are not filed or determined in a case until after the initial stages when the debtor's eligibility is decided and that the value of the collateral could therefore not be looked to because the court would have to rely on the debtor's valuation. (The creditor cited no reason why that valuation could not be challenged.)

The court rejected these arguments and held that the term *secured debts* referred to debts that are allowed secured claims, as discussed in Chapter 10, and are limited to the value of the collateral for those claims. The court found that, because a debtor could almost always create a security interest, practically at will, it would undermine the intent of the congressional limitations to allow the debtor to convert unsecured claims to secured claims in order to qualify for chapter 13. This case was later followed by all of the Courts of Appeals that have decided the issue to date.

Although the holding of those courts may often be helpful to consumer debtors with similar situations, at least as many debtors have the opposite problem, in view of the lower limit on unsecured debts for chapter 13 eligibility. These debtors will want to argue that Congress meant that "secured debts" could just as easily mean the total liability on a claim, whether secured or unsecured, before that claim is divided into its secured and unsecured parts. This result, too, has support in some court decisions.

Courts have also disagreed regarding whether a debt that is secured by property of someone other than the debtor should be considered to be a secured debt for eligibility purposes. Some courts have decided that such debts should be considered to be secured debts, as contemplated by that section, and others have decided that they should be considered unsecured debts because they are not secured by the debtor's property.

Further problems may arise in determining whether debts are liquidated or noncontingent and therefore count toward the debt limitations. The Code defines neither term, and thus state laws may come into play. All debtors who file chapter 13 cases have a common interest—to classify the maximum number of debts as nonliquidated or contingent.

The clearest cases regarding whether a debt is liquidated are at the extremes. A note as to which a court judgment has been entered and to which the debtor has no disputes or defenses is perhaps the paradigm of a liquidated debt. A claim for personal injuries and pain and suffering that has not been decided by a court is clearly unliquidated. Between the extremes, however, there is more doubt. Many of the legal definitions of *liquidated* suggest that a debt is not liquidated when the amount owed is neither agreed on nor fixed by operation of law. Even if the defenses go to only a part of the amount due, these definitions indicate that the debt as a whole should be considered unliquidated because its precise amount is not settled.

The question of contingency is somewhat more complicated. Generally, a contingent debt is one that depends on some future event that may never occur. An example is an agreement to pay a debt if, and only if, another person does not do so. In many states, cosigners on debts are in this position. The exact status of a debt must always be determined by both the applicable law and the facts. A dispute may arise regarding whether the condition on which the debt is contingent has occurred. This may in turn depend on whether valid reasons justified nonpayment by a principal debtor. Alternatively, the court may find that, due to known facts, the outcome of another proceeding need not be awaited for it to decide that the condition has occurred. It may also find that, as a matter of state law, the creditors need not pursue other assets or co-obligors before looking to the debtor for payment.

It is essential for the debtor to avoid eligibility issues when possible. This may sometimes be accomplished simply by filing separate cases for a husband and wife rather than filing a joint petition. Because the debt limitation amounts would then apply separately to the debts of each—rather than to their combined debts, as in a joint case—the total amount of combined debt permitted can be increased to the extent that the debts owed are not joint obligations. If a large injury judgment is imminent, a chapter 13 petition may be filed before it is entered, even if a bankruptcy is not then contemplated, to preserve the option if it later becomes necessary. Debtors should be wary of agreeing to settlements or judgments that could push their liquidated debt totals near the limit. Because the key date is the date that the petition is filed, other actions, such as settlements of disputed amounts, may still be taken after the bankruptcy case is filed without affecting the debtor's eligibility for chapter 13.

A debtor with unsecured debts above the limit must occasionally file a chapter 7 case to deal with some debts, in the hopes that the chapter 7 case will be sufficient. If it is not, the debtor may then be eligible to file a chapter 13 case because the unsecured debts have been discharged in the prior chapter 7 case. However, if a chapter 13 case closely follows a chapter 7 case in such circumstances, a court may perceive the two filings as a subterfuge to avoid the chapter 13 dollar limitations.

PAYMENTS TO UNSECURED CREDITORS

No single question under the Code stirred more debate in its early years than the issue of how much the debtor must pay unsecured creditors in a chapter 13 plan. Hundreds of courts debated the question and came to a fairly consistent, if vague, result. That result has now been made a part of the Code, and the issue will probably recede, except in occasional cases.

The Best Interests of Creditors Test

One standard regarding how much unsecured creditors should receive in a chapter 13 case is known as the best interests of creditors test. The Code provides that, if all other requirements are met, the court "*shall* confirm a plan if . . . the value, as of the effective date of the plan, of property to be paid under the plan on account of each allowed unsecured claim is not less than the amount that would be paid on the claim [in a chapter 7 case]." This test was inserted into the Code to ensure that general unsecured creditors would not be harmed by a debtor's choice of chapter 13 over chapter 7. By giving such creditors payments with a present value equivalent to the value of the debtor's nonexempt property—that is, including interest to compensate for delay in their receipt—the Code gives them as much as they would have received in a chapter 7 liquidation.

Because the court must compare the chapter 13 distributions to the outcome of a chapter 7 case, the appropriate date for valuing the nonexempt property that would be distributed to creditors is the filing date of the chapter 13 petition because the filing date is the date of valuation in a chapter 7 case. Property acquired after the petition is filed should not be included in the determination of what creditors would receive for purposes of the best interests of creditors test.

Moreover, the court must take into account the costs of sale that would be incurred by a chapter 7 trustee, which could include a capital gains tax on the increase in value of the property since the debtor acquired it. Although questions might arise regarding which claims to consider in determining whether this test is met, there is no doubt that, unless the proposed plan meets the standard, a creditor may challenge it, and the court need not confirm it.

The Good Faith Test

Many courts were dissatisfied that the best interests of creditors test looked only to the debtor's assets and not to income. Faced with plans proposing little or no payment to unsecured creditors from debtors who clearly had sufficient income to make substantial payments, they devised a wide variety of standards for confirming plans, under the general standard of the Code that the plan be proposed in good faith. These standards often required "substantial" or "meaningful" payments to creditors holding unsecured claims; in one court, no plan proposing less than 70 percent payment of such claims was approved.

At the other end of the spectrum, many courts refused to view the good faith test as having any relevance to the amount paid to unsecured creditors. These courts and most commentators looked to the more specific language of chapter 13 as being dispositive of what unsecured creditors must be paid. They pointed out that, although some references in the legislative history of the Code showed congressional intent to encourage or enable debtors to make substantial payments to unsecured creditors, there was no indication whatsoever that this was required. Those courts did not permit the good faith test to preclude taking advantage of the plain provisions of a statute. Rather, they held that good faith means honesty in fact and the absence of extraordinary circumstances, such as fraud, malfeasance, or concealment of assets.

In addition, some of the courts that totally rejected use of the good faith test as a quantitative measure of payments of unsecured claims looked to the practical consequences. Perhaps most importantly for low-income debtors, requiring meaningful or substantial payments threatened to become a barrier to the other benefits of chapter 13, such as the right to cure defaults or the right to cramdown regarding secured creditors, which is discussed in Chapter 10. Low-income debtors could have been found, generally, to be too poor to be filing in good faith.

In view of these conditions, some courts found that meaningful payments to unsecured creditors should not be required of debtors who are unable to make them, at least if the chapter 13 plan serves any special rehabilitative purpose. In a similar vein, other courts found that when no payments are made to any creditors, the case is merely a disguised liquidation and there is no reason to allow it to proceed under chapter 13. Some of these courts dismissed or converted such cases on jurisdictional grounds. Most of these courts would presumably agree that when the debtor makes some legitimate use of chapter 13, such as saving a home from foreclosure or providing for other payments to secured creditors, a chapter 13 case is permissible even when the debtor makes no payments to unsecured creditors.

One thing nearly all courts have agreed on is that a creditor that holds an unsecured claim that is not dischargeable in chapter 7 may not argue that, because its claim will be discharged in chapter 13, it will receive less than it would receive in a chapter 7 liquidation. The courts have pointed to the plain language of the Code, which considers the amount that the creditor "would be paid" in the chapter 7 case, not whether the creditor would still have the right to pursue a nondischargeable claim after the case.

Finally, a substantial number of courts have held that whether unsecured creditors receive meaningful payments is a component of the good faith test but that the court must consider all of the facts and circumstances of each case to determine whether chapter 13 has been abused. The circumstances that various courts have listed as relevant include the following:

1. Whether the percentage paid to unsecured creditors is "meaningful"
2. The debtor's ability to pay
3. Whether the debtor is making his or her best effort
4. Whether the debtor is making an "honest and sincere effort"
5. The debtor's present and potential earnings
6. Whether the payments meet a rule-of-thumb requirement of 10 percent of take-home pay
7. The length of the proposed plan
8. Whether the debtor has been in bankruptcy before, especially if the six-year bar to a chapter 7 case is applicable
9. Whether the debtor is attempting to obtain a discharge of debts that are not dischargeable under chapter 7
10. The amount and type of debt involved
11. The extent to which secured claims are involved
12. The relation of attorney's fees and administrative costs to the amount paid to unsecured creditors
13. Whether the debtor has created preferences or preferred classes of creditors
14. The availability of property that could be liquidated
15. Whether the case is a disguised chapter 7 case

Consideration of all the circumstances, which apparently appealed to many bankruptcy courts as a compromise between the extreme positions on this question, meant different things to different judges. A decision to weigh all of the circumstances did not yield a clear and discernible standard by which the debtor could predict whether a plan would be approved or whether a chapter 13 case would be worthwhile. Moreover, it burdened the courts with innumerable subjective questions that, to be dealt with fairly, would take a great deal of time and expense to decide.

Ultimately, most Courts of Appeals addressed the good faith issue. The appellate courts settled on a fairly liberal version of the all-of-the-circumstances compromise, holding that the percentage of payment on unsecured claims is one factor to examine, but it is never the only factor. All of these decisions left open the possibility of a plan that provides zero or nominal payments to unsecured creditors in cases in which they are necessary and appropriate to achieve the debtor's goals.

The Ability-to-Pay Test

Some of the issues that so troubled the courts that interpreted the good faith test were resolved by the 1984 amendments to the Bankruptcy Code. In a new subsection, courts were given express instructions regarding whether and how to take into account the debtor's income. At the same time, by adding a new subsection separate and apart from the good faith standard, Congress made clear its intent that the good faith test revert to its more traditional meaning, which did not concern the size of the debtor's payments.

The new subsection provides that if, and only if, an unsecured creditor or the chapter 13 trustee objects to confirmation of the plan, the court must determine whether the plan either (1) pays the objecting creditor in full or (2) commits to the plan all of the debtor's "disposable income" for the next three years. The Code defines *disposable income* as income that is not reasonably necessary for the maintenance or support of the debtor or the debtor's dependents. If a debtor is engaged in business, the term also excludes funds necessary for the continuation, preservation, and operation of the business.

This new provision makes clear that a debtor need not have enough income to make substantial payments or, indeed, any payments to unsecured creditors. If a debtor has no disposable income, then a plan may be confirmed without payments to unsecured creditors if the debtor meets other requirements of chapter 13. The legislative history expressly states that this so-called zero-payment plan is permissible in certain circumstances.

The procedure for objections under the new provisions is the same as that for other objections to confirmation. It requires that objections be filed with the court and mailed to the debtor, the debtor's attorney, and the trustee. They must be filed within a time set by the court. Objections are normally based on the debtor's schedules of current income and expenditures, so it behooves the debtor to complete those portions of the forms carefully, with both the ability-to-pay test and feasibility test, which is discussed below, in mind. Because only the trustee or the holder of an allowed unsecured claim may file an objection, a creditor who has not filed a claim does not have the right to object to confirmation.

Once an objection is filed, the debtor may defeat the objection by proving one of two things. First, the debtor may show that an objecting creditor will be paid in full. Obviously, this will be true if all unsecured claims are paid in full. It may also be true if the objecting claimant can be classified separately as discussed below, and paid in full, even if other creditors will not receive full payment. It may occasionally be worthwhile for the debtor to amend the plan to add such classification to satisfy the troublesome creditor, especially if the debtor anticipates difficulty in meeting the alternative disposable income standard. However, if the trustee objects to confirmation, the full-payment test will likely require that all filed unsecured claims be paid in full.

Second, if an objection under the ability-to-pay test is filed and the full payment standard cannot be met, a plan of at least three years' duration is probably mandatory. The court must then determine whether the debtor has committed to the plan all of his or her "projected disposable income."

Because changes in income or expenses can rarely be foreseen, the court normally looks to the debtor's current financial situation to decide this issue. Although the legislative history contains little indication concerning what expenses may be considered to be reasonably necessary and therefore properly deductible from the debtor's income, the court's inquiry under the ability-to-pay test is usually limited to determining whether debtors have included expenses for luxuries in their budgets, rather than whether they conform to some predetermined level of expenses. Courts cannot reasonably or fairly make decisions beyond that regarding what expenses are more necessary or truly necessary. Different debtors will have widely varying expenses for housing and transportation, depending on their age, mobility, and place of residence, yet all but luxury-style residences should be considered necessary. Similarly, some debtors will feel that parochial school or other items are absolutely required. The court can realistically go no further than deciding whether clearly unnecessary luxuries are included in the budget, and they should not attempt to do so. If the debtor's total expenses are average or less than average, it is doubtful that the court should even look at the expenses individually because such debtors could only afford luxuries by making sacrifices in some other part of their budgets.

The court decisions under the new provisions have generally followed these principles. It has been held that the debtor need not commit to the plan every last dollar that is not necessary for expenses and may preserve a small cushion ($117 per month in one case) to guard against life's unexpected events. Nor should the debtor be expected to commit income that may never be received because its receipt is uncertain or speculative. On the other hand, courts have denied confirmation to debtors who paid $1,000 per month in private-school tuitions, contributed $140 per month to their church, made monthly investments in stocks and retirement accounts, and made payments on a $17,000 sports car.

Finally, the ability-to-pay provisions also provide for unanticipated changes in the debtor's income or expenses. The Code was also amended to permit a debtor, unsecured creditor, or trustee to seek modification of the plan, raising or lowering payments, if the debtor's circumstances change substantially. Thus, when the debtor's financial condition has improved substantially and unexpectedly after confirmation, an unsecured creditor can move for a modification that increases the debtor's payments. As a practical matter, however, this section is used primarily by debtors who seek to lower payments because of lower income or higher expenses. The trustee and the creditors usually have no knowledge of changes in the debtor's situation.

A few courts have tried to plan for possible increases in the debtor's incomes by requiring that payments increase by the same percentage as the income or by some percentage of any additional income that the debtor receives. These court decisions are misguided for several reasons. First, the legislative history gives no indication that such automatic increases were contemplated; the mechanism discussed in the proposal that led to the 1984 amendments was the motion to modify the plan. Second, such automatic increases would create monitoring and verification problems, making it difficult for the court or the trustee to know when or if the debtor had completed payments under the plan. Finally, an automatic increase provision could not take into account inflation or other expenses that could decrease the debtor's real disposable income. A 3 percent salary increase in a period when the cost of living increases by 6 percent is a decrease in real income that leaves the debtor less able to afford plan payments. It is for these reasons that the only proper method for increasing plan payments is a case-by-case approach through motions to modify chapter 13 plans.

The ability-to-pay test should lay to rest problems that had made chapter 13 virtually unavailable to low-income debtors in some districts. It should now be clear that, if the other specific requirements of chapter 13 are met, no debtor is too poor to file a chapter 13 case.

Continued Viability of the Good Faith Test

Although use of the good faith test to challenge the amount of a debtor's payment to unsecured creditors should be put to rest by the ability-to-pay test, creditors will undoubtedly continue to invoke that test to challenge other perceived debtor abuses. Some courts have read the new ability-to-pay test as simply eliminating certain issues—those going to whether minimal payments to unsecured creditors evidence bad faith—from the all-of-the-circumstances examination of good faith. However, even when courts continue to evaluate all of the circumstances, the inquiry into good faith should be limited to such issues as the debtor's honesty in completing the schedules and the debtor's intention to effectuate the proposed chapter 13 plan. Nonetheless, some courts will continue to impose limitations that are based on subjective judgments about the appropriate purposes for which a debtor may use chapter 13.

Payments to Unsecured Priority Creditors

The debtor must normally pay one group of unsecured claims in full through the chapter 13 plan. The Code requires that the plan provide for payment in full of all claims entitled to priority under the Code, unless the claim holder agrees otherwise.

The most common types of priority claims in chapter 13 cases are tax claims and claims for administrative expenses, such as the debtor's attorney's fees or the trustee's fees. Debtors who have been in business may also owe priority debts for wages or consumer deposits. Although attorney's fees and trustee's fees are to be expected in most chapter 13 cases, the requirement that other priority claims be paid in full may be difficult for some debtors to meet.

It should be noted, however, that the Code does not require that priority creditors receive the present value of their claims—that is, the claims plus interest—over the course of the plan, as does the best-interests-of-creditors test. Nor does it require that priority claims be paid before other claims. A debtor may sometimes want to provide for payment of large priority claims only after the secured claims are paid in full. If the debtor is then unable to complete the plan for some reason, there is a better chance that the secured claims will have been satisfactorily dealt with by the time the plan fails. In this case, the debtor may seek a hardship discharge, as discussed in Chapter 3, or may choose to convert the case to chapter 7. If the debtor selects either of these alternatives, priority claims need not be paid in the bankruptcy case, although some priority taxes may not be discharged.

The debtor should generally provide for payment of priority claims before general unsecured claims are paid, however. Then, if the plan fails before it can be completed, there will be a greater chance that priority claims have been paid in full or almost paid in full, which could keep open the option of modifying the plan because any modified plan must also provide for full payment of priority claims. Alternatively, if the debtor seeks a hardship discharge or converts to chapter 7, taxes that would not have been discharged will no longer be owed if they have already been paid in the chapter 13 plan.

Clearly, a priority creditor need not be paid if it fails to file a claim. Occasionally, taxing authorities will fail to file claims for priority income or other taxes; in such cases, provided that the taxes were properly scheduled and the taxing authority had notice of the case, the taxes are discharged when the plan is completed, just as any other unsecured claim. A similar result occurs when a taxing authority fails to file a claim for the full amount that it later claims is owed. Generally, if the omitted amounts derive from a different year or a different transaction, the courts will not allow them to be added to the taxing authority's proof of claim by amendment after the claims deadline has passed.

CLASSIFICATION OF CLAIMS

One of the powers that chapter 13 gives debtors is the right to designate classes of claims. In essence, this is the right to treat some claims better than others in the chapter 13 plan. This right is subject to an important limitation, however. The plan may not "discriminate unfairly" against any class of claims. Generally, this means that if certain claims are placed in a separate class for preferred treatment, some distinguishing characteristic of those claims must justify that preferred treatment, making it "fair." Otherwise, one of the cardinal principles of bankruptcy, equality among creditors, would be undermined.

Unfortunately, chapter 13 gives little indication of what should be considered to be fair. Because it allows classes of unsecured claims, it does make clear that all unsecured claims need not be in the same class. The Code also refers to a provision in chapter 11 that provides for classification of claims in chapter 11 cases. That section, in turn, provides a little more guidance. A claim may be placed in a class only if it is "substantially similar" to other claims in the class, and a separate class of small unsecured claims may be created for administrative convenience.

Although helpful, none of these guidelines fully prepared bankruptcy courts for all of the types of classifications that consumers would propose in chapter 13 cases. Some classifications have posed few problems; it is clear that secured claimants and priority claimants have greater rights in bankruptcy than unsecured claimants. Separate classifications of such claims merely carry forward the policies evident in the Code.

Claims with Cosigners

The most commonly proposed classification that the courts have confronted has been that providing for favored treatment (usually 100 percent payment) to creditors who have obtained cosigners on their claims. Because in consumer cases these cosigners are almost always the debtors' close friends or relatives, it is not surprising that debtors wanted to place a higher priority on payment of these debts to avoid the bad feelings or embarrassment that could be engendered if the creditor sought payment from their cosigners. Debtors in such cases argued that, for them, there was a substantial difference between these and other unsecured claims.

Although the courts had not been particularly sympathetic to these arguments, Congress apparently did agree with them. The 1984 amendments to the Code specifically permit separate classification of claims with cosigners. The Senate report on the bill recognized that practical differences exist between cosigned claims and other claims and that these differences cause debtors to pay creditors voluntarily outside the plan if classification is not permitted, thereby jeopardizing their ability to make plan payments. These practical differences were found to justify separate classification. Because some courts have held that creditors may proceed against cosigners in chapter 13 unless the plan proposes to pay the claim in full, including interest, separate classification of such claims can also presumably be used to pay interest on them when no other creditors receive interest under the plan.

Other Classifications

Debtors in early chapter 13 cases have also proposed a number of other types of classifications. Several have classified separately debts that would likely be nondischargeable in a chapter 7 case or in both chapters 7 and 13. Although these claims are not given priority in liquidation, such classifications have been allowed.

For example, plans proposing favored treatment of child support arrearages were approved based on the nondischargeability of such debts and the different enforcement mechanisms available, such as contempt of court. Courts have found that the strong public policy in favor of obtaining funds for child support claims, including those assigned to government bodies, dictated that they could be classified separately and paid more than other unsecured claims.

Similarly, separate classification of student loan debts has been allowed. Many of the same arguments applicable to child support debts apply to student loans. Like child support, the exception to the chapter 13 discharge for student loans is not based on some fault of the debtor and is not intended to punish the debtor. The student loan exception was passed as part of a budget act as a way of providing revenues to the government. Therefore, it is entirely in keeping with this purpose to allow separate classification and greater payments, which will increase the amount that the government collects on such debts. At least one court has also pointed out that separate classification has another reasonable basis: Absent payment of a student loan, a debtor is often ineligible to obtain other financial assistance or to return to school. For some courts, it has been sufficient that the debt is nondischargeable in chapter 13 and that the debtor therefore has a significant interest in paying as much of it as possible.

Other proposals have involved preferred treatment to creditors with a special relationship to the debtor or with claims of a special nature. Courts have approved more favored treatment for doctors, landlords, trade creditors necessary for continued operation of a business, attorneys, and even banks from whom future credit is needed. Such decisions have been justified by the fact that these debts were more likely to be paid in the nonbankruptcy world and that the plan or even the debtor's well-being might be endangered without payment to such creditors—for example, if the only doctor in town refused treatment because of a discharged debt. However, some courts might decide these cases differently.

Classification may also be used to designate which portion of a claim for federal taxes a debtor wishes to pay. The debtor generally wishes to classify tax claims to make sure that priority and secured tax claims are paid before unsecured tax claims. The Supreme Court has held that a chapter 11 debtor may so designate the payments under its plan, so a chapter 13 debtor should also be able to designate which tax years are provided for in the plan.

Payments Outside the Plan

Another type of provision that may be a classification is the designation of certain claims to be paid outside the plan. This means that the debtor will make payments on these claims directly to the creditor, instead of through the trustee. These provisions may offer a number of advantages. They usually save the debtor from paying the trustee's fees and costs, normally about 9 to 10 percent, on such debts. This factor may be important when the payments on one debt, such as a home mortgage, are particularly large. Payments outside the plan may also avoid the delays that are sometimes encountered when payments are made through the trustee. In any case, to the extent that the plan provides a creditor with a greater benefit from having payments made outside the plan, that designation does constitute a classification subject to the unfair discrimination test.

Practical Considerations

It is generally in the debtor's interest to classify some claims. Large secured claims may be paid outside the plan to avoid considerable trustee expenses. It is usually advantageous to pay other secured claims—when liens cannot be avoided—and claims that are not dischargeable in chapters 13 or 7 before general unsecured claims. Then, after the chapter 13 case, or if later circumstances force a conversion to chapter 7 or dismissal, the debtor may have paid off or at least reduced the claims that would be most troublesome in chapter 7 or outside of bankruptcy. In addition, the debtor usually wants to provide for early payment of priority claims at least before other unsecured claims. Once these are paid, if circumstances change, the debtor may choose to modify the plan to terminate earlier, assuming that the other mandatory requirements of chapter 13 have already been met. If priority claims have not yet been paid in full, such modification is not available; the options may be limited to a hardship discharge, as discussed in Chapter 3, conversion to chapter 7, or dismissal.

In view of the courts' general hostility to special treatment for certain unsecured debts, the debtor may not be able to provide for such treatment in the plan. However, other alternatives that accomplish a similar result may be available. The debtor may be able to propose a plan that gives a low percentage payment to all unsecured creditors and then make voluntary payments outside the plan to the preferred creditors. Because the plan would not provide for these payments, however, the debtor would not be bound to make them. Nor could the debtor formally promise the creditor that the payments would be made without running afoul of the reaffirmation provisions of the Code. (Reaffirmation is discussed later in Chapter 13.) A creditor who received continued voluntary payments is unlikely to deny services on the basis of a bankruptcy. Thus, as long as the payments are not provided for in the plan or binding on the debtor and the plan otherwise complies with chapter 13 (it might run afoul of the ability-to-pay test if an objection is raised on that basis), there should be no impediment to voluntarily giving preferred treatment to particular creditors outside the plan.

FEASIBILITY OF THE PLAN

The consumer debtor must also be aware of the feasibility standard. This provision of the Code requires that the court confirm a plan only if "the debtor will be able to make all payments under the plan and to comply with the plan." If the plan does not meet this standard, confirmation may be denied.

The property and budget figures listed on the schedules must show sufficient income or other financial resources to enable the debtor to make the proposed payments. If the debtor does not present the evidence necessary to convince the court that payments can be made, the plan may be found to be not feasible. Similarly, if the plan calls for a very large lump-sum payment at the end of the plan but offers no reasonable explanation of how the debtor will fund it, the plan will be found not to meet the feasibility test. The court may consider whether such necessaries as potential medical expenses and clothing have been provided for and whether there is sufficient "cushion" or "play" in the budget to cover unexpected expenses and inflation. Finally, it may simply find the debtor's expense estimates to be unreasonably low.

In view of such possible scrutiny, it is important to note on the schedules of income and expenditures such facts as coverage of all medical expenses by medical assistance, receipt of food stamps and emergency fuel grants, and any other noncash variations from a normal budget. Even with these, a "cushion" for unexpected expenses is virtually unheard of for low-income people. The best way of showing ability to make payments is to begin making the monthly payments before the confirmation hearing, as the Code now requires. If a debtor has demonstrated an ability to pay the monthly amounts provided in the plan, then few courts will deny him or her the opportunity to at least try to comply with the plan.

All of these considerations dictate careful construction of a reasonable budget that, if possible, allows a small cushion over and above the required plan payments. Because the court may also look to ability to pay if an objection is filed under that provision, however, this cushion should not be overly large, or the court may decide that the debtor could pay more into the plan. Ultimately, the debtor must steer a course between feasibility and ability to pay to create the optimum chance of confirmation. The feasibility ceiling on payments may not be far above the ability-to-pay floor.

OTHER PLAN PROVISIONS

Payment of Debtor's Income Directly to Trustee

The Code provides that, after confirmation, the court may order any entity from whom the debtor receives income to pay all or part of that income directly to the trustee. This order, called a *wage order*, is often sought by private attorneys who represent debtors (with the client's concurrence) to ensure that they receive their own fees, which are priority administrative expenses. The court may sometimes view these payments as a sign of the debtor's seriousness, and thus they may help obtain confirmation. In some courts, they are almost a requirement.

Most courts require that a separate application or motion be filed to obtain a wage order. Because it is a court order, the court can enforce compliance with the wage order by a recalcitrant employer, if necessary.

An issue that arose regarding this subsection is whether it overrides the provisions of the Social Security Act and of other federal laws that prohibit assignment or attachment of benefits. Congress has amended the Social Security Act to make clear that a payment order cannot be entered with respect to such benefits. However, other benefits, such as public assistance benefits, can be subject to such an order.

It is important to remember that the debtor may dismiss a chapter 13 case at any time as a matter of right if the case has not been converted from another chapter. Therefore, the debtor always retains the right to end the assignment of benefits or of any other income almost instantly.

Payment of Interest and Penalties

Postpetition interest, late fees, and other charges are not normally considered to be part of a creditor's claim. Carried over from case law under the prior Bankruptcy Act is the principle that such charges are in the nature of penalties that will not be enforced by the bankruptcy court, which is a court of equity. Not even priority claims, such as unsecured debts for taxes, are entitled to interest.

Under the Bankruptcy Code, a few exceptions to this general rule exist. As discussed earlier in this chapter, a debtor may have to pay interest to meet the best-interests-of-creditors test if the debtor has a substantial amount of nonexempt property. In addition, the Code may require payment of interest, possibly at the contract rate, to give secured creditors the present value of their allowed secured claims or to cure a default on a long-term debt.

Thus, in drafting a plan, the debtor must be aware of several possibilities regarding interest rates. Particular claims may be entitled to no interest (such as most unsecured claims), to interest at a rate necessary to meet a present-value test, or possibly to interest at the contract rate.

Length of Plan

Although it contains provisions that set maximum limits on the length of plans, chapter 13 contains no minimum time period. A plan may not exceed three years in length, unless the court specifically finds that there is good cause for a longer plan. In this case, the court may approve a plan of up to five years. Many courts require that a separate application and order be filed to obtain approval of a plan of more than three years in length, although it may be possible to incorporate the approval into the plan confirmation process.

Good cause for a longer plan may exist when the debtor needs the additional time to complete the payments necessary under the plan confirmation standards. It may also exist if four or five years is the minimum reasonable time in which a debtor can cure a default on a long-term debt, such as a mortgage. However, the debtor's desire to pay more to unsecured creditors may not be sufficient cause, especially because a debtor can continue to pay creditors voluntarily after the end of the plan, if the debtor chooses, without being bound to do so.

Plans that last less than three years may be confirmed as long as they comply with the other tests of chapter 13, including the ability-to-pay test. A plan may last only 18 months or it may consist of only one payment, liquidating property designated by the debtor, if unsecured creditors are paid in full or if no party objects.

Liquidation of Property in Chapter 13

Nonbankruptcy law occasionally prevents a debtor from selling property to realize exempt equity or to pay creditors. This may occur, for example, if only one of two cotenants by the entirety wishes to sell property that can be conveyed only by both spouses under state law. It may also occur when the debtor cannot complete a sale of real estate in time to prevent an imminent foreclosure.

In such cases, a chapter 13 plan that provides for the liquidation of property is often a solution. Filing the petition will stay all proceedings against the property, allowing time for a sale. The plan may then provide for the method of sale and the distribution of the proceeds, as well as the trustee's use of the power to sell entireties property in certain circumstances, if necessary.

It is clear that property may be liquidated in a chapter 13 plan. It is less clear whether the debtor must submit some income to the trustee in such cases, as required by other provisions of chapter 13. To be safe, the plan should provide for at least minimal payments in addition to the liquidation of property. Even when a mortgage will be cured and satisfied by the sale of property, the court may still require maintenance of current payments until the sale takes place. In any case, the sale of property through a chapter 13 plan is often a useful device, especially when an impending foreclosure threatens the loss of a large equity that was built up over years of ownership.

Use and Possession of Property of the Estate

One of the principal advantages of chapter 13 is that the debtor has the right to possession of all property of the estate, whether exempt or nonexempt. (Exempt property is discussed in Chapter 9.) The Code specifically provides that "the debtor shall remain in possession of all property of the estate." Although the Code speaks only of "remaining" in possession, it also applies to property that the estate acquires after commencement of the case. The entire thrust of chapter 13 is to transfer to the debtor virtually all of the powers and rights that the trustee would otherwise have with respect to property of the estate.

Debtors are free to use, sell, or lease property of the estate as they ordinarily did before the case. As mentioned above, however, parties with interests in such property have a right to adequate protection if the property is used. "On request," the court may prohibit or condition the use of a home or a car, for example, by requiring fire or collision insurance to protect a secured party against damage resulting from use. Such issues are normally decided at a hearing that might occur in conjunction with a hearing on a party's request for relief from the automatic stay; the party may be entitled to relief if adequate protection is not furnished. In any case, the issues are similar to those in a hearing on relief from the stay, which are discussed in Chapter 8.

EXECUTORY CONTRACTS AND UNEXPIRED LEASES

Another important feature of chapter 13 provides that the debtor has the power to assume or reject any executory contract or unexpired lease. This power may be exercised only by the trustee in a chapter 7 case, in which an executory contract or unexpired lease is automatically deemed to be rejected unless the trustee assumes it within 60 days after the case is commenced. A default or anticipated difficulties with respect to an executory contract or unexpired lease may be a prime reason for choosing chapter 13.

Executory Contracts

The Code does not define exactly the term *executory contract*, and whether a particular contract is executory is sometimes an important question. Generally speaking, an executory contract is one "on which performance remains due to some extent on both sides." Perhaps the classic example of an executory contract is the unexpired lease, which is specifically included. Another common example is an agreement to purchase real estate that has not yet gone to a closing or settlement. Other definitions have looked mainly to whether the debtor has other than an obligation to pay money for property and services already received before the bankruptcy. If so, the contract is executory.

There are several types of executory contracts into which consumer debtors routinely enter. They include real estate leases, purchase and sale agreements for real estate, options for the sale of real estate or other property, most automobile leases, layaway contracts, contingent fee contracts with attorneys, insurance contracts, personal services contracts, installment payment contracts for cemetery plots, book clubs, magazine subscriptions, health clubs, appliance or motor vehicle service contracts that are paid for in installments, and (if they are not considered credit sales) rent-to-own contracts. There is considerable dispute regarding whether an agreement not to compete with a former employer may be rejected as an executory contract.

Another type of contract that might present problems under this section is the land installment sales agreement, in which a debtor pays for property in installments, receiving a deed only after making most or all of the payments to the seller. A number of courts have held such arrangements to be executory contracts and have required debtors who wish to maintain them to cure defaults promptly. However, the court's ruling may depend on the nature of the agreement and the applicable state law. In many places, courts consider such transactions to be similar to taking a mortgage and to fall within the scope of secured claims, which are covered by other Code sections.

Assumption of an Executory Contract or Lease

The debtor often has much to gain from assuming an executory contract or unexpired lease. For example, it is usually advantageous to keep a lease in effect if moving would cause a hardship or if the lease has favorable terms. This may be particularly true in a rent-control jurisdiction or in public housing because the debtor's occupancy may not otherwise be terminable even at the end of the lease term. (The debtor may also be allowed to stay beyond the term of a lease due to the operation of the automatic stay during the course of the plan.)

The court's approval is required for the debtor to assume an executory contract or lease. The debtor must be willing to assume the burdens as well as the benefits of the contract; a debtor may not assume only its favorable aspects. To assume a lease or executory contract, the debtor must be willing and able to promptly cure any default or must provide adequate assurance that the default will be promptly cured. If there has been a default, the debtor must also compensate the other party for any actual pecuniary loss resulting from the default and must provide adequate assurance of future performance under the contract or lease. This assurance is not required if no default exists.

Finally, the nondebtor party to the contract or lease may argue that it cannot be assumed because it was validly terminated before the bankruptcy. This issue is particularly likely to arise when the debtor files bankruptcy on the eve of an eviction. Courts have not agreed on whether this argument is correct, but most have decided that, if it was possible for the debtor to maintain the tenancy by a payment of money on the date of the petition, the lease may be assumed.

Rejection of an Executory Contract or Lease

Problems are less likely to arise when the debtor chooses to reject an executory contract. This choice may be advantageous in a variety of situations because many of the types of executory contracts listed above are unfair and burdensome to consumers. It may also be possible to reject contracts that impose restrictions on the debtor, such as a covenant not to compete with a former employer or business in which the debtor was involved.

The rejection of an executory lease or contract gives the other contracting party a damage claim. The rejection is deemed to be a breach of the contract as of the time immediately before the filing of the petition. As with any claim, the debtor may object to the amount claimed. If the contract is secured, however, and will be provided for in the plan, the claim may have to be paid in full through the plan to secure confirmation.

Leases

The rejection of a lease is advantageous to a debtor mainly when the debtor plans to move or has vacated the premises before the end of the lease. The unpaid rent from the period before the bankruptcy usually becomes a general unsecured claim, which is often paid little or nothing during the case. The lessor's damages for lost future rents are limited to one year's rent or 15 percent of the rent due for the remaining term of the lease, whichever is less.

Payment for the period after the case is filed is treated somewhat differently. During the time between filing of the case and the debtor's rejection (and also after rejection, if the debtor stays on), the lessor is entitled to the reasonable rental value of the property, often called *use and occupancy payments*. The rent agreed on previously is generally taken to be the fair value, but the court may be persuaded to set it at a higher or lower level. If the rent provided for in the lease is greater than the fair value of the premises, it may thus be to the debtor's advantage to reject the lease (or simply not assume it) but remain in occupancy paying rent, if the lessor agrees or the court allows the automatic stay to remain in effect. In any case, once set, this claim will probably be considered an administrative expense, and thus, in a chapter 13 case, it must be paid in full if filed as a priority claim unless the case is dismissed, converted, or ended by a hardship discharge.

Procedure and Tactics

In a chapter 13 case, the debtor is not normally required to choose assumption or rejection until confirmation of the plan. However, the other party may force an earlier election by requesting the court to set a specified date by which the choice must be made. Although courts do not agree on this point, a lessor might seek relief from the stay before a decision on assumption or rejection, arguing that its interest in the property is not adequately protected. Few parties in consumer cases take advantage of either method of forcing an election.

It is normally to the debtor's advantage to wait until the last possible moment before choosing assumption or rejection, at least with leases. By waiting, the debtor keeps all options open and also postpones the time by which defaults must be cured as part of an assumption. The nondebtor party to the executory contract or lease is bound to honor the contract until it is rejected. During the period before assumption of a lease, the debtor can save money, making an immediate or prompt cure of the default easier. Alternatively, the savings can finance a move to another home.

As discussed earlier, the debtor-lessee also builds up a debt for use and occupancy, usually at the agreed rate of rental payments, during this interim period. Current payments of this rent debt after the bankruptcy is filed satisfy the debtor's only obligation to the lessor at this time and usually keep the lessor satisfied to let the proceedings run their course, especially if the lessor is told that back rent payments will eventually be paid under the chapter 13 plan. A lessor who is satisfied with this arrangement is unlikely to exercise the right to seek adequate protection or to force an early election of assumption or rejection.

After weighing the factors involved, the debtor usually should assume or reject the lease by the time of confirmation. If this is done, the consequences described above will transpire. If not, it is somewhat less clear what will happen. The automatic stay is presumably still in effect, but the debtor's failure to assume the lease when given the opportunity might be considered to be cause for relief from the stay.

CHAPTER 13 CASES AFTER PRIOR BANKRUPTCIES

One last important distinction between chapters 13 and 7 is the debtor's right to file a chapter 13 case within six years of a prior bankruptcy case. This right exists because the Code provisions that bar a chapter 7 discharge within six years after any chapter 7 case and many chapter 13 cases are clearly inapplicable in chapter 13, which has no comparable provision. Every court that has considered whether a chapter 13 case may be filed within six years after a prior bankruptcy has agreed that this is the only possible meaning of the statutory provisions.

Nevertheless, the hostility of some courts to what they perceive as abuse of chapter 13 has carried over to cases filed shortly after prior bankruptcies. Despite the statute's clear authorization, at least one court has denied confirmation of a plan that proposed full payment of debts that had not been discharged in an earlier chapter 7 case. The court found that the chapter 7 case and the subsequent chapter 13 case combined to effectuate a plan that resulted in no payment to unsecured creditors. By that court's definition, the plan failed the good faith test, which was discussed earlier in this chapter. However, most courts have found nothing improper in the filing of a chapter 13 case after an earlier chapter 7 case, at least when the chapter 13 case is not a disguised liquidation. At most, the earlier case should be considered in the determination of whether the later chapter 13 case is filed in good faith. The Supreme Court has held that there is no *per se* bar to such a filing and that any allegations of abuse must be proved in connection with an objection to confirmation under the good faith standard.

The filing of a chapter 13 case during a still-pending chapter 7 case, on the other hand, is presumably not permitted. But when the debtor has already received a discharge in a prior chapter 7 case, the fact that the case has not been administratively closed should not affect the debtor's right to file a subsequent chapter 13 case.

A number of advantages to the debtor spring from the right to file a chapter 13 case after a chapter 7 case. The most obvious is the possibility of refuge from creditors in bankruptcy court when a chapter 7 discharge is not available. Another possibility is that of successive chapter 13 cases, with one commenced, if necessary, immediately after discharge or dismissal of a previous case. This could be particularly useful if new and unanticipated debts—such as a tort judgment or medical bills—arise after the first chapter 13 case is underway, if debts not discharged in the first chapter 13 case continue to cause insurmountable problems for the debtor, or if problems develop in the first case. The first case may then be dismissed, as the debtor has a right to do, and a new chapter 13 or chapter 7 case could be commenced. However, if a request for relief from the automatic stay was filed in the first case, no new case may be started for 180 days after the voluntary dismissal of that case.

In considering these possible courses of action, the debtor's attorney should be aware that an unsympathetic court may find them to be not in good faith and may deny confirmation of the plan in the later chapter 13 case. (The good faith test could not be used to bar a chapter 7 discharge after a dismissed chapter 13 case, however.) If it appears that the debtor has willfully incurred many new debts with the specific intent of filing a new chapter 13 case to discharge them, a court may be quite receptive to creditor arguments that the successive petitions are part of a fraudulent scheme and that confirmation should be denied. In such cases, debtors may run a significant risk not only of dismissal, but also of an involuntary conversion to chapter 7.

CONFIRMATION OF THE PLAN

The chapter 13 plan confirmation order is binding on the debtor and all creditors. Once the appeal period has passed, it is a final determination regarding all issues that could have been raised in opposition to confirmation. No creditor may later challenge the plan by arguing that it did not comply with some provision of chapter 13, such as the good faith requirement. Even if a creditor has not been provided all that it is entitled to receive under the statute—such as present value interest for secured creditors—the creditor that does not assert those rights in time will lose them, just as parties in other proceedings may lose rights by default. Because noncompliance with any provision of chapter 13 or other applicable provisions of the Bankruptcy Code may be raised as an objection to confirmation under the Code, a creditor has few if any ways to challenge a confirmed plan other than under the very narrow grounds provided for seeking revocation of confirmation.

However, even a provision of a confirmed plan may not be sufficient to invalidate a creditor's properly filed claim. Some courts have held that the only method contemplated for challenging a filed proof of claim is the process of objecting to the claim. Other courts have allowed the provisions of a confirmed plan to govern over an inconsistent claim.

The binding effect of confirmation can be important in requiring creditors to abide by the terms of the plan, even after it has been concluded. If a plan provides that certain payments under the plan will cure a mortgage default, thereby bringing the debtor current on the mortgage, a mortgage lender may not add extra charges or prepetition claims to the ongoing mortgage payments during the plan or after it has been completed, as some attempt to do. The debtor must be treated as if the default had not occurred and he or she is current on payments. Debtors who have cured mortgages should be alert to any charges added to their payments that may be related to the earlier default. If such charges are imposed, the debtor may need to enforce the terms of the confirmation order, reopening the chapter 13 case if it has already been completed.

Chapter 12

OTHER TYPES OF LITIGATION IN THE BANKRUPTCY COURT

THE BANKRUPTCY COURT'S EXPANDED POWERS

Under the Bankruptcy Act of 1898, consumer bankruptcy cases were almost always handled routinely by all parties involved, more as matters of administrative processing than as proceedings involving legal issues to be litigated. Few contested disputes arose in these cases, and most of those that did arise were resolved not in the bankruptcy courts, but rather in state courts because of the limited jurisdiction of the bankruptcy referees under the Act. Virtually the only litigated matters that involved consumer debtors pertained to the discharge of particular debts, and even these cases were forced into bankruptcy courts only by relatively recent amendments to the Act.

All of this has changed radically under the Bankruptcy Code. Not only does the Code make the basic bankruptcy case a more attractive alternative for consumer debtors, but also other provisions in the Bankruptcy Reform Act have brought about a major expansion of many different kinds of consumer litigation in the bankruptcy courts.

Central to this change was the greatly expanded jurisdiction of the bankruptcy courts under the 1978 act. (A court's jurisdiction determines the types of cases that it can decide.) In the years since the Code was enacted, these courts have heard numerous and varied claims of types never before brought before them, including damage claims for injury to property or for unfair trade practices, consumer protection actions, actions to rescind contracts, and class actions under the Civil Rights Acts for enforcement of rights provided by federal welfare programs.

The bankruptcy courts were generally quick to recognize and exercise their increased jurisdiction in these cases, although a few resisted. Only when no significant relation existed between the lawsuit and the bankruptcy's purpose or success was jurisdiction found to be lacking.

New uncertainties arose in 1982 with the Supreme Court's decision in a case called *Northern Pipeline Construction Co. v. Marathon Pipe Line Co.*, which declared the entire bankruptcy jurisdictional scheme to be unconstitutional. For almost two years after that decision, the bankruptcy system operated under makeshift emergency jurisdictional rules that were themselves of questionable constitutionality. Finally, on July 10, 1984, a new jurisdictional structure was enacted as part of the Bankruptcy Amendments and Federal Judgeship Act of 1984. The new scheme creates a host of different issues, not the least of which is the constitutionality of some of its own provisions under the *Marathon* case. This chapter considers some of the issues, not discussed elsewhere in this guide, that are most likely to arise in bankruptcy litigation, including bankruptcy court litigation of issues under nonbankruptcy law.

ADVANTAGES OF THE BANKRUPTCY COURT AS A FORUM

Depending on the circumstances, the bankruptcy court may be a preferable forum for the litigation of many types of cases that involve consumer debtors. When the debtor is in bankruptcy and has a choice of forums, a number of factors should be considered. Even if a debtor is not in bankruptcy, the litigation advantages offered by the federal bankruptcy forum may be so great that they justify filing a bankruptcy petition even if it might not otherwise be needed.

In many districts, the bankruptcy judges and federal judges may be much more sympathetic to the consumer's case than judges in other local courts. Not only do bankruptcy judges regularly see the problems of debtors in trouble, but also they are generally more aware of the unfair creditor practices that often take place. Many bankruptcy judges are pleased to be presented with novel and creative cases that provide a change of pace from routine bankruptcy matters and a means for ruling on unfair practices.

In addition, most bankruptcy judges are far more knowledgeable in commercial law and often in consumer law than the average state judge because the cases they see usually involve such issues. For bankruptcy judges who are not yet familiar with consumer law, the concentration of a significant number of consumer cases in their courts will soon enhance their expertise. In addition, both bankruptcy and federal judges may be more disposed than state judges to consider carefully bona fide legal arguments on behalf of debtors because of lower case loads and greater availability of law clerk assistance.

Litigation in the bankruptcy case may provide a method of avoiding a forum in which the debtor has little chance of prevailing. In a rural area, it may be the only way to avoid a hostile state judge who hears every case filed in that particular locality. It may also provide a means to avoid courts that have become high-volume mills (usually for the benefit of the debtor's adversaries) for eviction, foreclosure, and collection cases.

BRINGING A MATTER BEFORE THE BANKRUPTCY FORUM

A dispute may be brought into the bankruptcy system in a number of ways. Depending on the nature of the dispute and the tactics of the parties, most litigation takes place through either lawsuits or motions within the bankruptcy case.

Removal

The most dramatic method of bringing a matter into bankruptcy court is through the removal (transfer) of an action already pending in another court to the bankruptcy court. Under the Bankruptcy Reform Act, nearly all actions pertaining to the debtor's finances may be removed to the district court in the jurisdiction in which the removed action is pending. The power to remove a case may be exercised by either the plaintiff or the defendant at any stage of the proceedings.

The removal of an action is often both a surprise and a problem for an opposing party who is unfamiliar with the bankruptcy system. It may also be an excellent way to permanently alter the course of state court litigation that has been going unfavorably. Once the action is removed, federal procedural law, which may be more favorable to the debtor's case, will govern. Substantive rights—such as the right to a jury trial—should be unaffected.

However, once a case has been removed, any of the other parties to the case can seek to have the case remanded (returned to the court in which it was previously being heard). Under the removal provisions, the court to which a claim or cause of action is removed may remand it "on any equitable grounds." The decision regarding whether to remand is generally based on such considerations as the convenience of the parties, federal court relations with state courts, judicial economy, and the likelihood of delay.

Litigation of Other Claims Commenced by the Debtor

Even if the time limit for removal has expired or the debtor has decided not to remove an action in state court (continuation of any action against the debtor is usually halted by the automatic stay), a dispute already pending elsewhere may still be brought into bankruptcy court. It is well established that the pendency of an action in one court does not bar a subsequent action in another for the same or similar relief.

The debtor may commence a lawsuit for damages or a lawsuit seeking other types of court orders to bring such a case before the bankruptcy forum. By becoming the plaintiff, the debtor is often able to frame the litigation in the most advantageous way. The debtor can bring virtually any type of action based on prepetition claims and on some postpetition claims into the federal bankruptcy system. Of course, the bankruptcy court can choose to abstain (not to decide the case), if it deems abstention to be appropriate.

Objections to Claims

Another way of raising issues in the bankruptcy forum is by objecting to claims filed by creditors. Many grounds for objections exist. In a chapter 13 case, for example, debtors may object to claims that they do not want to pay if the claims have not been filed on time, or if they do not otherwise conform to the rules. However, courts sometimes find that some other filing by the creditor serves as a timely informal proof of claim. The Code also permits objections to claims on various other grounds.

An objection to late claims is particularly valuable for handling creditors that claim priority in chapter 13; otherwise, priority claims must be paid in full. Because the IRS seems to have difficulty responding to bankruptcy filings, much of the litigation on the timeliness of claims involves tax claims in chapter 13. In some cases, courts have precluded the IRS from amending a timely claim for one tax year to include claims for other types of taxes or for the same taxes due in other years.

Further, the Code provides that no claim may be allowed to the extent that it is unenforceable against the debtor. This means that the debtor may assert, as objections to claims, any defenses or grounds why the debt should not be paid, for resolution by the bankruptcy court.

INVOLUNTARY BANKRUPTCY CASES

In addition to permitting debtors to file their own bankruptcy cases, the Bankruptcy Code sometimes permits creditors to force an *involuntary bankruptcy case* for an individual. Involuntary bankruptcy cases against consumers, in which creditors force the liquidation of a debtor's nonexempt assets, were extremely rare under the prior Bankruptcy Act. Although the requirements for commencing an involuntary bankruptcy have been relaxed somewhat under the Bankruptcy Code, such cases continue to be uncommon.

Creditors are not eager to file involuntary consumer cases for a number of reasons. First, the prerequisites are not easy to meet. A single creditor may file an involuntary case only if the debtor has fewer than 12 unsecured creditors and only if the creditor holds a noncontingent, undisputed, unsecured claim of at least $5,000. If the debtor has 12 or more creditors that hold claims that are totally or partially unsecured, three of them with noncontingent, undisputed claims aggregating at least $5,000 must join in the petition. That claims subject to bona fide dispute may not be included was made clear by specific language added in the 1984 amendments to the Bankruptcy Code. Moreover, an involuntary bankruptcy may never be filed against a farmer. It also appears that an involuntary petition cannot be filed against a husband and wife jointly.

Second, creditors rarely wish to force consumers into bankruptcy because of all the advantages that consumers can obtain under the Bankruptcy Code. Thus, trying to use bankruptcy to collect a claim could backfire on the creditor; at best, bankruptcy only allows the creditor to share the debtor's assets with all other creditors. In many states, these assets do not include property that is exempt under the federal bankruptcy exemptions, leaving less for creditors than would be available under state law execution procedures.

Third, bringing an involuntary bankruptcy can be very risky for the petitioning creditor. If the petition is not successful (the court may dismiss the case or decide not to hear it), the court is authorized to award to the debtor attorney's fees and costs and compensatory and punitive damages.

In those rare instances in which a consumer faces an involuntary bankruptcy petition, the first decision that must be made is whether to contest the case. Debtors may be better off going through with the bankruptcy and taking advantage of the numerous provisions available to them, particularly if a creditor has acted without much knowledge of the bankruptcy laws. In such cases, the debtor would not contest the petition but might wish to exercise the absolute right to convert the liquidation case to chapter 13.

A debtor who does contest the involuntary petition must file an answer to it. Otherwise, the petition may be granted automatically by default. The debtor may be able to raise a number of defenses. If the petition has been filed by only one creditor, the debtor may show that more than 12 creditors hold unsecured claims and that one petitioning creditor is therefore not sufficient. Most consumers have more than 12 creditors, counting utilities, friends, and so on. However, the court may allow other creditors to join in to make up the requisite number. If a creditor knows that more than 12 creditors exist but nonetheless files as a single petitioning creditor, the court may dismiss the petition as filed in bad faith.

The debtor might also challenge the petition on the grounds that some of the creditors hold contingent claims or claims subject to a bona fide dispute and that these claims disqualify them from filing as petitioners. Certain claims—such as unliquidated injury claims and claims against guarantors of notes on which there has been no default—are rather clearly contingent because they depend on the occurrence of future events.

The debtor may also contest the basic allegation of the petition, which the creditors have the burden of proving: that the debtor is generally not paying debts as they come due. This is called the *equity test* of insolvency. Its meaning is not entirely clear because it is a new concept in American bankruptcy law. It has generally been the rule that, even if a debtor is insolvent under a balance-sheet test (having liabilities greater than assets), the debtor may still be found to be paying debts as they come due. Moreover, the failure to pay one or only a small percentage of creditors is not considered to be a "general" failure to pay debts as they come due. However, when only a single creditor is not being paid, involuntary bankruptcy may be granted under one of the following circumstances:

1. The creditor is the debtor's only creditor.
2. The creditor is a significant creditor and special circumstances—such as fraudulent conduct—exist.
3. The debtor admits inability to pay other creditors.

Court decisions under the Code have tended to adopt these tests. In determining whether debts are being paid as they come due, the debtor's defenses against the claims can be very important. If the debtor succeeds in these defenses, the debt has not come due and need not have been paid. Finally, courts have held that making partial payments to all creditors is not paying those debts as they come due. However, the result might be different if the creditors agreed to the partial payments because then only these partial payments would be due.

Of course, in defending against an involuntary bankruptcy, the debtor's attorney may aggressively use the weapons that the Code provides. Through counterclaims, debtors may quickly let petitioning creditors know that they will seek attorney's fees and damages. These damages may presumably include compensation for the anxiety and the loss of reputation or credit standing that the debtor will probably suffer as a result of the petition. Consumers should then be able to inquire into such issues as a petitioning creditor's bad faith in filing and perhaps its assets, which are relevant to awards of punitive damages. Because involuntary cases against consumers are almost never filed, the court may be sympathetic to a claim for punitive damages when the drastic remedy of involuntary bankruptcy is wrongfully invoked. If damages are sought and awarded in these cases, involuntary consumer bankruptcies will continue to be rare.

DISMISSAL OF BANKRUPTCY CASES

Voluntary Dismissal

Akin to questions regarding debtors who do not wish to be brought into bankruptcy court is the question of when a debtor may extricate himself or herself from a bankruptcy that was voluntarily commenced.

In chapter 13, the answer to this question is simple. Under the Code, the debtor may obtain a dismissal on request in any chapter 13 case that has not been converted from another chapter. Even when creditors oppose dismissal or seek to convert the case, the debtor's election to dismiss must be honored.

Chapter 7 cases present a somewhat more complicated picture. The court may dismiss a case only after notice to creditors and a hearing and only for good cause. What constitutes cause for dismissal has been a matter of some dispute. A number of courts have decided that cause does not exist in cases in which the debtor sought only to refile a petition after paying a favored creditor or to include debts incurred after the first petition was filed. Some courts have required the consent of all creditors for a dismissal to be be obtained, although such a blanket rule seems too broad.

Most courts have been more liberal, allowing dismissal in any case in which no creditor objects after receiving notice of the request for dismissal. At least one court stated that cause need not be shown in such cases. These courts have generally required the debtor to pay the trustee for any expenses incurred, and at least a few have stated that the trustee has no right to object to dismissal if these expenses are paid, though others have decided otherwise. As a practical matter, there is rarely an objection to dismissal in cases in which the debtor has no significant nonexempt assets.

Involuntary Dismissal or Conversion to Chapter 7

Involuntary dismissal may occur for a number of reasons in chapter 7 and chapter 13 cases. Probably the most common causes are failure to pay the filing fees or chapter 13 payments, failure to file appropriate papers—

such as the schedules or the chapter 13 plan—and failure to appear at a meeting of creditors. However, when some reasonable excuse for delay or nonpayment is raised, a motion to dismiss on these grounds is normally denied. Further, it is clear that involuntary dismissals are discretionary with the court, rather than mandatory. Except perhaps in egregious cases of repeated bankruptcies in which the debtor does not follow through, dismissals in such cases usually do not affect the debtor's right to file another bankruptcy case. Of course, the limitations on the debtor's eligibility to file within 180 days of certain dismissals, as discussed in Chapter 2, do apply. In a chapter 13 case, there is always a possibility that the court might convert the case to chapter 7, rather than dismiss it.

Dismissal may also occur after the debtor fails to obtain confirmation of a chapter 13 plan, usually when the court has found that the confirmation standards cannot be met. Debtors in these cases decline or do not request the opportunity to present an amended plan that is satisfactory to the court, effectively leaving themselves in the same position as if no plan had been filed; thus, the case cannot proceed, at least not under chapter 13.

Occasionally, a creditor in a consumer case moves for dismissal. Although chapter 7 cases are subject to dismissal in limited circumstances for substantial abuse, only the court or the U.S. trustee can raise that issue, as discussed below. Some creditors seek to circumvent that limitation by moving to have chapter 7 cases dismissed under other parts of the Code, on the grounds that they were filed in bad faith. These motions should be denied as an attempt to circumvent the limitation on creditor's motions under the substantial abuse provisions, which were intended to prevent improper dismissal motions by creditors.

Dismissal for Substantial Abuse of the Provisions of Chapter 7

In what was certainly the most novel and controversial provision of the 1984 consumer bankruptcy amendments to the Code, Congress for the first time in recent memory limited the debtor's previously absolute right to file a liquidation bankruptcy case. A new section of the Code establishes the substantial abuse test. This test permits a bankruptcy court to dismiss a chapter 7 case after notice to the debtor and a hearing, on its own motion or on motion of the U.S. trustee and not at the request or even the suggestion of any other party, if the court finds that granting relief under chapter 7 would be a substantial abuse of its provisions.

Despite the significant theoretical change in philosophy that this section represents, its practical effects should be slight because it is directed at only a tiny percentage of the consumer bankruptcies that are filed. The purpose of the new section may be ascertained from its lengthy legislative history, which gives important guidance regarding what is and is not intended by the substantial abuse test.

The idea of totally barring a debtor from chapter 7 relief originated in proposals by the consumer credit industry. These proposals and the legislation that first embodied them had several key elements. First, a creditor could obtain dismissal of a bankruptcy petition by filing a motion. Second, dismissal would be ordered in any case in which a consumer could pay a "reasonable portion" of his or her debts (excluding first mortgage debts); this was defined as 50 percent of those debts. Third, the determination of this ability to pay would assume a five-year repayment period, even if the debts came due in shorter periods. Finally, the court was to decide these matters based on the debtor's "anticipated future income."

The ultimate legislative product rejected each of these concepts. A case may be dismissed under the substantial abuse provisions only by the court acting on its own initiative after reviewing the petition and schedules—including the schedule of current income and expenditures—or on a motion filed by the U.S. trustee. The legislative history suggests that this limitation is intended to prevent creditors from using motions to dismiss or the threat of such motions to harass or bargain with the debtor. If a creditor does request dismissal, the court may not be able to dismiss the case.

In practice, if the court can make its determination on substantial abuse as soon as the pertinent schedules are filed, this problem should not arise because few creditors would learn of the bankruptcy and suggest dismissal that early in the case. It is likely that the courts will delegate the duty of reviewing the schedules to law clerks or clerks of the court, who would not be considered parties in interest.

The final statute also rejected the idea that a chapter 7 case should be dismissed if a debtor could pay only a portion of his or her debts or could pay those debts only if they were stretched out over five years. In describing what was meant by the term *substantial abuse* in the Senate's version of the bill (which adopted more of the creditor proposals than the final statute), the Senate Report limited the term to those debtors who could meet their debts "without difficulty as they came due." Other portions of the legislative history also show that Congress had no intent to reduce debtors to minimal standards of living to force them to pay their debts.

Finally, Congress rejected the concept of future income. A court is not to prognosticate about the debtor's prospects for income and expenses over the next five years. It is to look only to the debtor's current financial situation, as reflected in the bankruptcy schedules.

Thus, as it finally emerged from Congress, the substantial abuse test is a narrowly targeted provision. It should affect only a few high-income debtors, such as the doctors and professional athletes who often appeared in creditors' congressional testimony. Low- and even middle-income debtors should have little difficulty in arguing that they do not fall within the statute's intended parameters, as described above.

The substantial abuse test applies only to debtors whose debts are primarily consumer debts. Thus, for debtors who have incurred most of their debts in business, through investment losses, or through liability for personal injuries or property damage, the section should not be a problem. A few courts have decided that debts secured by real estate are not consumer debts. At least one court has stated that this focus on consumer debtors also means that the section should not be applied when the debtor is ineligible for chapter 13, particularly if the debtor also cannot formulate a viable chapter 11 plan.

The early cases that dealt with substantial abuse are most notable for their total failure to discuss the legislative history of the new provisions, especially the language of the Senate Report. Instead, the courts focused on high-income debtors with extravagant life-styles, sometimes denying chapter 7 relief even when debtors could not repay all of their debts.

One early case that approached the drafters' intent stated that a case should not be dismissed under the substantial abuse provisions unless the debtor could afford a three-year chapter 13 plan that could pay 100 percent of the claims against the debtor. A number of other courts also seem to have adopted this approach, finding substantial abuse based on a debtor having income sufficient to fund a 100 percent plan. Other courts have unfortunately developed even more expansive definitions of substantial abuse and have dismissed cases even when debtors could pay only some of their debts under a three-year chapter 13 plan. One appellate court decided that a chapter 7 case may be dismissed for substantial abuse when the debtor could get by and pay 100 percent of the debts with "good, old-fashioned belt tightening" and other available state remedies. These cases have completely lost sight of the congressional intent in enacting the substantial abuse provision. More appropriately, other courts have held that the debtor's ability to fund a chapter 13 plan is not enough by itself to dictate a finding of substantial abuse.

Some courts have found substantial abuse in situations in which the debtor was not fully honest in preparing the petition and schedules. A number have held that a determination of substantial abuse must be based on an examination of the totality of the circumstances. This standard, however, has encouraged some judges to make essentially value-based decisions about the purposes of a given debtor's use of credit.

In any case, a dismissal based on substantial abuse does not forever prevent a debtor from filing a bankruptcy case. If the debtor's circumstances change, he or she is free to file again at any time.

BANKRUPTCY APPEALS

The 1984 legislation altered not only the jurisdictional scheme applicable to initial bankruptcy proceedings but also the avenues available for appeals from decisions of the bankruptcy court. These avenues depend on the judicial district in which a proceeding is litigated.

Appeals from the Bankruptcy Court

The normal forum for appeals from decisions of a bankruptcy court is the federal district court for the area in which the bankruptcy court is located. (In some cases, instead of an appeal, a party must file objections to proposed findings of fact and conclusions of law; slightly different rules apply in these cases.) An innovation of the 1978 act—the bankruptcy appellate panel—has been retained to a limited degree. An appeal that would otherwise go to the district court may be heard by an appellate panel of three bankruptcy judges if the judges for a particular area have set up such a panel and all parties consent that it be heard there instead of the district court.

Appeals from the District Court or a Bankruptcy Appellate Panel

Appeals from the district courts and from bankruptcy appellate panels are heard in the circuit courts of appeals. Complicated federal appellate jurisdictional statutes determine whether and when during the case a particular lower court decision may be appealed.

Chapter 13

THE BANKRUPTCY DISCHARGE: PROTECTING IT AND USING IT

The principal goal of most bankruptcies is the discharge, which frees the debtor from personal liability on almost all debts. This clean slate gives debtors the fresh start that bankruptcy is meant to provide. The Bankruptcy Code expanded the protections of the discharge in an effort to help debtors further and to prevent creditors and others from vitiating its benefits.

The discharge and its fruits are not quite absolute, however, nor are they automatic in every bankruptcy case. Under certain limited circumstances, the court may deny a discharge, or the discharge may be inapplicable to some debts. Even after it is granted, in rare instances the discharge may be revoked.

This chapter covers two aspects of the discharge: the difficulties that can arise in obtaining it and the benefits it can provide for consumer debtors.

OBJECTIONS TO DISCHARGE IN CHAPTER 7 CASES

As discussed earlier in Chapter 7, the procedure for obtaining a discharge is normally quite simple. In a chapter 7 case, a discharge order is usually entered about 60 days after the first date set for the meeting of creditors, assuming that no objection to discharge has been filed by that time. In a chapter 13 case, the discharge is granted after the debtor completes payments under a confirmed plan or on application by the debtor for a hardship discharge. In both chapters, the court may choose to hold a discharge hearing, but it is not required to do so unless the debtor decides to reaffirm a debt.

In chapter 7 only, a serious obstacle may arise from an objection to the discharge. These objections, which are quite rare, may be raised by a lawsuit within the bankruptcy case filed by the U.S. trustee, the bankruptcy trustee, or a creditor. In view of the wording of the Code, it may be possible for the court to deny a discharge on its own initiative if it knows of facts that would bar the debtor from that relief. However, such active partisanship of the court is very unusual; the court normally acts as a neutral arbiter of disputes brought before it, rather than as a participant.

If a discharge is denied in a chapter 7 case, the effect is quite serious. The debtor loses any nonexempt property to creditors, and creditors that are not paid in full may still pursue the debtor after the bankruptcy for the remaining amounts due. Although property that the debtor claims as exempt cannot be taken to satisfy these creditors (this might well protect all of the debtor's property), any property acquired after the bankruptcy could be subjected to process.

Grounds for Objecting to Discharge

Of all of the grounds for denial of discharge that are listed in the Code, the first is not applicable in consumer cases. This provision, which prohibits a discharge in chapter 7 if the debtor is not an individual, is meant simply to deny a discharge to corporations or partnerships. (The prohibition on nonindividuals does not apply to the estate of a deceased debtor, which is entitled to the benefits of the debtor's discharge.) The remaining grounds are discussed below in the order in which they appear in the statute.

Intentional Concealment, Transfer, or Destruction of Property

Probably the most common objection to discharge is that the debtor has intentionally transferred or concealed assets to prevent creditors from obtaining access to them in bankruptcy. This blatant fraudulent conduct strikes at the very heart of the bankruptcy law, defeating its purpose of distributing nonexempt property to creditors.

Several limitations to this bar to discharge are present both explicitly and implicitly in the law. First, the debtor must have committed the act with actual intent to hinder, delay, or defraud a creditor or officer of the estate. Intent cannot be presumed simply on the basis of the debtor's financial condition. Without this very specific intent, a discharge will not be denied.

Many of the recent cases under this provision have examined the debtor's prebankruptcy conversion of assets that are nonexempt into assets that are exempt in bankruptcy. Several of the decisions turn on whether the exemption planning was done with intent to defraud creditors. Given that the debtor has control over the timing of a voluntary bankruptcy, it would appear to be unfair to require that the debtor maintain nonexempt assets to satisfy creditors' claims in bankruptcy when the debtor could protect those assets under state or federal law by making them exempt before the petition. The courts have taken a fairly subjective approach to this issue, depending on the amount of money shielded from creditors, with a good deal of discretion afforded to the bankruptcy court.

Exemption planning obviously must be distinguished from the transfer of assets completely out of the debtor's name for little or nothing in return, particularly if the debtor has some access to or full use of those assets. The courts have denied a discharge when there has been an obvious dissipation of assets in contemplation of bankruptcy or a suspicious transfer to relatives for little or nothing in return. However, if the debtor has recovered virtually all of the property transferred before the bankruptcy is filed and truthfully discloses the transfers, the debtor should not be denied a discharge under this subsection.

Finally, the challenged action must have taken place within one year before the bankruptcy or sometime after the bankruptcy was filed, and it must have involved property that would have been available to creditors. If the debtor had no equity in the property, the bar to discharge is usually not considered applicable. The same result would presumably be reached with respect to property that the debtor could claim as exempt. (Exemption claims are discussed in Chapter 9.)

Unjustified Failure to Keep Financial Books or Records

The Code provides for denial of discharge if the debtor has "concealed, destroyed, mutilated, falsified, or failed to keep or preserve any recorded information" concerning his or her finances, but only if the act or the failure to act was not justified under the circumstances. The exception to the general rule, which excuses the failure to keep records if it was "justified," has prevented the application of this subsection in most consumer cases.

Most consumers, of course, do not keep books and records in the conventional sense. What they have, at most, is a collection of receipts, canceled checks, loan documents, and payment books. A consumer debtor who has any of these documents may honestly say that books or records have been kept. Because this provision is really directed at independent businesses and, perhaps, gamblers, even a total lack of records has been excused in the cases of wage earners and other low-income people. As long as the debtor did not have any particular reason to anticipate the need for records and there are other ways to ascertain the debtor's financial affairs, this provision should present few problems in consumer cases.

Dishonesty in Connection with the Bankruptcy Case

Not surprisingly, the Code does not treat kindly debtors who attempt to perpetrate a fraud on the bankruptcy court. Those who make a false oath (commit perjury), present false claims, give or take bribes, or withhold records are denied a discharge. This provision clearly extends to the bankruptcy statements and schedules, which are submitted under oath.

However, like many of the other bars to discharge, the false oath objection is limited by its terms and by court decisions to the more serious types of cases. The false oath must be in regard to a matter that is material to the proceedings and that could have a real effect on creditors and the estate. The false oath must be intentional; false answers resulting from carelessness or ignorance do not prevent a debtor's discharge. Finally, the false oath must be in connection with the administration of the case itself; fraudulent conduct in connection with a particular debt can be grounds only for an exception to the discharge of that debt, as discussed below.

Failure to Explain Loss or Deficiency of Assets

This provision barring discharge is often grouped with the previous two relating to the debtor's honesty with regard to the bankruptcy case. Once a creditor shows that an asset has been lost or dissipated, the debtor must explain the loss or dissipation. Courts that have interpreted this section have been concerned primarily with debtors who previously had large amounts of property or money, a situation which few consumer debtors have ever experienced. In most consumer cases, the obvious use of any diminishing assets was for basic living expenses. Even if this were not the case, this subsection is not intended as a vehicle through which the court may pass judgment on the wisdom of the debtor's expenditures.

Refusal to Obey Court Orders or to Testify

If the debtor refuses to comply with direct court orders, a discharge may be denied. This unusual situation arises most often when a debtor has been ordered to turn over property that he or she expected to keep in the bankruptcy and that the debtor may no longer even possess. For example, debtors who were poorly advised under the old Act sometimes spent tax refunds that they received after filing their cases. When those refunds were not exempt, they constituted property of the estate that the court ordered turned over to the trustee. If the debtor was unable to deliver the amount of the refund within a reasonable time, the discharge was often denied.

Debtors who refuse to testify may also be denied a discharge. However, if a debtor properly invokes the privilege against self-incrimination, discharge cannot be denied unless immunity is first offered for the matter concerning which the privilege was invoked. Debtors presumably also will not be ordered to answer questions when other privileges—such as the attorney-client privilege—are properly invoked as a reason for not testifying.

Commission of Prohibited Acts in Connection with Another Bankruptcy Case Concerning an Insider

Debtors who have committed any of the fraudulent acts listed in the previous sections within one year before filing their cases or sometime after filing their cases are barred from discharge if the acts were committed in connection with another case concerning an insider. The Code defines *insider* to include relatives and partners as well as partnerships and corporations of which the debtor is a director, officer, or person in control.

Although this section is undoubtedly directed principally at debtors who have been involved in bankrupt corporations and partnerships, it could also be applied to occasional consumer cases. These would most likely involve a husband and wife or other related persons who committed the specified fraudulent acts.

Prior Discharge in Chapter 7, Chapter 11, or Their Predecessors

This subsection contains a six-year prohibition against successive bankruptcy discharges. It is important to note that it applies only to prior cases in which a discharge was granted. If a prior bankruptcy case was terminated without a discharge—by dismissal, for example—this objection to discharge may not be raised. Moreover, this section does not bar discharge following prior discharges under chapter 13 or under the old Chapter XIII. As with all of the provisions that govern objections to discharge, this section has no applicability when the debtor seeks a chapter 13 discharge. Finally, it should be noted that the six-year period runs from the date that the earlier bankruptcy case was commenced, not from the date of the discharge.

Prior Discharge in Chapter 13 or Old Chapter XIII

The Code also bars a chapter 7 discharge in many cases when the debtor has received a discharge under chapter 13 or its predecessor within the previous six years. Again, this subsection applies only if the earlier case proceeded to a discharge.

A significant exception to this general rule has been added to allow a chapter 7 discharge when the previous case paid unsecured debts in full or in large part. Thus, if 100 percent of the allowed unsecured claims were paid in the previous case, this subsection is not applicable. Similarly, if the actual payments under the previous chapter 13 plan comprised at least 70 percent of the allowed unsecured claims in that case and the court finds that the plan was proposed by the debtor in good faith and was the debtor's best effort, a subsequent chapter 7 discharge within six years is not barred. The drafters of the Code anticipated that a debtor could receive this best-effort determination when the original chapter 13 plan was confirmed.

Written Waiver of Discharge

Finally, the court may deny a discharge based on a court-approved written waiver of discharge executed after the order for relief. This section has no applicability to the purported waivers of bankruptcy rights that creditors obtained in granting loans. Given the strict standards set forth for the reaffirmation of even a single debt, which are discussed later in this chapter, it is highly unlikely that many waivers of discharge will be approved.

The court will presumably approve a waiver of discharge only when it seems likely that no discharge could be granted anyway. Thus, it may be a method of settling a complaint objecting to discharge that would disclose damaging or embarrassing facts about the debtor. Even in these cases, a debtor may be able to obtain a better settlement, excepting only debts to particular creditors from the discharge.

Filing Fees

Under the prior Bankruptcy Act, an additional ground for denial of discharge was the failure to pay filing fees. This provision has been eliminated under the Code.

In practical terms, however, the elimination of the provision has resulted in few changes. The original purpose of eliminating this bar to discharge was to allow bankruptcies for debtors who could not afford to pay the filing fee. But Congress ultimately decided that the filing fee must be paid. Thus, most courts have dismissed cases in which the filing fee has not been paid.

REVOCATION OF DISCHARGE

Even more rare than an objection to the discharge is a complaint seeking revocation of the discharge. Such a complaint must be filed within a relatively short time. It must allege the existence of one of the limited circumstances that allow revocation. Specifically, the discharge may be revoked only if one of the following is true:

1. The debtor obtained the discharge through fraud, and the requesting party was not aware of it until after the discharge.
2. The debtor knowingly and fraudulently failed to report the acquisition of property that would be property of the bankruptcy estate.
3. The debtor failed to obey an order of the court.

To obtain revocation of a discharge for fraud, it is not sufficient to show that the debtor's fraud rendered a particular debt nondischargeable; the plaintiff must show that the bankruptcy discharge itself would not have been granted without the fraud. The creditor must also allege fraud with particularity, including the time, place, and contents of any false representation as well as its consequences. In addition, the party requesting revocation of discharge must not have learned of the fraud before the discharge was entered.

A lawsuit raising any of these allegations must be filed within one year of the discharge. If the case is closed after one year from the date of the discharge, the second and third grounds set forth above may be raised until the date that the case is closed.

EXCEPTIONS TO DISCHARGE

Somewhat less serious than an objection to the discharge is the problem of particular debts that are not covered by the discharge. But depending on their nature and extent, debts excepted from discharge can seriously undermine the benefits that a bankruptcy would otherwise provide.

Differences between Chapters 7 and 13

One of the important features of chapter 13 is the inapplicability of many of the chapter 7 provisions that exclude certain types of debts from the effect of the discharge. If the debtor earns a chapter 13 discharge by completing a confirmed plan, all debts provided for in the plan are discharged. The only exceptions to the discharge are alimony and support obligations that are not dischargeable in chapter 7, debts for educational loans and grants not dischargeable in chapter 7, debts for drunk driving debts not dischargeable in chapter 7, certain criminal restitution debts, and long-term debts that are cured under the plan but have a final payment that is due after the last payment of the plan. The chapter 7 discharge exceptions listed in this paragraph are discussed in detail below.

However, this chapter 13 full-compliance discharge cannot be granted unless all debts given priority under the Code's priority provisions—such as many taxes—are also paid in full because a plan must normally provide for full payment of such debts. Thus, in a sense, those debts too are not dischargeable through a normal chapter 13 discharge.

All other debts that are excepted from discharge in chapter 7 and are discussed below are included in the normal chapter 13 discharge. This difference, as discussed in Chapter 5, can be an important factor in the choice of chapter 13 rather than chapter 7, or in the decision to convert from chapter 7 to chapter 13. However, some courts have taken the presence of debts that are allegedly nondischargeable under chapter 7 into consideration in ruling on whether the plan has been filed in good faith, as discussed earlier in Chapter 11.

This difference between chapters 7 and 13 does not exist if the debtor obtains a chapter 13 hardship discharge. In such cases, the exceptions to discharge are the same as in chapter 7. The debtor is also excused from the requirement, not present in chapter 7, that all priority debts be paid.

How Exceptions to Discharge Are Raised

The Bankruptcy Code makes an important distinction between two categories of exceptions to discharge. The first category consists of debts that are excepted from the discharge regardless of whether anyone raises the issue during the bankruptcy case. The exceptions that fall into this category, each of which is discussed below, are those for taxes, debts not listed by the debtor, alimony and support, fines and penalties, student loans, certain debts incurred through drunk driving, debts for which a discharge was denied or waived in a prior bankruptcy, and certain debts owed to agencies that regulate federal depository institutions. Creditors that hold claims covered by these exceptions are free to assert them against the debtor after the bankruptcy, without the permission of the bankruptcy court.

The second category of exceptions consists of debts that are excluded from the discharge only if their nondischargeability is raised and determined during the bankruptcy case. The debts that fall into this category are those incurred by false pretenses or false financial statements, claims for fraud on the part of fiduciaries, and claims for willful and malicious injuries. The rules require that these nondischargeability issues be raised by a lawsuit within the bankruptcy case. The deadline for commencing this proceeding is 60 days after the first date set for the meeting of creditors. The court always gives at least 30 days' notice of this deadline, which the court may extend for good cause only if the extension is requested before the deadline passes. This notice is normally combined with the notice of the meeting of creditors.

If a creditor does not file a lawsuit alleging nondischargeability of a claim before the deadline or any extension, the claim is permanently discharged, and the debtor may raise the deadline as a complete defense to any later dischargeability lawsuit. Even if the creditor did not receive proper notice of the deadline, it is strictly applied by the courts if the creditor had timely notice of the bankruptcy case.

The rules permit the debtor or any creditor to file a complaint to determine dischargeability of a debt. For the types of dischargeability exceptions that a creditor need not raise during the bankruptcy case, the debtor may wish to seek to have such issues settled. The debtor may prefer to resolve dischargeability questions in the bankruptcy court, which is often a more sympathetic forum than the one later chosen by the creditor. (The debtor may also attempt to transfer a later case brought by the creditor to the bankruptcy forum.) An action brought by the debtor seeking a court decision on the dischargeability of a particular debt is not governed by the deadline discussed above, which is applicable only to the dischargeability complaints that must be filed in the bankruptcy court.

Debts That Are Excepted from Discharge

Taxes

Taxes are the debts that are most frequently nondischargeable in bankruptcy cases. Not all taxes are nondischargeable, however. A rather complicated series of cross-references within the Code can be followed to the conclusion that only the types of taxes listed below are nondischargeable in consumer cases:

1. Any tax for which the debtor did not file a return, if required, or that the debtor attempted to evade

2. Any tax with respect to which the debtor filed a late return within two years before filing of the bankruptcy

3. Taxes on income or gross receipts (a) for which a return, if re-

quired, is last due within three years of filing of the bankruptcy, (b) assessed within 240 days before filing of the bankruptcy, or (c) not yet assessed, but assessable after filing of the bankruptcy

4. Property taxes assessed before commencement of the case and last payable without penalty less than one year before filing for bankruptcy

5. Excise taxes (a) On transactions for which a return is required and last due less than three years before the bankruptcy, or (b) On transactions for which no return is required and that occurred less than three years before the bankruptcy

6. Taxes that must be collected or withheld by the debtor, such as employment "trust fund" taxes (income taxes and Federal Insurance Contributions Act [FICA] withholding) or sales taxes

Any penalties related to the taxes listed above are also nondischargeable, unless the penalty is solely punitive in nature. Erroneous refunds of nondischargeable taxes are similarly nondischargeable. The treatment of interest is not as clear; some courts have found that it is dischargeable, and others that it is not. However, postbankruptcy interest on nondischargeable tax debts is clearly nondischargeable.

In view of the relative intricacy of these provisions, the wise debtor will check his or her particular situation with an experienced bankruptcy attorney. When significant amounts of money are involved, it may pay to delay filing until one or more of the time periods listed above has expired. For the purpose of calculating time limits under the various provisions, taxes are found to be payable from the date that the relevant tax return is due, rather than the date on which quarterly estimated payments are required. In addition, because taxes in the last four categories are priority claims, a chapter 13 plan must normally provide for their full payment.

Although most property taxes do not come within these provisions, state laws generally provide that unpaid property taxes automatically become statutory liens on the real estate that is the subject of the tax. Therefore, for all practical purposes, these tax debts cannot be eliminated by a bankruptcy discharge.

Debts Incurred through False Pretenses, Fraud, or False Financial Statements

The exception dealing with false pretenses, fraud, and false financial statements has given rise to more court decisions than any other exception. Generally speaking, the Code upholds a creditor's timely filed lawsuit seeking a determination that a debt is nondischargeable if the debt is for obtaining money, property, services, or an extension, renewal, or refinancing of credit by false pretenses, a false representation, fraud, or a false financial statement.

Litigation concerning these questions has decreased markedly in consumer cases for two reasons. First, debts that are not dischargeable under this subsection in chapter 7 may now be discharged in chapter 13. Second, creditors who file nondischargeability complaints based on this subsection and lose are often required to pay attorney's fees to the debtor's counsel, as discussed below.

False Financial Statements

To prevail on a complaint alleging nondischargeability due to a false financial statement, a creditor must prove that the transaction met every criterion set out in the Code's provisions. In many cases, it has been difficult for creditors to accomplish this. The provisions are described below.

The Debtor Obtained Money, Property, Services, or an Extension, Renewal, or Refinancing of Credit

The first fact that the creditor must allege and prove is that the debtor obtained money, property, services, or an extension, renewal, or refinancing of credit through the use of the allegedly false statement. If the creditor has given up nothing in the transaction, the exception to discharge is not applicable.

The most important aspect of this element is its applicability to refinancing transactions, which are very common in the world of consumer credit. By adding the words "extension, renewal, or refinancing of credit, to the extent obtained," Congress intended to include the entire refinanced debt in some, but not all, refinancing transactions. This marked a change in the law that had prevailed in many bankruptcy courts; only the amount of the refinanced loan that was "fresh cash" had previously been held to be nondischargeable.

The apparent intent of the provision as now worded is to make the entire refinanced loan nondischargeable only when the creditor agreed to refinance because of detrimental reliance on the false financial statement. Thus, especially in cases in which the refinancing was initially suggested by the creditor or was required by state law when new funds were advanced, a strong argument may be made that the refinancing itself was not detrimental to the creditor and was not obtained by the consumer as a result of any alleged falsehoods. A number of courts have adopted these arguments in finding only the "new money" or "fresh cash" nondischargeable.

The "fresh cash" argument received a substantial boost from the 1984 amendments to the Code. They seemingly made clear that refinancing obligations were not covered by the exception to the extent that credit had already been obtained previously without fraud or a false financial statement.

The Statement Was Materially False and in Writing

The creditor cannot prevail simply by proving that a debtor's statement was false. The statement must be in writing, and it must be materially false. Small omissions are usually insufficient to meet this test. Similarly, a false statement that is irrelevant to the decision about whether to grant credit is not material. Thus, a debtor contesting this element should be entitled to inquire into the creditor's scoring systems and methods to determine what effect the falsehood actually had.

The Statement Concerned the Financial Condition of the Debtor or an Insider

This requirement is similar to the previous one. The statement must concern the debtor's financial condition. False information in a deed or contract is insufficient. A statement that has no bearing on the finances of the debtor or an insider is not sufficient to bar dischargeability of the debt, no matter how false or distorted.

The Creditor Reasonably Relied on the False Statement

Creditors often cannot prove that they reasonably relied on the debtor's false statement. This test encompasses two facts that the creditor must prove: that the creditor in fact relied on the statement and that this reliance was reasonable.

Thus, when a creditor relies on the consumer's past record of dealing with the creditor or on other information, this standard is not met. If a loan or refinancing is offered and agreed to before the false statement is made, no reliance can be shown. Often, other information possessed by the creditor, such as a credit report, indicates that the debtor's financial statement is false, and if the creditor had reason to know that the statement was false, it could not have reasonably relied on it. Similarly, if the financial statement was perfunctorily completed for the file and the creditor made no real reference to it, no reliance can be shown. This may be the case when the creditor takes a lien and relies on the value of the property subject to the lien rather than on the debtor's ability to make payment.

Even if the creditor shows that it did rely on the statement, that reliance may not have been reasonable. If the creditor did not obtain a credit report or check any information given by the debtor, its reliance may not have met this standard. If the creditor told the debtor not to worry about listing every debt owed on the financial statement, it could not have reasonably relied on that statement.

The Debtor Had Intent to Deceive

Finally, the creditor must prove that the debtor had an actual intent to deceive it through the use of the false financial statement. If the debtor's false disclosure was innocently or carelessly made, the debt is dischargeable, although some courts have considered a "reckless indifference" to the truth to be equivalent to intentional falsehood. Thus, debtors who failed to list debts because they thought a spouse or relative was responsible for paying them were found to be without intent to deceive. Similarly, debtors who made a good faith effort but omitted debts, such as taxes, in answering ambiguous questions were entitled to discharge of the debts involved. If the debtor acts in good faith, even seriously inaccurate estimates of assets or liabilities do not constitute intentional deception. The debtor may also have simply assumed that the creditor knew of debts from prior statements or other sources.

Probably the most common defense against the question of intent arises out of the practices of creditors who mislead debtors about the purpose of the financial statement. Some finance companies require a financial statement for future use in bankruptcy proceedings, rather than for making the decision to grant credit. These creditors typically provide a form that has little space for listing debts, and they advise the debtor not to worry if the list is not complete. Some creditors describe the form as a mere formality or as a list of credit references. These companies then retain the form for use in a bankruptcy case in which they challenge the dischargeability of the debt, hoping that the debtor will reaffirm, rather than pay an attorney to litigate the matter. When such conduct can be shown, there is no intent to deceive on the part of the debtor, nor is there reasonable reliance on the part of the creditor.

False Pretenses or Fraud

Similar to cases dealing with false financial statements are those challenging dischargeability on the basis of false pretenses, false representations, or actual fraud. These complaints are usually based on information that the debtor conveyed orally, in writing, or by conduct, but not in a written financial statement.

A chapter 7 debtor will be denied the discharge of a particular debt under this section if it is shown that the creditor provided money, property, services, or an extension, renewal, or refinancing of credit due to an intentionally and materially false statement by the debtor on which the creditor reasonably relied. This standard is basically the standard for fraud in other areas of the law.

Debtors who have obtained money in their businesses through deliberate misrepresentations about security interests or about the use that would be made of the funds have been denied discharge on those debts. Loans obtained through willful misrepresentations about other intended activities may also be nondischargeable. In addition, an intentional failure to disclose a material fact may constitute false pretenses. Debtors who fail to disclose significant facts about a transaction or about unrecorded mortgages on real estate have been denied discharges of debts incurred in that fashion.

Just as with false financial statements, the creditor must prove all of the components of the exception to discharge in each case. The creditor must prove both intent on the part of the debtor and reasonable reliance on the part of the person who was allegedly deceived. It is not sufficient to show that the debtor wrote a bad check. It must also be shown that the check induced the transfer of money, property, or credit; if it was given in payment of an antecedent debt, no false pretenses exist. Furthermore, the intent requirement is not satisfied unless the debtor knew when the check was issued that it would not be honored. The fact that a representation or promise later turns out to be one that the debtor does not fulfill is not sufficient to show intent. Otherwise, almost every debt would be nondischargeable under this exception.

Credit Cards and Other Credit Use with No Intent to Pay

One of the classic types of false pretenses is the obtaining of money, goods, or services on credit with no intent to pay. These debts must be distinguished from debts that the debtor later finds himself or herself unable or unwilling to pay. Debts incurred through false pretenses were incurred through an intentionally false representation that they would be paid. Because such a representation may be found to have been implied, rather than expressed, it is not surprising that difficult problems of proof arise regarding intent and regarding exactly when the debtor decided that the debt would not be paid.

In consumer cases, these issues arise most frequently when credit cards are involved, particularly if there is evidence of an unusual buying spree shortly before the bankruptcy. It is not uncommon for creditors to allege that this use of credit constitutes a knowing misrepresentation, on which they reasonably relied, that the debt could and would be paid.

The creditor must produce evidence that proves these allegations. The 1984 amendments to the Code made this burden far easier for creditors to meet when the debtor allegedly "loaded up" before bankruptcy. Whenever a debtor incurs consumer debts in excess of $500 to a single creditor for luxury goods or services within 40 days before filing a bankruptcy or receives cash advances of more than $1,000 on an open-ended credit plan within 20 days before filing, there is a presumption that the debts were incurred through false pretenses.

Luxury goods or services are defined in this subsection as goods and services that are not reasonably acquired for the support or maintenance of the debtor or the debtor's dependents. Therefore, the presumption would not arise if the debtor purchased more than $500 worth of ordinary clothing or a necessary major appliance. Similarly, when a debt is incurred to refinance an earlier debt within 40 days before bankruptcy, the presumption does not arise, even if the earlier debt was to purchase luxury goods or services, because those goods and services were not obtained during the 40-day period. Even when the subsection's standards are met, the debtor may disprove the presumption. It may be overcome if the debtor can show that a sudden change in circumstances occurred after the transaction or that bankruptcy had not been contemplated until after the transaction when the debtor consulted counsel. It should be overcome whenever the court is convinced that the debtor honestly intended to pay the debt.

The presumption is not operative unless the creditor files a timely dischargeability lawsuit. The amendments did not alter the Code's language providing that a claim of nondischargeability under the fraud sections is lost if not raised during the bankruptcy case.

Problems that might be caused by the presumption may usually be avoided by delaying the bankruptcy until after the applicable time period has passed. However, the time period is only relevant to the automatic presumption. Debts incurred before that period may still be found to be nondischargeable for fraud or false pretenses, but in such cases, the creditor must prove all of the facts necessary to show fraud.

To show fraudulent intent, it is not sufficient to prove simply that the debt was incurred and not paid; that much is true of all dischargeable debts. And absent a foolish admission on the part of the debtor, it is almost impossible to prove the debtor's intent through direct evidence or statements that the debtor has made. These difficulties have led courts to look to circumstantial evidence.

The courts have considered several indicia as strong evidence of fraudulent intent. The first of these is a surge of credit use shortly before the bankruptcy. When a debtor suddenly resigned from her job and left home to travel extensively on credit without notifying anyone of her whereabouts, it was not hard for the court to infer intent, despite a defense that these activities were the result of mental illness. Similarly, if a debtor makes $1,000 worth of credit purchases, most of which are gift certificates used not for others but for himself, the court will find this behavior to be more than a little suspicious. A few courts have gone so far as to say that any substantial use of credit, at least by a sophisticated debtor, when the debtor should have known that he or she would be unable to pay, constitutes false pretenses.

A second indication of fraudulent intent is the use of a credit card after it is no longer permitted by the credit contract, either because the credit limit has been exceeded or because the creditor has instructed the debtor to destroy, return, or cease using the card. Some courts have held that this use constitutes intentional false representation to the merchant that the card is being used in compliance with the terms of the contract and is therefore fraudulent by itself. The evidence of fraud is much stronger when the debtor ceases to make purchases in excess of $50, the amount at which merchants customarily call for credit approval. Of course, proof that the debtor consulted an attorney or other evidence that the debtor contemplated bankruptcy at the time of the credit use is quite helpful to the creditor's cause.

A debtor may raise a number of arguments in defense against such claims. Most courts have decided that merely exceeding the credit limit is not sufficient to constitute false pretenses. If the creditor has acquiesced in such use of the credit card over a period of months, the creditor should be prohibited from later challenging dischargeability or it should be found that the contract was changed by the parties' conduct. One appellate court has ruled that debts incurred through credit card use cannot be excepted from discharge unless the use occurs after an unequivocal revocation of credit card privileges. A debtor's honest belief that he or she could and would pay, even if that belief is ill-founded, negates any fraudulent intent. An absence of fraudulent intent is also evidenced in many cases by the return of the credit cards when requested.

In applying these guidelines, courts have seldom found it difficult to separate the dishonest debtors from the honest ones.

Public Benefits Overpayments

Another type of fraud problem that may arise in the cases of low-income debtors involves past overpayments of Social Security, unemployment, welfare, or other benefits. In many cases, the amount that was erroneously paid is deducted from future benefits, often causing considerable hardship.

When determining whether debts for overpayments should be discharged, the bankruptcy court applies the same standards as in other cases in which fraud is alleged. These standards may be quite different from those applied by the agency that administers the benefits; many agencies, including the Social Security Administration (SSA), may decide to deduct erroneous payments even if the debtor was not at fault. They may use a fault standard that is far less favorable to the debtor than that used in bankruptcy.

Any overpayment that is the result of an administrative error should clearly be discharged under this standard. No exception to discharge arises solely because the debt is owed to a government agency. Following these principles and despite the continued opposition of the SSA, courts have consistently ruled that Social Security overpayments are dischargeable unless a successful dischargeability challenge is made under the fraud provisions of the Code.

However, debtors who fraudulently obtain benefits by intentionally and falsely representing that they are unemployed are usually denied a discharge of overpayment if a dischargeability lawsuit is filed. Courts are likely to extend this rule to those who do not report new employment, at least if it can be shown that they were aware of their duty to do so, under the theory that such failure constitutes a continuing misrepresentation. Other intentional falsehoods in the application regarding eligibility for benefits can also lead to an exception from discharge. On the other hand, fraud cannot be assumed simply because a debtor has erroneously received payments while working or because the agency has incorrect information.

Award of Attorney's Fees in Fraud Dischargeability Cases

Some creditors continue to believe that they can obtain a settlement reaffirming all or part of a debt simply by filing a complaint alleging nondischargeability due to a false financial statement, false pretenses, or fraud because many such cases have not been defended in the past. For this reason, Congress passed a new provision of the Bankruptcy Code that requires a creditor to pay the debtor's attorney's fees if the debtor prevails and the creditor's complaint alleging a false financial statement, false pretenses, or fraud was not "substantially justified."

The purpose of this provision is to prevent a creditor from bringing a questionable case to exploit the debtor's need to pay a lawyer to assert a meritorious defense to a dischargeability case; thus, whenever a creditor does not have significant evidence to support its claim, the creditor should be obliged to pay the debtor's attorney. Otherwise, the debtor will have lost money even when the case is won.

Creditors Not Listed or Scheduled by the Debtor

Debts owed to most creditors that are not listed or scheduled in the bankruptcy case are excepted from the discharge. This general rule underscores the importance for the debtor of filing a complete and accurate list of debts. At least one appellate court has held that this exception applies not only to the schedules themselves, but also to any mailing label matrix required by local rules. Although the exception is expressly applicable only to chapter 7 cases, failure to list a creditor may have similar consequences in chapter 13. Creditors that are never listed and are thus not informed of the bankruptcy need not file a complaint to raise this ground for nondischargeability.

Fortunately, there are a number of exceptions to this exception. If the debtor does not know and cannot, with reasonable diligence, determine a creditor's name or address, the unknown information need not be listed. However, the fact of the debt and whatever information the debtor does know must be listed, along with a statement that the supplied information is the extent of the debtor's knowledge and perhaps a description of efforts taken to obtain the missing information.

The debt will also be discharged, even though not listed, if the creditor has actual knowledge, either from the debtor or from someone else, that the bankruptcy has been filed and knows about the case in time to file a proof of claim or, if the claim is nondischargeable and a dischargeability lawsuit is required, in time to file a suit. Because the deadline for claims is presently 90 days after the first date set for the meeting of creditors (or later) and in some cases there is no deadline under the rules, most creditors can still be notified of the case even if they are not discovered until well after the case is filed. Creditors that seek to fall within the time limit for filing a nondischargeability lawsuit must prove not only that they did not have timely notice, but also that their claims are in fact nondischargeable under one of the listed exceptions.

The Code specifically requires that the creditor receive actual notice of the case if the debt is not duly scheduled. Notice is sometimes, but not always, considered to be received if an agent—for example, a collection agent or attorney—receives notice. However, it is not enough to show that the creditor receives a newspaper that lists bankruptcies, unless perhaps it is also shown that the creditor reads these lists regularly. It is therefore safest to list the creditor itself in the bankruptcy schedules, though the agent or attorney may also be listed.

If a creditor is not scheduled at the outset of a case, the schedules should be amended, and the debtor should be sure to send a copy of the notice of the meeting of creditors to the creditor by certified mail to ensure actual notice. If a discharge has already been granted, the debtor may still file an amendment up to the time that the case is closed or even afterward. Even if the schedules are not amended, actual notice sent and received within the time limits should be sufficient under the wording of the Code.

In some districts in which the practice is not to have creditors file claims when the debtor has no nonexempt assets, courts have ruled that all otherwise dischargeable claims are discharged in these cases, even if they are not listed in the debtor's schedules. The rationale is that the only notice that unscheduled creditors miss is a notice not to file a proof of claim and a notice of a deadline for dischargeability objections that the creditors do not have. Therefore, they suffer no harm from the lack of notice. In other words, under the language of the Code, the creditor has not been denied the right to file a timely proof of claim.

If the creditor is duly scheduled, it is irrelevant whether it receives notice. The courts have ruled that minor irregularities, such as misspellings or incorrect amounts listed as due, do not render improper the listing of a particular creditor. It has generally been decided that if the creditor's identity can be reasonably ascertained, the listing is sufficient. However, listing a creditor's address as that of its attorney or in care of its attorney may not be sufficient. Moreover, if the debtor knows that the debt has been assigned (transferred to another creditor), the new creditor must be listed. If the debtor lists an incorrect address, the court may inquire whether the debtor exercised reasonable diligence in completing the schedules.

Of course, a claim that is not discharged solely because it was not listed in a chapter 7 case may be included and discharged in a subsequent bankruptcy.

Fraud as a Fiduciary, Embezzlement, and Larceny

The fourth exception to discharge involves fraud or defalcation while acting in a fiduciary capacity—such as a corporate officer or trustee—and embezzlement or larceny while not in a fiduciary capacity. The exception based on fraud or defalcation is rarely invoked in cases involving consumers because few consumers have acted as fiduciaries. A sales employee who has misappropriated funds is thus not a fiduciary, though someone who takes goods on consignment may be one. When a true fiduciary relationship is created by the law, there is little doubt that the section applies.

The terms *larceny* and *embezzlement* have been added to this exception, and are applicable to nonfiduciaries as well as fiduciaries. The extent of their use has yet to be fully explored, however. *Larceny* is not necessarily defined in the same way in bankruptcy as it is in state law. It is defined as a matter of federal common law as taking property from its rightful owner willfully and with fraudulent intent. *Embezzlement* is the fraudulent taking of property belonging to another by a person in lawful possession of that property. As under the other exceptions discussed above, the creditor must prove actual fraudulent intent in order to prove embezzlement.

In any case, for this exception to apply, a lawsuit must be filed during the bankruptcy case within the time limits set by the Bankruptcy Rules.

Alimony, Maintenance, or Support Owed to a Spouse, Former Spouse, or Child

The Code excepts from discharge in both chapter 7 and chapter 13 alimony, maintenance, or support payments owed to a spouse, former spouse, or child of the debtor in connection with a separation agreement, divorce decree, order of a court of record, administrative determination made by a government body, or property settlement.

This exception to discharge does not apply to debts for alimony, support, or maintenance owed to most other entities, even if they have been assigned by the spouse or the child or by operation of law. Thus, debts owed under palimony decisions to persons who were never validly married to the debtor are not excepted from discharge, nor are debts to putative spouses—for example, spouses in a void marriage. Similarly, debts that pass to a former spouse's heirs after his or her death are not included in the exception. In some cases, such as divorce decrees that give the nondebtor spouse a right to pension benefits, courts have ruled that no debt is owed, and therefore no debt can be discharged, because the divorce decree actually divided up the future benefits between the spouses so that each spouse owns his or her share.

Child support rights transferred to public welfare departments in cases in which the debtor's children receive public assistance are included within this exception to discharge. Thus, the most a bankruptcy can do with respect to these debts is provide protection during a reasonable payment plan under chapter 13. This protection can be very valuable in areas where overzealous prosecutors and judges harass and even incarcerate those who, because of unemployment or other problems, have allowed their dependents to become public charges. It also now appears that most alimony and spousal support rights that are assigned to the state cannot be discharged. A 1984 amendment to the Code eliminated any question about whether other support order obligations, such as those arising in paternity cases, may be discharged. All such obligations arising from support orders of any court of record or from administrative determinations of a government body are now clearly nondischargeable.

Most disputes under this subsection concern whether the debt is for alimony, maintenance, or support as opposed to being a property settlement debt, which is dischargeable. As with any exception to discharge, the complaining party must establish that the debt is nondischargeable. The designation of a debt as alimony or property settlement by a state court decree or agreement is not binding in the dischargeability determination; a court can look behind such language to determine the real nature of the debt.

The main indicators that courts consider in determining whether the debt is a support payment rather than a property settlement are the following:

1. Whether the payments terminate on death or remarriage of the spouse who receives them
2. Whether payments are contingent on the nondebtor spouse's future earning abilities
3. Whether payments are to be periodic over a long period of time rather than in a lump sum
4. Whether the payments are designated as being for such purposes as medical care, mortgage, or other needs of the spouse who receives them

Each of these factors indicates that support, based on the spouse's needs, is involved, not a property settlement. The existence of those needs at the time of the agreement is, by itself, often sufficient for a finding that an obligation was intended for the purpose of support. Another factor that courts may find relevant is the parties' tax treatment of the payments. A spouse who treats a marital obligation as alimony may be prohibited from later contending that the obligation was a property settlement.

If the intent of an agreement is to provide support, it is irrelevant whether such support is required by law. On the other hand, if the court finds that payments are to compensate for a spouse's property interest, they will be designated as dischargeable property settlement debts.

Spouses or former spouses often disagree about the nature of a hold-harmless agreement in which one spouse agrees to pay marital debts and then later claims that they were discharged in a bankruptcy. Whether the responsibility for these debts is more in the nature of a support payment or a property settlement is determined using similar criteria. For these debts to be determined to be nondischargeable, most courts have held that payment of them must be necessary to support the nondebtor spouse at the time of the agreement or order. If the debtor spouse had agreed to pay current mortgage, utility, insurance, and tax payments, for example, these payments are deemed to be support. This conclusion is bolstered if the nondebtor spouse is unemployed or if the agreement provides for payment through the court, with noncompliance punishable by contempt. Other cases in which courts have found an intent to provide support have involved such debts as payments for life insurance policies that name the debtor's spouse and children as beneficiaries, payments for medical treatment after the divorce, and debts for furniture used by the former spouse and children, when the intent was to relieve the spouse from the burden of paying them, and the spouse waived the right to periodic alimony payments.

On the other hand, when the intent was simply to divide assets and previous liabilities, the debt is dischargeable, especially if there is no apparent benefit intended for the nondebtor spouse. Courts have generally ruled that business debts and debts incurred during the marriage for medical expenses, furniture and other household items, and transportation are dischargeable. Once these debts are discharged, any action to collect them is enjoined under the discharge provisions of the Code.

One type of divorce debt that has usually been found to be in the nature of support and thus nondischargeable arises from attorney's fees payable by one spouse to the other's attorney, at least when the first spouse has been awarded alimony or support. The attorney's fees are generally deemed to rise or fall with the determination on the primary debt. Other courts have reasoned that the award of fees is based on the need of one spouse or the duty of the other to support.

Bankruptcy debtors, potential debtors, and their spouses will naturally want to keep these principles in mind when negotiating marital settlements. Obtaining a large property settlement in return for reduced alimony may be a short-lived victory if obligations under the former are discharged in bankruptcy soon afterward. Although labels are not binding on the court, at least some deference may be given to how the various obligations are labeled in the agreement.

Willful and Malicious Injury

The sixth category of debts excepted from discharge consists of debts for willful and malicious injury by the debtor to another or to the property of another. This exception encompasses a narrow class of debts in which the debtor's conduct was both intentional and such that it intended to harm an entity or its property or would necessarily produce such harm.

Most of the litigation under this exception has centered on whether specific conduct was willful and malicious. At one end of the spectrum, assault and battery is clearly willful and malicious. At the other end, negligence and even gross negligence are not. Thus, few liabilities that arise from automobile accidents are excepted from discharge under this subsection, even if the debtor was driving while intoxicated, driving without insurance, or violating various traffic laws. Even a reckless disregard for the safety of others is usually not sufficient to except the debt from discharge.

Although the court decisions indicate that a case-by-case analysis must be made to determine whether conduct was willful and malicious, proof that an act was done intentionally may not be enough. The ultimate outcome usually depends on the nature of the act. The intentional setting of a fire is obviously sufficient, but breaches of contractual rights, even if intentional, generally fall short of the standard. Most courts have adopted a definition of willful and malicious injury as injury that involves the intentional doing of a wrongful act, which necessarily causes injury, without just cause or excuse.

Perhaps the most common attempts to use this exception in consumer cases arise from alleged conversions (wrongful use or taking) of collateral that secures debts. It was probably the common use of these allegations in cases in which consumers innocently disposed of such property that led to the requirement that the willful and malicious exception be raised during the bankruptcy case if it is to be raised at all.

It is clear that the willful and malicious standard is applicable to conversion cases. Although a technical conversion may occur whenever a debtor disposes of collateral, no matter how small its value, more is required to bring the discharge exception into play. The debt will not be excepted from discharge unless the debtor understood that the creditor had rights to the property and he or she acted with a specific intent to harm or defraud the creditor. Moreover, if the debt is excepted, it should be nondischargeable only to the extent of the value of the collateral converted if that value is less than the debt.

Courts have disagreed regarding whether punitive damages are also nondischargeable. Some courts have ruled that they are not because a wholly private penalty cannot be the basis of a nondischargeability judgment. Others have ruled that the entire debt resulting from the conduct is nondischargeable.

Finally, only willful and malicious acts of the debtor—not those of employees, children, or others—can lead to a finding of nondischargeability. This represents a change from the prior law, which sometimes denied the discharge of debts for willful and malicious acts of partners, children, and others for whom the debtor was legally responsible under state law.

Fines and Penalties

One of the less frequently used exceptions covers fines and penalties owed to government bodies and for their benefit. By its terms, this exception is limited to purely punitive, as opposed to compensatory, assessments. However, the Supreme Court ruled that a restitution order in a welfare fraud case constitutes a nondischargeable fine or penalty within the meaning of this section. This exception may extend to fines imposed by administrative agencies as well as by courts.

Many penalties and fines are dischargeable in a chapter 13 case. However, arguments are frequently raised about whether court-imposed payments are debts within the meaning of the Bankruptcy Code. The Supreme Court has laid most of these arguments to rest by ruling that debts for restitution orders imposed as a condition of probation in a criminal proceeding are dischargeable in chapter 13. Shortly after it was rendered, this decision was partially overruled by Congress through an amendment that made restitution debts included in a sentence on the debtor's conviction of a crime nondischargeable in chapter 13. Other restitution debts, such as those imposed in pretrial diversion programs, remain dischargeable in chapter 13. Fines, except federal criminal fines, also remain dischargeable in chapter 13.

Not included in this exception are two specific kinds of tax penalties. Those relating to a tax that is dischargeable are also dischargeable, as are any tax penalties relating to a transaction or event that occurred more than three years before the bankruptcy filing.

Student Loans

The exception to discharge for student loans resulted from publicity over a supposed flood of bankruptcies in the early seventies filed by students who were just finishing their education with the purpose of discharging their student loans before they started earning money. The exception has had several different wordings and, as last amended, covers an "educational benefit, overpayment or loan" that is "made, insured or guaranteed by a governmental unit, or made under any program funded in whole or in part by a governmental unit or a nonprofit institution, or for an obligation to repay funds received as an educational benefit, scholarship or stipend." This language was intended to broaden the scope of the exception to cover most, if not all, student loans, at least when the loan recipient is the debtor.

Student Loans in Chapter 7

The Code makes student loan debts nondischargeable in chapter 7 bankruptcy cases unless the loan first came due more than seven years before filing or unless repayment would cause the debtor "undue hardship." The plain language of the applicable section provides that a debt that came due more than seven years before the bankruptcy filing is dischargeable. Although student loans usually first become due shortly after graduation, extensions and consolidations can occasionally cause confusion regarding whether the seven years has passed.

Generally, the first date that payments became due is the critical point of reference. Later consolidations are irrelevant, even if the first payment on the consolidation was due less than seven years before the bankruptcy. However, courts have suspended the running of the time period when payment has been deferred by reenrollment after the initial period has begun to run.

Regardless of whether the debtor is confused about passage of the requisite seven years, it is essential to achieve clarity on this issue with the applicable creditors. In some cases, there is no dispute because all parties agree that the loan is dischargeable as it is undeniably more than seven years old. In that event, a stipulation, letter, or other confirmation of an agreement is essential because the lending institution, guarantee agency, or some other creditor may not keep adequate records that reflect the discharge and may therefore seek to collect in the future.

If there is any dispute about whether the seven years have passed, the debtor must decide whether to seek a bankruptcy court ruling on dischargeability. The debtor's other potential course of action is simply to wait and see if the creditor recommences collection efforts following the bankruptcy and then to raise the discharge defense in the applicable state or federal forum.

If the debtor desires a bankruptcy court determination, there is no time limit to commence a proceeding to resolve the dischargeability issue. In fact, the applicable rule even speaks of allowing cases to be reopened to obtain determinations on issues related to dischargeability.

The other exception to the nondischargeability of student loans is available when excepting the debt from discharge would cause the debtor or the debtor's dependents "undue hardship." Courts have long struggled to define this term. Although most courts agree that *undue* means more than the garden-variety hardship that arises from the expense of future payments, each judge seems to bring a unique set of values to the process of defining and implementing the applicable standard.

The earliest and most influential attempt to catalog the relevant considerations proposed a three-part assessment involving mechanical, good-faith, and policy tests. It has frequently been stated that to obtain discharge on the basis of undue hardship, a debtor must prevail under all three tests.

The proposed mechanical test essentially involves a consideration of the debtor's current ability to meet the terms of the debt without deprivation together with an analysis of future income potential, other resources, educational and work skills, marketability of skills, health, and expected future financial responsibilities. In implementing the mechanical test, most courts focus on current income and expenses as a predictor of future income. Several courts have stated that undue hardship exists whenever a debtor would have to live at or below the poverty level to repay the loan. To the extent that marketability of work skills is a relevant consideration under the mechanical test, the fact that a vocational or trade school education is worthless should be an important consideration in favor of discharge.

The good-faith test requires proof that the debtor has made his or her best effort to pay the debt in the past. Most courts have given this test relatively little attention, and it is hard to see how this essentially value-based judgment is relevant to the question of future hardship. For low-income debtors who did not make past payments, it should be sufficient to establish that the debtor had no ability to pay.

Finally, the policy test involves an inquiry into whether discharge of the debt would undermine the legislative intent behind the student loan exception to discharge. Because the intent was primarily to prevent discharges for wealthy or middle-class students who try to discharge large student loan debts without payment just before they begin lucrative careers, cases coming close to that paradigm rarely meet with much sympathy from the bankruptcy court. Most low-income debtors can easily meet this test.

In essence, the three-part test requires the evaluation of the totality of the circumstances. Other courts have separately concluded that the totality of the circumstances is relevant without adopting the three-part test.

The only court of appeals to extensively consider the definition of undue hardship came up with a three-part test that closely resembles the analysis above. It is framed as follows:

> (1) that the debtor cannot maintain, based on current income and expenses, a "minimal" standard of living . . . if forced to repay the loans; (2) that additional circumstances exist indicating that this state of affairs is likely to persist for a significant portion of the repayment period of the student loans; and (3) that the debtor has made good faith efforts to repay the loans.

In general, low-income debtors should seek to have the court focus on their income and expenses as the basis for a determination of undue hardship. At least one court has stated that a presumption of undue hardship exists for debtors whose income falls below the federal poverty guideline. Other courts have focused on the question of whether a low-income debtor is likely to be able to resume making payments in the foreseeable future. Any debtor who can demonstrate some unique misfortune, medical problem, or underprivilege should bring it to the attention of the court. Every effort should be made to establish lack of job skills, lack of available jobs, disabilities, and other factors that make it improbable that a low-income debtor will have better prospects in the future.

In evaluating student loans that were incurred for vocational school education, two additional considerations related to discharge are appropriate. First, the debtor's undue hardship argument may be strengthened if the student loan arose from a private vocational school that closed down or defrauded the student. Not only do courts sense the unfairness involved in making a student repay a loan for a valueless education, but also the absence of acquired skills makes it less likely that the debtor will be able to obtain employment that permits future loan repayment. In fact, under recent federal legislation, the debtor may be excused from paying such a loan, even without a bankruptcy case. Evidence that a student obtained no benefit from a trade school education is relevant to the mechanical test because it suggests a lack of skills necessary to obtain income for future repayment. It is also relevant to the policy test because valueless vocational school education is outside the congressional concern about highly skilled professionals who shed loan obligations before beginning lucrative careers.

Second, if it is unlikely that a debt will be found dischargeable (and especially in chapter 13 when payments on the debt will be made), the debtor should consider whether there are defenses to the debt based on the school's fraud or some other grounds, particularly if there is a close relationship between the school and the lender. If possible, the debtor should consider an objection based on school-related defenses—for example, breach of contract, warranty, fraud, or unfair trade practice—to the proof of claim filed by the originating lender or guarantee agency. A decision that disallows the claim based on a valid defense is as good or better than a decision that the loan is dischargeable.

Student Loans in Chapter 13

In the past, because student loan debts were dischargeable on completion of a chapter 13 bankruptcy plan, chapter 13 was an attractive option for those who sought to deal with student loan debt burdens. However, recent changes in the law have eliminated many of the advantages of the chapter 13 option. Chapter 13 now incorporates the chapter 7 student loan provisions. Student loans that would be nondischargeable in chapter 7 are also nondischargeable in chapter 13.

Nevertheless, student loan issues continue to arise when chapter 13 is filed for other reasons. In some cases, a bankruptcy plan may still provide advantages during the term of the plan, even if the debt is ultimately nondischargeable.

Given that chapter 13 simply incorporates the chapter 7 provisions, issues of dischargeability of student loans in chapter 13 should be treated almost identically to those arising under chapter 7. As in chapter 7, the debtor will have to request a finding of undue hardship for the debt to be found dischargeable during the bankruptcy case.

Additionally, the change to chapter 13 making student loans nondischargeable contains a "sunset provision" under which it ceases to be effective on October 1, 1996. If Congress does not extend this provision, debtors in chapter 13 cases that are still pending on October 1, 1996, can reasonably argue that their student loan debts are discharged on completion of the plan because the dischargeability exception will no longer exist when they receive their discharges.

The fact that student loans are nondischargeable in chapter 13 does not mean that they cannot be paid in chapter 13 plans. Thus, the debtor can propose treatment of a student loan creditor during a bankruptcy plan that is no different than treatment of any other unsecured creditor. The creditor will not be entitled to additional regular payments outside the plan before the debtor's discharge.

However, if the student loan is nondischargeable, it is in the debtor's interest to ensure that as much as possible of the loan is paid during the bankruptcy. This frequently means that the debtor should propose a plan that classifies the student loan separately and pays it at a higher percentage than other unsecured debts. Several courts have explicitly ruled that a separate classification in favor of a student loan creditor does not "discriminate unfairly" within the meaning of chapter 13's classification provisions. At least one court has held that a reasonable basis for the separate classification exists because the debt is nondischargeable and because, absent payment, the debtor may be unable to return to school to obtain a degree. However, other courts have disagreed.

Health Education Assistance Loans

Congress created a different exception to discharge for a particular type of student loan. No bankruptcy discharge may be granted for a Health Education Assistance Loan (HEAL) debt within five years after the date that repayment is to begin. During this five-year period, no hardship discharge is available for these loans. Even after the five years, the loan is dischargeable only if the bankruptcy court finds that denial of a discharge would be unconscionable. This nondischargeability provision has been held to apply in chapter 13 as well as in chapter 7. Because the provision makes discharge available after five years based on unconscionability, a discharge should be possible in a chapter 13 case that is filed within five years if the discharge is not entered until after the five-year period has expired. Several courts have held that a determination regarding discharge of a HEAL debt can only be made at the conclusion of a chapter 13 plan.

Several other health education assistance programs have similar provisions. Debts that arise from those programs are nondischargeable under the same rules as are applicable to HEAL debts.

Debts Incurred through Drunk Driving

As a result of increased public concern about the social problem of drunk drivers, the 1984 bankruptcy amendments added an exception to the chapter 7 discharge for debts incurred through drunk driving. A 1990 amendment to the statute made the exception to discharge applicable in chapter 13 cases as well. The same amendment broadened the exception to include unlawful driving while under the influence of a drug or other substance but also narrowed it to include only debts for death or personal injury.

The specific terms of this subsection narrow its scope somewhat. The exception applies only if the debtor operated the vehicle and the operation was unlawful due to intoxication. At a minimum, this presumably requires that the debtor met the legal standard for intoxication in the jurisdiction in which the accident occurred. These standards vary and may not even exist in every jurisdiction. When they do exist, there may be disputes about how the standard is to be applied, especially if it is not labeled "intoxication." A judgment or consent decree often does not specify whether the standard was met. There is then the question of whether this issue may later to litigated separately to determine dischargeability under this provision.

Debts That Existed at Time of Denial or Waiver of Discharge in Prior Bankruptcy Cases

The Code contains another exception to discharge that is rarely seen. It is relevant only if the debtor has been denied a discharge in a prior bankruptcy case, which rarely occurs in consumer cases. If the debtor has been denied a discharge, any debt that existed when the prior bankruptcy was filed may not be discharged in a later bankruptcy.

This exception does not apply if discharge was denied in the prior case only because of the six-year bar to consecutive bankruptcies or because of failure to pay filing fees. Nor does it apply when a dischargeable debt was reaffirmed in a prior bankruptcy case. Similarly, the exception does not apply when a previous case was dismissed, with or without prejudice, if a discharge was not waived or denied in that case.

Debts Emerging from Responsibilities to Federal Depository Institutions

The last two exceptions to discharge in chapter 7 are rarely, if ever, applicable in consumer cases. They were added to the Code as part of the congressional response to the savings and loan crisis in order to help the Federal Deposit Insurance Corporation (FDIC) and other regulators recover assets to pay the cost of the bailout.

The Code excepts from discharge debts that emerged from fraud or defalcation in a fiduciary capacity related to the debtor's responsibility to a depository institution or credit union when that debt is memorialized in a "final judgment, unreviewable order, consent order, decree or . . . settlement agreement." It also excepts debts for malicious or reckless failure to maintain the capital of insured depository institutions, unless such responsibility has been terminated by an act of the applicable regulatory agency.

Debts Made Nondischargeable by Other Statutes

Congress has passed several other statutory provisions that may make debts nondischargeable in bankruptcy under chapters 7 or 13. Statutes that make student loan debts nondischargeable in some circumstances outside of the Code's own provisions are discussed above. Similarly, certain obligations that arise from retention bonuses paid to military officers were made nondischargeable when the discharge is entered less than five years from the date that the retention agreement is terminated. Because these provisions contain language that makes them applicable when a discharge is entered within five years, they will not apply in a chapter 13 case that is filed within five years if the discharge is not entered until after the five-year period has expired.

THE PROTECTIONS OF THE DISCHARGE

Effects on Discharged Claims

For most debts discharged in bankruptcy cases, the protections of the discharge can only be described as sweeping. They extend to a wide range of debts: all debts that arose before the bankruptcy petition was filed in a chapter 7 case, except those made nondischargeable by the provisions discussed above. *Debt* is defined as any liability on a claim, and *claim* is very broadly defined to include any right to payment or any right to an equitable remedy if the remedy gives rise to a right to payment, regardless of whether that right is reduced to judgment, liquidated, unliquidated, fixed, contingent, matured, unmatured, disputed, undisputed, legal, equitable, secured, or unsecured.

Disputes arise in numerous contexts in which the debtor's prepetition conduct has consequences that are undiscovered or even undiscoverable until after a petition is filed or a case is closed. Many courts have concluded that such circumstances create dischargeable claims in bankruptcy. Whether they are discharged, however, may depend on whether the creditor receives appropriate notice of the bankruptcy.

In chapter 13, the normal discharge covers all debts "provided for in the plan," except alimony and support, restitution included in a sentence on the debtor's conviction of a crime, most debts connected with intoxicated driving, and long-term debts cured in the plan on which the last payment is due after the last payment under the plan is due. Because some uncertainty exists regarding whether an unsecured debt is "provided for" if no payment on that debt is possible in the plan, it is a good idea to include at least a nominal amount for all unsecured creditors in every chapter 13 plan.

The discharge operates to obviate the personal liability of the debtor. It does not eliminate valid liens against the debtor's property that have not been avoided, paid, or modified during the bankruptcy. Thus, a mortgage continues to be valid after a chapter 7 case, though the creditor can no longer sue the debtor if the property fails to satisfy the debt. If a chapter 13 plan provides for the creditor to retain a lien, that lien remains valid until the allowed claim is paid.

However, as discussed in Chapter 9, exempt property may not be reached after the case even by most creditors that hold nondischargeable claims. It is protected from any prebankruptcy "debt of the debtor," except debts for taxes, those for alimony and support, and those secured by a lien that was not voided in the bankruptcy. In fact, these protections are granted to debtors even when a discharge has been denied because they are not contingent on a discharge being granted.

For both chapter 7 and chapter 13 cases, the discharge section contains additional effectuating provisions. The discharge automatically voids any judgment obtained at any time to the extent that the judgment is a determination of the debtor's personal liability on a discharged debt. (However, a judgment can be a lien on property as well as a determination of personal liability, and that lien is not automatically void. It may often be avoidable through a separate motion within the bankruptcy case, as discussed in Chapter 9.)

Thus, even if a creditor proceeds to judgment after the bankruptcy, that judgment would be void. Although this means that the debtor need take no action to protect against a judgment, the best course would be to seek to eliminate the judgment as early as possible, perhaps in the bankruptcy court, because even a void judgment may cause various kinds of problems for the debtor until it is removed from the court's records.

The provision that voids judgments is self-effectuating, and no further action is required by the debtor with respect to judgments already entered before the bankruptcy case. A diligent record search to check the status of judgments should also turn up the debtor's bankruptcy, which voids all judgments against him or her, at least if all of the proceedings occurred in the same locality. Nonetheless, in some areas it is advisable and customary to notify the court of the discharge or otherwise record its existence where a judgment is recorded.

The discharge puts into effect a broad prohibition of the commencement or continuation of any legal action, the employment of process, or any act to collect, recover, or offset any discharged debt as a personal liability of the debtor or from property of the debtor. This section was intended to cover not only legal proceedings, but also any other acts of creditors, such as dunning, harassment, withholding of further credit, threatening or instituting criminal proceedings, and the like, whether directed at the debtor or at anyone else. It has already been broadly construed to cover acts that are related only indirectly to the discharged debt but that could harm the debtor because of the debt's previous existence. Violation of the prohibition is contempt of court, punishable by awards of damages and attorney's fees to the injured party.

However, this section does not bar the enforcement of valid liens against the debtor's property if they have not been modified or avoided in the bankruptcy. These security interests are limited to property acquired before the bankruptcy, regardless of any clause that would otherwise cover property acquired later.

For debtors with interests in community property, the discharge is even broader; it covers prebankruptcy creditors' claims against any community property acquired after the bankruptcy case that would have been included in the bankruptcy estate, even if only one spouse has filed a bankruptcy petition. The only exceptions to this broad rule are claims excepted from discharge in the debtor spouse's case and claims that would not have been discharged if the nondebtor spouse had filed. These provisions also mean that all creditors of both spouses should be listed in the schedules to prevent nondischargeability problems under the provisions that pertain to unlisted creditors, as discussed above.

Reaffirmation and Security Interests That Survive Bankruptcy

Some of the most persistent problems under the previous Bankruptcy Act were those arising through the reaffirmation of debts by consumer debtors. By using a variety of coercive levers—such as threats of repossession, collection activities directed at cosigners, and refusal to lend more money without reaffirmation—creditors routinely lured debtors into giving up the protections of their bankruptcy discharge by making new and binding promises to pay debts that had been discharged.

This problem was recognized by both the Bankruptcy Commission, which proposed a total bar against reaffirmation agreements, and Congress. Although the Code does not completely bar reaffirmation agreements, it does restrict them significantly under the theory that reaffirmation is rarely a wise step for the debtor.

Requirements for Reaffirmation

The Code sets forth a number of requirements that must be followed before a reaffirmation is binding. First, there must be an agreement between the debtor and the creditor that is valid under applicable nonbankruptcy law. That agreement is usually a contract in which the debtor agrees to pay the debt, even though it is discharged. The requirements of the Code also apply to other postbankruptcy contracts that effectively constitute a renewed obligation to pay a prebankruptcy debt. Without an agreement, there can be no reaffirmation; in such cases, neither the debtor nor the creditor may seek court approval of reaffirmation. Only the debtor may apply to the court for approval of the reaffirmation when that approval is still necessary.

The reaffirmation agreement must be made before the discharge. By the terms of the Code, a reaffirmation agreement is not enforceable unless entered into before the discharge. In addition, at the discharge hearing the court must inform the debtor of the right not to enter into the agreement and of the legal effects of the agreement and any default that might occur. Once the discharge has been granted, reaffirmation is no longer possible; the discharge may not be revoked to provide for reaffirmation.

Several other requirements exist for an enforceable reaffirmation agreement. The agreement must contain a clear and conspicuous statement advising the debtor that the agreement may be rescinded (canceled by the debtor) at any time before the discharge or within 60 days after the agreement is filed with the court, whichever is later, by giving notice to the creditor. The agreement must then be filed with the court if it was not rescinded during the time permitted.

Finally, in all debt reaffirmations, there are two additional requirements. If an attorney has negotiated the reaffirmation, the agreement filed with the court must be accompanied by the attorney's affidavit that the reaffirmation represents a fully informed and voluntary agreement by the debtor and will not impose an undue hardship on the debtor or the debtor's dependents.

If the agreement was not negotiated by an attorney, the court must approve the agreement as not imposing an undue hardship on the debtor or the debtor's dependents and as being in the debtor's best interests. The only exception to this rule is for reaffirmation of certain consumer debts that are secured by real property. It is not clear whether this exception applies when the agreement is negotiated by an attorney because the exception appears only in the provision pertaining to reaffirmations that are not negotiated by an attorney.

The Undue Hardship and Best Interests Tests

Because the tests for approval of reaffirmation of consumer debts that are not secured by real property were new, the courts had to determine what circumstances are sufficient to satisfy them. To do this, they have looked to a number of factors.

Principally, courts have sought to determine the debtor's reasons for wanting to reaffirm. If the debtor seeks only to satisfy a moral obligation or to protect a cosigner, courts have generally found that reaffirmation is not in the debtor's best interests. The possibility of undisclosed pressure from creditors, cosigners, and others has weighed heavily in these cases, and the courts have pointed out that the absence of reaffirmation does not prevent the debtor from voluntarily making whatever payments he or she chooses. It only serves to prevent the debtor from being bound by an agreement to pay should he or she become unable or unwilling to pay.

Cases in which debts are secured by the debtor's property have presented more difficult problems. Courts have often looked to whether the property was a necessity for the debtor and whether reaffirmation was necessary to keep the property. In one case, reaffirmation was allowed on a debt secured by vehicles necessary for the debtor's employment but denied on a debt secured by an expensive television.

Even with debts secured by necessary property, courts have looked askance at reaffirmation agreements to pay more than the value of the property without a showing that some other method, such as redemption (discussed in Chapter 10), was not possible. Other courts have flatly refused to approve reaffirmations for amounts in excess of the value of the collateral. It appears that such agreements have been proposed mainly in cases in which the debtor's counsel was lazy, incompetent, or both in not exploring better alternatives for the debtor.

Factors to Consider

Debtors should be extremely cautious about entering into reaffirmation agreements. Before 1979, many debtors entered into ill-advised reaffirmations; the numerous cases in which courts have disapproved reaffirmations since then suggest that attorneys have not always been as wary of reaffirmation as the courts have been.

It is usually best to avoid reaffirmations, if possible. The debtor can often obtain the desired result by simply maintaining voluntary payments on a debt without reassuming the legal obligation. For example, a creditor cannot pursue a codebtor if the debtor's payments remain current. Many courts have held that property subject to a security interest may not be repossessed if payments are up to date. If there is any doubt on this issue, a chapter 13 filing should be considered to handle the secured claim.

Secured Debts without Reaffirmation

For various reasons, secured debts may exist after bankruptcy in which neither reaffirmation nor redemption has taken place. This may occur because the debtor does not choose to again be personally obligated to pay the debt. It may also occur because the creditor refuses to agree to reaffirmation.

In such cases, the question arises concerning whether the creditor may foreclose on its still-existing lien due to a "bankruptcy clause" in the contract that creates an automatic default when the debtor files a bankruptcy case even without a default in payments under the contract. These contractual default clauses are not favored under the Code, but some creditors have argued that they may still be used to foreclose on collateral even if there has been no default in payments.

Debtors can overcome this potential problem in several ways. The best way, which is usually preferable to reaffirmation, is a redemption agreement that does not provide for reaffirmation. Although it probably cannot be required to do so, a creditor may enter a binding agreement not to foreclose as long as contractual payments are made.

Even when creditors are not willing to enter into such agreements, they will usually take no action against the debtor as long as payments are current. Some court decisions have simply stated, using various reasons, that foreclosure is not permissible while the debtor is current with payments. An experienced bankruptcy attorney should know whether those decisions are binding on creditors in a particular region. A final alternative is to file a new chapter 13 case, under which the debtor could retain the property and cure the default. Sometimes, the mere threat of a chapter 13 case, in which the creditor might be paid less or more slowly, is enough to persuade a recalcitrant creditor to agree to the debtor's continuing payments without reaffirmation.

If the debtor does fall behind on payments after the bankruptcy case, the creditor is, of course, entitled to enforce a valid lien. A new bankruptcy case under chapter 13 may also be available at that time as an option.

Protection against Discrimination Based on Bankruptcy

In addition to the other protections of the discharge, the Code contains a specific provision that bars some types of discrimination based on a person's bankruptcy. The Code provides that, with a few uncommon exceptions, a government body may not discriminate against a bankruptcy debtor when granting "a license, permit, charter, franchise, or other similar grant" and may not discriminate with respect to employment against an individual solely because that person is or has been a bankruptcy debtor or has not paid a debt that is dischargeable in bankruptcy.

This provision is clearly directed at government bodies—whether federal, state, or local—and does not cover private entities. However, a second provision of the law prohibits private employers from employment discrimination based on bankruptcy, insolvency before a bankruptcy, or nonpayment of a debt discharged or dischargeable in bankruptcy. This section is most often helpful when employers are unhappy with court orders to deduct chapter 13 payments from a debtor's paycheck and forward them to the chapter 13 trustee. It will also help in those rare cases in which debtors owe debts to their employers or to persons or institutions closely affiliated with their employers. As in any employment discrimination case, there may still be the difficult problem of proving why an employer took a particular action, especially when the employer presents other reasons for its action against the debtor. The court may have to evaluate whether the reasons presented are the true motivations for the employer's action and, if so, whether those reasons are valid.

In addition to the question of who may or may not discriminate, there is also a good deal of uncertainty about how broad the scope of the protection really is. What is covered by the phrase "license, permit, charter, franchise, or other similar grant"? Such matters as the issuance of a driver's license and employment are clearly covered, but what about the provision of various public benefits, such as welfare or Social Security when the agency has been denied repayment of a debt by the discharge, or the granting of a student loan when a previous loan debt was discharged? What about utility service provided by public entities? May a deposit be required of debtors who have discharged debts when it is not required of others? The courts have differed in answering these questions.

The principle of the fresh start should be applicable to virtually any type of public benefit or government action. As discussed below, the law has already been broadly interpreted to include the right to live in public housing and the right to receive a transcript from a university to which a student loan was owed. Denial of various other government benefits, services, or privileges has also been found to be discriminatory. It is also clear that the section extends not just to discrimination based on the bankruptcy, but also to discrimination based on an unpaid debt that was discharged in bankruptcy.

One important limitation should be noted, however. The section bars discrimination only when it is *solely* based on the bankruptcy or on nonpayment of a dischargeable debt. When other factors are involved, unless they can be shown to be pretexts and not the real reasons for the challenged action, the debtor will have a difficult case, especially because the legislative history specifically states that factors such as future financial ability may be considered if applied nondiscriminatorily. For example, a law cannot require only debtors who have filed bankruptcies to obtain automobile insurance. However, if all persons who do not have assets sufficient to pay a judgment are required to obtain insurance, then debtors who filed bankruptcies are not treated differently. And if a debt is not discharged in a bankruptcy, discrimination based on that debt is not prohibited by this section.

Finally, when the discrimination provisions do not apply, the discharge order may still prevent the challenged action. Whenever it can be shown that the denial or other act directed at a debtor was intended to coerce payment of the discharged debt, the act is in violation of the discharge order and should therefore be considered a contempt of court.

Particular Problems Relating to Discharge Protections

Driver's Licenses

One of the more common uses of bankruptcy is to prevent the loss of or to regain a driver's license that is jeopardized by state laws that require debtors to pay court accident judgments if they do not have insurance. These laws typically provide that an operator's license and sometimes vehicle registration are suspended until a judgment arising from a motor vehicle accident is paid. The Supreme Court has held that, if the debt is discharged in bankruptcy, the license can no longer be denied.

Some courts have more recently held that any other discrimination based on a discharged debt—such as a requirement that special insurance or a bond be purchased before a license can be granted—is also prohibited because the discrimination would tend to frustrate the congressional purpose of giving debtors a fresh start. Other courts have disagreed.

Similarly, a license cannot be withheld on the basis of nonpayment of traffic tickets that are dischargeable in chapter 13 cases. In these situations, the law has been read to mean that the debtor involved should be treated as if the discharged debt never existed. Thus, for a debtor who needs a driver's license but cannot pay a judgment or fines, bankruptcy can be an ideal solution. However, if the license was suspended or revoked for some reason other than the nonpayment of money, such as points assessed after particular traffic violations, the bankruptcy will not resolve that problem.

Student Loans and College Transcripts

A persistent problem under the prior Bankruptcy Act concerned college students and graduates who were refused transcripts from educational institutions because of discharged student loans. Assuming that a transcript falls under the phrase "license, permit, charter, franchise, or other grant," the law is now clear that a public institution cannot deny a transcript. Similarly, a public entity's denial, based on the bankruptcy, of further student loans might be prohibited, although not all courts have agreed on this.

Moreover, withholding a transcript is not a valid means for a private educational institution to induce payment of a debt. The discharge order prohibits "any act" to collect a debt after discharge. Indeed, as soon as a bankruptcy case is filed, acts to collect a debt are prohibited by the automatic stay, which is discussed in Chapter 8.

One additional argument that a debtor might face from a private college that is withholding a transcript is that the school is not trying to coerce payment of the debt, but rather is simply exercising its right to refuse to enter into new transactions with the debtor. This argument could be attacked as a pretext to cover up an actual intent to coerce payment. Unlike a creditor that decides not to extend further credit or services, the college puts nothing new at risk in releasing a transcript. The fee is normally paid in advance, and there is no chance whatsoever of creditor harm. Finally, the debtor might argue that the right to a transcript is a property right that is received in conjunction with the degree or with enrollment. If the debtor claims this right as exempt, as discussed in Chapter 9, a good argument exists that a creditor may not withhold such property, which is also property of the estate, from the debtor.

Thus, debtors are afforded significant new protections with respect to college transcripts under the Code. Since its enactment, the courts have largely made this problem a thing of the past.

Public and Private Housing

Many of the issues that arise with respect to student loans are also involved in disputes concerning the right to remain in public or private housing after discharge. A strong argument can be made that the right to remain in public housing is in essence a grant of the subsidy that makes possible lower rents. Further, it is well established in court decisions and HUD regulations that tenants may be evicted from public housing only for valid cause. Thus, it is not surprising that the discrimination provisions have been used to prevent eviction of public housing tenants who discharged rent arrearages through bankruptcy.

Like private colleges, private landlords present somewhat more difficult problems. In most places, the landlord has no obligation to renew a lease, and the landlord may assert its right to evict the tenant at the end of the lease for any reason, including bankruptcy. Although it is clear that relief from the automatic stay must be obtained to evict during the pendency of the bankruptcy case, after the case the debtor must find some other protection.

The possible arguments to the contrary are similar to those in the context of student loans. If the debtor can show that the landlord has tried to coerce payment of the discharged debt by threatening eviction, protection may be obtained under the discharge order. In many places, the debtor can also assert a right to remain based on state law. For example, in most rent-control jurisdictions, the tenant may only be evicted for good cause. Some court decisions in these areas have stated that, when the discharged debt is the only possible basis for the eviction, the eviction must be seen as a means to compel payment and is thus prohibited. Similarly, the debtor can argue that the eviction is improper because it is in retaliation for the debtor's exercise of rights granted under the law. As long as the debtor posts adequate security for future rent and otherwise complies with the lease, this argument may be persuasive. Of course, if the debtor anticipates a problem with his or her landlord, the best course of action may be to file a chapter 13 case to take advantage of its additional options with respect to leases, as discussed earlier in Chapter 11.

Social Security, Welfare, and Other Government Benefits

Debtors sometimes have debts to local, state, or federal government agencies that arise from various public benefit programs and that they wish to discharge. These debts may arise from a general duty to reimburse for such benefits, which exists under some state laws, or from an overpayment that the debtor is required to repay.

These debts are usually dischargeable because, absent certain kinds of fraud, they do not fall within any of the exceptions to discharge, which were discussed earlier in this chapter. It seems clear that any future denial or reduction of benefits because of the discharge would fall squarely within the prohibitions of the discrimination and discharge provisions.

Criminal Proceedings, Fines, and Incarceration

In some cases, the tricky problem of dealing with criminal or quasi-criminal proceedings during or after bankruptcy is encountered. During the bankruptcy, these problems may sometimes be handled with the automatic stay if the proceedings represent attempts to collect money from the debtor. Both during and after the case, the discrimination provisions may also be applicable. Assuming that the right to be free from incarceration is a "license," then the state cannot incarcerate a debtor due to a debt that was discharged. Similarly, driver's license suspensions, based on dischargeable unpaid traffic fines should be found to violate these provisions. To the extent that it can be shown that a criminal or contempt proceeding is for the purpose of collecting a discharged debt, these proceedings are in violation of the discharge order.

However, as discussed elsewhere in this chapter, the court must first find that the restitution order is a dischargeable debt. The Supreme Court has held that it is not dischargeable in a chapter 7 case but the debt may be dischargeable in a chapter 13 case if it was not imposed on conviction of a crime.

If those hurdles are overcome, along with the reluctance of federal courts to interfere with state criminal cases, the bankruptcy could give the debtor significant protections in the many cases in which creditors and local authorities attempt to use criminal or contempt proceedings to coerce payments. However, emotions in such cases may run high, and enforcement of the bankruptcy protections may not always be easy.

Enforcement of the Discharge Protections

In almost every case in which the debtor's discharge rights are being violated, it is wise to take some type of protective action. Even though a judgment obtained on a discharged debt is void, that judgment could also cause an illegal but harmful garnishment of the debtor's wages or a seizure of the debtor's property. Thus, it is a good idea to assert the protections of the discharge as early as possible.

The first decision that arises in such cases is where to enforce the debtor's rights. Although the issue could be raised in the state court in which a proceeding is already pending, it is usually preferable to go to the bankruptcy court, which is likely to be more sympathetic to the debtor's concerns. The bankruptcy court clearly has jurisdiction over any proceeding relating to the debtor's bankruptcy, and a state court proceeding may often be removed to the bankruptcy court.

Several remedies may be possible in the bankruptcy court in addition to simply defending a removed action. The federal court may be permitted to issue a writ of habeas corpus to release a debtor who is incarcerated in state proceedings. A court may issue an order against private parties or state officials. Finally, violators of the discharge order can be held in contempt of court. The remedies for civil contempt include damages and attorney's fees, even when the contempt is not willful.

Thus, the bankruptcy court does not offer assistance to debtors only during their bankruptcy cases. Its expanded reach enables it to provide a full measure of protection as long as it is needed in relation to the bankruptcy and the debts discharged therein. Consumer debtors can turn to the bankruptcy court to solve many of their problems, applying a law that, unlike most, is designed principally to benefit those unfortunate people who so often find themselves victimized elsewhere.

Chapter 14

ATTORNEYS AND THEIR FEES IN CONSUMER BANKRUPTCY CASES

THE ADVISABILITY OF HAVING A LAWYER

Bankruptcy laws are, unfortunately, quite complicated, a fact demonstrated by the length of this book. Indeed, numerous issues may arise in consumer bankruptcy cases that could not be discussed in this guide because they are too technical or are specific to debtors in only a few states.

In addition, the law changes constantly as a result of new amendments to the Bankruptcy Code or court decisions. Readers are thus cautioned that statements in this book are the author's best explanation of the law at the time that the book was published.

For these reasons, it is advisable for bankruptcy debtors to be represented by lawyers, if at all possible. Unfortunately, lawyers are not inexpensive, and for some, there is simply no way to pay an attorney's fee. To compound their problems, the woeful state of funding for legal services to poor people has left most legal aid and legal services programs with insufficient resources to handle most bankruptcy cases.

For anyone who is able to obtain a good attorney to handle a bankruptcy case, the cost of the attorney's fee is well worth the price. A good bankruptcy attorney is well versed in the possible complications that might arise in what seems to be a simple and straightforward case. A good bankruptcy attorney is aware of recent changes in the law and of court decisions in the local courts. A good bankruptcy attorney can usually find ways of making a bankruptcy case more productive and effective than it would be if the debtor tried to handle it without an attorney, ultimately saving the debtor many hundreds or thousands of dollars more than the attorney's fee. Finally, having a good bankruptcy attorney can bring debtors the peace of mind that results from knowing their cases are being handled without the mistakes that they might make on their own.

Debtors who attempt to file bankruptcy cases without attorneys risk any number of pitfalls. At a minimum, these may result in wasted time and effort if a case is dismissed due to mistakes in filing the papers. In other cases, debtors may lose the benefit of discharge for uncommon sorts of debts that are not listed, or they may lose the opportunity to eliminate liens on their property. In the worst situations, mistakes may cost the debtor's family its car or even its home.

AVOIDING DEBT COUNSELING, CREDIT REPAIR, AND BANKRUPTCY-RELATED SCAMS

The desperate situations of many debtors and the high price of attorneys have left debtors easy prey for a variety of unscrupulous operators who are all too willing to take their last remaining dollars. These operators appear in a number of types of businesses, but all offer the lure of a cheap, easy way to make financial problems disappear. They invariably leave the debtor poorer and, in many cases, much worse off than before they rendered their "services."

Perhaps the most common are those who advertise that they can help debtors file bankruptcy cases without an attorney. At best, these individuals have some familiarity with the forms used in bankruptcy cases and know generally how to fill them out. However, they do not have the legal training necessary to recognize problems or advise the debtor about bankruptcy law. They do not know when a case requires more than the standard steps they take in every case. They cannot advise the debtor of ways to eliminate liens or pursue more complicated procedures. They cannot go to court or defend the debtor if a creditor attempts to oppose the bankruptcy or take advantage of the debtor. They cannot give advice that could save the debtor hundreds or thousands of dollars in the long run. A bankruptcy filed with only the help of nonattorneys often fails to accomplish even its basic purposes, thus leaving the debtor worse off than before.

At worst, many of these "typing services" or "paralegals" are interested only in separating debtors from their money. They claim to be able to stop evictions, foreclosures, repossessions, and collection actions, and they do not even explain that they will do so by having the debtor file a bankruptcy case. When such cases are filed, they do not follow up with the necessary forms, and the cases are quickly dismissed, often making it harder for the debtor to file a legitimate bankruptcy case in the future.

Closely related are operations that offer "credit repair" or credit counseling but are not associated with the established nonprofit credit counselors in the community. These outfits promise to make credit problems go away and to obtain new credit for those who have bad credit records. However, they know no magic tricks. At best they may obtain an expensive "secured" credit card, which can be used as long as the card user keeps enough money in a special account to cover the amount charged on the card. In other words, customers get to pay a fee to obtain a card with which they can borrow money from themselves at a very high interest rate in order to buy something that they had enough money to purchase with cash. In most cases, customers do not even receive this dubious benefit, and the operators simply fail to deliver on their promises after taking the customer's money.

Other rip-off artists sell as magic cures to debt problems services that consumers could obtain free or at minimal expense. After taking the consumer's money, some offer only a referral to a bankruptcy attorney, who is often not a particularly competent one. Others who claim that they can help consumers with bad credit to find housing, give lists of apartments taken directly from newspaper advertisements.

Finally, some operators claim that they can solve the consumer's problems through a debt-consolidation loan, which often means a home-equity loan or a refinancing of the debtor's first mortgage. As discussed in Chapter 5, these loans can be colossal mistakes, turning debts that can be discharged in bankruptcy into mortgages that cannot be eliminated or trading debts with no interest charges or small interest charges for debts with high interest rates. The brokers or lenders who push these loans on debtors with poor credit histories usually reward themselves with large fees and charges for their services.

HOW TO FIND A GOOD BANKRUPTCY LAWYER

Just as there are good doctors and bad doctors, good teachers and bad teachers, good auto mechanics and bad auto mechanics, so too there are good lawyers and bad lawyers. Indeed, the legal profession has a fairly large number of members who are barely competent or downright incompetent at what they do. Once a lawyer graduates from law school and passes the bar exam, which is not difficult in many places and does not test many skills that a lawyer needs, there is no mechanism to check whether a lawyer can represent clients adequately, except for whatever supervision the lawyer receives from his or her employer.

Just as there is no simple, guaranteed way of finding a good doctor, there is no simple, guaranteed way to find a good lawyer. However, the debtor can take various steps to avoid incompetents. A debtor who diligently follows the steps outlined below can be reasonably sure of finding someone who can ably handle a consumer bankruptcy case.

Availability of Free Legal Services

For low-income debtors, legal services may be available at little or no cost through government-funded legal services and legal aid offices. Unfortunately, because of funding cuts during the 12 years of Republican rule in the White House, these programs do not have enough lawyers to handle even a small fraction of the legal problems that people bring to them.

In some areas, the efforts of legal services programs are supplemented by lawyers who contribute some of their time to handling cases for low-income people, without charging fees, *pro bono* (for the public good). These programs usually work in conjunction with free legal aid or legal services programs. Therefore, a first step for low-income debtors who seek a bankruptcy attorney should be a call or visit to the local office that provides free legal services for poor people. These offices can be located through the phone book or through social services agencies or political officials.

It is surprising to some people that the attorneys employed by legal services offices are generally capable and knowledgeable. There is much competition for the few legal services jobs available among dedicated people who could make more money elsewhere but have chosen to pursue a career helping others. If a legal services office does handle bankruptcy cases, chances are good that they are handled well. Although *pro bono* attorneys who work with legal services offices may not be as experienced in handling consumer bankruptcy cases, there are usually some mechanisms in place to ensure the quality of their services. Finally, even when no free legal help is available, a legal services office may be a good source for a referral to a competent private lawyer.

Finding a Good Private Attorney

It is very difficult for a layperson to assess an attorney's abilities and qualifications. Unlike in shopping for a car or a television, there is no Consumers Reports that rates attorneys. Similarly, the services offered by attorneys are not standardized; one cannot simply look for the best price and be assured that the services will always be the same, even in a simple consumer bankruptcy case. Nor will the attorney who charges the most necessarily be better than one who charges less.

How can a consumer find a good attorney? Probably the best way is similar to the way one would find a good doctor or other professional:

through the knowledge of others in the field who are familiar with an attorney's work. Attorneys are far more able than laypeople to recognize both good and bad legal work. Just as one might get a referral to a specialist physician from a general practitioner, a consumer client can seek the opinion of attorneys they know regarding who can handle a consumer bankruptcy case skillfully. The best source of this advice would be a respected attorney who does not handle bankruptcy cases.

Other good sources of information are professionals who are regularly involved in consumer bankruptcy cases. Every area has a chapter 13 trustee who administers chapter 13 cases for the court. It is not difficult to find out the name and address of the trustee from the federal bankruptcy court clerk. The trustee, who may or may not be an attorney, may be happy to recommend a good attorney. Similarly, every area has people, some of whom are attorneys, designated as trustees for chapter 7 bankruptcy cases; their names should be available from the court. They, too, could recommend attorneys or perhaps handle consumer bankruptcy cases themselves. Trustees are generally, but not always, capable of doing a good job in consumer bankruptcy cases, so it is worth checking a little on a trustee who recommends himself or herself.

Another good indicator is participation in professional activities. If an attorney has taught bankruptcy courses for other attorneys or has written articles for professional publications, that is a very good sign that the attorney's work is respected by his or her peers. Participation in such activities as attorney committees or professional organizations concerned with bankruptcy law is another indicator of someone who is knowledgeable in the field.

A source of information that is not particularly helpful in finding a good attorney is advertising. In fact, many of the attorneys who advertise the most are not very good; the best attorneys get most or all of their cases through word-of-mouth referrals. At most, attorney advertising will identify some of the bankruptcy attorneys in the area.

Another poor indicator of quality is the number of bankruptcy cases a firm or attorney handles. Although it might seem that an attorney with a lot of cases must be good, some of the bankruptcy lawyers with the largest caseloads are also the worst. These lawyers are sometimes more interested in attracting clients than in doing a thorough job on their cases, and they do little or nothing to fight for a client once the client has paid the attorney's fee. The large number of cases handled by these lawyers may indicate only an effective advertising campaign, luring in consumer debtors who are not sophisticated enough to know better. On the other hand, some firms that handle a large number of cases do an excellent job.

Finally, the price of an attorney's services should not be a prime consideration. The attorney who offers the lowest price may do so only because cases are handled in a routine way that does not give enough attention to problems or special situations, or the attorney may fail to explain things adequately to clients. The difference in price among attorneys for a consumer bankruptcy case is usually no more than a few hundred dollars. For debtors who can afford more than the lowest price, the money saved by hiring a better attorney may be many times the difference in fees.

Consumers may wish to interview attorneys about their qualifications and how their cases would be handled before making a final decision on which attorney to retain. Many bankruptcy attorneys offer a free initial consultation. Besides questions about the topics mentioned above, consumers might ask generally what the attorney could accomplish through their bankruptcy case, how the attorney would proceed, and what their other alternatives are. Another useful question is how often the court dismisses cases filed by the attorney. A significant percentage (more than 20 percent to 30 percent) of dismissals in chapter 13 cases is a sign that the attorney may not be doing much to fight for his or her clients. (Chapter 7 cases are rarely dismissed.)

ARRANGEMENTS FOR THE ATTORNEY'S FEE

Bankruptcy attorney's fees are unusual in several ways. Unlike most clients of private attorneys, bankruptcy clients always face serious financial problems. They may have great difficulties in paying even modest fees. Attorneys must be paid in advance in most chapter 7 cases in which no assets will be distributed to creditors; the debt for these prebankruptcy services is dischargeable, and any attempt to collect the debt after the case is filed would violate the automatic stay, which is discussed in Chapter 8.

Another unusual aspect of bankruptcy attorney's fees is the requirement that all fees be disclosed to the court and approved by the court.

A third key difference in chapter 13 cases and in occasional chapter 7 cases is the possibility for payment of attorney's fees through the court's administration of the bankruptcy. Most typically, this means the payment of fees as a priority claim through the debtor's chapter 13 plan, which provides one solution for the debtor who is unable to pay all or even part of the fee in advance.

Initial Fee Arrangements

As in any other matter, it is very important for an attorney and client to discuss and have a clear understanding of fee arrangements as early as possible. This discussion normally occurs at the first interview with the attorney. Many attorneys have preprinted retainer agreements or brochures that they give to clients at this initial consultation; they spell out exactly which services are covered by the attorney's basic fee and what charges will be made for additional services, should they prove necessary. These written materials and all fee arrangements should be consistent with any previous advertisements or representations that the attorney has made.

The Basic Fee

Many attorneys begin the process of setting fees by deciding on a reasonable basic fee for these services that are necessary in every bankruptcy case. This fee covers the initial consultation with the debtor and advice about the alternatives to bankruptcy, the consequences of bankruptcy, whether to file, and under what chapter to file. It also encompasses preparation of the initial papers—such as the petition, schedules, statement of affairs, and chapter 13 plan—as well as any factual investigation necessary for that task. In addition, the basic fee includes compensation for attendance at the meeting of creditors, the chapter 13 confirmation hearing, and the discharge hearing, when required. Finally, this fee is deemed to encompass ancillary minor and routine tasks and advice to the debtor throughout the course of the case.

Typical Fees

Although there are great variations in the amounts charged to cover these basic services, the range in chapter 7 cases is usually from $300 to $800, and many courts set an informal limit between $400 and $700. Some attorneys and courts consider it appropriate to add a small increment to this fee in joint cases for a husband and wife or when other complications make the case more difficult than average to prepare. In chapter 13 cases, basic fees generally range from $600 to $1,500, but in very complicated cases they may be up to $5,000 or more.

An attorney can usually predict other services that will be necessary—such as motions to avoid liens or the filing of a homestead deed— once the facts of the debtor's case are known. The fees for such services, assuming that they will proceed routinely, should also be set in advance. An agreement for a percentage contingency fee is sometimes appropriate, but no such agreement may override the court's duty to determine whether fees are reasonable.

Finally, the attorney and the client should agree on an arrangement for fees, usually at an hourly rate prevalent in the community, should complications arise. Complications might include a motion for relief from the automatic stay or a dischargeability complaint. In every case, the debtor should be advised of all costs that are likely to be incurred, including the necessary filing fees, as well as possible costs for title searches and appraisals.

Method of Payment

In a chapter 7 case, the attorney usually wants to be paid all or most of the fee before the filing. This means that the debtor must also pay the entire filing fee in advance because installment filing fee payments are not permitted when the debtor has given any money or property to an attorney for services in connection with the case. The attorney's fee may be paid in ways other than cash from the client. It may be paid by a third party, such as a friend or relative. The debtor may also give the attorney a security interest in property, may transfer property outright to the attorney, or may even barter services with the attorney.

An attorney may also be compensated through payment from the debtor's bankruptcy estate. As discussed below, this arrangement is common in chapter 13 cases. It is feasible in a consumer chapter 7 case only if the debtor has sufficient nonexempt property to pay all priority administrative expenses in full. Because debtors, if they receive good advice, normally protect their nonexempt property by converting it to exempt property or by filing a chapter 13 petition, this method of payment in consumer chapter 7 cases is quite rare.

COURT SUPERVISION OF BANKRUPTCY ATTORNEY'S FEES

One aspect of bankruptcy attorney's fees that is somewhat unusual is the close court supervision of the fees charged. Monitoring and, when appropriate, commenting on attorney's fee applications is one of the primary duties of the U.S. trustee's office. This supervision of attorney's fees in bankruptcy arises mainly from an unfortunate history of abuse and overreaching by the bankruptcy bar.

The purpose of the monitoring is twofold. First, it was designed to prevent bankruptcies in which the debtor has significant assets from becoming boondoggles for the lawyers involved. Scandals in which little, if anything, was left for creditors by the time the attorneys finished compensating themselves have left the bankruptcy courts quite sensitive to this problem. Second, the scrutiny of fees paid by the debtor is based on a recognition that bankruptcy clients are particularly vulnerable to attorney overreaching. Court oversight now prevents much of that overreaching.

Disclosures Required

Both the Bankruptcy Code and the Federal Rules of Bankruptcy Procedure have strict requirements for disclosure of all fees. The Code requires any attorney who represents a debtor in a bankruptcy case or in connection with a bankruptcy case to file a statement of all compensation paid or agreed to in connection with services rendered within one year before filing, or to be rendered, which are related to the bankruptcy. The same section requires disclosure of the source of all such compensation.

In addition, when the attorney seeks compensation from the bankruptcy estate, including payment through a chapter 13 plan, the attorney must provide a detailed statement of the services rendered and expenses incurred to justify the amount requested.

Bankruptcy Court Review of Fee Disclosures and Requests

All fees paid by the debtor that are related to the bankruptcy case are subject to review. Any payments that exceed the reasonable value of services rendered may be ordered returned to either the debtor or the estate, whichever is appropriate.

Although the Bankruptcy Rules provide that such an order may be made on the court's own initiative, it most often occurs after a request by the bankruptcy trustee or the U.S. trustee. In many districts, the court specifically requires the trustee to recommend whether an attorney's fee should be approved, and it has been held that this is part of the U.S. trustee's function of supervising the administration of bankruptcy cases. The executive office for the United States trustees has announced that it considers the monitoring of debtors' attorneys' fees to be a very important part of the U.S. trustee's job.

One aspect of reviewing fees simply involves the question of whether the fees charged are reasonable in relation to the services involved. Bankruptcy courts have broad discretion in determining appropriate levels of compensation. As discussed above, most judges have a range of rates that they consider to be fair for the basic services involved in a consumer bankruptcy case.

Courts also concern themselves with preventing abuse of the bankruptcy process by attorneys at the expense of debtors or creditors. In pursuit of this goal, bankruptcy judges have remedied conduct that ranges from unfair advertising to incompetence to outright fraud.

For example, the fees of an attorney who had deceptively advertised his fees were limited in all of his cases to the low fees advertised. Other attorneys who failed to attend hearings or to cooperate with trustees, misrepresented their fees, or allowed their clients to be seriously prejudiced have been denied all fees and ordered to reimburse their clients for costs incurred. When services rendered have been harmful or worthless to the debtor, all fees have been denied. Similarly, when attorneys have acted unethically in other aspects, their requested fees have not been allowed, and when attorneys failed to disclose accurately the fees charged, those fees have been reduced or denied.

Finally, courts have also begun to police the fees and conduct of nonattorneys who provide debtors with "advice" or "services" in connection with bankruptcy cases, which are then often filed *pro se* (without a lawyer). On motion by the U.S. trustee or on request of disgruntled "clients," the Code, often combined with state unfair trade practice statutes, can be an effective weapon against the unauthorized practice of law and the abusive practices of these "clinics," "debt counselors," "typing services," and other operations that prey on the misfortunes of financially troubled people.

PAYMENT OF ATTORNEY'S FEES THROUGH THE CHAPTER 13 PLAN

An important feature of chapter 13 that is not usually present in consumer chapter 7 cases is the possibility of paying the debtor's attorney from the property of the estate. The payment of all or part of the fee in installments is often the only way a financially strapped debtor can pay the fee at all. The fact that the attorney has some assurance, though hardly a complete guarantee, that the fee will be paid in this manner makes him or her more comfortable about taking the client's case without advance payment of all or most of the fee.

Fees That Can Be Paid through the Plan

The debtor's attorney normally classifies his or her fee among the administrative expenses that are entitled to priority under the Code. Not only does this mean that the fee must be paid in full for a chapter 13 discharge, but also it usually means that the fee will be paid before most other creditors receive payment.

However, an administrative expense priority can only be given to fees for services that benefit the estate, as opposed to services that benefit only the debtor. Virtually all of the basic services in a chapter 13 case do benefit the estate—that is, prepetition advice about bankruptcy, preparation of the initial papers and plan, and attendance at the meeting of creditors and the confirmation hearing. Courts rarely question payment of the entire basic fee as an administrative expense. Fees for other activities to preserve the estate or the functioning of the plan—such as objections to claims or modifications of the plan—warrant administrative expense priority.

Courts impose one other requirement: that there be some estate to be benefited. Many courts find an abuse of the system when all or almost all of the debtor's payments go toward payment of the attorney's fee. The use of chapter 13 simply as a device for collecting fees, with little or no benefit to any creditors, may be looked on with disfavor as little more than a disguised liquidation and akin to past abuses in which the primary beneficiaries of a bankruptcy plan were the attorneys involved.

Procedure for Obtaining Payment of Fees through the Plan

The current Bankruptcy Rules require that a debtor's attorney who seeks compensation for services from the estate—that is, through the plan—must file an application for those fees, including a detailed statement of services rendered, the time and costs expended, and the amounts requested. The Code also requires at least some type of notice to all parties that fees are sought from the estate, giving them an opportunity to request a hearing to raise any questions they might have.

After confirmation of a chapter 13 plan, there are sometimes circumstances that require the debtor's attorney to do work that was not originally anticipated. When this occurs, the attorney may make an application for additional fees if the work is compensable from the estate.

OTHER SOURCES OF ATTORNEY'S FEES IN BANKRUPTCY CASES

A final source of attorney's fees that many bankruptcy practitioners overlook is the opposing party. Most practitioners are aware of the Bankruptcy Code provisions that provide for attorney's fees to prevailing debtors in certain circumstances—such as proceedings to enforce the automatic stay, discussed in Chapter 8; certain dischargeability complaints, discussed in Chapter 13; and involuntary bankruptcy petitions, discussed in Chapter 12—but they are often less knowledgeable about the myriad of other federal and state laws that provide for attorney's fees to prevailing consumers who bring certain types of lawsuits and win. Altogether, there are nearly one hundred such federal statutes and many more state statutes.

Among the most important of these laws are state and federal consumer protection laws. An attorney's thorough familiarity with debtor's rights under these laws can result in important benefits for the attorney's clients, and those clients may not have to pay additional attorney's fees to obtain those benefits.

On the federal level, the most important of these statutes is the Truth in Lending Act, which allows for damages and sometimes the cancellation of home mortgages when creditors violate the act. Other federal consumer protection statutes that provide for attorney's fees include the Magnuson-Moss Warranty Act, the Fair Debt Collection Practices Act (discussed briefly in Chapter 5), the Equal Credit Opportunity Act, and the Fair Credit Reporting Act.

Many state laws have similar provisions. These include usury laws, laws prohibiting unfair and deceptive practices, and laws regulating collection practices or landlord-tenant relationships. In most cases, claims under these statutes may be reserved by the debtor as exempt property and then pursued by the debtor in the bankruptcy court or elsewhere.

DEALING WITH YOUR BANKRUPTCY LAWYER

Debtors should understand what will happen in their bankruptcy cases, and a good attorney normally explains the basics of the procedures to them. An attorney should also be reasonably available to answer clients' questions throughout the case.

At the same time, debtors should recognize that most attorneys have quite a few clients and many matters to handle, so their time is not unlimited. If clients have questions or things they need to discuss with the attorney, it is best to deal with them all at one time, rather than in a long series of phone calls, or to put them in a letter that the attorney can answer at a convenient time. Debtors must also recognize that there are not absolute answers to every legal question and that an attorney may only be able to say what will probably happen or what courts usually do or what creditors usually do.

Finally, an attorney's work can only be as good as the information that the attorney receives. If debtors forget to list creditors, the attorney usually cannot discover them, and their claims may not be discharged in bankruptcy. There are many other examples of situations in which giving less than complete information can hurt the debtor's case. Communications to an attorney are confidential, and the best policy for a debtor is to hide nothing from his or her attorney. The debtor should make every effort to answer the attorney's questions as completely and truthfully as possible.

Chapter 15

CONSUMERS' RIGHTS IN BUSINESS BANKRUPTCY CASES

With increasing frequency, consumers have claims against businesses that have filed bankruptcy, or they are affected by someone else's bankruptcy filing. Consumers with claims against retailers, service companies, financial institutions, farmers, or individuals are halted in the pursuit of those claims. Tenants discover that their landlord is in bankruptcy and services to their building have stopped.

The rights of consumers as creditors or other interested participants in bankruptcy cases involve different perspectives and often different legal issues than when consumers are bankruptcy debtors. This chapter deals with some of the issues that consumer debtors will face in the bankruptcy cases of businesses and others.

THE AUTOMATIC STAY

As soon as an entity has filed a bankruptcy petition, the consumer and the consumer's attorney are subject to the far-reaching impact of the automatic stay. Virtually all legal proceedings against the debtor and other collection efforts must cease until the bankruptcy court grants relief. Violators of the stay risk contempt, actual damages, costs and attorney's fees, and possibly punitive damages. (The scope of the stay is discussed in detail in Chapter 8.)

Formal notice of the filing is not required to subject an attorney or creditor to the automatic stay. Once a creditor has received any indication that a bankruptcy has been filed, he or she should assume that the stay is in effect unless the nonexistence of a filing has been determined by inquiry at the bankruptcy court.

In virtually every instance, the bankruptcy court must grant permission for relief from the stay before litigation or other action to collect claims from the debtor may be taken. Nevertheless, the filing of a bankruptcy does not necessarily prevent continuing or even starting litigation to determine liability or, in some instances, taking action to collect on debts. In cases in which state court litigation is well advanced, consumers may wish to seek relief from the stay to continue the litigation in the state court for the limited purpose of deciding the amount of the claim. In other cases, there may be advantages to pursuing the litigation in the bankruptcy court.

FILING A PROOF OF CLAIM

Generally speaking, to share in the distribution of the bankruptcy estate, a creditor must file a proof of claim. The Bankruptcy Code's definition of a claim is very broad.

A claim should be filed even if the consumer has no judgment against the debtor, has not begun litigation, or is not certain of the exact amount of the claim. If the consumer has begun litigation or has obtained a judgment outside the bankruptcy proceeding, proof of claim must still be filed in the bankruptcy court.

The claim must be made on Official Form 10, a copy of which may be found in Appendix B, or on a substantially similar document. The form is relatively simple and self-explanatory. It should be filed by the consumer with the court, not with the trustee, unless a local rule exists to the contrary.

In cases under chapters 7, 12, or 13, the proof of claim must be filed within 90 days after the first date set for the meeting of creditors. A few exceptions to this deadline exist. The one most likely to be encountered is a no-asset notice. In a chapter 7 case, if it appears that the debtor has no assets to distribute, the notice of the meeting of creditors may indicate that proofs of claim need not be filed, that creditors will be notified if it later appears that there will be assets for distribution, and that notice of a time for filing will then be given.

The first date set for the meeting of creditors, which sets the clock running for the chapter 7 and chapter 13 proof of claim, is usually 20 to 60 days after the filing of the bankruptcy petition. If the debtor has listed the consumer as a creditor, the consumer should receive notices of the meeting from the court. Otherwise, the consumer must check the court files to determine the date.

In a chapter 11 case, the court sets the deadline for filing proofs of claim and may extend the time for good cause. The deadline for filing may be set in the chapter 11 plan and may become an order of the court upon confirmation of the plan, rather than in a separate court order. A creditor whose claim is listed in the schedule of liabilities in a chapter 11 case and not noted as disputed, contingent, or unliquidated need not file a claim. Filing a claim is still advisable, however. Business debtors often do not value the claim as highly as consumer creditors or do not give it the priority that the creditors may claim. Further, if the case is converted to chapter 7, as many chapter 11 cases are, only claims actually filed by the creditor in chapter 11 are deemed to be filed in the chapter 7 case. At the time of conversion, a new claim date will be set for those who have not previously filed claims.

Certain claims are entitled to priority. They are paid in the order of priority set by the Code before payment to most unsecured creditors. In making a proof of claim, the consumer creditor should take care to claim any priorities, which are discussed below. Unless there is an objection, a proof of claim is allowed. Therefore, the claim should be for as high an amount and with as high a priority as good faith permits.

Postpetition Claims as Administrative Expenses

Most consumer claims against businesses in bankruptcy arise before the filing of the bankruptcy petition. However, some claims, especially injury claims that are of a continuing nature—such as debt collection harassment or claims involving illegal housing conditions—may continue or may arise after the filing.

After the debtor files for bankruptcy, the debtor's property and the proceeds, rents, and profits from the property become part of the bankruptcy estate. During the pendency of the case, the business will be operated either by a trustee or, more likely, by the corporate entity or the individual debtor as a "debtor in possession" in chapter 11. Claims arising after the filing of the petition and before confirmation are considered to be claims against the bankruptcy estate and are considered to be administrative expenses as a cost or expense of preserving the estate. Administrative expenses receive the highest priority and are paid before all other unsecured claims.

A proof of claim should be filed that indicates that the claim arose postpetition, both by setting out the date that the claim accrued and by labeling the claim "(administrative)." The claim should also indicate that it is a priority. A motion or application should then be filed, requesting an order that designates the claim as an administrative expense and orders payment.

Even administrative expenses, however, are ordinarily paid after the claims of secured creditors with valid liens on the debtor's property. For example, if the bankruptcy estate consists of an apartment building and the sale of the building does not generate enough funds to pay off the mortgage holders, then neither the administrative expenses nor the unsecured claims will be paid. An exception to this rule allows certain expenses of preserving and disposing of the secured property to be paid before the secured claim is paid.

This exception provides that the reasonable and necessary costs of preserving and disposing of property that secures an allowed secured claim may be recovered by the party that incurs the expense to the extent that the expenditure benefits the secured creditor. Claims are made most commonly for continued utility services, other costs of maintaining the business as a going concern, costs of storage of the property, and costs of selling the property. In one case, the court allowed tenants of a building complex in Puerto Rico to recover costs for building security directly from the landlord's secured creditor. In doing so, the court recognized that security is essential for the building to be preserved in good condition. The good condition of the building then benefits not only the tenants, but also the secured creditor. Consequently, the secured creditor was forced to pay, at least to the extent of its benefits.

This principal can be applied to other essential building maintenance. For example, repair of a leaking roof or a broken pipe can be crucial to maintain a building in good condition. Similarly, the maintenance of utilities benefits a secured creditor by preventing broken water pipes. Tenants may use this rationale to force payment for such items by the secured creditor.

The Consumer Priority

The Bankruptcy Code provides certain consumers with priority as creditors in bankruptcy proceedings. Consumer creditors are given priority after claims made by five other categories of preferred creditors, including claims of the attorneys and professionals who administer the case and claims by employees for wages and benefits. The consumer priority gives individual creditors priority for claims up to $900 for prebankruptcy deposits made in connection with the purchase, lease, or rental of property or services intended for personal, family, or household use.

Before the adoption of the Code, consumer creditors who could not persuade the bankruptcy court to return deposits paid to bankrupt retailers were relegated to unsecured creditor status. The bankruptcies of large retailers—such as W.T. Grant—which gave rise to numerous claims by consumers who had given the debtor deposits without being aware that those deposits were not specifically held by the retailer for refund, prompted Congress to act. Consumer advocates earlier in the decade had brought this problem to the attention of the public and Congress. Subsequent commentators explained that a consumer priority was necessary because consumer losses in the bankruptcy of large retailers could not have been avoided by consumers who did not have the resources to conduct credit checks on retailers before making consumer deposits. Congress met these problems by providing for a consumer priority.

The few reported cases that have considered issues pertaining to the consumer priority provisions of the Bankruptcy Code have interpreted them broadly. Each member of a household or family has a separate $900 maximum; the family or household is not limited to one priority claim. The scope of the priority is also interpreted liberally. The purchase of a yacht for personal use in a lease/purchase transaction has been held to give rise to a consumer priority. In another case, in recognizing a consumer priority for deposits given to a residential home builder, the court concluded that Congress did not intend to limit the priority to transactions with retail merchants.

The consumer should claim the priority at the time the proof of claim is filed, by conspicuously marking it as a priority claim. The claim is then allowed unless the debtor in possession, trustee, or a party in interest—such as another creditor—objects to the claim. Upon such objection, after notice and hearing, the court rules on whether the priority was properly claimed.

CHAPTER 11 BANKRUPTCY

Businesses that file bankruptcy cases usually file a petition under chapter 11, a reorganization chapter that allows them to restructure their debts and assets and to discharge some debts. However, although a chapter 11 case is, in theory, a reorganization, which suggests that at least some consumer claims will be paid, in most cases the debtor goes out of business, and no payments are made to unsecured creditors.

Although similar in some ways to chapter 13, chapter 11 cases are considerably more complex than consumer bankruptcy cases for obvious reasons. Not only are the debts and assets larger and more numerous, but also additional procedures are involved. Because there is usually no trustee appointed to run the business and look after creditor's rights, a committee of the major creditors is often appointed. Occasionally, if many consumers have claims that add up to a large amount, they may have a representative on this committee.

The other major difference is that the chapter 11 plan is put up for a vote of all of the creditors, who are sent ballots and a "disclosure statement" explaining the plan, as well as the plan. There are various rules about how many votes must be obtained, but it is important to note that a plan cannot be confirmed unless the holders of priority claims, such as consumer deposit claims, wage claims, and administrative claims, (1) receive immediate full payment of the priority claim under the plan,

(2) vote as a group to accept deferred payment in full, or (3) each, individually, agree or vote to accept lesser payment.

PROBLEMS OF TENANTS OF BANKRUPT LANDLORDS

As the real estate market declines in various parts of the United States, owners of private housing frequently file for bankruptcy. Often, tenants receive no official notice of the bankruptcy. They may begin to notice that the building is no longer receiving services—such as utilities, trash pickup, and repairs—and that no one is collecting the rent. A call to the landlord or the landlord's attorney may reveal that the landlord has filed a bankruptcy petition. The following discussion of tenant's rights in that situation emphasizes methods of ensuring the continuation of needed services.

After filing the bankruptcy petition, the debtor in possession is theoretically responsible for managing the assets of the bankruptcy estate. The real estate is frequently mortgaged well beyond its value, so there is no equity remaining for unsecured creditors. Therefore, the mortgage holders are the other parties most involved in the case.

The law requires whoever manages the building—whether it is a chapter 11 debtor in possession, a trustee, or a mortgage lender in the process of foreclosure—to comply with all state and local laws, including housing codes, health and safety laws, and the like. If the manager fails to provide services, tenants can contact local code enforcement authorities, who are permitted to enforce local laws notwithstanding the automatic stay. They may also ask the bankruptcy court to force compliance with local laws. The mortgage lender is sometimes an important ally in these efforts, especially if the bankruptcy debtor is still running the building, because it too has an interest in ensuring the condition of the building does not deteriorate.

As in chapter 13 cases, a chapter 11 debtor has the right to assume or reject leases. (This right is discussed in Chapter 11.) If the landlord wishes to assume the lease, he or she must fully comply with all the lease terms and must promptly cure any defaults or give assurance that defaults will be promptly cured.

In some situations, landlords in bankruptcy may wish to eliminate tenants in the hopes of replacing them with tenants who will pay higher rent. Tenants of a landlord in chapter 11 who are faced with a rejection of the lease are given important rights by the Bankruptcy Code.

If the trustee or debtor in possession rejects the lease, the Code allows the tenant to remain in possession as long as the tenant would have had the right to unilaterally renew the lease under nonbankruptcy law. Tenants who receive section 8 housing subsidies, tenants in rent-controlled housing, or tenants under statutes such as New Jersey's, which requires "cause" for eviction, have a right to continued occupancy as long as their rent payments are maintained and other lease provisions are not breached. The Code thus protects tenants from eviction, despite rejection of their leases. Moreover, if the landlord rejects the lease, the Code allows tenants to deduct from lease payments damages that result from the rejection, such as lost security deposits and services that tenants have to pay for because the landlord has not. Finally, the courts have ruled that filing bankruptcy does not protect a landlord from rent-control regulations.

CONCLUSION

The importance of a business chapter 11 case to a consumer depends on how much is at stake. If the consumer has only a small claim, of a few hundred dollars, the best thing to do may be simply to file a proof of claim, a simple and costless matter. If more money is at stake, the best route is to consult a good bankruptcy lawyer. The lawyer may advise that little can be done beyond filing a proof of claim, but there may be other steps that the consumer can take.

For tenants of a landlord who has filed a bankruptcy case, it is probably a good idea to consult an attorney at the first sign of a serious disruption in services. When there are numerous tenants, the costs of an attorney can be shared and thus should not be a large burden. An attorney can often take steps to greatly improve the situation of tenants, who have significant rights under the law.

MAJOR STATE AND LOCAL EXEMPTIONS AVAILABLE IN BANKRUPTCY

This appendix summarizes the major exemptions that were available under nonbankruptcy exemption schemes when this book was written. Not every exemption available is listed, and exemption laws are sometimes changed. In some states, property held as tenants by the entireties may be exempted when state exemptions are chosen, at least from debts of only one spouse, as discussed in Chapter 9. Residents of some states may alternatively choose the federal exemptions that are listed in Chapter 9 if their state has not prohibited that choice. The availability of federal exemptions in each state is noted below. All of the exemptions are available for each debtor, unless otherwise stated.

Debtors who use a state or local exemption scheme also have the benefit of federal nonbankruptcy exemptions. These exemptions protect:

- Social Security benefits
- veteran's benefits
- railroad retirement annuities and pensions
- civil service retirement benefits
- military annuities and survivor's benefits
- other less common federal benefits

In addition, all pension plans covered by the Employee Retirement Income Security Act are protected in bankruptcy.

ALABAMA

Are federal bankruptcy exemptions available? No

Homestead exemption: $5,000 per person for an area not larger than 160 acres

Vehicle exemption: None

Household item exemptions: $3,000; necessary wearing apparel

Other significant exemptions: Certain pension plans, insurance, and benefits

ALASKA

Are federal bankruptcy exemptions available? No

Homestead exemption: Up to $54,000 per family for one residence

Vehicle exemption: $3,000 in one vehicle worth $20,000 or less

Household item exemptions: $3,000; $1,000 in jewelry

Other significant exemptions: certain pension plans, insurance, and benefits; liquid assets of $1,400 if the debtor has no earnings; $2,800 for tools of trade

ARIZONA

Are federal bankruptcy exemptions available? No

Homestead exemption: $100,000 per debtor or married couple

Vehicle exemption: $1,500

Household item exemptions: $4,000; $500 in clothing; $1,000 in engagement and wedding rings; various other items

Other significant exemptions: Certain pension plans, insurance, and benefits; $100 in a bank account; $2,500 for tools of trade

ARKANSAS

Are federal bankruptcy exemptions available? Yes

Homestead exemption: $800 for unmarried debtors; $1,250 for married debtors; plus rural homestead up to 80 acres or urban homestead up to one-quarter acre

Vehicle exemption: $1,200 in one vehicle

Household item exemptions: Wearing apparel; wedding bands not over one-half carat (may use wild-card exemption for any property)

Other significant exemptions: Certain pension plans, insurance, and benefits; $750 for tools of trade; $200 for unmarried debtor in any property; $500 for married debtor or head of household in any property

CALIFORNIA

Are federal bankruptcy exemptions available? No

Two alternative exemption schemes are available. A husband and wife filing jointly must choose the same alternative, and a married debtor filing separately can choose the second alternative only if both spouses give up the right to claim the first alternative in any bankruptcy case.

Alternative 1

Homestead exemption: $75,000 for a debtor who is a member of a family unit if at least one other member of the family unit owns no other homestead or owns only a community property interest with the debtor; $100,000 for debtors over 55 with income under $15,000 (or, if a couple, $20,000), for debtors over 65, or for disabled debtors; $50,000 for all other debtors (spouses may not double exemption)

Vehicle exemption: $1,200 (may not be doubled for spouses)

Household item exemptions: All items if ordinarily and reasonably necessary to and personally used by debtor and family at principal residence; $2,500 for jewelry, heirlooms, and artwork; health aids (spouses may not double monetary exemption)

Other significant exemptions: Certain pension plans, insurance, and benefits; $2,500 for tools of trade

Alternative 2

Homestead exemption: $7,500

Vehicle exemption: $1,200 in one vehicle

Household item exemptions: Up to $200 per item; $500 for jewelry

Other significant exemptions: Certain pension plans, insurance, and benefits; wild-card exemption of $400 plus unused homestead exemption for any property; $750 for tools of trade; health aids

COLORADO

Are federal bankruptcy exemptions available? No

Homestead exemption: $20,000

Vehicle exemption: $1,000 if vehicle is used for debtor's occupation

Household item exemptions: $1,500; $750 for clothing; $500 for jewelry; $300 for fuel and food

Other significant exemptions: Certain pension plans, insurance, and benefits; $1,500 for tools of trade; health aids

CONNECTICUT

Are federal bankruptcy exemptions available? Yes

Homestead exemption: None

Vehicle exemption: None

Household item exemptions: Necessary clothing and household goods

Other significant exemptions: Certain pension plans, insurance, and benefits; tools of trade; health aids

DELAWARE

Are federal bankruptcy exemptions available? No

Homestead exemption: None (may use wild-card exemption for any property)

Vehicle exemption: None (may use wild-card exemption for any property)

Household item exemptions: Wearing apparel (may also use wild-card exemption for any property)

Other significant exemptions: Certain pension plans, insurance, and benefits; $5,000 wild-card exemption for any property; $50–75 for tools of trade

DISTRICT OF COLUMBIA

Are federal bankruptcy exemptions available? Yes

Homestead exemption: None

Vehicle exemption: $500 for head of family or householder if vehicle is used in debtor's business

Household item exemptions: $300 for head of household and $300 per family member in wearing apparel; food and fuel for three months

Other significant exemptions: Certain pension plans, insurance, and benefits; $200 for tools of trade; $200 for stock or materials for business

FLORIDA

Are federal bankruptcy exemptions available? No

Homestead exemption: 160 acres outside a municipality or one-half acre inside a municipality

Vehicle exemption: None (may use wild-card exemption for any personal property)

Household item exemptions: None (may use wild-card exemption for any personal property)

Other significant exemptions: Certain pension plans, insurance, and benefits; $1,000 for any personal property; all wages deposited in the debtor's bank account

GEORGIA

Are federal bankruptcy exemptions available? No

Homestead exemption: $5,000

Vehicle exemption: $1,000 (may also use wild-card exemption for any property)

Household item exemptions: $3,500, no item worth more than $200; $500 for jewelry

Other significant exemptions: Certain pension plans, insurance, and benefits; wild-card exemption of $400 plus unused homestead exemption for any property; $500 for tools of trade

HAWAII

Are federal bankruptcy exemptions available? Yes

Homestead exemption: $30,000 for married person, head of household, or person over 65; $20,000 for others

Vehicle exemption: $1,000 in one vehicle

Household item exemptions: Necessary clothing, books, appliances, and household furnishings of family; $1,000 in jewelry

Other significant exemptions: Certain pension plans, insurance, and benefits; tools of trade

IDAHO

Are federal bankruptcy exemptions available? No

Homestead exemption: $30,000

Vehicle exemption: $1,500 in one vehicle

Household item exemptions: $4,000 for furniture and appliances that are reasonably necessary, no item over $500; portraits and heirlooms, no item over $500; $250 in jewelry

Other significant exemptions: Certain pension plans, insurance, and benefits; $1,000 for tools of trade; health aids

ILLINOIS

Are federal bankruptcy exemptions available? No

Homestead exemption: $7,500

Vehicle exemption: $1,200 in one vehicle

Household item exemptions: Wearing apparel of debtor and debtor's family (may also use wild-card exemption for any property)

Other significant exemptions: Certain pension plans, insurance, and benefits; $2,000 wild-card exemption for any property of the debtor; $750 for tools of trade; health aids

INDIANA

Are federal bankruptcy exemptions available? No

Homestead exemption: $7,500; any interest in a tenancy by the entirety unless both tenant spouses are in bankruptcy

Vehicle exemption: None (may use wild-card exemption for any property)

Household item exemptions: None (may use wild-card exemption for any property)

Other significant exemptions: Certain pension plans, insurance, and benefits; $4,000 wild-card exemption for any tangible personal property or other real estate and $100 in liquid assets, but not to the extent that the homestead exemption plus these exemptions exceed

$10,000; health aids; any interest in a tenancy by the entirety unless both tenant spouses are in bankruptcy

IOWA

Are federal bankruptcy exemptions available? No

Homestead exemption: one-half acre in a city or town or 40 acres outside a city or town

Vehicle exemption: $5,000 in one vehicle, minus any exemption for wages, tax returns, and musical instruments

Household item exemptions: $2,000; $1,000 in clothing; engagement or wedding ring

Other significant exemptions: Certain pension plans, insurance, and benefits; health aids; $100 in bank deposits; tax refunds up to $1,000

KANSAS

Are federal bankruptcy exemptions available? No

Homestead exemption: One acre in a city or town or 160 acres of farm land

Vehicle exemption: $20,000 in one vehicle if used for transportation to work

Household item exemptions: Items at the debtor's principal residence that are reasonably necessary; $1,000 in jewelry

Other significant exemptions: Certain pension plans, insurance, and benefits; $7,500 for tools of trade

KENTUCKY

Are federal bankruptcy exemptions available? No

Homestead exemption: $5,000 (may also use wild-card exemption for any property)

Vehicle exemption: $2,500 (may also use wild-card exemption for any property)

Household item exemptions: $3,000 (may also use wild-card exemption for any property)

Other significant exemptions: Certain pension plans, insurance, and benefits; $1,000 wild-card exemption for any property; $300 for tools of trade

LOUISIANA

Are federal bankruptcy exemptions available? No

Homestead exemption: $15,000 per person or married couple

Vehicle exemption: Only if used for trade

Household item exemptions: Items used by debtor and family; $5,000 in wedding and engagement rings

Other significant exemptions: Certain pension plans, insurance, and benefits; tools of trade

MAINE

Are federal bankruptcy exemptions available? No

Homestead exemption: $7,500; $60,000 for debtors over 60 or disabled debtors

Vehicle exemption: $1,200 in one vehicle

Household item exemptions: Items under $200 per item; $500 in jewelry, plus wedding and engagement rings (may also use wild-card exemption for household property)

Other significant exemptions: Certain pension plans, insurance, and benefits; $1,000 for tools of trade; $400 wild-card exemption for any property; up to $4,500 of unused homestead exemption for additional household items; tools of trade

MARYLAND

Are federal bankruptcy exemptions available? No

Homestead exemption: $500 (may also use wild-card exemption for any property)

Vehicle exemption: None (may use wild-card exemption for any property)

Household item exemptions: None (may use wild-card exemption for any property)

Other significant exemptions: Certain pension plans, insurance, and benefits; $5,500 wild-card exemption for any property; $2,500 for tools of trade

MASSACHUSETTS

Are federal bankruptcy exemptions available? Yes

Homestead exemption: $100,000 (may not be doubled for joint tenants); $150,000 for debtors over 65 or disabled debtors

Vehicle exemption: $700 if vehicle is necessary to maintain employment

Household item exemptions: $3,000; wearing apparel and beds necessary to family

Other significant exemptions: Certain pension plans, insurance, and benefits; $500 in a bank account; $125 in cash or additional bank deposit; $500 for tools of trade

MICHIGAN

Are federal bankruptcy exemptions available? Yes

Homestead exemption: $3,500

Vehicle exemption: None

Household item exemptions: $1,000; food and fuel for six months

Other significant exemptions: Certain pension plans, insurance, and benefits; $1,000 for tools of trade; $1,000 in building and loan shares if no homestead is claimed

MINNESOTA

Are federal bankruptcy exemptions available? Yes

Homestead exemption: One acre in a city or 160 acres outside a city

Vehicle exemption: $2,000 in one vehicle

Household item exemptions: $4,500

Other significant exemptions: Certain pension plans, insurance, and benefits; some earnings deposited in a bank account for 20 days after debtor is paid; $5,000 for tools of trade

MISSISSIPPI

Are federal bankruptcy exemptions available? No

Homestead exemption: $30,000

Vehicle exemption: None (may use wild-card exemption for any tangible personal property)

Household item exemptions: None (may use wild-card exemption for any tangible personal property)

Other significant exemptions: Certain pension plans, insurance, and benefits; $10,000 wild-card exemption for any tangible personal property; husbands, wives, widows, and widowers may claim exemption of $30,000 in proceeds of former residence

MISSOURI

Are federal bankruptcy exemptions available? No

Homestead exemption: $8,000 (may not be doubled for co-owners); or $1,000 for mobile home

Vehicle exemption: $500 in one vehicle

Household item exemptions: $1,000; $500 in jewelry (may also use wild-card exemption for any property)

Other significant exemptions: Certain pension plans, insurance, and benefits; wild-card exemption of $400 plus $850 if head of family plus $250 per unmarried dependent under 18 for any property; $2,000 for tools of trade; health aids

MONTANA

Are federal bankruptcy exemptions available? No

Homestead exemption: $40,000

Vehicle exemption: $1,200 in one vehicle

Household item exemptions: $4,500, no item worth more than $600

Other significant exemptions: Certain pension plans, insurance, and benefits; $3,000 for tools of trade; health aids

NEBRASKA

Are federal bankruptcy exemptions available? No

Homestead exemption: $10,000

Vehicle exemption: None (debtors not claiming homestead may use wild-card exemption for any property)

Household item exemptions: Immediate personal possessions and necessary wearing apparel; $1,500 in other household goods; provisions and fuel for six months (debtors not claiming homestead may also use wild-card exemption for any property)

Other significant exemptions: Certain pension plans, insurance, and benefits; $2,500 wild-card exemption for any property for debtors who do not claim homestead; $1,500 for tools of trade

NEVADA

Are federal bankruptcy exemptions available? No

Homestead exemption: $95,000

Vehicle exemption: $1,000 in one vehicle

Household item exemptions: $3,000

Other significant exemptions: Certain pension plans, insurance, and benefits; $4,500 for tools of trade

NEW HAMPSHIRE

Are federal bankruptcy exemptions available? No

Homestead exemption: $5,000

Vehicle exemption: $1,000

Household item exemptions: $2,000 plus clothing, beds and bedding, cooking stove, heating stove, and refrigerator; $400 in fuel and provisions; $500 in jewelry

Other significant exemptions: Certain pension plans, insurance, and benefits; $1,200 for tools of trade

NEW JERSEY

Are federal bankruptcy exemptions available? Yes

Homestead exemption: None

Vehicle exemption: None

Household item exemptions: $1,000; plus wearing apparel (may also use wild-card exemption for any personal property)

Other significant exemptions: Certain pension plans, insurance, and benefits; $1,000 wild-card exemption for any personal property

NEW MEXICO

Are federal bankruptcy exemptions available? Yes

Homestead exemption: $20,000 if debtor is married, widowed, or supporting another

Vehicle exemption: $4,000 (may also use wild-card exemption for any personal property)

Household item exemptions: Clothing and furniture; $2,500 in jewelry (may also use wild-card exemption for any personal property)

Other significant exemptions: Certain pension plans, insurance, and benefits; $500 wild-card exemption for any personal property, plus $2,000 wild-card exemption for those who do not own homestead for any property; $1,500 for tools of trade; health aids

NEW YORK

Are federal bankruptcy exemptions available? No

Homestead exemption: $10,000

Vehicle exemption: $2,400 in one vehicle

Household item exemptions: $5,000, but no more than one radio, one television, and one refrigerator

Other significant exemptions: Certain pension plans, insurance, and benefits; $600 for tools of trade (to be deducted from household item amount); health aids; cash or equivalent up to $2,500 to the extent that a debtor who does not claim a homestead does not use all of the $5,000 household item exemption; health aids

NORTH CAROLINA

Are federal bankruptcy exemptions available? No

Homestead exemption: $7,500

Vehicle exemption: $1,000 in one vehicle, unless purchased within 90 days of bankruptcy

Household item exemptions: $2,500, plus $500 per dependent up to $2,000 (may also use wild-card exemption for any property)

Other significant exemptions: Certain pension plans, insurance, and benefits; wild-card exemption of $2,500, less any amount used for homestead exemption, for any property; $500 for tools of trade; health aids

NORTH DAKOTA

Are federal bankruptcy exemptions available? No

Homestead exemption: $80,000

Vehicle exemption: $1,200

Household item exemptions: Clothing; food and fuel for one year; head of family may claim $1,000 but only by giving up higher wild-card exemption

Other significant exemptions: Certain pension plans, insurance, and benefits; $5,000 wild-card exemption available to head of family for any personal property ($2,500 for single person), unless household goods, crops or grain, or tools of trade exemption is taken; $7,500 exemption if no homestead exemption is taken; $1,000 for tools of trade, but only by giving up higher wild-card exemption; health aids

OHIO

Are federal bankruptcy exemptions available? No

Homestead exemption: $5,000

Vehicle exemption: $1,000 in one vehicle

Household item exemptions: Wearing apparel, beds and bedding not over $200 per item; $300 for cooking unit and $300 for refrigerator; plus $1,500 for debtors claiming homestead and $2,000 for debtors not claiming homestead in items not exceeding $200, with the exception of $400 for one item of jewelry

Other significant exemptions: Certain pension plans, insurance, and benefits; $400 wild-card exemption for any property; $750 for tools of trade; $400 in cash or equivalent; health aids

OKLAHOMA

Are federal bankruptcy exemptions available? No

Homestead exemption: One-quarter acre in a city or town or 160 acres outside a city or town

Vehicle exemption: $3,000 in one vehicle

Household item exemptions: Unlimited for household and kitchen furniture; $4,000 in wearing apparel

Other significant exemptions: Certain pension plans, insurance, and benefits; $5,000 for tools of trade; health aids

OREGON

Are federal bankruptcy exemptions available? No

Homestead exemption: $15,000 (maximum of $20,000 for joint owners)

Vehicle exemption: $1,200 in one vehicle

Household item exemptions: $1,450; $900 in wearing apparel, jewelry, and personal items; food and fuel for 60 days (may also use wild-card exemption for any personal property, but not to increase another exemption on an item of property)

Other significant exemptions: Certain pension plans, insurance, and benefits; wild-card exemption of $400 for any personal property, but not to increase another exemption; $750 for tools of trade; health aids; $5,000 in otherwise exempt funds deposited in a bank

PENNSYLVANIA

Are federal bankruptcy exemptions available? Yes

Homestead exemption: None

Vehicle exemption: None (may use $300 wild-card exemption for any property)

Household item exemptions: Wearing apparel (may also use $300 wild-card exemption for any property)

Other significant exemptions: Certain pension plans, insurance, and benefits; $300 wild-card exemption for any property

PUERTO RICO

Are federal bankruptcy exemptions available? Yes

Homestead exemption: $1,500 for head of family

Vehicle exemption: Only if used in debtor's occupation

Household item exemptions: $100 in chairs, tables, desks; $200 in necessary furniture, stove, beds; wearing apparel; provisions for one month; refrigerator; kitchen appliances; washing machines under $200; radios under $100; televisions under $250

Other significant exemptions: Certain pension plans, insurance, and benefits; $300 for tools of trade

RHODE ISLAND

Are federal bankruptcy exemptions available? Yes

Homestead exemption: None

Vehicle exemption: None

Household item exemptions: $1,000, plus wearing apparel

Other significant exemptions: Certain pension plans, insurance, and benefits; $500 for tools of trade

SOUTH CAROLINA

Are federal bankruptcy exemptions available? No

Homestead exemption: $5,000

Vehicle exemption: $1,200 in one vehicle

Household item exemptions: $2,500; plus $500 in jewelry

Other significant exemptions: Certain pension plans, insurance, and benefits; $1,000 in cash or liquid assets for debtors without homestead; $750 for tools of trade; health aids

SOUTH DAKOTA

Are federal bankruptcy exemptions available? No

Homestead exemption: One acre in a town or 160 acres outside a town

Vehicle exemption: None (may use wild-card exemption for any property)

Household item exemptions: Wearing apparel; food and fuel for one year; plus $200 or wild-card exemption for any personal property

Other significant exemptions: Certain pension plans, insurance, and benefits; $4,000 wild-card exemption to head of family for any personal property if certain specific exemptions are not claimed ($2,000 for single person)

TENNESSEE

Are federal bankruptcy exemptions available? No

Homestead exemption: $5,000 ($7,500 limit in shared home for joint debtors)

Vehicle exemption: None (may use wild-card exemption for any personal property)

Household item exemptions: Wearing apparel (may also use wild-card exemption for any personal property)

Other significant exemptions: Certain pension plans, insurance, and benefits; $4,000 wild-card exemption for any personal property; $750 for tools of trade; health aids

TEXAS

Are federal bankruptcy exemptions available? Yes

Homestead exemption: One acre urban or 200 acres rural per family (100 acres for a single person)

Vehicle exemption: None (may use wild-card exemption for any personal property)

Household item exemptions: None (may use wild-card exemption for any personal property)

Other significant exemptions: Certain pension plans, insurance, and benefits; $30,000 wild-card exemption per family for most types of personal property ($15,000 for single person); tools of trade

UTAH

Are federal bankruptcy exemptions available? No

Homestead exemption: $8,000 for head of family, plus $2,000 for spouse and $500 for each other dependent

Vehicle exemption: $1,500 in one vehicle if used for debtor's work (not including commuting)

Household item exemptions: One washer and dryer; one refrigerator; one freezer; one stove; $500 in additional household items; all wearing apparel, beds, and bedding; food and fuel for three months

Other significant exemptions: Certain pension plans, insurance, and benefits; $1,500 for tools of trade; health aids

VERMONT

Are federal bankruptcy exemptions available? Yes

Homestead exemption: $30,000

Vehicle exemption: $2,500 (may also use wild-card exemption for any property)

Household item exemptions: $2,500 plus stove, heating appliances, re-frigerator, freezer, water heater; wedding ring; $500 in other jewelry (may also use wild-card exemption for any property)

Other significant exemptions: Certain pension plans, insurance, and benefits; $400 plus $7,000 of unused exemption amounts for motor vehicles, tools of trade, jewelry, and household items as wild-card exemption for any property; $5,000 for tools of trade; $700 in bank deposits; health aids

VIRGIN ISLANDS

Are federal bankruptcy exemptions available? Yes

Homestead exemption: $30,000, limited to one-quarter acre urban or five acres rural

Vehicle exemption: None

Household item exemptions: $3,000; wearing apparel

Other significant exemptions: Certain pension plans, insurance, and benefits; tools of trade

VIRGINIA

Are federal bankruptcy exemptions available? No

Homestead exemption: $5,000, plus $500 for each dependent

Vehicle exemption: $2,000 (may also use wild-card exemption for any personal property)

Household item exemptions: $5,000; $1,000 for wearing apparel; wedding and engagement rings (may use wild-card exemption for any personal property)

Other significant exemptions: Certain pension plans, insurance, and benefits; $5,000 plus $500 per dependent from unused homestead exemption as wild-card exemption for any personal property; $10,000 for tools of trade; health aids

WASHINGTON

Are federal bankruptcy exemptions available? Yes

Homestead exemption: $30,000

Vehicle exemption: $2,500 in no more than two vehicles

Household item exemptions: $2,700 (not doubled for community property owned by spouses); wearing apparel, including no more than $1,000 in furs and jewelry

Other significant exemptions: Certain pension plans, insurance, and benefits; $1,000 wild-card exemption for any property, not more than $100 of which can be used for cash or liquid assets; $5,000 for tools of trade

WEST VIRGINIA

Are federal bankruptcy exemptions available? No

Homestead exemption: $7,500

Vehicle exemption: $1,200 in one vehicle (may also use wild-card exemption for any property)

Household item exemptions: $1,000, no item to exceed $200; $500 in jewelry (may also use wild-card exemption for any property)

Other significant exemptions: Certain pension plans, insurance, and benefits; $400 plus unused homestead amounts as wild-card exemption for any property; $750 for tools of trade; health aids

WISCONSIN

Are federal bankruptcy exemptions available? Yes

Homestead exemption: $40,000 (may not be doubled for husband and wife in same household)

Vehicle exemption: $1,200, plus unused household items exemption amount

Household item exemptions: $5,000

Other significant exemptions: Certain pension plans, insurance, and benefits; $1,000 in bank accounts; $7,500 for tools of trade

WYOMING

Are federal bankruptcy exemptions available? No

Homestead exemption: $10,000

Vehicle exemption: $2,000

Household item exemptions: $2,000; $1,000 in wearing apparel and wedding rings

Other significant exemptions: Certain pension plans, insurance, and benefits; $2,000 for tools of trade

Appendix B

OFFICIAL CONSUMER BANKRUPTCY FORMS

FORM 1. VOLUNTARY PETITION

United States Bankruptcy Court	VOLUNTARY PETITION
_____ **District of** _____	

IN RE (Name of debtor -- If individual, enter: Last, First, Middle)	NAME OF JOINT DEBTOR (Spouse) (Last, First, Middle)
ALL OTHER NAMES used by the debtor in the last 6 years (Include married, maiden, and trade names)	ALL OTHER NAMES used by the joint debtor in the last 6 years (Include married, maiden, and trade names)
SOC. SEC./TAX I.D. NO. (If more than one, state all)	SOC. SEC./TAX I.D. NO. (If more than one, state all)
STREET ADDRESS OF DEBTOR (No. and street, city, state, and zip code)	STREET ADDRESS OF JOINT DEBTOR (No. and street, city, state, and zip code)
COUNTY OF RESIDENCE OR PRINCIPAL PLACE OF BUSINESS	COUNTY OF RESIDENCE OR PRINCIPAL PLACE OF BUSINESS
MAILING ADDRESS OF DEBTOR (If different from street address)	MAILING ADDRESS OF JOINT DEBTOR (If different from street address)

LOCATION OF PRINCIPAL ASSETS OF BUSINESS DEBTOR (If different from address listed above)	VENUE (Check one item)
	___ Debtor has been domiciled or has had a residence, principal place of business, or principal assets in this District for 180 days immediately preceding the date of this petition or for a longer part of such 180 days than in any other District.
	___ There is a bankruptcy case concerning debtor's affiliate, general partner, or partnership pending in the District.

INFORMATION REGARDING DEBTOR (Check applicable items)

TYPE OF DEBTOR
- ___ Individual
- ___ Joint (Husband & Wife)
- ___ Partnership
- ___ Other: _____

- ___ Corporation Publicly Held
- ___ Corporation Not Publicly Held
- ___ Municipality

NATURE OF DEBT
- ___ Non-Business/Consumer
- ___ Business -- Complete A & B below

A. TYPE OF BUSINESS (Check one item)
- ___ Farming
- ___ Professional
- ___ Retail/Wholesale
- ___ Railroad
- ___ Transportation
- ___ Manufacturing/ Mining
- ___ Stockbroker
- ___ Commodity Broker
- ___ Construction
- ___ Real Estate
- ___ Other Business

B. BRIEFLY DESCRIBE NATURE OF BUSINESS

CHAPTER OR SECTION OF BANKRUPTCY CODE UNDER WHICH THE PETITION IS FILED (Check one item)

- ___ Chapter 7
- ___ Chapter 9
- ___ Chapter 11
- ___ Chapter 12
- ___ Chapter 13
- ___ Sec. 304 -- Case Ancillary to Foreign Proceeding

FILING FEE (Check one item)
- ___ Filing fee attached.
- ___ Filing fee to be paid in installments (applicable to individuals only). Must attach signed application for the court's consideration certifying that the debtor is unable to pay fee except in installments. Rule 1006(b). See Official Form No. 3.

NAME AND ADDRESS OF LAW FIRM OR ATTORNEY

Telephone No.

NAME(S) OF ATTORNEY(S) DESIGNATED TO REPRESENT THE DEBTOR (Print or Type Names)

- ___ Debtor is not represented by an attorney.

STATISTICAL/ADMINISTRATIVE INFORMATION (28 U.S.C. § 604)
(Estimates Only) (Check applicable items)

THIS SPACE FOR COURT USE ONLY

- ___ Debtor estimates that funds will be available for distribution to unsecured creditors.
- ___ Debtor estimates that after any exempt property is excluded and administrative expenses paid, there will be no funds available for distribution to unsecured creditors.

ESTIMATED NUMBER OF CREDITORS

1-15	16-49	50-99	100-199	200-999	1000-over
___	___	___	___	___	___

ESTIMATED ASSETS (In thousands of dollars)

Under 50	50-99	100-499	500-999	1000-9999	10,000-99,000	100,000-over
___	___	___	___	___	___	___

ESTIMATED LIABILITIES (In thousands of dollars)

Under 50	50-90	100-499	500-999	1000-9999	10,000-99,000	100,000-over
___	___	___	___	___	___	___

EST. NO. OF EMPLOYEES -- CH. 11 & 12 ONLY

0	1-19	20-99	100-999	1000-over
___	___	___	___	___

EST. NO. OF EQUITY SECURITY HOLDERS -- CH. 11 & 12 ONLY

0	1-19	20-99	100-499	500-over
___	___	___	___	___

Name of Debtor _____

Case No. _____

(Court use only)

FILING OF PLAN

For Chapter 9, 11, 12 and 13 cases only. Check appropriate item.

__ A copy of debtor's proposed plan dated _____ is attached.   __ Debtor intends to file a plan within the time allowed by statute, rule, or order of the court.

PRIOR BANKRUPTCY CASE FILED WITHIN LAST 6 YEARS (If more than one, attach additional sheet.)

Location Where Filed	Case Number	Date Filed

PENDING BANKRUPTCY CASE FILED BY ANY SPOUSE, PARTNER, OR AFFILIATE OF THIS DEBTOR (If more than one, attach additional sheet.)

Name of Debtor	Case Number	Date
Relationship	District	Judge

REQUEST FOR RELIEF

Debtor requests relief in accordance with the chapter of title 11, United States Code, specified in this petition.

SIGNATURES

ATTORNEY

x _____

Signature   Date _____

INDIVIDUAL/JOINT DEBTOR(S)

   I declare under penalty of perjury that the information provided in this petition is true and correct.

x _____

Signature of Debtor   Date _____

x _____

Signature of Joint Debtor   Date _____

EXHIBIT "A" (To be completed if debtor is a corporation requesting relief under chapter 11.)
__ Exhibit "A" is attached and made a part of this petition.

TO BE COMPLETED BY INDIVIDUAL CHAPTER 7 DEBTOR WITH PRIMARILY CONSUMER DEBTS (See P.L. 98-353 §322)

   I am aware that I may proceed under chapter 7, 11, 12, or 13 of title 11, United States Code, understand the relief available under each such chapter, and choose to proceed under chapter 7 of such title.

   If I am represented by an attorney, exhibit "B" has been completed.

x _____

Signature of Debtor   Date _____

x _____

Signature of Joint Debtor   Date _____

EXHIBIT "B" (To be completed by attorney for individual chapter 7 debtor(s) with primarily consumer debts.)

   I, the attorney for the debtor(s) named in the foregoing petition, declare that I have informed the debtor(s) that (he, she, or they) may proceed under chapter 7, 11, 12, or 13 of title 11, United States Code, and have explained the relief available under each such chapter.

x _____

Signature of Attorney   Date _____

Official Form 6, Summary

UNITED STATES BANKRUPTCY COURT

_____ District of _____

In re _____,   Case No. _____
                          Debtor   (If known)

SUMMARY OF SCHEDULES

Indicate as to each schedule whether that schedule is attached and state the number of pages in each. Report the totals from Schedules A, B, D, E, F, I, and J in the boxes provided. Add the amounts from Schedules A and B to determine the total amount of the debtor's assets. Add the amounts from Schedules D, E, and F to determine the total amount of the debtor's liabilities.

NAME OF SCHEDULE	ATTACHED (YES/NO)	NO. OF SHEETS	AMOUNTS SCHEDULED		
			ASSETS	LIABILITIES	OTHER
A - Real Property			$		
B - Personal Property			$		
C - Property Claimed as Exempt					
D - Creditors Holding Secured Claims				$	
E - Creditors Holding Unsecured Priority Claims				$	
F - Creditors Holding Unsecured Nonpriority Claims				$	
G - Executory Contracts and Unexpired Leases					
H - Codebtors					
I - Current Income of Individual Debtor(s)					$
J - Current Expenditures of Individual Debtor(s)					$

Total Number of Sheets of ALL Schedules _____

Total Assets $ _____

Total Liabilities $ _____

In re _____, Case No. _____
　　　　　　Debtor　　　　　　　　　　　　　　　　　　　　(If known)

SCHEDULE A -- REAL PROPERTY

Except as directed below, list all real property in which the debtor has any legal, equitable, or future interest, including all property owned as a cotenant, community property, or in which the debtor has a life estate. Include any property in which the debtor holds rights and powers exercisable for the debtor's own benefit. If the debtor is married, state whether husband, wife, or both own the property by placing an "H," "W," "J," or "C" in the column labeled "Husband, Wife, Joint, or Community." If the debtor holds no interest in real property, write "None" under "Description and Location of Property."

Do not include interests in executory contracts and unexpired leases on this schedule. List them in Schedule G -- Executory Contracts and Unexpired Leases.

If an entity claims to have a lien or hold a secured interest in any property, state the amount of the secured claim. See Schedule D. If no entity claims to hold a secured interest in the property, write "None" in the column labeled "Amount of Secured Claim."

If the debtor is an individual or if a joint petition is filed, state the amount of any exemption claimed in the property only in Schedule C -- Property Claimed as Exempt.

DESCRIPTION AND LOCATION OF PROPERTY	NATURE OF DEBTOR'S INTEREST IN PROPERTY	H, W, J, or C	CURRENT MARKET VALUE OF DEBTOR'S INTEREST IN PROPERTY, WITHOUT DEDUCTING ANY SECURED CLAIM OR EXEMPTION	AMOUNT OF SECURED CLAIM

Total　$

(Report also on Summary of Schedules.)

SCHEDULE B -- PERSONAL PROPERTY

Except as directed below, list all personal property of the debtor of whatever kind. If the debtor has no property in one or more of the categories, place an "x" in the appropriate position in the column labeled "None." If additional space is needed in any category, attach a separate sheet properly identified with the case name, case number, and the number of the category. If the debtor is married, state whether husband, wife, or both own the property by placing an "H," "W," "J," or "C" in the column labeled "Husband, Wife, Joint, or Community." If the debtor is an individual or a joint petition is filed, state the amount of any exemptions claimed only in Schedule C -- Property Claimed as Exempt.

Do not list interests in executory contracts and unexpired leases on this schedule. List them in Schedule G -- Executory Contracts and Unexpired Leases.

If the property is being held for the debtor by someone else, state that person's name and address under "Description and Location of Property."

TYPE OF PROPERTY	NONE	DESCRIPTION AND LOCATION OF PROPERTY	H, W, J, or C	CURRENT MARKET VALUE OF DEBTOR'S INTEREST IN PROPERTY, WITHOUT DEDUCTING ANY SECURED CLAIM OR EXEMPTION
1. Cash on hand.				
2. Checking, savings or other financial accounts, certificates of deposit, or shares in banks, savings and loan, thrift, building and loan, and homestead associations, or credit unions, brokerage houses, or cooperatives.				
3. Security deposits with public utilities, telephone companies, landlords, and others.				

In re _____,   Case No. _____
             Debtor   (If known)

SCHEDULE B — PERSONAL PROPERTY
(Continuation Sheet)

TYPE OF PROPERTY	N O N E	DESCRIPTION AND LOCATION OF PROPERTY	H, W, J, or C	CURRENT MARKET VALUE OF DEBTOR'S INTEREST IN PROPERTY, WITHOUT DEDUCTING ANY SECURED CLAIM OR EXEMPTION
4. Household goods and furnishings, including audio, video, and computer equipment.				
5. Books; pictures and other art objects; antiques; stamp, coin, record, tape, compact disc, and other collections or collectibles.				
6. Wearing apparel.				
7. Furs and jewelry.				
8. Firearms and sports, photographic, and other hobby equipment.				
9. Interests in insurance policies. Name insurance company of each policy and itemize surrender or refund value of each.				
10. Annuities. Itemize and name each issuer.				
11. Interests in IRA, ERISA, Keogh, or other pension or profit sharing plans. Itemize.				
12. Stock and interests in incorporated and unincorporated businesses. Itemize.				
13. Interests in partnerships or joint ventures. Itemize.				
14. Government and corporate bonds and other negotiable and nonnegotiable instruments.				
15. Accounts receivable.				
16. Alimony, maintenance, support, and property settlements to which the debtor is or may be entitled. Give particulars.				
17. Other liquidated debts owing debtor including tax refunds. Give particulars.				
18. Equitable or future interests, life estates, and rights or powers exercisable for the benefit of the debtor other than those listed in Schedule of Real Property.				
19. Contingent and noncontingent interests in estate of a decedent, death benefit plan, life insurance policy, or trust.				
20. Other contingent and unliquidated claims of every nature, including tax refunds, counterclaims of the debtor, and rights to setoff claims. Give estimated value of each.				
21. Patents, copyrights, and other intellectual property. Give particulars.				
22. Licenses, franchises, and other general intangibles. Give particulars.				
23. Automobiles, trucks, trailers, and other vehicles and accessories.				
24. Boats, motors, and accessories.				
25. Aircraft and accessories.				

In re _____,   Case No. _____
         Debtor   (If known)

SCHEDULE B -- PERSONAL PROPERTY
(Continuation Sheet)

TYPE OF PROPERTY	N O N E	DESCRIPTION AND LOCATION OF PROPERTY	H, W, J, or C	CURRENT MARKET VALUE OF DEBTOR'S INTEREST IN PROPERTY, WITHOUT DEDUCTING ANY SECURED CLAIM OR EXEMPTION
26. Office equipment, furnishings, and supplies.				
27. Machinery, fixtures, equipment, and supplies used in business.				
28. Inventory.				
29. Animals.				
30. Crops -- growing or harvested. Give particulars.				
31. Farming equipment and implements.				
32. Farm supplies, chemicals, and feed.				
33. Other personal property of any kind not already listed. Itemize.				

_____ continuation sheets attached   TOTAL | $

(Include amounts from any continuation sheets attached. Report total also on Summary of Schedules.)

SCHEDULE C -- PROPERTY CLAIMED AS EXEMPT

Debtor elects the exemption to which debtor is entitled under:
(Check one)

_____ 11 U.S.C. § 522(b)(1):   Exemptions provided in 11 U.S.C. § 522(d). **Note:** These exemptions are available only in certain states.

_____ 11 U.S.C. § 522(b)(2):   Exemptions available under applicable nonbankruptcy federal laws, state or local law where the debtor's domicile has been located for the 180 days immediately preceding the filing of the petition, or for a longer portion of the 180-day period than in any other place, and the debtor's interest as a tenant by the entirety or joint tenant to the extent the interest is exempt from process under applicable nonbankruptcy law.

DESCRIPTION OF PROPERTY	SPECIFY LAW PROVIDING EACH EXEMPTION	VALUE OF CLAIMED EXEMPTION	CURRENT MARKET VALUE OF PROPERTY WITHOUT DEDUCTING EXEMPTION

Total | $

313

Official Form 6, Schedule D

In re _____ ,   Case No. _____
                    Debtor   (If known)

SCHEDULE D -- CREDITORS HOLDING SECURED CLAIMS

State the name, mailing address, including zip code, and account number, if any, of all entities holding claims secured by property of the debtor as of the date of filing of the petition. List creditors holding all types of secured interests such as judgment liens, garnishments, statutory liens, mortgages, deeds of trust, and other security interests. List creditors in alphabetical order to the extent practicable. If all secured creditors will not fit on this page, use the continuation sheet provided.

If any entity other than a spouse in a joint case may be jointly liable on a claim, place an "X" in the column labeled "Codebtor," include the entity on the appropriate schedule of creditors, and complete Schedule H -- Codebtors. If a joint petition is filed, state whether husband, wife, both of them, or the marital community may be liable on each claim by placing an "H," "W," "J," or "C" in the column labeled "Husband, Wife, Joint, or Community."

If the claim is contingent, place an "X" in the column labeled "Contingent." If the claim is unliquidated, place an "X" in the column labeled "Unliquidated." If the claim is disputed, place an "X" in the column labeled "Disputed." (You may need to place an "X" in more than one of these three columns.)

Report the total of all claims listed on this schedule in the box labeled "Total" on the last sheet of the completed schedule. Report this total also on the Summary of Schedules.

___ Check here if debtor has no creditors holding secured claims to report on this Schedule D.

CREDITOR'S NAME AND MAILING ADDRESS INCLUDING ZIP CODE	CODEBTOR	H, W, J, or C	DATE CLAIM WAS INCURRED, NATURE OF LIEN, AND DESCRIPTION AND MARKET VALUE OF PROPERTY SUBJECT TO LIEN	CONTINGENT	UNLIQ.	DISPUTED	AMOUNT OF CLAIM WITHOUT DEDUCTING VALUE OF COLLATERAL	UNSECURED PORTION, IF ANY
ACCOUNT NO.								
			VALUE $					
ACCOUNT NO.								
			VALUE $					
ACCOUNT NO.								
			VALUE $					

___ continuation sheets attached

Subtotal (Total of this page) $ _____

Total (Use only on last page) $ _____

(Report total also on Summary of Schedules)

In re _____,   Case No. _____
　　　　　　　Debtor　　　　　　　　　　　　　　　　　　　　(If known)

SCHEDULE E -- CREDITORS HOLDING UNSECURED PRIORITY CLAIMS

A complete list of claims entitled to priority, listed separately by type of priority, is to be set forth on the sheets provided. Only holders of unsecured claims entitled to priority should be listed in this schedule. In the boxes provided on the attached sheets, state the name and mailing address, including zip code, and account number, if any, of all entities holding priority claims against the debtor or the property of the debtor, as of the date of the filing of the petition.

If any entity other than a spouse in a joint case may be jointly liable on a claim, place an "X" in the column labeled "Codebtor," include the entity on the appropriate schedule of creditors, and complete Schedule H -- Codebtors. If a joint petition is filed, state whether husband, wife, both of them, or the marital community may be liable on each claim by placing an "H," "W," "J," or "C" in the column labeled "Husband, Wife, Joint, or Community."

If the claim is contingent, place an "X" in the column labeled "Contingent." If the claim is unliquidated, place an "X" in the column labeled "Unliquidated." If the claim is disputed, place an "X" in the column labeled "Disputed." (You may need to place an "X" in more than one of these three columns.)

Report the total of claims listed on each sheet in the box labeled "Subtotal" on each sheet. Report the total of all claims listed on this Schedule E in the box labeled "Total" on the last sheet of the completed schedule. Repeat this total also on the Summary of Schedules.

___ Check here if debtor has no creditors holding unsecured priority claims to report on this Schedule E.

TYPES OF PRIORITY

___ **Extensions of credit in an involuntary case**
Claims arising in the ordinary course of the debtor's business or financial affairs after the commencement of the case but before the earlier of the appointment of a trustee or the order for relief. 11 U.S.C. § 507(a)(2).

___ **Wages, salaries, and commissions**
Wages, salaries, and commissions, including vacation, severance, and sick leave pay owing to employees, up to a maximum of $2000 per employee, earned within 90 days immediately preceding the filing of the original petition, or the cessation of business, whichever occurred first, to the extent provided in 11 U.S.C. § 507(a)(3).

___ **Contributions to employee benefit plans**
Money owed to employee benefit plans for services rendered within 180 days immediately preceding the filing of the original petition, or the cessation of business, whichever occurred first, to the extent provided in 11 U.S.C. § 507(a)(4).

___ **Certain farmers and fishermen**
Claims of certain farmers and fishermen, up to a maximum of $2000 per farmer or fisherman, against the debtor, as provided in 11 U.S.C. § 507(a)(5).

___ **Deposits by individuals**
Claims of individuals up to a maximum of $900 for deposits for the purchase, lease, or rental of property or services for personal, family, or household use, that were not delivered or provided. 11 U.S.C. § 507(a)(6).

___ **Taxes and Certain Other Debts Owed to Governmental Units**
Taxes, customs duties, and penalties owing to federal, state, and local governmental units as set forth in 11 U.S.C. § 507(a)(7).

CREDITOR'S NAME AND MAILING ADDRESS INCLUDING ZIP CODE	CODEBTOR	H, W, J, or C	DATE CLAIM WAS INCURRED AND CONSIDERATION FOR CLAIM	CONTIN.	UNLIQ.	DISPUTED	TOTAL AMOUNT OF CLAIM	AMOUNT ENTITLED TO PRIORITY
ACCOUNT NO.								
ACCOUNT NO.								

Sheet no. _____ of _____ sheets attached to Schedule of Creditors Holding Priority Claims

Subtotal (Total of this page)　$

Total (Use only on last page of the completed Schedule E.)　$

(Report total also on Summary of Schedules)

In re _____,   Case No. _____
           Debtor   (If known)

SCHEDULE F -- CREDITORS HOLDING UNSECURED NONPRIORITY CLAIMS

State the name, mailing address, including zip code, and account number, if any, of all entities holding unsecured claims without priority against the debtor or the property of the debtor, as of the date of filing of the petition. Do not include claims listed in Schedules D and E. If all creditors will not fit on this page, use the continuation sheet provided.

If any entity other than a spouse in a joint case may be jointly liable on a claim, place an "X" in the column labeled "Codebtor," include the entity on the appropriate schedule of creditors, and complete Schedule H--Codebtors. If a joint petition is filed, state whether husband, wife, both of them, or the marital community may be liable on each claim by placing an "H," "W," "J," or "C" in the column labeled "Husband, Wife, Joint, or Community."

If the claim is contingent, place an "X" in the column labeled "Contingent." If the claim is unliquidated, place an "X" in the column labeled "Unliquidated." If the claim is disputed, place an "X" in the column labeled "Disputed." (You may need to place an "X" in more than one of these three columns.)

Report total of all claims listed on this schedule in the box labeled "Total" on the last sheet of the completed schedule. Report this total also on the Summary of Schedules.

____ Check here if debtor has no creditors holding unsecured non priority claims to report on this Schedule F.

CREDITOR'S NAME AND MAILING ADDRESS INCLUDING ZIP CODE	C O D E B T O R	H, W, J, or C	DATE CLAIM WAS INCURRED AND CONSIDERATION FOR CLAIM. IF CLAIM IS SUBJECT TO SETOFF, SO STATE.	C O N T I N.	U N L I Q.	D I S P U T E D	AMOUNT OF CLAIM
ACCOUNT NO.							
ACCOUNT NO.							
ACCOUNT NO.							
ACCOUNT NO.							
ACCOUNT NO.							

_____ continuation sheets attached

Subtotal (Total of this page)	$
Total (Use only on last page)	$

(Report total also on Summary of Schedules)

In re _____, Case No. _____
  Debtor   (If known)

SCHEDULE F -- CREDITORS HOLDING UNSECURED NONPRIORITY CLAIMS
(Continuation Sheet)

CREDITOR'S NAME AND MAILING ADDRESS INCLUDING ZIP CODE	C O D E B T O R	H, W, J, or C	DATE CLAIM WAS INCURRED AND CONSIDERATION FOR CLAIM. IF CLAIM IS SUBJECT TO SETOFF, SO STATE.	C O N T I N.	U N L I Q.	D I S P U T E D	AMOUNT OF CLAIM
ACCOUNT NO.							
ACCOUNT NO.							
ACCOUNT NO.							
ACCOUNT NO.							
ACCOUNT NO.							
ACCOUNT NO.							

_____ continuation sheets attached

Subtotal (Total of this page)	$
Total (Use only on last page)	$

(Report total also on Summary of Schedules)

Official Form 6, Schedules G, H

In re _____,   Case No. _____
                     Debtor   (If known)

SCHEDULE G – EXECUTORY CONTRACTS AND UNEXPIRED LEASES

Describe all executory contracts of any nature and all unexpired leases of real or personal property. Include any timeshare interests.

State nature of debtor's interest in contract, i.e., "Purchaser," Agent," etc. State whether debtor is the lessor or lessee of a lease.

Provide the names and complete mailing addresses of all other parties to each lease or contract described.

NOTE: A party listed on this schedule will not receive notice of the filing of this case unless the party is also scheduled in the appropriate schedule of creditors.

___ Check here if debtor has no executory contracts or unexpired leases.

NAME AND MAILING ADDRESS, INCLUDING ZIP CODE, OF OTHER PARTIES TO LEASE OR CONTRACT.	DESCRIPTION OF CONTRACT OR LEASE AND NATURE OF DEBTOR'S INTEREST. STATE WHETHER LEASE IS FOR NONRESIDENTIAL REAL PROPERTY. STATE CONTRACT NUMBER OF ANY GOVERNMENT CONTRACT.

SCHEDULE H -- CODEBTORS

Provide the information requested concerning any person or entity, other than a spouse in a joint case, that is also liable on any debts listed by debtor in the schedules of creditors. Include all guarantors and co-signers. In community property states, a married debtor not filing a joint case should report the name and address of the nondebtor spouse on this schedule. Include all names used by the nondebtor spouse during the six years immediately preceding the commencement of this case.

___ Check here if debtor has no codebtors.

NAME AND ADDRESS OF CODEBTOR	NAME AND ADDRESS OF CREDITOR

In re _____,   Case No. _____
                     Debtor   (If known)

SCHEDULE I -- CURRENT INCOME OF INDIVIDUAL DEBTOR(S)

The column labeled "Spouse" must be completed in all cases filed by joint debtors and by a married debtor in a chapter 12 or 13 case whether or not a joint petition is filed, unless the spouses are separated and a joint petition is not filed.

Debtor's Marital Status:	DEPENDENTS OF DEBTOR AND SPOUSE		
	NAMES	AGE	RELATIONSHIP

Employment:	DEBTOR	SPOUSE
Occupation:		
Name of Employer:		
How long employed:		
Address of Employer:		

Income: (Estimate of average monthly income)	DEBTOR	SPOUSE
Current monthly gross wages, salary, and commissions (pro rate if not paid monthly.)	$_____	$_____
Estimated monthly overtime	$_____	$_____
SUBTOTAL	$_____	$_____
LESS PAYROLL DEDUCTIONS		
a. Payroll taxes and social security	$_____	$_____
b. Insurance	$_____	$_____
c. Union dues	$_____	$_____
d. Other (Specify: _____)	$_____	$_____
SUBTOTAL OF PAYROLL DEDUCTIONS	$_____	$_____
TOTAL NET MONTHLY TAKE HOME PAY	$_____	$_____
Regular income from operation of business or profession or farm (attach detailed statement)	$_____	$_____
Income from real property	$_____	$_____
Interest and dividends	$_____	$_____
Alimony, maintenance or support payments payable to the debtor for the debtor's use or that of dependents listed above.	$_____	$_____
Social security or other government assistance (Specify) _____	$_____	$_____
Pension or retirement income	$_____	$_____
Other monthly income (Specify) _____	$_____	$_____
_____	$_____	$_____
TOTAL MONTHLY INCOME	$_____	$_____

TOTAL COMBINED MONTHLY INCOME $_____   (Report also on Summary of Schedules)

Describe any increase or decrease of more than 10% in any of the above categories anticipated to occur within the year following the filing of this document:

In re _____ ,   Case No. _____
                    Debtor   (If known)

SCHEDULE J – CURRENT EXPENDITURES OF INDIVIDUAL DEBTOR(S)

Complete this schedule by estimating the average monthly expenses of the debtor and the debtor's family. Pro rate any payments made bi-weekly, quarterly, semi-annually, or annually to show monthly rate.

___ Check here if a joint petition is filed and debtor's spouse maintains a separate household. Complete a separate schedule of expenditures labeled "Spouse."

Rent or home mortgage payment (include lot rented for mobile home)	$ _____
Are real estate taxes included? Yes _____ No _____	
Is property insurance included? Yes _____ No _____	
Utilities Electricity and heating fuel	$ _____
Water and sewer	$ _____
Telephone	$ _____
Other _____	$ _____
Home maintenance (repairs and upkeep)	$ _____
Food	$ _____
Clothing	$ _____
Laundry and dry cleaning	$ _____
Medical and dental expenses	$ _____
Transportation (not including car payments)	$ _____
Recreation, clubs and entertainment, newspapers, magazines, etc.	$ _____
Charitable contributions	$ _____
Insurance (not deducted from wages or included in home mortgage payments)	
Homeowner's or renter's	$ _____
Life	$ _____
Health	$ _____
Auto	$ _____
Other _____	$ _____
Taxes (not deducted from wages or included in home mortgage payments)	
(Specify) _____	$ _____
Installment payments: (In chapter 12 and 13 cases, do not list payments to be included in the plan)	
Auto	$ _____
Other _____	$ _____
Other _____	$ _____
Alimony, maintenance, and support paid to others	$ _____
Payments for support of additional dependents not living at your home	$ _____
Regular expenses from operation of business, profession, or farm (attach detailed statement)	$ _____
Other _____	$ _____
TOTAL MONTHLY EXPENSES (Report also on Summary of Schedules)	$ _____

(FOR CHAPTER 12 AND 13 DEBTORS ONLY)

Provide the information requested below, including whether plan payments are to be made bi-weekly, monthly, annually, or at some other regular interval.

A. Total projected monthly income	$ _____
B. Total projected monthly expenses	$ _____
C. Excess income (A minus B)	$ _____
D. Total amount to be paid into plan each _____	$ _____
(interval)	

In re _____,   Case No. _____
                    Debtor   (If known)

DECLARATION CONCERNING DEBTOR'S SCHEDULES

DECLARATION UNDER PENALTY OF PERJURY BY INDIVIDUAL DEBTOR

    I declare under penalty of perjury that I have read the foregoing summary and schedules, consisting of _____ sheets (total shown on summary page plus 1), and that they are true and correct to the best of my knowledge, information, and belief.

Date _____   Signature: _____
                                                                Debtor

Date _____   Signature: _____
                                                          (Joint Debtor, if any)

    [If joint case, both spouses must sign]

Penalty for making a false statement or concealing property: Fine of up to $500,000 or imprisonment for up to 5 years or both. 18 U.S.C. §§ 152 and 3571.

Official Form 7

FORM 7. STATEMENT OF FINANCIAL AFFAIRS

UNITED STATES BANKRUPTCY COURT
_____ DISTRICT OF _____

In re _____,   Case No. _____
                (Name)   (If known)
                        Debtor

STATEMENT OF FINANCIAL AFFAIRS

This statement is to be completed by every debtor. Spouses filing a joint petition may file a single statement on which the information for both spouses is combined. If the case is filed under chapter 12 or chapter 13, a married debtor must furnish information for both spouses whether or not a joint petition is filed, unless the spouses are separated and a joint petition is not filed. An individual debtor engaged in business as a sole proprietor, partner, family farmer, or self-employed professional, should provide the information requested on this statement concerning all such activities as well as the individual's personal affairs.

Questions 1 - 15 are to be completed by all debtors. Debtors that are or have been in business, as defined below, also must complete Questions 16 - 21. **Each question must be answered. If the answer to any question is "None," or the question is not applicable, mark the box labeled "None."** If additional space is needed for the answer to any question, use and attach a separate sheet properly identified with the case name, case number (if known), and the number of the question.

DEFINITIONS

"*In business.*" A debtor is "in business" for the purpose of this form if the debtor is a corporation or partnership. An individual debtor is "in business" for the purpose of this form if the debtor is or has been, within the two years immediately preceding the filing of this bankruptcy case, any of the following: an officer, director, managing executive, or person in control of a corporation; a partner, other than a limited partner, of a partnership; a sole proprietor or self-employed.

"*Insider.*" The term "insider" includes but is not limited to relatives of the debtor; general partners of the debtor and their relatives; corporations of which the debtor is an officer, director, or person in control; officers, directors, and any person in control of a corporate debtor and their relatives; affiliates of the debtor and insiders of such affiliates; any managing agent of the debtor. 11 U.S.C. § 101(30).

1. Income from employment or operation of business

None

☐

State the gross amount of income the debtor has received from employment, trade, or profession, or from operation of the debtor's business from the beginning of this calendar year to the date this case was commenced. State also the gross amounts received during the **two years** immediately preceding this calendar year. (A debtor that maintains, or has maintained, financial records on the basis of a fiscal rather than a calendar year may report fiscal year income. Identify the beginning and ending dates of the debtor's fiscal year.) If a joint petition is filed, state income for each spouse separately. (Married debtors filing under chapter 12 or chapter 13 must state income of both spouses whether or not a joint petition is filed, unless the spouses are separated and a joint petition is not filed.)

AMOUNT   SOURCE (if more than one)

2. Income other than from employment or operation of business

None

☐

State the amount of income received by the debtor other than from employment, trade, profession, or operation of the debtor's business during the **two years** immediately preceding the commencement of this case. Give particulars. If a joint petition is filed, state income for each spouse separately. (Married debtors filing under chapter 12 or chapter 13 must state income for each spouse whether or not a joint petition is filed, unless the spouses are separated and a joint petition is not filed.)

AMOUNT   SOURCE

3. Payments to creditors

None

☐

a. List all payments on loans, installment purchases of goods or services, and other debts, aggregating more than $600 to any creditor, made within **90 days** immediately preceding the commencement of this case. (Married debtors filing under chapter 12 or chapter 13 must include payments by either or both spouses whether or not a joint petition is filed, unless the spouses are separated and a joint petition is not filed.)

NAME AND ADDRESS OF CREDITOR	DATES OF PAYMENTS	AMOUNT PAID	AMOUNT STILL OWING

None

☐

b. List all payments made within **one year** immediately preceding the commencement of this case to or for the benefit of creditors who are or were insiders. (Married debtors filing under chapter 12 or chapter 13 must include payments by either or both spouses whether or not a joint petition is filed, unless the spouses are separated and a joint petition is not filed.)

NAME AND ADDRESS OF CREDITOR AND RELATIONSHIP TO DEBTOR	DATE OF PAYMENT	AMOUNT PAID	AMOUNT STILL OWING

4. Suits, executions, garnishments and attachments

None

☐

a. List all suits to which the debtor is or was a party within **one year** immediately preceding the filing of this bankruptcy case. (Married debtors filing under chapter 12 or chapter 13 must include information concerning either or both spouses whether or not a joint petition is filed, unless the spouses are separated and a joint petition is not filed.)

CAPTION OF SUIT AND CASE NUMBER	NATURE OF PROCEEDING	COURT AND LOCATION	STATUS OR DISPOSITION

None

☐

b. Describe all property that has been attached, garnished or seized under any legal or equitable process within **one year** immediately preceding the commencement of this case. (Married debtors filing under chapter 12 or chapter 13 must include information concerning property of either or both spouses whether or not a joint petition is filed, unless the spouses are separated and a joint petition is not filed.)

NAME AND ADDRESS OF PERSON FOR WHOSE BENEFIT PROPERTY WAS SEIZED	DATE OF SEIZURE	DESCRIPTION AND VALUE OF PROPERTY

5. Repossessions, foreclosures and returns

None

☐

List all property that has been repossessed by a creditor, sold at a foreclosure sale, transferred through a deed in lieu of foreclosure or returned to the seller, within **one year** immediately preceding the commencement of this case. (Married debtors filing under chapter 12 or chapter 13 must include information concerning property of either or both spouses whether or not a joint petition is filed, unless the spouses are separated and a joint petition is not filed.)

NAME AND ADDRESS OF CREDITOR OR SELLER	DATE OF REPOSSESSION, FORECLOSURE SALE, TRANSFER OR RETURN	DESCRIPTION AND VALUE Of PROPERTY

6. Assignments and receiverships

None

☐

a. Describe any assignment of property for the benefit of creditors made within **120 days** immediately preceding the commencement of this case. (Married debtors filing under chapter 12 or chapter 13 must include any assignment by either or both spouses whether or not a joint petition is filed, unless the spouses are separated and a joint petition is not filed.)

NAME AND ADDRESS OF ASSIGNEE	DATE OF ASSIGNMENT	TERMS OF ASSIGNMENT OR SETTLEMENT

None

☐

b. List all property which has been in the hands of a custodian, receiver, or court-appointed official within **one year** immediately preceding the commencement of this case. (Married debtors filing under chapter 12 or chapter 13 must include information concerning property of either or both spouses whether or not a joint petition is filed, unless the spouses are separated and a joint petition is not filed.)

NAME AND ADDRESS OF CUSTODIAN	NAME AND LOCATION OF COURT CASE TITLE & NUMBER	DATE OF ORDER	DESCRIPTION AND VALUE OF PROPERTY

Official Form 7

7. Gifts

None

☐

List all gifts or charitable contributions made within **one year** immediately preceding the commencement of this case except ordinary and usual gifts to family members aggregating less than $200 in value per individual family member and charitable contributions aggregating less than $100 per recipient. (Married debtors filing under chapter 12 or chapter 13 must include gifts or contributions by either or both spouses whether or not a joint petition is filed, unless the spouses are separated and a joint petition is not filed.)

NAME AND ADDRESS OF PERSON OR ORGANIZATION	RELATIONSHIP TO DEBTOR, IF ANY	DATE OF GIFT	DESCRIPTION AND VALUE OF GIFT

8. Losses

None

☐

List all losses from fire, theft, other casualty or gambling within **one year** immediately preceding the commencement of this case **or since the commencement of this case**. (Married debtors filing under chapter 12 or chapter 13 must include losses by either or both spouses whether or not a joint petition is filed, unless the spouses are separated and a joint petition is not filed.)

DESCRIPTION AND VALUE OF PROPERTY	DESCRIPTION OF CIRCUMSTANCES AND, IF LOSS WAS COVERED IN WHOLE OR IN PART BY INSURANCE, GIVE PARTICULARS	DATE OF LOSS

9. Payments related to debt counseling or bankruptcy

None

☐

List all payments made or property transferred by or on behalf of the debtor to any persons, including attorneys, for consultation concerning debt consolidation, relief under the bankruptcy law or preparation of a petition in bankruptcy within **one year** immediately preceding the commencement of this case.

NAME AND ADDRESS OF PAYEE	DATE OF PAYMENT, NAME OF PAYOR IF OTHER THAN DEBTOR	AMOUNT OF MONEY OR DESCRIPTION AND VALUE OF PROPERTY

10. Other transfers

None

☐

List all other property, other than property transferred in the ordinary course of the business or financial affairs of the debtor, transferred either absolutely or as security within **one year** immediately preceding the commencement of this case. (Married debtors filing under chapter 12 or chapter 13 must include transfers by either or both spouses whether or not a joint petition is filed, unless the spouses are separated and a joint petition is not filed.)

NAME AND ADDRESS OF TRANSFEREE, RELATIONSHIP TO DEBTOR	DATE	DESCRIBE PROPERTY TRANSFERRED AND VALUE RECEIVED

11. Closed financial accounts

None

☐

List all financial accounts and instruments held in the name of the debtor or for the benefit of the debtor which were closed, sold, or otherwise transferred within **one year** immediately preceding the commencement of this case. Include checking, savings, or other financial accounts, certificates of deposit, or other instruments; shares and share accounts held in banks, credit unions, pension funds, cooperatives, associations, brokerage houses and other financial institutions. (Married debtors filing under chapter 12 or chapter 13 must include information concerning accounts or instruments held by or for either or both spouses whether or not a joint petition is filed, unless the spouses are separated and a joint petition is not filed.)

NAME AND ADDRESS OF INSTITUTION	TYPE AND NUMBER OF ACCOUNT AND AMOUNT OF FINAL BALANCE	AMOUNT AND DATE OF SALE OR CLOSING

12. Safe deposit boxes

None

☐

     List each safe deposit or other box or depository in which the debtor has or had securities, cash, or other valuables within **one year** immediately preceding the commencement of this case. (Married debtors filing under chapter 12 or chapter 13 must include boxes or depositories of either or both spouses whether or not a joint petition is filed, unless the spouses are separated and a joint petition is not filed.)

NAME AND ADDRESS OF BANK OR OTHER DEPOSITORY	NAMES AND ADDRESSES OF THOSE WITH ACCESS TO BOX OR DEPOSITORY	DESCRIPTION OF CONTENTS	DATE OF TRANSFER OR SURRENDER, IF ANY

13. Setoffs

None

☐

     List all setoffs made by any creditor, including a bank, against a debt or deposit of the debtor within **90 days** preceding the commencement of this case. (Married debtors filing under chapter 12 or chapter 13 must include information concerning either or both spouses whether or not a joint petition is filed, unless the spouses are separated and a joint petition is not filed.)

NAME AND ADDRESS OF CREDITOR	DATE OF SETOFF	AMOUNT OF SETOFF

14. Property held for another person

None

☐

     List all property owned by another person that the debtor holds or controls.

NAME AND ADDRESS OF OWNER	DESCRIPTION AND VALUE OF PROPERTY	LOCATION OF PROPERTY

15. Prior address of debtor

None

☐

     If the debtor has moved within the **two years** immediately preceding the commencement of this case, list all premises which the debtor occupied during that period and vacated prior to the commencement of this case. If a joint petition is filed, report also any separate address of either spouse.

ADDRESS	NAME USED	DATES OF OCCUPANCY

* * * * * * * * * *

[If completed by an individual or individual and spouse]

I declare under penalty of perjury that I have read the answers contained in the foregoing statement of financial affairs and any attachments thereto and that they are true and correct.

Date _____   Signature _____
                            of Debtor

Date _____   Signature _____
                            of Joint Debtor
                            (if any)

* * * * * * * * * *

Penalty for making a false statement: Fine of up to $500,000 or imprisonment for up to 5 years, or both. 18 U.S.C. § 152 and 3571

Form 8. CHAPTER 7 INDIVIDUAL DEBTOR'S STATEMENT OF INTENTION

UNITED STATES BANKRUPTCY COURT
_____ DISTRICT OF _____

In re _____,   Case No. _____
            (Name)   (If known)
                        Debtor

INDIVIDUAL CHAPTER 7 DEBTOR'S STATEMENT OF INTENTION

1. I, the debtor, have filed a schedule of assets and liabilities which includes consumer debts secured by property of the estate.

2. My intention with respect to the property of the estate which secures those consumer debts is as follows:

a. Property to be Surrendered.

Description of property	Creditor's name
1. _____	_____
2. _____	_____
3. _____	_____

b. Property to Be Retained. [Check applicable statement of debtor's intention concerning reaffirmation, redemption, or lien avoidance.]

Description of property	Creditor's name	Debt will be reaffirmed pursuant to § 524(c)	Property is claimed as exempt and will be redeemed pursuant to § 722	Lien will be avoided pursuant to § 522(f) and property will be claimed as exempt
1. _____	_____	___	___	___
2. _____	_____	___	___	___
3. _____	_____	___	___	___
4. _____	_____	___	___	___
5. _____	_____	___	___	___

3. I understand that § 521(2)(B) of the Bankruptcy Code requires that I perform the above stated intention within 45 days of the filing of this statement with the court, or within such additional time as the court, for cause, within such 45-day period fixes.

Date: _____

_____
Signature of Debtor

FORM 10. PROOF OF CLAIM

UNITED STATES BANKRUPTCY COURT _____ **District of** _____	**PROOF OF CLAIM**
In re (Name of Debtor)	Case Number

NOTE: This form should not be used to make a claim for an administrative expense arising after the commencement of the case. A "request" of payment of an administrative expense may be filed pursuant to 11 U.S.C. § 503.

Name of Creditor _(The person or entity to whom the debtor owes money or property)_	___ Check here if you are aware that anyone else has filed a proof of claim relating to your claim. Attach copy of statement giving particulars.
Name and Address Where Notices Should Be Sent	___ Check here if you have never received any notices from the bankruptcy court in this case. ___ Check here if the address differs from the address on the envelope sent to you by the court.
Telephone No.	**THIS SPACE IS FOR COURT USE ONLY**

ACCOUNT OR OTHER NUMBER BY WHICH CREDITOR IDENTIFIES DEBTOR:

Check here if this claim ___ replaces ___ amends a previously filed claim dated:_____

1. BASIS FOR CLAIM
- ___ Goods sold
- ___ Services performed
- ___ Money loaned
- ___ Personal injury/wrongful death
- ___ Taxes
- ___ Other (Describe briefly)

- ___ Retiree benefits as defined in 11 U.S.C. § 1114(a)
- ___ Wage, salaries, and compensations (Fill out below)

Your social security number _____
Unpaid compensation for services performed
from _____ to _____
(date)   (date)

2. DATE DEBT WAS INCURRED:

3. IF COURT JUDGMENT, DATE OBTAINED:

4. CLASSIFICATION OF CLAIM. Under the Bankruptcy Code all claims are classified as one or more of the following: (1) Unsecured nonpriority; (2) Unsecured Priority; (3) Secured. It is possible for part of a claim to be in one category and part in another.
CHECK THE APPROPRIATE ITEM OR ITEMS that best describe your claim and STATE THE AMOUNT OF THE CLAIM.

___ SECURED CLAIM $ _____
   Attach evidence of perfection of security interest
   Brief Description of Collateral:
   ___ Real Estate ___ Motor Vehicle ___ Other (Describe briefly)

Amount of arrearage and other charges included in secured claim above,
if any $ _____

___ UNSECURED NONPRIORITY CLAIM $ _____
   A claim is unsecured if there is no collateral or lien on property of the debtor securing the claim or to the extent that the value of such property is less than the amount of the claim.

___ UNSECURED PRIORITY CLAIM $ _____
   Specify the priority of the claim.
   ___ Wages, salaries, or commissions (up to $2000, earned not more than 90 days before filing of the bankruptcy petition or cessation of the debtor's business, whichever is earlier) -- 11 U.S.C. § 507(a)(3)
   ___ Contributions to an employee benefit plan -- 11 U.S.C. § 507(a)(4)
   ___ Up to $900 of deposits toward purchase, lease, or rental of property or services for personal, family, or household use -- 11 U.S.C. § 507(a)(6)
   ___ Taxes or penalties of governmental units -- 11 U.S.C. § 507(a)(7)
   ___ Other -- 11 U.S.C. §§ 507(a)(2), (a)(5) -- (Describe briefly)

5. TOTAL AMOUNT OF CLAIM AT TIME CASE FILED:
$ _____ (Unsecured) $ _____ (Secured) $ _____ Priority $ _____ (Total)

___ Check here if claim includes prepetition charges in addition to the principal amount of the claim. Attach itemized statement of all additional changes.

6. CREDITS AND SETOFFS: The amount of all payments on this claim has been credited and deducted for the purpose of making this proof of claim. In filing this claim, claimant has deducted all amounts that claimant owes to debtor.

7. SUPPORTING DOCUMENTS: Attach copies of supporting documents, such as promissory notes, purchase orders, invoices, itemized statements of running accounts, contracts, court judgments, or evidence of security interests. If the documents are not available, explain. If the documents are voluminous, attach a summary.

8. TIME-STAMPED COPY: To receive an acknowledgment of the filing of your claim, enclose a stamped, self-addressed envelope and copy of this proof of claim.

THIS SPACE IS FOR COURT USE ONLY

Date	Sign and print the name and title, if any, of the creditor or other person authorized to file this claim (attach copy of power of attorney, if any)

Penalty for Presenting Fraudulent Claim: **Fine of up to $500,000 or imprisonment for up to 5 years, or both. 18 U.S.C. §§ 152 and 3571.**

INDEX

Abandonment of property, in chapter 7 cases, 21
Ability-to-pay test, 197–199
Adequate assurance, utility's right to discontinue service for lack of, 135–136
Adequate protection
    under chapter 13, 181–182
    relief from automatic stay for lack of, 131–132
Administrative claims, 44
Administrative expenses, postpetition claims as, in chapter 11 bankruptcy cases, 283–284
Alimony, exception from discharge, 246–248
Allowed secured claims, 172–175
    cash collateral held by creditors and, 175–176
    concept of, 172–173
    cramdown and. See Cramdown
    procedure for determining, 173–175
        date of valuation and, 174
        method of valuation and, 174–175
Amendments
    to claim of exemption, 153–154
    to statement or schedules, 101
American Savings Bank, Nobleman v., 173, 181
Anti-alienation provision, 11, 12
Appeals
    from bankruptcy court, 9–10, 225
    from district court or bankruptcy appellate panel, 225
Assets. See also Bankruptcy estate; Property
    failure to explain loss or deficiency of, as grounds for

objection to discharge in chapter 7 cases, 230
nominal, 22
sale of, in chapter 7 cases, 22
Attachment, 43, 66
Attorney(s), 269–280. See also Attorney fees
    dealing with, 280
    finding, 271–274
        free legal services and, 272
        private attorneys, 272–274
    forms signed by, 98
    reasons for having, 269–270
Attorney fees, 274–280
    basic, 275
    court supervision of, 276–278
        disclosures required for, 277
        review of disclosures and requests and, 277–278
    cure of defaults on long-term debts and, 186
    disclosure of, 97, 277–278
        court review of, 277–278
    in fraud dischargeability cases, 243
    initial arrangements for, 274–275
    in involuntary bankruptcy cases, 220–221
    payment method for, 276
    payment through chapter 13 plan, 278–279
        fees which can be paid through plan, 278–279
        procedure for obtaining, 279
    sources of, in bankruptcy cases, 279–280
    typical, 275–276
Automatic stay, 56, 121–134
    in chapter 7 cases, 20
    in chapter 11 cases, 281–282
    in chapter 13 cases, 30

    codebtors and, 125–126
    permission to proceed with acts prohibited by, 30–31
    creditor's motion for relief from, 104
    duration of, 122
    enforcement of, 128–129
    exceptions to, 126–127
    notice of, 100–101, 127–128
    purpose of, 121–122
    relief from. See Relief, from automatic stay
    rent-to-own transactions and, 187
    scope of, 122–125
Automatic turnover, 101
Automobile loan defaults, remedies for, 79–80
Avoidance, 156–169
    debtor's right to use trustee's avoiding powers and, 160–169
        fraudulent transfers and, 164–166
        liens securing fines, penalties, and forfeitures and, 168
        postpetition transfers and, 166–167
        preferences and, 162–164
        setoff and, 167–168
        statutory liens and, 161–162
        "strong-arm" clause and, 160–161
    exemption of property recovered by trustee and, 159
    general principles of, 156
    of judicial liens, 157–158
    of nonpossessory, nonpurchase-money security interests, 158–159
    of postpetition transfers, 166–167
    preferences and, 75, 162–164

preservation of avoided transfers
or recovered property and,
169
procedure for, 156–157
of transfers of exempt property,
101–102

Bank accounts, freezing of, 175–176
Bankruptcy
advantages of, 55–57
alternatives to, 62–69
budgeting and payment
agreements as, 67
credit counseling agencies as,
67–68
defending against disputed
debts as, 69
lack of action as, 62–67
refinancing of debts as, 68
disadvantages of, 57–62
discrimination after. See Discrimination, after bank-
ruptcy
dispelling myths about, 54–55
overcoming stigma of, 53–54
Bankruptcy Act of 1898, 215
Bankruptcy Act of 1978, court's
powers under, 215–216
Bankruptcy Amendments and
Federal Judgeship Act of
1984, 216
Bankruptcy appellate panel, appeals
from, 225
Bankruptcy Code, 5–6, 215
trustee's duties and, 14
Bankruptcy court, 7–10
appeals from, 9–10, 225
dismissal by, 221–224
of chapter 13 cases, 36, 113–
114
involuntary, 221
for substantial abuse of
chapter 7 provisions, 222–
224
voluntary, 221
involuntary bankruptcy cases in,
218–221
litigation of cases outside
bankruptcy in, 215–218
advantages for, 216–217
claims commenced by debtor
and, 217–218
objections to claims and, 218
removal and, 217
powers of, 7, 8–9, 215–216
status under amended Bankruptcy
Reform Act, 7–8

supervision of attorney fees by.
See Attorney fees
Bankruptcy estate, 10–13. See also
Assets; Property
pensions and spendthrift trusts
and, 11–12
sale of assets of, in chapter 7
cases, 22
tax refunds and earned income
tax credit and, 12–13
Bankruptcy Reform Act of 1898, 8
Bankruptcy Reform Act of 1978, 8,
217
1984 amendments to, 7–8
Benefit plans, 11–12, 149
Best interests of creditors test, 96
payments to unsecured creditors
in chapter 13 cases and,
194
Best interests of debtor test, reaffirmation of debts and, 260
Budget analysis, 48
Budgeting, 67
Business bankruptcy cases, consumers' rights in. See Chapter
11 bankruptcy cases

Cash collateral, held by creditors,
allowed secured claims and,
175–176
Cause, relief from automatic stay
for, 130–131
Chapter 7 bankruptcy cases, 6, 17–
25
as alternative to chapter 13 cases,
193
attorney fees in, 274–276
chapter 13 cases filed after, 211–
212
closing of, 25
commencement of, 17–20
initial forms and, 19–20, 81
persons who may file cases,
17–19
considerations favoring, 70–71
conversion of chapter 13 cases to,
34–36, 113, 221–222
conversion to chapter 13 cases,
30
court seizures of property and, 79
creditors meeting and, 20–21
events following, 21–25, 108–
109
discharge in. See Discharge, in
chapter 7 cases
distribution in, 22–25
first steps after filing, 20

forms required for
petition, 82–83
to start case, 19–20, 81
statement of intention with
respect to property securing
debts and, 176–177
objections to claims of creditors
in, 103
objections to discharge in. See
Discharge
redemption in, 102, 177–180
installment payments and, 178
limitations of, 177–178
purpose of, 177
refusal to agree to continued
installment payments and,
178–179
uses of, 179–180
retaining nonexempt property in,
104
substantial abuse of provisions in,
dismissal for, 222–224
trustee in. See Trustee, in chapter
7 cases
unsecured debts and, 79
utility bills and, 79
wage garnishments and, 79
Chapter 11 bankruptcy cases, 6,
281–287
automatic stay in, 281–282
debtor in possession in, 383
filing proof of claim in, 282–285
prior discharge in, as grounds for
objection to discharge in
chapter 7 cases, 231
tenants of bankrupt landlords
and, 286–287
use by consumer debtors, 72–73
Chapter 13 bankruptcy cases, 6, 27–
37, 189–213
attorney fees in, 274–276. See
also Attorney fees
automatic stay protecting
codebtors in, 125–126
automobile loan defaults and
repossessions and, 79–80
classification of claims in, 201–204
claims with cosigners and,
201–202
payments outside plan and, 203
practical considerations
regarding, 203–204
commencement of, 27–30
conversion from chapter 7
case and, 30
initial forms and, 28–30
persons who may file, 27–28

confirmation hearing in, 32, 109–110

considerations favoring, 71–72

conversion of chapter 7 cases to, 30

conversion to chapter 7 cases, 34–36, 113, 221–222

court seizures of property and, 79

cramdown and. *See* Cramdown

creditors meeting and, 31–32

debtor's failure to complete plan and, 33–36
  conversion to chapter 7 and, 34–36, 113
  dismissal and, 36
  hardship discharge and, 33–34
  modification of plan and, 34

discharge in. *See* Discharge, in chapter 13 cases

dismissal of, 36, 113–114

eligibility for, 27–28, 190–193
  debt limitations and, 191–193
  regular income and, 190–191

executory contracts in, 208–209, 210–211
  assumption of, 209, 210–211
  rejection of, 209–211

first steps after filing, 30–31

forms required for, to start case, 81

leases in, 209–211
  assumption of, 209, 210–211
  rejection of, 209–211

liquidation of property in, 207

modification of plan in, 112

mortgage delinquencies and foreclosures and, 80

objections to claims of creditors in, 103

payment of debtor's income directly to trustee in, 205–206

payment of interest and penalties in, 206

payments under, 31, 99
  commencement of, 105
  to unsecured creditors. *See* Unsecured debts, in chapter 13 cases

plan administration in, 110–114
  inability to complete plan and, 112–114
  modification of plan and, 111
  postpetition claims and, 110–111
  trustee payments to creditors and, 110

plan and, 94–97

confirmation of, 213

feasibility of, 204–205

length of, 206–207

modification of, 32–33, 111

provisions for filing, 29–30

refusal by court, 95–96

requirements for, 94–95

transactions after filing, 32–33

after prior bankruptcies, 211–212

prior discharge in, as grounds for objection to discharge in chapter 7 cases, 232

priority or secured claims in, 108

reorganization and, 133

tax debts and, 80

trustee in. *See* Trustee, in chapter 13 cases

use and possession of property of estate in, 207–208

utility bills and, 79

wage garnishments and, 79

Chapter 13 bankruptcy cases, prior discharge in, as grounds for objection to discharge in chapter 7 cases, 231, 232

Child support
  in chapter 13 cases, 202
  exception from discharge, 246

Claims
  classification in chapter 13 cases. *See* Chapter 13 bankruptcy cases, classification of claims in
  definition of, 256–257
  filing proof of, in chapter 11 bankruptcy cases, 282–285
  objections to, 103
  postpetition
    as administrative expenses, in chapter 11 bankruptcy cases, 283–284
    in chapter 13 cases, 110–111
  priority, filing in chapter 13 cases, 108
  secured. *See also* Allowed secured claims; Cramdown
    filing in chapter 13 cases, 108

Codebtors
  in chapter 13 cases, automatic stay and, 125–126
  claims with, in chapter 13 cases, 201–202
  list of, 88

Collateral. *See* Allowed secured claims; Secured debts

Collection letters and telephone calls, 63–64

College transcripts, discharge and, 264

Commission, of trustee, 61

Community property, 47
  bankruptcy estate and, 10
  in chapter 7 cases, 24
  effects of discharge and, 258

Complaints, on dischargeability, 102–103

Confirmation hearing, in chapter 13 cases, 32, 109–110

Consolidation loans, 68

Consumer(s). *See also* Debtor(s)
  priority in business bankruptcy cases, 284–285
  rights in business bankruptcy cases. *See* Chapter 11 bankruptcy cases

Consumer credit counseling, 67–68
  reasons to avoid, 270–271

Consumer protection laws, 279–280

Contempt of court proceedings, automatic stay and, 126

Contingent debts, limitations on, eligibility for chapter 13 and, 193

Contracts
  executory. *See* Executory contracts
  rent-to-own, 88, 186–187

Co-owners
  nondebtor, 11
  tenancy in common and, 46

Corporations, property owned by, 47

Costs. *See also* Fees
  of filing petition, 61

Court orders, refusal to obey, as grounds for objection to discharge in chapter 7 cases, 230–231

Cramdown, 180–186
  claims not secured only by debtor's principal residence and, 180–184
    adequate protection requirement and, 181–182
    limitations on debts secured only by debtor's principal residence and, 180–181
    provisions dealing with allowed secured claims provided for by plan and, 182–184
  right to cure defaults on long-term debts and, 184–186
    amount necessary to effectuate cure, 185–186

maintaining current payments
on debts being cured and,
185
mortgages, after acceleration
or foreclosure judgment,
184–185
time permitted for, 185
Credit
effect of bankruptcy on, 54, 58–
59
use without intent to pay,
exception of debts from
discharge and, 240–242
Credit counseling agencies, 67–68
reasons to avoid, 270–271
Creditors
best-interests-of-creditors test
and, 96, 194
in chapter 7 cases, claims filed
by, 22
equity among, 7
favored, paying, 78
list of, 85, 86
litigation of disputes with, 57
motion for relief from automatic
stay made by, 104
notification of automatic stay,
100–101, 127–128
objections to claims of, 103
payments to, in chapter 13 cases,
110
relief from automatic stay sought
by. See Relief, from
automatic stay
secured. See Secured debts
unsecured. See Unsecured debts
vote of, in chapter 11 cases, 285–
286
Creditors meeting [section 341(a)
meeting], 105–108
in chapter 7 cases, 20–21
events following, 21–25, 108–
109
notice of, 20
in chapter 13 cases, 31–32
notice of, 31
preparation for, 105–106
procedure for, 106–108
Credit repair, reasons to avoid, 270–
271
Credit unions, debts emerging from
responsibilities to, exception from discharge, 256
Criminal proceedings
automatic stay and, 126
discharge and, 266
nonautomatic stays and, 127

Damages, in involuntary bankruptcy
cases, 220–221
Debt(s), 42–45
definition of, 256
dischargeability of. See Discharge
disputed, defending against, 69
frequently overlooked, 50–51
further, delaying petition and, 77–
78
limitations on, eligibility for
chapter 13 and, 191–193
list of, 85–86, 87
medical, after bankruptcy, 60
postpetition, conversion of
chapter 13 cases to chapter
7 cases and, 35
priority. See Priority debts
reaffirmation of. See Reaffirmation of debts
refinancing, 68, 271
secured. See Secured debts
tax. See Taxes
unsecured. See Unsecured debts
Debt amount, chapter 13 cases and,
28, 71
Debtor(s). See also Codebtors
ability to pay, 96
avoidance by. See Avoidance
bankruptcy as remedy for, 3–4
benefits of bankruptcy for, 4–5
equity of, 43
financial picture of. See Financial
picture
forms signed by, 98
Debtor in possession, 283
Declaration page, 89
Default(s)
on long-term debts, right to cure,
184–186
remedies for, 79–80
Default judgment, 65
Depository institutions, debts
emerging from responsibilities to, exception from
discharge, 256
Disability benefits, exemption of,
148–150
Discharge, 55, 114, 227–267
actions following, 117
in chapter 7 cases, 25
discharge hearing and, 25
effects of, 257–258
exceptions to, 25, 250–253
granting of, 25
objections to. See Discharge,
objections to discharge in
chapter 7 cases

in chapter 13 cases, 36–37, 71–72
absence of bars to, 28
discharge hearing and, 37
effects of, 257–258
exceptions to, 233–234, 253–
254
revocation of, 36
complaints on dischargeability
and, 102–103
exceptions to, 25, 36, 233–256
alimony, maintenance, or
support owed to spouse,
former spouse, or child,
246–248
chapter 7 and 13 compared
and, 133–134
creditors not listed or scheduled by debtor, 244–245
debts emerging from responsibilities to federal depository
institutions, 256
debts existing at time of
denial or waiver of dis-
charge in prior bankruptcy
cases, 255
debts incurred through drunk
driving, 255
debts incurred through false
pretenses, fraud, or false
financial statements, 236–
243
debts made nondischargeable
by other statutes, 256
fines and penalties, 249–250
fraud as fiduciary, embezzlement, and larceny, 245–246
raising, 234–235
student loans, 250–255
taxes, 235–236
willful and malicious injury,
248–249
hardship, in chapter 13 cases, 33–
34, 112–113
notice of, 117
objections to discharge in chapter
7 cases, 227–233
failure to pay filing fees and,
232–233
grounds for, 228–232
prior discharge as grounds for,
231–232
protections of, 256–267
criminal proceedings, fines,
and incarceration and, 266
against discrimination based
on bankruptcy, 262–263
driver's licenses and, 263–267

effects on discharged claims
and, 256–258
enforcement of, 266–267
exempt property and, 170
government benefits and, 265
public and private housing
and, 264–265
reaffirmation and security
interests surviving bank-
ruptcy and, 258–261
secured debts without
reaffirmation and, 261
student loans and college
transcripts and, 264
revocation of, 233
waiver of
as grounds for objection to
discharge in chapter 7
cases, 232
in prior bankruptcy case,
exception of debts from
discharge in present case
and, 255
Discharge hearing, 114–116
in chapter 7 cases, 25
procedure at, 116
reaffirmation of debts and, 115–
116
Disclosure
of attorney fees. See Attorney
fees
of expenses, 88, 89
full, importance of, 51–52
of income, 88–89
Discrimination
after bankruptcy, 59–60
medical debts and, 60
protections against, 59–60
protection against, 262–263
Dismissal. See Bankruptcy court,
dismissal by
Disposable income, 96
definition of, 197
Distribution, in chapter 7 cases, 22–
25
District court, appeals from, 225
Dividends, 23
Driver's licenses, discharge and,
263–264
Drunk driving, debts incurred by,
exception from discharge,
255

Earned income tax credit, exclusion
from estate, 13
Embezzlement, exception from
discharge, 245, 246

Emergency filings, 82
Employee benefit plans, 11–12, 149
Employee Retirement Income
Security Act (ERISA), plans
established under, 11–12,
149
Entireties property, 47
Equal Credit Opportunity Act, 280
Equity
of debtor, 43
relief from automatic stay for
lack of, 132–133
Equity test of insolvency, 220
ERISA. See Employee Retirement
Income Security Act
(ERISA)
Estate. See Bankruptcy estate
Eviction, 64
Exceptions, to discharge. See
Discharge, exceptions to
Executory contracts, 87
in chapter 13 cases, 208–211
assumption of, 209, 210–211
rejection of, 209–211
Exemptions. See also Exempt
property
enhancement of, 155–169
debtor's avoiding powers and.
See Avoidance
exemption planning for, 155–156
federal, 143–151
of accrued dividend, interest,
or loan value of life
insurance, 148
of any property, 147
of disability, retirement, and
other benefits replacing
wages, 148–150
of health aids, 148
of homestead, 144–145
of household goods and
similar items, 145–146
of jewelry, 146
of motor vehicles, 145
of rights to compensation for
injury or losses, 150–151
of tools of trade, 147
of unmatured life insurance,
147–148
listed by state, 289–306
nonbankruptcy. See
Nonbankruptcy exemptions
of pension plans, 11–12
planning, 76–77, 155–156
procedure for claiming, 153–155
allowance of exemptions and,
154–155

amending claims and, 153–154
initial claim and, 153
objections to exemptions and,
154
purposes of, 142
of spendthrift trusts, 12
state versus federal, 143
wild-card, 146, 147
Exempt property, 141–170
avoidance of transfers of, 101–102
definition of, 142
list of, 84–85
possession of, 138
protection of, after discharge, 170
Expenses, disclosure of, 88, 89
Extensions, filing for, 97–98

Fair Credit Reporting Act, 58, 280
Fair Debt Collection Practices Act,
63, 280
False pretenses, debts incurred
through, exception from
discharge, 236–237, 239–243
Feasibility standard, for chapter 13
plans, 204–205
Federal laws, 5, 279–280. See also
Bankruptcy Code
Federal Rules of Bankruptcy
Procedure, 5
Official Forms and, 5
Fees. See also Attorney fees; Filing
fee; Noticing fee
court, 61
cure of defaults on long-term
debts and, 185–186
payment of, in chapter 13 cases,
206
trustee's commission, 61
Filing fee, 81
for amendments, 101
application to pay in installments, 97
for chapter 13 case, 28–29
for chapter 7 cases, 19
failure to pay, as grounds for
objection to discharge in
chapter 7 cases, 232–233
Final judgment orders and decrees,
appeal from, 9
Financial books and records
false, debts incurred through,
exception from discharge,
236–239
unjustified failure to keep, as
grounds for objection to
discharge in chapter 7
cases, 229–230

Financial picture
    assembling information about,
        48–51
        additional sources of informa-
            tion for, 51
        debts frequently overlooked
            in, 50
        property frequently overlooked
            in, 49–50
    importance of knowing, 41–42
Fines
    discharge and, 249–250, 266
    liens securing, avoidance of, 168
Fixtures, 45
Foreclosure, 64
    in chapter 13 cases, 112
    programs offering assistance to
        prevent, 69
    remedies for, 80
Forfeitures, liens securing, avoidance
    of, 168
Forms, 81–98. See also Official
    Form(s); Petition; specific
    types of bankruptcy cases
    required to start cases, 81–82
        emergency filings and, 82
    signing, verifying, and filing, 98
Fraud
    in connection with bankruptcy
        case, as grounds for
        objection to discharge in
        chapter 7 cases, 230
    debts incurred through, exception
        from discharge, 236–237,
        239–243
    as fiduciary, exception from
        discharge, 245
Fraudulent transfers, 75–76
    avoidance of, 164–166
Free legal services, 272
Fresh start concept, 7
Full disclosure, importance of, 51–52

Garageman's liens, 43
Garnishment, 66
Going bare, 67
Good faith test
    of ability to pay student loans,
        252
    continued viability of, 199–200
    payments to unsecured creditors
        in chapter 13 cases and,
        194–197
Government benefits
    definition of public assistance
        and, 149–150

discharge and, 265
    overpayments of, exception from
        discharge, 242–243

Hardship discharge, in chapter 13
    cases, 33–34, 112–113
Harm, forestalling, timing of
    petition and, 78
Health aids, exemption of, 148
Health Education Assistance Loans
    (HEAL), 254–255
Hearings
    confirmation, in chapter 13 cases,
        32, 109–110
    discharge. See Discharge hearing
    modification of chapter 13 plan
        and, 111
Homestead exemption, 144–145
Homestead pourover, 147
Household goods, exemption of,
    145–146
Housing, discharge and, 264–265
Hunt, Local Loan Co. v., 7

Incarceration, discharge and, 266
Income
    disclosure of, 88–89
    disposable, 96
        definition of, 197
    eligibility for chapter 13 and,
        190–191
    payment directly to trustee, in
        chapter 13 cases, 205–206
    protection from unsecured
        creditors, 55–56
Indubitable equivalent, 131
Injury, rights to compensation for,
    exemption of, 150–151
Insiders, commission of prohibited
    acts concerning, as grounds
    for objection to discharge in
    chapter 7 cases, 231
Intangible personal property, 46
Interest
    computation of, cure of defaults
        on long-term debts and, 186
    payment of, in chapter 13 cases,
        206
Interim trustee, for chapter 7 cases,
    20
Internal Revenue Service (IRS). See
    Taxes
Involuntary bankruptcy cases, 218–
    221
    contesting, 219–221

Jewelry, exemption of, 146
Joint filing, 73–74
Joint ownership with right of
    survivorship, 46–47
Joint tenants, 46–47
Judges, 7
Judicial liens, 43, 66
    avoidance of, 157–158
Junior lienholders, 43

Landlords, bankrupt, tenants of,
    286–287
Larceny, exception from discharge,
    245–246
Lawsuits, 65–67. See also Bank-
    ruptcy court, litigation of
    cases outside bankruptcy in
    disputed debts and, 69
Lawyers. See Attorney(s); Attorney
    fees
Lease-purchase agreements, cure of
    defaults on, 184
Leases
    in chapter 13 cases, 209–211
        assumption of, 209, 210–211
        rejection of, 209–211
    relief from automatic stay and,
        133–134
    unexpired, 87
Legal actions. See also Criminal
    proceedings
    automatic stay and, 122–123
    contempt of court, automatic
        stay and, 126
    following discharge, 117
Legal services. See Attorney(s);
    Attorney fees
Levies, 43
Lien(s), 42–43
    in chapter 7 cases, 21–22
    effects of discharge and, 258
    garageman's, 43
    judicial, 43, 66
        avoidance of, 157–158
    nonpossessory, avoidance of, 158–
        159
    securing fines, penalties, and
        forfeitures, avoidance of,
        168
    statutory, 43
        avoidance of, 161–162
    tax, 43
Lien priority, 43
Life insurance
    accrued dividend, interest, or loan
        value of, exemption of, 148

unmatured, exemption of, 147–148

Liquidated debts, limitations on, eligibility for chapter 13 and, 192–193

Liquidation. *See* Chapter 7 bankruptcy cases

Liquidation of property, in chapter 13 cases, 207

Litigation, of disputes with creditors, 57

Local laws, 5

Local Loan Co. v. Hunt, 7

Losses, rights to compensation for, exemption of, 150–151

Luxury goods or services, definition of, 241

Magnuson-Moss Warranty Act, 280

Maintenance, exception from discharge, 246–248

Malicious injury, exception from discharge, 248–249

Marathon Pipe Line Co., Northern Pipeline Construction Co. v., 8, 216

Matrix, 81

Mechanical test, of ability to pay student loans, 251–252

Medical debts, after bankruptcy, 60

Moral obligation, feelings of, 60–61

Mortgages, 42–43. *See also* Foreclosure

cure of defaults on, 184–185

delinquencies and, remedies for, 80

Motor vehicles, exemption of, 145

Myths, dispelling, 54–55

Nobleman v. American Savings Bank, 173, 181

Nominal-asset cases, 22

Nonautomatic stays, 127

Nonbankruptcy exemptions, 151–153

federal bankruptcy modification of, 151–152

of property not subject to process, 152–153

Nondischargeable debts, priority debts distinguished from, 44–45

Nonexempt property, retaining in chapter 7 cases, 104

Nonfinal judgment orders and decrees, appeal from, 9–10

Nonpossessory liens, avoidance of, 158–159

Nonpossessory security interest, 43

Nonpurchase-money security agreements, avoidance of, 158–159

Nonpurchase-money security interests, 43

Northern Pipeline Construction Co. v. Marathon Pipe Line Co., 8, 216

Notice

of appointment of trustee, 99

of automatic stay, 100–101, 127–128

in chapter 7 cases, 20

of creditors meeting, 99

in chapter 7 cases, 20

in chapter 13 cases, 31

of discharge, 117

in chapter 7 cases, 25

in chapter 13 cases, 37

Notice of Appointment of a Trustee, 99

Notice of the Meeting of Creditors, 99

Noticing fee, 81

for chapter 7 cases, 19

for chapter 13 cases, 29

Objections

to claims filed by creditors, 218

to discharge in chapter 7 cases. *See* Discharge

to exemptions, 154

Official Form(s), 5, 82, 307–327. *See also specific Official Forms*

Official Form 1 (voluntary petition), 308–309

Official Form 6, 83–89, 310–321

amendments to schedules, 101

declaration concerning debtor's schedules, 321

declaration concerning schedules, 89

Schedule A, 83, 311

Schedule B, 83–84, 311–313

Schedule C, 84–85, 313

Schedule D, 85–86, 314

Schedule E, 85–86, 87, 315

Schedule F, 85–86, 316–317

Schedule G, 87–88, 318

Schedule H, 88, 318

Schedule I, 88–89, 319

Schedule J, 88, 89, 320

summary of schedules, 89, 310

Official Form 7 (statement of financial affairs), 89–93, 322–325

Official Form 8 (statement of intention), 93–94, 176–177, 326

Official Form 10 (proof of claim), 327

Partnerships, property owned by, 47–48

Payment(s)

of attorney fees. *See* Attorney fees

under chapter 13 cases. *See* Chapter 13 bankruptcy cases

Payment agreements, 67

Penalties

exception from discharge, 249–250

liens securing, avoidance of, 168

for violation of automatic stay, 128–129

Pensions, 11–12, 149

Personal property (personalty), 45–46

intangible, 46

list of, 83–84

Petition, 82–83

for chapter 13 case, 28

for chapter 7 cases, 19

cost of filing, 61

creditors not listed or scheduled by debtor and, exception from discharge, 244–245

timing of, 74–78

anticipation of further debts and, 77–78

exemption planning and, 76–77

forestalling harm and, 78

fraudulent acts, transfers of property, and preferences and, 75–76

paying favored creditors and, 78

voluntary (Official Form 1), 308–309

Plan, in chapter 13 cases. *See* Chapter 13 bankruptcy cases

Policy test, of ability to pay student loans, 252

Possessory security interest, 43

Postpetition claims, in chapter 13 cases, 110–111

Postpetition transfers, avoidance of, 166–167

Preferences, avoidance of, 75, 162–164

Present value, of payments to unsecured claims in chapter 13 cases, 29

Priority, as to liens, 43

Priority debts, 44–45
    filing claims in chapter 13 cases and, 108
    nondischargeable debts distinguished from, 44–45
    payments to unsecured creditors in chapter 13 cases and, 200–201

Proof of claim (Official Form 10), 327

Property, 45–46. See also Assets; Bankruptcy estate
    abandonment of, in chapter 7 cases, 21
    acts directed against, automatic stay and, 123–124
    community. See Community property
    court seizures of, remedies for, 79
    debtor's equity in, 43
    entireties, 47
    exempt. See Exemptions; Exempt property
    frequently overlooked, 49–50
    included in bankruptcy estate, 10–13
    intentional concealment, transfer, or destruction of, as grounds for objection to discharge in chapter 7 cases, 228–229
    liquidation of, in chapter 13 cases, 207
    loss in bankruptcy, 55, 57–58
    nonexempt, retaining in chapter 7 cases, 104
    personal, 45–46, 83–84
    protection from unsecured creditors, 55–56
    real. See Cramdown; Real property
    recovered. See Recovered property
    redemption of. See Chapter 7 bankruptcy cases, redemption in
    securing debts, statement of intention with respect to, 176–177

turnover of, 137–139
    automatic, 101
    general rule for, 137
    possession after, 138–139
    procedure for, 137–138
    use and possession of, in chapter 13 cases, 207–208

Property ownership, 46–48
    community property and, 47
    joint ownership with right of survivorship, 46–47
    obtaining after bankruptcy, 54–55
    sole ownership, 46
    tenancy by the entireties, 47
    tenants in common and, 46
    after turnover, 138–139

Public assistance. See Government benefits

Public housing, discharge and, 264–265

Punitive damages, in involuntary bankruptcy cases, 221

Purchase-money security interests, 43

Radloff, Toibb v., 72–73

Rake v. Wade, 186

Reaffirmation of debts, 115–116
    caution against, 108
    discharge and, 258–261
    factors to consider about, 260–261
    requirements for, 259–260
    undue hardship and best interests tests and, 260
    use of, 115

Real property, 45
    cramdown and. See Cramdown
    list of, 83

Recovered property
    avoidance of, 169
    exemption of, 159
    preservation of, 169–170

Redemption, in chapter 7 cases. See Chapter 7 bankruptcy cases, redemption in

Refinancing, 68

Relief, 6
    from automatic stay, 129–134
        for cause, 130–131
        creditor's motion for, 104
        for lack of adequate protection, 131–132
        for lack of equity and lack of need for effective reorganization, 132–133

leases and, 133–134

Removal, 217

Rent-to-own transactions, 88, 186–187

Reorganization. See also Chapter 11 bankruptcy cases; Chapter 13 bankruptcy cases
    relief from automatic stay and, for lack of need for, 132–133

Repossession, 64–65
    remedies for, 79–80

Reputation, effect of bankruptcy on, 58–59

Retirement benefits, exemption of, 148–150

Revocation, of discharge, 233

Scams, avoiding, 270–271

Section 341(a) meeting. See Creditors meeting (section 341(a) meeting)

Secured debts, 42–44, 171–187. See also Allowed secured claims; Cramdown
    allowed secured claim and. See Allowed secured claims
    cash collateral held by creditors and, 175–176
    chapter 13 cramdown and. See Cramdown
    eliminating or modifying, 56
    filing claims in chapter 13 cases and, 108
    limitations on, eligibility for chapter 13 and, 192
    without reaffirmation, after bankruptcy case, 261
    redemption in chapter 7 cases and. See Chapter 7 bankruptcy cases, redemption in
    statement of intention with respect to property securing consumer debt and, 176–177

Security deposits, required by utilities, 61, 136

Security interests, 43
    avoidance of, 163–164
    definition of, 164, 181

Senior lienholder, 43

Setoffs
    avoidance of, 167–168
    bank's retention of right of, 175–176

Signatures, on forms, 98

Social Security. *See* Government benefits
Sole ownership, 46
Spendthrift trusts, 12
Spouses
    community property and. *See* Community property
    joint filing by, 73–74
    tenancy by the entireties and, 47
Standing trustee, 14
State laws, 5, 280
    exemptions available under, list of, 289–306
State lines, filing suits across, 8
Statement(s), amendments to, 101
Statement of financial affairs (Official Form 7), 89–93
Statement of intention (Official Form 8), 93–94, 176–177, 326
Statutory liens, 43
    avoidance of, 161–162
Stays
    automatic. *See* Automatic stay
    nonautomatic, 127
Stigma of bankruptcy, overcoming, 53–54
Straight bankruptcy. *See* Chapter 7 bankruptcy cases
"Strong-arm" clause, 160–161
Student loans
    in chapter 13 cases, 202, 253–254
    discharge and, 264
    exception from discharge, 250–255
        in chapter 7 cases, 250–253
        in chapter 13 cases, 253–254
        Health Education Assistance Loans, 254–255
Substantial abuse test, 222–224
Summary of schedules, 89
Support
    in chapter 13 cases, 202
    exception from discharge, 246–248

Taxes
    automatic stay and, 125
    bankruptcy estate and
        refunds in, 12–13
        tax credits in, 13
    exception of tax debts from discharge and, 235–236

remedies for tax debts and, 80
    tax liens and, 43
Tenancy by the entireties, 47
Tenants, of bankrupt landlords, 286–287
Tenants in common, 46
Testimony, refusal to give, as grounds for objection to discharge in chapter 7 cases, 230–231
Timing
    extensions and, 97–98
    of petition. *See* Petition, timing of
Toibb v. Radloff, 72–73
Tools of trade
    definition of, 159
    exemption of, 147
Transfers
    avoidance of. *See* Avoidance
    fraudulent. *See* Fraudulent transfers
Trust, property owned in, 47
Trustee, 14–15
    avoiding powers of. *See* Avoidance
    in chapter 7 cases
        claims filed with, 22
        duties of, 14
        interim, 20
        sale of property by, 22
    in chapter 13 cases
        duties of, 14
        payments to creditors by, 105, 110
    commission of, 61
    notice of appointment of, 99
    objections to exemptions by, 154
    payment of income directly to, in chapter 13 cases, 205–206
    property recovered by. *See* Recovered property
        exemption of, 159
    recommendations for attorneys from, 273
    standing, 14
    turnover of property to. *See* Property, turnover of
United States, 15
Truth in Lending Act, 279–280
Turnover, of property. *See* Property, turnover of

Undue hardship test, reaffirmation of debts and, 260
United States trustee, 15
Unsecured debts, 44
    in chapter 13 cases, 79, 194–201
        ability-to-pay test and, 197–199
        best interests of creditors test and, 194
        good faith test and, 194–197, 199–200
        priority creditors and, 200–201
    remedies for, 79
Use and occupancy payments, 210
Utilities, 134–136
    bills from, remedies for, 79
    debtor's right to services from, 135
    security deposits required by, 61
    shutoff of, 65
    state assistance programs for, 69
    utility's right to discontinue services for lack of adequate assurance, 135–136

Valuation, determination of allowed secured claims and, 174–175
    date of valuation and, 174
    method of valuation and, 174–175
Violations, of automatic stay, 128–129
    willful, 128
Vocational school education, student loans incurred for, 253
Voluntary bankruptcy, 6
Voluntary petition (Official Form 1), 308–309

Wade, Rake v., 186
Wage garnishments, 66
    remedies for, 79
Wage order, 205
Wage replacement benefits, exemption of, 148–150
Waiver, of discharge. *See* Discharge, waiver of
Welfare benefits. *See* Government benefits
Wild-card exemption, 146, 147
Willful injury, exception from discharge, 248–249

ABOUT THE AUTHOR

Henry J. Sommer is a Supervising Attorney and Head of the Consumer Law Project at Community Legal Services, Inc., in Philadelphia, where he has specialized in the areas of bankruptcy and consumer law.

He has also served as a Lecturer in Law at the University of Pennsylvania Law School, where he taught a seminar on bankruptcy law. He has taught at numerous continuing legal education programs, including programs for bankruptcy judges presented by the Federal Judicial Center, the annual New York University Bankruptcy Workshop and programs presented by the Southeastern Bankruptcy Law Institute, the Executive Office of the United States Trustees, and Federal Reserve Board, the National Conference of Bankruptcy Judges, the American Law Institute, the Pennsylvania Bar Institute, the National Consumer Law Center, and the law schools of the University of Kentucky and Villanova University.

Mr. Sommer received an A.B. magna cum laude from Harvard College in 1971 and a J.D. cum laude from Harvard Law School in 1974. He is a member, appointed by the Chief Justice of the Supreme Court, of the Federal Judicial Conference Advisory Committee on Bankruptcy Rules. He is a director of the National Association of Consumer Bankruptcy Attorneys, the vice-president of the Consumer Bankruptcy Assistance Project, a member of the National Bankruptcy Conference, and a fellow of the American College of Bankruptcy, and he has served on the Federal Reserve Board Consumer Advisory Council.

Mr. Sommer is also the author of *Consumer Bankruptcy Law and Practice* (4th ed., 1992), a one volume practice guide published by the National Consumer Law Center in Boston; *Collier Family Law and the Bankruptcy Code*; and many articles on consumer bankruptcy in *The Practical Lawyer* and other publications. He is a contributing author to *Collier on Bankruptcy, Collier Bankruptcy Manual*, and the *Matthew Bender Debtor-Creditor Law Treatise*. He has testified about consumer bankruptcy at the invitation of congressional committees on many occasions, and he has appeared as a bankruptcy expert on numerous national and local television and radio shows.